ROYAL HISTORICAL SOCIETY
STUDIES IN HISTORY
SERIES
No. 46

JAMES GORDON BENNETT AND THE
NEW YORK HERALD

A Study of Editorial Opinion
in the Civil War Era
1854-1867

James Gordon Bennett in 1851
(Photograph by Brady),
Courtesy of Library of Congress.

JAMES GORDON BENNETT AND THE *NEW YORK HERALD*

A Study of Editorial Opinion in the Civil War Era 1854-1867

Douglas Fermer

ROYAL HISTORICAL SOCIETY

THE BOYDELL PRESS · WOODBRIDGE
ST MARTIN'S PRESS · NEW YORK

© Douglas Fermer 1986

First published in 1986

Printed in Great Britain

Published by
The Boydell Press
an imprint of Boydell & Brewer Ltd
PO Box 9 Woodbridge Suffolk IP12 3DF
and St Martin's Press Inc
175 Fifth Avenue New York NY10010

US ISBN 0-312-18079-9
UK ISBN 0 86193 203 X

Library of Congress Cataloging-in-Publication Data

Fermer, Douglas.
    James Gordon Bennett and the New York Herald

    Bibliography: p.
    Includes index.
    1. United States—History—Civil War,
    1861–1865—Journalists. 2. Bennett, James Gordon,
    1795–1871. 3. New York Herald (New York, N.Y. : 1840) I.
    Title. E609.F47 1987
    070.4'499737   86-6609
    ISBN 0-312-43955-5

Printed in Great Britain by Short Run Press Ltd, Exeter

CONTENTS

LIST OF ILLUSTRATIONS

ACKNOWLEDGEMENTS

Without implying any liability for errors, I tender my sincere thanks to:

Professor Maldwyn A. Jones of University College, London, who suggested the subject and supervised the doctoral thesis from which this book grew. His guidance and criticism have made inroads on even the author's dreary obtuseness, and it is not his fault if his attempts to enlighten me have all too often met the proverbial fate of the farmer leading his horse to water.

Professor Esmond Wright of the Institute of United States Studies and Professor Peter J. Parish of the University of Glasgow, who examined the original thesis. Professor Parish in particular gave me the benefit of a stringent criticism of the text.

Mr. W. B. Rainforth, whose gifted teaching of US history first interested me in the subject and whose advice and continued interest have been greatly appreciated.

Mr. J. O. Rhys for his hardihood above and beyond the call of friendship in reading the first draft.

The staff of the British Library, and most particularly of the Newspaper Library at Colindale. In my many months spent there poring over the files of the *Herald, Tribune* and *Times* I never received service which was less than courteous and efficient.

The staffs of the D.M.S. Watson Library (UCL), the Senate House Library, the Institute of Historical Research, the London School of Economics and Croydon Public Library.

In the USA, the staffs of the New York Public Library, the New York Historical Society and the Library of Congress, Washington D.C.

Mrs. J. Bevis and Mrs. M. Cocking for typing services.

Mrs. Christine Linehan of Studies in History for guiding the book through the final stages of production.

Last, but by no means least, Mrs. J. Godden, Executive Editor of Studies in History, who has laboured to give my idiosyncratic scribblings some resemblance to the English language.

My research, including a sojourn in the USA, was made possible by a grant from the Department of Education and Science.

The frontispiece is reproduced by permission of the Library of Congress, and Plates A-E by permission of the British Library.

Douglas Fermer

The Society records its gratitude to the following, whose generosity made possible the initiation of this series: The British Academy; The Pilgrim Trust; The Twenty-Seven Foundation; The United States Embassy Bicentennial Funds; The Wolfson Trust; several private donors.

The publication of this volume has been assisted by a further grant from the Twenty-Seven Foundation.

We live under a government of men
and morning newspapers.

– Wendell Phillips

INTRODUCTION

Seeing a crowd of curious people following James Gordon Bennett one day in the 1850s, a bystander reflected that 'the people of the United States would go farther and give more to see him than they would to see the President or any member of the United States Senate'.[1] In those days before radio, cinema or television, the editor of a great New York daily newspaper enjoyed considerable prestige. The provincial papers largely waited on the New York press. In republican America editors alone customarily referred to themselves in the imperial plural as 'we'.

Bennett could be seen coming or going in his carriage to his office in the heart of Manhattan, at the corner of Fulton and Nassau Streets. Here were the headquarters of the newspaper he owned and edited; the front of the building bearing his name in large letters underneath the title NEW YORK HERALD.[2] Bennett was tall, well dressed, slightly stooped but quick and nervous in his movements, with long silver hair and a grey chin beard which helped protect him from a bronchial ailment.[3] He was self-conscious about being cross-eyed, though when his enemies made fun of this feature he snapped that it resulted from trying to follow their political movements.[4] His enemies were legion, but he had defied their attacks. The *Herald,* as everyone knew, had the largest daily circulation of any paper in the country, or in the world.[5]

Bennett's success had made him wealthy. He maintained costly establishments in town and country, horses, yachts and that most expensive appendage, an heir apparent who was also his namesake.[6] Yet only two decades previously he had started the *Herald* with a capital of $500 in a dingy cellar, his desk made of a board resting on

[1]George W. Bungay, *Off-Hand Takings* (NY 1854), p. 389.

[2]The *Herald* occupied these premises from 1841 until 1867. Illustration in H.C. Brown, *Glimpses of Old New York* (NY 1917), p. 375.

[3]Bungay, pp. 389-90; Isaac C. Pray, *Memoirs of J.G. Bennett and His Times* (NY 1855), p. 454.

[4]In fact the condition seems to have been caused by proof-reading as a clerk in Boston in 1820-1 and by intensive reading later in life, see Pray, pp. 41, 87. Bennett's sensitivity about his strabismus may account for the comparative rarity of photographs of him.

[5]On circulation figures see Appendix 1.

[6]James G. Bennett Junior was born in 1841. A second boy, Cosmo, died in 1859. Bennett had one daughter, Jeanette. His country residence at Washington Heights on the upper part of Manhattan Island was purchased in 1858 — see Don C. Seitz, *The James Gordon Bennetts* (NY 1928), pp. 203, 214.

flour barrels, and acting as his own editor, reporter, clerk and salesman.[7] In those early days he had written freely in the *Herald* of his own career. He had been born at New Mill, Banffshire, Scotland, in September 1795, and he liked to portray his life in romantic terms, telling how as a dreamy Scots youth raised on a cultural diet of Byron, Napoleon, Benjamin Franklin and Sir Walter Scott he had taken ship to America in 1819 and had by sheer enterprise worked his way up from poverty and failure.[8] This picture rang false to his rivals, who regarded him as immoral, ambitious and unscrupulous. Bennett's valuation of himself was ironic too in portraying in print an impudent and extroverted character, whereas outside a small circle of friends and family he was in reality aloof, austere and devoted to his work.

More than a century after his death, a romantic interpretation of his career seems even more out of place, but for other reasons. In an age increasingly aware of the influence of the 'mass media' the founder of the *Herald* demands attention.

In Bennett's lifetime the United States grew remarkably, and not just in land area. Population grew, both from natural increase and heavy immigration, from just under four million in 1790 to over thirty-one million in 1860, and the growth was most marked in the cities. In 1860 one American in every twenty-five lived in New York City, which had become the third largest city in the world.[9] Americans generally were probably better schooled in basic literacy than any of the peoples of Europe, and improved kerosene lamps made leisure reading easier.[10] The canal, railway, steamship, telegraph and improved cylinder printing presses ensured that people inhabiting a vast land were brought into closer contact with each other than ever before. In 1833 fewer than 30,000 people in New York City bought a daily

---

[7]James Parton, 'The New York Herald', *North American Review,* 102 (April 1866), 373-419, reprinted in the same author's *Famous Americans of Recent Times* (Boston 1867), pp. 261-305.

[8]On Bennett's early life the major source is Pray, pp. 25 ff. See also Oliver Carlson, *The Man Who Made News* (NY 1942), chs. 1-3.

[9]As compared with one in seventy in 1800; see *American Annual Cyclopedia for 1861,* p. 525.

[10]The growth of the public school system in the 1850s is described in Arthur C. Cole, *The Irrepressible Conflict, 1850-65* (NY 1934). Illiteracy ran at about 9% throughout the nation at this period among whites over the age of twenty, according to Frank L. Mott, *American Journalism* (NY 1962), p. 304, quoting Edwin Leigh, 'Illiteracy in the United States' in *Report of the Commissioner of Education, 1870* (Washington 1875), pp. 467-502. In New York City an 1872 estimate put adult illiteracy at 6% — which in absolute terms meant that something like 60,000 New Yorkers over the age of ten could barely write their own names, see Charles L. Brace, *The Dangerous Classes of New York* (NY 1872), pp. 31-2.

newspaper: in 1860 that figure had multiplied ten times to 300,000.[11] Bennett's newspaper embodied even as it reported the changes of an era. One New Yorker reflected that 'the diverse races of men certainly seem tending toward development into a living organic unit with railroads and steampackets for a circulating system, telegraph wires for nerves, and the London *Times* and New York *Herald* for a brain'.[12]

New York City pioneered a new kind of journalism in the 1830s, aimed at providing cheap newspapers which would appeal to the widest possible readership. Within New York Bennett's *Herald*, founded in 1835, became pre-eminently successful in this field. Bennett aimed to make the *Herald* an institution in its own right: the medium through which the daily thought and activities of the people of the United States would find expression, in short, the forum of American democracy. Whatever judgement one may pass on the nature and quality of his achievement, there is no doubt that his venture won support from the people of New York in the most direct manner possible – they bought his paper in unprecedented numbers.

The importance of Bennett's contribution to the development of the modern newspaper has long been recognised by historians of journalism. If anything they have overrated his role as an innovator at the expense of his real significance as a successful exploiter of the opportunities for the development of a cheap press. The three major biographies of Bennett to date have been by journalists. Quite naturally they have dealt mostly with his personal history and professional techniques, and have tended to concentrate on the 1830s and '40s, the period of the 'newspaper revolution' and the founding and initial development of the *Herald*. The first was completed by a contemporary, Isaac C. Pray, in 1855, when Bennett still had seventeen years to live.[13]

Although the first chapter of this study offers a sketch of the earlier period of Bennett's editorship of the *Herald*, my main object is to deal with the period from 1854 until after the Civil War, when Bennett transferred the active duties of management to his son. But I have not aimed simply at carrying on the story where Pray left off. Rather I have used the *Herald* files and manuscript collections unused by (or

[11]Alfred M. Lee, *The Daily Newspaper in America* (NY 1937), table xvii. The percentage of the population was roughly 10% and 25% respectively.

[12]Allan Nevins and Milton H. Thomas eds., *The Diary of George Templeton Strong* (NY 1952), vol 2 p. 409, entry for 10 Aug 1858.

[13]On Pray's work see Appendix 2. This and other Bennett biographies are discussed in the bibliographical essay.

unavailable to) previous biographers in an attempt to view familiar historical events from a little-canvassed vantage point. The Civil War era is so often written of from the perspective of the Republican North or the secessionist South that one can easily forget that the nation's largest city often reflected a 'plague on both your houses' mentality. New York City has always stood slightly apart, with its own wry, materialist viewpoint on the affairs of the rest of the country, and nowhere was this spirit better expressed than in Bennett's newspaper. The pages of the *Herald* afford us a chance to see not just the unfolding story of the sectional conflict but what New Yorkers felt were the issues in that conflict and how they responded to them. Through its columns we can learn something of the interplay of the city and federal politics which had some important effects nationally, especially in the crisis of 1860-1. The *Herald* also offers a key to understanding how Americans of the 1850s and '60s thought about their society, their country and its future as a world power. It testifies that expansionism and negrophobia were quite as common in the urban North as the plantation South.

Nor was the *Herald* merely a passive reporter of events. I hope to show how Bennett's personality and what he judged to be the interests of the *Herald* shaped editorial policies which were an important part of the history of those days. Because we tend to think of political history in terms of parties, and because the *Herald* cannot be neatly classified with a party label, historians have never accorded the paper the importance it had to contemporaries, for whom indeed Bennett was a household name. We shall see that the *Herald* really deserves a prominent place in the inner history of the Pierce and Buchanan administrations, that it helped to shape as well as to record the sectional crisis, and has some claim to be considered the voice of the 'loyal opposition' in the wartime North. The relationship of four successive Presidents with the *Herald* is in any case a fascinating political study.

Two questions may be raised. Is a study of the editorial attitudes of the *Herald* likely to be anything more than a recounting of the fluctuating opinions of a wilful and roguishly eccentric old man? And how important is the editorial as a historical document anyway? After all it was Bennett himself who made it a truism that it is *news* that sells newspapers and that the expression of a political opinion in an editorial is less important commercially than having the fastest and fullest information possible on the front page. As James Parton wrote in 1866:

> The power of the editorial lessens as the intelligence of the people increases. The prestige of the editorial is gone . . . our

journalists already know that editorials neither make nor mar a daily paper: that they do not much influence the public mind, nor change many votes, and that the power and success of a newspaper depend wholly and absolutely upon its success in getting and skill in exhibiting the news. The word *newspaper* is the exact and complete description of the thing which the true journalist aims to produce. The news is his work; editorials are his play.[14]

Samuel Bowles of the Springfield *Republican* agreed decidedly that the *Herald* was 'worthless in editorial judgment'.[15] A standard modern work on journalism pronounces that 'the *Herald* was remembered not so much for *what* it said as for *how* it said it. Bennett's contributions [to journalism] were largely technical.'[16]

Historians have tended to comb the *Herald* files for their news value, but when considering editorial opinion in the Civil War era have centred discussion around Horace Greeley's New York *Tribune* (witness the small mountain of literature about Greeley). The *Tribune* was admittedly a Bible of Republican opinion in the 1850s. Its weekly edition sold in huge numbers (163,000 in one week in 1856)[17] throughout the Northern States, diffusing its principles in rural northwestern areas as well as in upstate New England. The historian James Ford Rhodes said that to read the *Tribune* was to understand the opinions of the nearly two million men who voted for Lincoln in 1860.[18] By contrast it became fashionable among articulate contemporaries and historians to treat lightly Bennett's importance as a political and social commentator.

And yet, though it would take a bold man to claim James Gordon Bennett as entirely representative of his generation, perhaps one should be suspicious of the painstaking earnestness with which intellectuals, fellow editors and political opponents denied his influence. The very intensity of the protests suggests that they feared his power as a maker and reflector of popular opinion. Together with the crowds which hooted Bennett's name and even his would-be assassins,[19] they

[14]Parton, 'The New York *Herald*' He added that 'it is not as a vehicle of opinion that the *Herald* has importance, but solely as a vehicle of news'.

[15]Springfield *Republican* 7 June 1872.

[16]Edwin Emery, *The Press and America* (Englewood Cliffs 1971), p. 173.

[17]W.T. Coggeshall, *The Newspaper Record* (Philadelphia 1856), pp. 149-50; Jeter A. Isely, *Horace Greeley and the Republican Party, 1853-61* (Princeton 1947), p. 338.

[18]James Ford Rhodes, 'Newspapers as Historical Sources', *Atlantic Monthly,* 103 (1909), 650-7.

[19]On attempts to kill Bennett see below, p. 37-8.

bought his paper if only to be appalled at and disagree with his views. The correspondence in the Bennett Papers in the New York Public Library suggests that the paper had a loyal readership which approved Bennett's views and admired his impatience of humbug.[20] It is worth remembering that although in 1856 the circulation of the *Herald*'s weekly edition was a mere eighth of the *Tribune*'s, on its home ground of New York City at that time the daily edition of the *Herald* sold almost exactly double the *Tribune*'s total.[21] The *Herald* outsold all other competitors in the city[22] and had considerable sales in the other cities of the eastern seaboard and some circulation in the South, where the *Tribune*'s anti-slavery views caused it to be proscribed. To repeat, no paper in the world had ever achieved the circulation built up by Bennett's *Herald* and its sales increased steadily throughout the period.

Parton, who thought that the day of the editorial was past, and who was no admirer of Bennett, apparently found no contradiction in bemoaning that 'he, if any one, – he more than anyone else – is the master in a free country'.[23] Lambert A. Wilmer, author of a volume published in 1859 which set out to expose the corruptions of 'Our Press Gang'[24] found it deplorable that 'every American has his newspaper oracle, as every African has his fetish, or talismanic counselor. Each has a superstitious reliance on the infallibility of his mysterious director; but neither can give any reason for implicitly submitting his judgement to such guidance.'[25] As to the *Herald*, continued Wilmer,

> This journal is read by people of all classes, and its power and influence are universally acknowledged. Although the *Herald* is denounced from one end of the country to the other as the most corrupt and profligate in existence, its opinions on almost every subject are often quoted as indisputable authority, and hundreds of other newspapers adopt its views and republish its statements without the least reservation.[26]

Bennett indeed was fully aware of his opportunity to influence the opinions of so many people. He was not innocent of the techniques by

---

[20]e.g. Anon to Bennett, 22 Feb 1844, Bennett Papers, NYPL.

[21]Coggeshall, pp. 149-50.

[22]Its daily edition overtook the NY *Sun* in the later '50s.

[23]Parton, 'The New York *Herald*'.

[24]Lambert A. Wilmer, *Our Press Gang* (Philadelphia 1859).

[25]*Ibid.*, p. 60.

[26]*Ibid.*, p. 79.

which 'impartial' front page news could act as bait for the hook of editorial opinion, but his personal attention to his editorials[27] and the amount of space devoted to them in the *Herald* belie any notion that he thought them obsolete or unimportant. Rather, he knew that the daily press had supplanted and surpassed the influence of the political pamphleteer, lecturer and stump speaker,[28] and that his voice in national affairs was louder through the *Herald* than it ever could have been in the more traditional paths of power in the Capitol at Washington.

Intellectuals might despise Bennett's lack of consistency, for at times he seemed to act in the belief that if anything is more stale than yesterday's news it is yesterday's opinions. He also enjoyed playing Devil's advocate. Greeley commented that the *Herald* amused the public 'by contradicting and refuting today all that it set forth as true yesterday, and charging on others as a crime what it has been doing itself'.[29] To such accusations Bennett replied blithely 'I print my paper every day'. He was not writing for posterity. He boasted that he intended never to be in a minority nor more than one day ahead of public opinion.

It may even be that while the *Tribune* was in the vanguard of reform the *Herald*, for all the individuality of its editor, represented the conservative mainstream of American thought. If to read the *Tribune* is to understand the nearly two million men who voted for Lincoln, to read the *Herald* is to gain some insight into the intellectual currency of a portion of the nearly three million who voted against him, of those Democrats who supported the war for the Union, and even of the soldiers of the Army of the Potomac who read the *Herald* more than any other paper. James Ford Rhodes himself judged that the *Herald* 'spoke for a potent public sentiment outside of New England'.[30] Significantly a newspaper directory in 1860 contained the comment that 'the tactics of the *Herald* have always been to court the popular voice, while those of the *Tribune* often defy it'.[31]

---

[27]Bennett's responsibility for editorial policy is discussed in chapter 1.

[28]Bennett steadfastly declined the offer of lecturing engagements, saying that the *Herald* was his one means of communicating with the public. He once described lecturing as 'wholesale boring' — *NYH* 6 March 1859.

[29]*New York Daily Tribune* 10 May 1861.

[30]James Ford Rhodes, *History of the United States from the Compromise of 1850* (London, 1893), vol. 3 p. 517.

[31]Daniel J. Kenny, *The American Newspaper Directory and Record of the Press* (NY 1861), p. 109.

8

Certainly the newspaper editorial is concerned with situations and decisions as they seem to be, and not with the facts as the historian understands them. Certainly it is written to a deadline for designed effect: but is this not an argument as much for as against its use as a key to the past? The editorial as a historical document has all the virtues as well as the vices of proximity to events.[32] Political historians are forever reminding us that elections are decided by relatively small shifts of opinion and polling behaviour. Does not this make the more intriguing the views of a paper which professedly stood as an 'armed neutral' between parties, ready to tilt the balance either way? In an age in which there were no opinion polls and in which election returns offer an ambiguous guide to the views of the electorate, editorials form a useful supplement to understanding the mental climate in which great political changes occurred. Bennett could express ideas which were morally repugnant to some of his contemporaries and are unacceptable now, but his historical importance should not therefore be underrated.

I have had to be highly selective in writing this study. Except in chapters 1 and 8 I have been little concerned with the *Herald*'s major function as a newsgatherer. Moreover, Bennett had something to say on several important topics every day for a period of years and his leaders form a body of literature exceeding that of any individual statesman of the time. Mark Twain, himself a sometime contributor to the *Herald*, once besought his readers to consider that:

> The matter that each editor of a daily paper in America writes in the course of a year would fill from four to eight bulky volumes. . Fancy what a library an editor's work would make, after twenty or thirty years service. Yet people often marvel that Dickens, Scott, Bulwer, Dumas, etc. have been able to produce so many books. If these authors had wrought as voluminously as the newspaper editors do, the result would be something to marvel at, indeed. How editors can continue this tremendous labor, this exhausting consumption of brain fibre (for their work is creative, and not a mere technical laying up of facts, like reporting), day after day, and year after year, is incomprehensible. Nobody,

[32]Some of the historiographical problems in studying past public opinion are examined in Lee Benson, 'An Approach to the Scientific Study of Past Public Opinion', in *Toward the Scientific Study of History* (NY 1972), pp. 105-59. Among discussions of the value of the newspaper to the historian are James Ford Rhodes, 'Newspapers as Historical Sources', which has special reference to this period; Allan Nevins, 'American Journalism and its Historical Treatment', *Journalism Quarterly*, 36 (1959), 411-22, 519; J. W. Piercy, 'The Newspaper as a Source of Historical Information', *Indiana Historical Bulletin*, 10 (1933), 387-96; Lucy M. Salmon, *The Newspaper and the Historian* (NY 1923); Will Irvin, *Propaganda and the News, or What Makes You Think So?* (NY 1936).

except he has tried it, knows what it is to be an editor . . . fancy
how you would feel if you had to pump your brains dry every day
in the week, fifty-two weeks in the year. It makes one low-
spirited simply to think of it.[33]

I can only hope to have given a fair sample of Bennett's views while
providing enough evidence from other newspapers, letters, diaries and
memoirs to put them in some meaningful historical context.

In trying to tell the story of the *Herald* over a dozen years I have
concentrated on the political affairs which dominated the era and in
which Bennett was so keenly interested, but it should be remembered
that he wrote almost as much about the opera, the turf, yachting (in
which his son excelled) and matters of local and topical interest as
about politics. Although the first two chapters of this study attempt a
broad introduction and leaven to the narrative which follows, I fear
that I have scarcely hinted at the rich variety of New York City's
social, business and cultural life as recorded in the *Herald* files. Nor
have I taken account of the *Herald*'s interpretations of European
affairs (as distinct from American foreign relations), though it led in
this field in consequence of its superior foreign news service,[34] nor of
its military commentaries during the Civil War. Alas, to have treated
these subjects at all adequately would have required a book twice as
long.

The editor of the New York *Herald* was a controversial character
in an era of bitterly partisan politics. I have not succeeded in giving an
impartial view of him, but were such an impartial study possible it
might make Bennett seem dull, and he was never that. I hope that the
following chapters provide sufficient evidence for the reader to form
an independent judgement. However imperfectly this book scratches
the surface of the subject it will have served its purpose if it spreads the
conviction that a comprehensive history of Bennett and his newspaper,
written by some historian capable of the task, would be both a highly
entertaining and very important contribution to the literature of
American history.

---

[33]*Roughing It,* ch 55.

[34]'For decades the special foreign news service of [the *Herald*] was unsurpassed;
even though it carried trivialities and scandal, one had to read it if one would be
posted as to events and political personalities in Europe,' O.G. Villard, *Some
Newspapers and Newspaper Men* (NY 1923), p. 275.

PART ONE

THE *HERALD* IN ITS TIME AND PLACE

1

AN EDITOR, A NEWSPAPER AND A REPUTATION

Journalism and Politics

When Bennett founded the *New York Herald* in 1835 he already had a great deal of journalistic experience.[1] Indeed, he remembered as a young man in Aberdeen in 1815 having written up a story on the battle of Waterloo. His Catholic parents had intended him for the church and had him educated at a seminary but Bennett balked at taking holy orders and had emigrated from Scotland in 1819. After teaching in Halifax, Nova Scotia and in Maine and spending a miserable time clerking and proof-reading in Boston he had been employed in 1822-3 on the Charleston (South Carolina) *Courier.* Harbour boats brought in newspapers in Spanish off the packet ships from Havana and Bennett translated items of news about affairs in the South American republics. Returning to New York, he failed in an attempt to found a commercial school but began writing for the *Sunday Courier.* He even raised enough capital to buy the paper but sold it back after a few weeks because it was unprofitable. Thereafter he was employed on the *National Advocate* and in 1827 obtained a job on M. M. Noah's[2] *Enquirer.* Apparently he and Noah did not get on well and when the paper's Washington correspondent was killed in a duel (having ridiculed the practice) Bennett was posted to cover affairs at the national capital. Here he made himself a reputation for his lively and informal pictures of Washington political and social life and his satires on 'good society'.[3]

When the *Enquirer* merged with Colonel James Watson Webb's[4] *Courier* in 1829 Bennett became an associate editor, in which capacity he added to his reputation for vivid and aggressive reporting. Covering a murder trial in Salem, Massachusetts, in 1830, he challenged the judge's right to exercise contempt of court powers over

---

[1]Bennett wrote about his own career in various issues of the *Herald.* Otherwise the two primary sources for this account are Isaac C. Pray, *Memoirs of J.G. Bennett and his Times* (NY 1855) and Frederic Hudson, *Journalism in the United States from 1690 to 1872* (NY 1873). See section E of the bibliography.

[2]See Isaac Goldberg, *Major Noah: American-Jewish Pioneer* (NY 1937).

[3]There is a brief memoir of Bennett's Washington days in Ben Perley Poore, *Perley's Reminiscences of Sixty Years in the National Metropolis* (Philadelphia 1886), vol. 1, pp. 57-8. See also Frederick D. Marbut, 'Early Washington Correspondents: Some Neglected Pioneers', *Journalism Quarterly,* 25 (1948), 369-74.

[4]Webb is well served in a scholarly biography by James L. Crouthamel, *James Watson Webb* (Middletown 1969).

the press, defending his right to publish facts and rumours about the case with the assertion 'The Press is the living Jury of the Nation'.[5]

In 1832 he established his own paper in New York, the *Globe*, selling at two cents, but abandoned it after two months. After contributing a few literary sketches to the *Mirror*[6] he tried his luck in Philadelphia. He bought shares in and edited the *Pennsylvanian* of that city in 1833 but gave up this venture after a year and returned to New York.

Even harder than Bennett's schooling in journalism had been his apprenticeship in politics. Although he was a professional news-paperman, up to 1834 Bennett's career revolved around politics, and consideration of this fact is vital to an understanding of what the *Herald* later became. In the 1820s newspapers contained a heavy proportion of political and mercantile matter.[7] News for its own sake was sparse and less prominent than party propaganda. Papers were relatively expensive at six cents each. They were aimed at the educated and politically aware minority and were usually controlled by party or business interests.[8] Bennett sought to make his mark in this field. From at least 1826 he was politically active and became a keen partisan of Andrew Jackson. Years later he wryly confessed to having been a 'rampant Jackson blockhead'.[9] He left the *National Advocate* because of its support for John Quincy Adams, Jackson's opponent, and as Washington correspondent for the *Enquirer* he did sterling propaganda work for the Jackson party during the 1828 election.[10]

Bennett also found time to be actively involved in New York City politics. He was a worker for the Tammany Hall Democrats in 1829 and rose to be a member of the Democratic Ward Committee in the city's first ward in 1831.[11] Upon a cue from Amos Kendall, President Jackson's confidant, it was Bennett who penned for the *Courier and Enquirer* the withering attacks on the second Bank of the United States which heralded Jackson's 'war' on that institution.[12] Bennett

[5] Wallace B. Eberhard, 'Mr. Bennett Covers a Murder Trial', *Journalism Quarterly*, 4 (1970), 457-63.

[6] Pray, pp. 152-9, reprints one of Bennett's contributions to the *Mirror*.

[7] For general surveys of the press at this period see Frank L. Mott, *American Journalism*, 3rd ed. (NY 1962), chs X, XI; and Edwin Emery, *The Press and America*, 3rd ed., (Englewood Cliffs 1972), ch 10.

[8] Elwyn B. Robinson, 'The Dynamics of American Journalism from 1787 to 1865', *Pennsylvania Magazine of History and Biography*, 61 (1937), 434-45.

[9] Pray, p. 134.

[10] *Ibid.*, pp. 104-5.

[11] *Ibid.*, pp. 80-1, 133.

[12] *Ibid.*, pp. 110, 125-8.

also strongly supported New Yorker Martin Van Buren to succeed John C. Calhoun as Jackson's Vice-President.

Bennett strove to bring himself to the favourable attention of the politicians in the hope that they would reward him by furthering his career in journalism, but his first ambitions failed. Having suggested the merger of the *Enquirer* with the *Courier*, he tried to undermine the new concern and Webb with the Tammany and Washington politicans, in the hope that they would finance a new Democratic organ and appoint him the editor. They did not, and Bennett stayed on restlessly as associate editor of the *Courier and Enquirer*.[13]

In 1831 he ruminated miserably in his diary 'I have endeavoured to secure a high position in parties, and to settle myself in life. . . I have always failed – why so?'[14]

The answer was that his ambition and independence were mistrusted, and not without reason. Even his opposition to the Bank was ambiguous. Bennett left the *Courier and Enquirer* in 1832 ostensibly because Webb favoured recharter of the Bank, contrary to Democratic party policy. Later (the time lapse was significant) Bennett publicly accused Webb of having been bribed by Nicholas Biddle, the Bank's president – a charge which Webb had difficulty in living down.[15] Yet throughout Jackson's first term, while he was publicly attacking the Bank in the *Courier and Enquirer*, Bennett was privately sending Biddle reports on the plans and attitudes of the Van Buren leaders in New York.[16] In return he was later to beg Biddle for a loan of $4,000 in order to establish his own paper. He confessed his unhappiness at playing second string to Webb and told the banker 'I am opposed to the Bank and must be so – but I suppose you understand that'.[17] Throughout his own later career he was always ready to pay for news, whatever the source.

[13]*Ibid.*, pp. 105-10; Crouthamel, *Webb*, pp. 30-1; Jerome Mushkat, *Tammany* (Syracuse 1971), p. 120.

[14]Bennett's fragmentary 'Diary of a Journey through New York. . . July 12 – August 18 1831' is preserved in the New York Public Library.

[15]Bennett's version of the Bank affair in Pray, pp. 147-50. Crouthamel examines the bribery charge in *Webb*, ch 4, and also in 'Did the Second Bank of the United States Bribe the Press?', *Journalism Quarterly*, 36 (1959), 35-44 and answers the question with a qualified 'No'.

[16]Most of the letters are in the Nicholas Biddle Papers, Library of Congress: see Bennett to Biddle 2, 21 Apr: 17 Oct; 9 Nov; 6 Dec 1829; 9 Apr: 30 May; 11, 25 Sept; 22 Oct; 10 Nov 1830; 9, 29 Nov; 1 Dec 1832; 17, 23 Sept; 14 Oct; 20 Nov; 3, 16 Dec 1833. Another letter dated 13 July 1829 is in the New York Historical Society Library. See also Thomas P. Govan, *Nicholas Biddle* (Chicago 1959), pp. 153-4.

[17]Bennett to Biddle 9 Nov 1832, Biddle Papers, LC.

The distrust which Bennett aroused was shown by the attacks launched on him by the regular Democratic New York *Standard* when he started the *Globe* in 1832 as a campaign sheet for Jackson and Van Buren. Ever 'self-willed and forward', he boasted to the party scribes that 'if I make up my mind to establish a paper, I wish you to understand that I shall ask no man the liberty of doing so'.[18] His own barbed pen and suspected duplicity undermined his potential value as a party man. Nevertheless he thought himself deserving of a reward. After the elections were over and the *Globe* disappeared Bennett importuned Vice-President Van Buren for the US consulship at Bremen. Nothing came of this.[19] Then he sought an editorial position on the *Washington Globe*, which was the special organ of President Jackson.[20] Bennett was refused, however, and it was the *Globe's* editor, Francis P. Blair, who advised him to try his talents in Philadelphia.[21]

On the *Pennsylvanian* in 1833, Bennett applied to Van Buren via an acquaintance, Jesse Hoyt, for a $25,000 loan, complaining that the editor of the NY *Standard* had been subsidised to the extent of $40,000 – 'With a fourth of that sum I would have done twice as much'. He was refused.

Muttering of ingratitude, Bennett appealed directly to Van Buren against the 'heartlessness' of the party and hinted that his support might be withdrawn.[22] Van Buren, apparently annoyed, wrote to Hoyt that 'if Mr. Bennett cannot continue friendly to me on public grounds and with perfect independence I can only regret it, but I desire no other support'.[23] In fact Bennett, while professing support for Van Buren,

---

[18]Pray, pp. 141 ff. Bennett's introductory prospectus for the *Globe,* 29 Oct 1832, in Hudson, pp. 409-10.

[19]Bennett to Van Buren 30 Nov 1832, Van Buren Papers, LC.

[20]Bennett to Van Buren 1 Dec 1832, *ibid.* Bennett to Senator Levi Woodbury 4 Dec 1832, Woodbury Papers, LC. Bennett asked Woodbury to use his influence with President Jackson. 'I should like such a position remarkably well', he wrote, and thought he 'would add a good deal of reputation and patronage to the *Globe'.* See also James E. Pollard, *The Presidents and the Press* (NY 1947), p. 169 and William E. Smith, *The Francis Preston Blair Family in Politics* (NY 1933), vol. 1, p. 111.

[21]Hudson, p. 414.

[22]Bennett to Jesse Hoyt 12 June; 27 July 1833; Bennett to Van Buren 6 Aug 1833, Pray, p. 161 ff. and Hudson, p. 411 ff. See also Bennett to Van Buren 22 Mar 1833, Van Buren Papers, LC.

[23]James Parton, *Life of Andrew Jackson* (NY 1861), vol 3, p. 596. See also Edwin Croswell to Van Buren, 7 June 1833, Van Buren Papers, expressing lack of confidence in Bennett. Croswell was editor of the Albany *Argus,* mouthpiece of the regular Democratic party in New York State. He considered Bennett 'worthless and dishonest'.

had been attacking the New York editors closest to him with great virulence and following an independent line on financial questions. Hoyt wrote to Bennett taking him to task for ruining his own chances and lecturing him that 'the Press has lost some portion of its hold upon public confidence; recent developments have had a tendency to satisfy the people that its conductors, or many of them, at least, are as negotiable as a promissory note. This impression can only be removed by a firm adherence to principle in adversity as well as prosperity.'[24]

Bennett's prospects were crushed and his pride wounded by what he considered harsh treatment. He wrote a petulant reply to Hoyt protesting 'the deadly hostility which you all have entertained towards me' because 'I happen to have been born in another country'.[25] He tried to take revenge by writing direct to President Jackson, attempting to convince him that Amos Kendall was intriguing against him. Kendall protested that the editor was mad and Jackson made it clear to Bennett that his faith in his adviser was unshaken. The President concluded that 'the Bank has bought up Benet' (sic).[26] The Washington Globe read Bennett out of the Democratic party.[27]

Professing disillusion and disgust with the 'hollow-heartedness and humbuggery' of politics and politicians,[28] Bennett was left to make his living by journalism alone. At this time New York City was undergoing a 'newspaper revolution' which sought to bring the newspaper to the masses, not merely to the businessmen and politicians.[29] While Bennett was still in Philadelphia in 1833 Benjamin H. Day founded the New York Sun ('It shines for ALL'). Largely apolitical, the Sun sold for just one cent. It was brightly written and concentrated on police court reports and other short, entertaining items, presenting to its readers the unique, ironic, spectacular and trivial aspects of life which the rather turgid and

[24]Jesse Hoyt to Bennett 16 Aug 1833; Pray, pp. 167-9.

[25]Bennett to Hoyt Aug 1833; Pray, p. 169.

[26]Bennett to Levi Woodbury, 10 Sept 1833, Woodbury Papers, LC; Bennett to Andrew Jackson, 10, 14 Sept; 4 Dec 1833; Jackson to Bennett, 12 Sept 1833; Amos Kendall to Jackson 12 Sept 1833: Jackson to Van Buren 8, 19 Sept 1833, all in Correspondence of Andrew Jackson, ed. J.S. Bassett (Washington 1931). See also Bennett to Van Buren 25, 27 Sept; 5 Oct 1833 in Van Buren Papers, LC.

[27]Pray, p. 170; Poore, Perley's Reminiscences, p. 133; W.E. Smith, The Francis Preston Blair Family, p. 123. For instances of attacks on Bennett see Washington Daily Globe 4, 7, 22 Sept; 23 Nov 1833.

[28]Hudson, p. 430.

[29]James L. Crouthamel, 'The Newspaper Revolution in New York, 1830-60', New York History, 45 (1964) 91-113.

didactic commercial and political papers neglected.[30] At that time the twelve daily papers in New York City had an average daily circulation of something over 2,000 each. None had more than 5,000. Day changed that. By 1834 the *Sun* had a daily circulation of 8,000, in 1835 nearly 20,000; more than the London *Times*.[31]

Seeing his opportunity, Bennett returned to New York, defying what his biographer called 'prejudice of a permanent character' against him.[32] He asked Day for a job, but was refused.[33] Horace Greeley, a young printer, was not interested in a partnership.[34] So Bennett started his own excursion into the Penny Press field solo.

The first number of the *Herald*, on 6 May 1835, declared its independence of party and its indifference to 'any election or candidate from president down to constable'. Such a rhetorical profession was not in itself original or revolutionary, but Bennett's brand of independence was. The *Herald* became the great politician-hating organ of the age. It made war on the whole class of politicians, puncturing their pretensions, embarrassing their schemes, insulting them and making them look foolish and criminal. In Scotland Bennett had been trained in a Catholic seminary,[35] and in the degeneracy of politicians he found a text on which he preached zealously for a lifetime. Over the years he sought to make his paper almost a fourth element in the constitutional system by invoking the power of the people to preserve the democratic system against the 'party wire pullers' who sought to 'beguile the masses'.[36]

He announced that 'political morals . . . are the grave of honour and the charnel-house of integrity'.[37] Every day for thirty years readers of the *Herald* were reminded that politicians were 'schemers',

[30]Frank M. O'Brien, *The Story of the Sun* (NY 1927); Mott, *American Journalism*, ch XII; Sidney Kobre, *Development of American Journalism* (Dubuque 1969), chs 7, 8.

[31]W. Coggeshall, *The Newspaper Record* (Philadelphia 1856); Daniel J. Kenny, *The American Newspaper Directory and Record of the Press* (NY 1861); O'Brien, p. 69; Pray, p. 172. In 1834 there were three other penny papers in New York besides the *Sun:* The *Transcript, The Man* and *The Jeffersonian. The Herald* became the sixteenth paper publishing in the city in 1835.

[32]Pray, p. 172.

[33]See Albert E. Coleman, 'A New and Authentic History of the *Herald* of the Bennetts', serialised in *Editor & Publisher,* 56-8 (29 Mar 1924 – 13 June 1925).

[34]James Parton, *The Life of Horace Greeley* (NY 1855), p. 151.

[35]Pray, pp. 31-2.

[36]*NYH* 14 Jan 1860; 11 Jan 1866.

[37]Pray, p. 468.

'tricksters', 'loafers', 'frauds', 'parasites', 'spoilsmen', 'thieves' and 'vagabonds', with many a choice adjective thrown in. 'For the people at large', Bennett proclaimed, 'the question is simply whether these politicians – these two hundred thousand hungry lawyers – are to be allowed to ruin the country or not'.[38] If in the 1820s the politicians drove the press the opposite seemed true in the 1850s. For this Bennett claimed credit. A little optimistically he told his readers in 1856 that 'the age of politicians is past and gone. We are at the beginning of a new period, in which all contests shall be decided by the independent press, working independently of parties and cliques and guided only by national instincts.'[39]

For Bennett was never indifferent to elections, and his 'national instincts' generally led him to support whichever party or candidate seemed the most popular. In 1840 he supported the Whig 'Log Cabin and Hard Cider' campaign and had the pleasure of helping to defeat Van Buren's bid for a second presidential term. The following chapters will deal with Bennett's role in politics in the 1850s and '60s and show how capriciously he could bestow his support on candidates who pleased him and withdraw it from those who did not. The politicians naturally hated Bennett as a demagogue and were outraged by his changing of sides, but they also had to fear him.[40] To their charges of treachery Bennett merely replied that they did not understand what he was at and that he owed no loyalty to any party. His revenge for his early experiences was long and sweet. He came to care only for the *Herald*, disdaining equally the idea of being controlled and those who sought to patronise him.[41] It is not unlikely that he made a system of caprice in politics partly in order to demonstrate and enjoy his independence.

Establishing the *Herald*

To create this independence it was first necessary to establish the *Herald* successfully and make it financially independent of the politicians. This Bennett did in three ways. Firstly, he provided a range of news coverage surpassing that of his rivals and presented his

[38]*NYH* 26 Mar 1856. See also *ibid.,* 7 April; 4 May 1859.

[39]*NYH* 8 Oct 1856.

[40]Francis P. Blair said of Bennett in 1856 'He don't seem to mix with the politicians, but he appears to know every thing that is going on around him' — quoted in Hudson, p. 239. On the politicians' fear of offending Bennett see also Edward Dicey, *Six Months in the Federal States* (London 1863), vol 1, pp. 32-3.

[41]New York *Spirit of the Times,* article reprinted in *NYH* 8 June 1872.

news more promptly and in a more appealing way. Secondly, he secured sufficient advertising patronage to make his paper a viable proposition and managed it on sound business principles. Thirdly, he demonstrated that he had the showman's ability to make himself an item of news and gave his paper notoriety by attacking the editors of other papers. Each of these topics deserves some discussion.[42]

The phenomenal success of Day's *Sun* suggested to Bennett that the Penny Press had only begun to tap the mass readership which New York City offered. The first number of the *Morning Herald*[43] made this analysis of the market:

> There are in this city at least 150,000 persons who glance over one or more newspapers every day. Only 42,000 daily sheets are issued to supply them. We have plenty of room, therefore, without jostling our neighbours, rivals or friends, to pick up at least twenty or thirty thousand for the *Herald*, and leave something for others who come after us. By furnishing a daily paper at... [a low price]... and making it at the same time equal to any of the high priced papers for intelligence, good taste, sagacity, and industry, there is not a person in the city, male or female, that may not be able to say, 'Well, I have got a paper of my own which will tell me about what's doing in the world. I'm busy now, but I'll put it in my pocket, and read it at my leisure'[44]

More crisply he later declared: 'That I *can* surpass every paper in New York, every person will acknowledge – that I *will* do so, I am resolved, determined.'[45]

---

[42]Two classic essays on the founding and rise of the *Herald* are Charles H. Levermore, 'The Rise of Metropolitan Journalism', *American Historical Review*, 6 (1900-1), 446-65 and Willard G. Bleyer, *Main Currents in the History of American Journalism* (NY 1927). See also James Melvin Lee, *History of American Journalism* (NY 1917), pp. 193-205; James Parton, 'The New York Herald', *North American Review*, 102 (Apr 1866), 373-419; Pray, ch XIV; Hudson, ch XXVII; Oliver Carlson, *The Man Who Made News: James Gordon Bennett 1795-1872* (NY 1942), ch 8; Louis M. Starr, 'James Gordon Bennett — Benificent Rascal', *American Heritage*, 6 (Feb 1955), pp. 32-7; Coleman, 'A New and Authentic History of the Herald', *loc. cit.* The general histories of journalism by Mott, Emery and Kobre, cited in notes 7 and 30 above, all contain notable essays on Bennett.

[43]The *New York Herald* began life as the *Morning Herald*. A fire put it out of business for a while in August 1835 and it resumed simply as the *Herald* (see *Herald* 31 Aug 1835). In 1837 it reverted to the title *Morning Herald* and only on enlargement in 1840 did it adopt the name New York Herald (*NYH* 21 Sept 1840). Possibly the name change had something to do with 'Moral War' — see below.

[44]*Morning Herald* 6 May 1835. In his 1832 prospectus for the NY *Globe* Bennett had ridiculed the huge, unwieldy commercial sheets as 'the pine barrens of intelligence and taste'.

[45]Pray, p. 468.

The *Herald* soon began to outdo the *Sun* in its sensational reports of crime and scandal, delighting in describing itself as 'saucy' and 'spicy'. 'I have seen human depravity to the core', trumpeted Bennett, 'I proclaim each morning . . . the deep guilt that is encrusting over society'.[46] The *Herald* became a muckraker on the calculation that the people of New York 'were more ready to seek six columns of the details of a brutal murder, or of testimony in a divorce case, or the trial of a divine for improprieties of conduct, than the same amount of words poured forth by the genius of the noblest author of the times'.[47]

The story which above all others made the *Herald*'s reputation was the Jewett-Robinson brothel murder of 1836.[48] Bennett's energetic personal reporting of this episode (during which, by the way, he is credited with originating the interview)[49] and his imaginative exploitation of the supposed 'mystery' of the culprit boosted *Herald* sales to 15,000 daily.

While cutting dramatically into the established preserve of the other penny papers Bennett also grasped that between the police courts on the one hand and the counting house and Congress on the other there lay unexploited a wide range of newsworthy human activity. He did not invent curiosity but he was perhaps the first man to demonstrate to the full its commercial value. He asserted the right of the reporter to go into spheres of society which had previously been regarded as private. The *Herald* spoke sternly of the follies and extravagances of the rich, yet it insinuated its reporters into dress balls and the fashionable watering places. The doings of the social elite, their manners and their dress, were reported with a mixture of irreverence and envy well calculated to appeal to female readers. High society was at first affronted by this intrusion but, knowing that to snub the ubiquitous *Herald* man could mean a cruel lampooning in the paper, it had to accept publicity as a fact of life and in time became educated to using it to advantage.[50]

---

[46]*NYH* 19 Aug 1836.

[47]Pray, p. 225.

[48]Bennett's sensational treatment of the case was sharply attacked in an anonymous 1844 pamphlet, *The Life and Writings of James Gordon Bennett, Editor of the New York Herald,* pp. 12-22. This pamphlet seems to have been subsidised by Bennett's rivals and sought to 'expose' him as a scoundrel chiefly by reprinting a series of spicy stories from the *Herald* files. There is a journalist's appreciation of Bennett's coverage in Alexander Woollcott, 'La Belle Helene and Mr. B', *While Rome Burns* (London 1934), pp. 180-7.

[49]Carlson, p. 146.

[50]Allan Nevins ed., *The Diary of Philip Hone* (NY 1936), pp. 289-90, 464-5. Hone, ex-mayor and social elitist, considered Bennett 'infamous' and a 'scoundrel'. The *Herald* had opposed his political aspirations.

Similarly, preachers and lecturers came to accept with a reluctance which now seems quaint that their orations would become public property through the *Herald* on the day after their delivery.[51] Bennett started regular reporting of religious affairs in 1839, though this in no way tempered the cocksure and blasphemous tone of the paper in its early days towards formal religion. (It was quite characteristic of the *Herald* to refer to the Pope as 'a decrepit, licentious, stupid, Italian blockhead').[52] Bennett's standard answer to criticisms of him by reformers, clergymen and politicians was that they owed the free dissemination of their views to the *Herald*. Speeches on important topics were printed with a fullness and impartiality which, though not above reproach, was unusual by the standards of the age.

Although Bennett disapproved editorially of prize fighting it received full publicity in his news columns. Sports such as horse racing and later yachting were given generous attention, though they had been deemed below the notice of the 'respectable' journals.[53] The theatre and the opera were also reported in the *Herald*, and the paper became deeply involved in the theatrical politics which were then so much a staple of New York life. Bennett had his first beating from an irate theatre manager in 1836. Thereafter, the *Herald*'s partiality involved it in a long series of law suits and embroilments including the Astor Place riots of 1850, the famous *Fry vs. Bennett* libel case of 1855 (in which the editor eventually had to pay $6,000 to the manager of the Astor Place Opera House) and Bennett's 'Theatre War' of 1865 arising from a property dispute with the showman Phineas T. Barnum.[54] Isaac C. Pray, sometime head of the *Herald*'s theatrical department, complained of the impossibility of making positive criticisms without offending managers or performers or both.[55] On the other hand the *Herald*'s favouritism or prejudice towards certain performers was regarded as venal by many. P.T. Barnum complained that the 'great Ogre of the *Herald*' ruled the theatre managers 'with a rod of iron' by blackballing or blackguarding those who presumed to have their handbills and posters printed elsewhere than in the *Herald*

[51]Hudson, p. 453.

[52]*Morning Herald* 14 May 1840.

[53]For general discussion see John R. Betts, 'The Technological Revolution and the Rise of Sport, 1850-1900', *Mississippi Valley Historical Review,* 40 (1953-4) 231-56. See also Hone, *Diary,* pp. 619-20, 870-1.

[54]On Fry see *NYH* 18, 25 Feb; 9, 14 Mar; 6 Oct 1855; Hudson, p. 753. On theatre war see *NYH* 2, 3, 9, 12 Oct; 8 Nov; 2 Dec etc. 1865; P.T. Barnum, *Struggles and Triumphs* (London 1869), ch XLI — a scathing attack on JGB; Don C. Seitz, *The James Gordon Bennetts* (NY 1928), ch VI; Carlson, p. 380.

[55]Pray, p. 463 and *passim*.

job printing office 'at Bennett's exorbitant prices'.[56]   Bennett's reputation recalls Artemus Ward's notorious comic encounter with a country editor:

> I was shaimfully aboozed by a editer in human form. He set my Show up steep & Kalled me the urbane & gentlemunly manajer, but when I, fur the purpuss of showin fair play all around, went to anuther offiss to git my hanbills printed, what duz this pussillanermus editer do but change his toon and abooze me like a Injun. He sed my wax wurks was a humbug & called me a horey-heded itinerent vagabone. I thort at fust I'd pollish him orf, but on reflectin that he cood pollish me much wuss in his paper, I giv it up.

By extending the concept of what was news and finding interesting ways of presenting it, Bennett forced the other papers to try to keep pace with him.[57]   The *Herald* was full of 'human interest': it offered something for everyone as no newspaper had ever attempted to do. Bennett's rivals soon learned that his extravagant boasts were backed by a 'rare natural gift, amounting almost to prescience'[58] for divining what news and ideas would sell. An exasperated editor once cried that 'It would be worth my while, sir, to give a million dollars, if the Devil would come and tell me every evening, as he does Bennett, what the people of New York would like to read about next morning.'[59]

Bennett had declared in 1835 that he intended to make a commercial newspaper for the millions, not for Wall Street.[60]   He realised too that 'there was more journalistic money to be made in recording gossip that interested bar-rooms, work-shops, race courses and tenement houses, than in consulting the tastes of drawing rooms and libraries'.[61]   At the same time, though, the *Herald* was in direct competition with the sixpenny papers. The editors of the commercial sheets disapproved of the *Herald*'s sensationalism and emphasis on immorality but also feared its intrusion into their own market.

The *Herald*'s resourcefulness in reporting local news did not diminish its coverage of national affairs. Politics were discussed as a

---

[56]Barnum, p. 668.

[57]Greeley's sour comment on the early *Herald* was that its news quality 'might be bad, and generally was; but it suited the multitude' — NY *Daily Tribune* 3 June 1872.

[58]NY *Sunday Mercury* 2 June 1872.

[59]Henry J. Raymond of the *Times,* quoted in Dicey, 1, p. 33.

[60]Pray, p. 194. For a discussion of the *Herald* as an exemplar of the 'democratic market society' see Michael Schudson, *Discovering the News* (NY 1978), ch 1.

[61]E.L. Godkin on Bennett, NY *Evening Post* 30 Dec 1899.

sport in the slang of the turf or prize ring and with the same jaunty mixture of personalities and gossip which Bennett had practised as a Washington correspondent. He soon had his own reporter stationed in that city.[62]   From 1837 news from Europe was rushed in by the *Herald*'s fleet of newsboats in the harbour, the *Teazer, Celeste* and *Boxer,* in competition with those of other papers.[63]   The first transatlantic steamship, the *Sirius,* arrived in New York from England in 1838. Bennett, fully alive to the commercial possibilities now opened, made the return journey on the ship (he now had sufficient staff to run the *Herald* in his absence) and organised a team of correspondents in Europe. In the same year the *Herald* extended its arrangements for covering internal news and exchanging bulletins with provincial papers throughout the Union.[64]

This enterprise was a serious menace to the sixpenny papers, but more threatening to them was Bennett's rude invasion of the holy precincts of Wall Street. His education in economics was used to advantage in discussing business matters. On 11 May 1835 Bennett made his first report on the money market.[65]   Very soon this item, describing the state of buying and selling various commodities in the informal jargon of bulls and bears, became a standard feature, and one for which Bennett was personally responsible.[66]   His disclosures of the affairs of the financial community and especially his listing of bankrupts brought accusations of blackmail and manipulation of the market and more law suits.[67]   In turn Bennett made a great deal of noise about exposing speculators to public wrath, but the *Herald* money articles survived controversy and proved of permanent value. Although the *Herald* was never quite 'respectable', a critic complained, 'the money article constantly lengthened, and increased in importance. It won for the little paper a kind of footing in broker's offices and bank parlors, and provided many respectable persons with an excuse for reading it.'[68]

[62]Marbut, 'Early Washington Correspondents', and *News from the Capital* (Carbondale 1971), pp. 44-5.

[63]T.H. Giddings, 'Rushing the Transatlantic News in the 1830s and 1840s', *New York Historical Society Quarterly,* 42 (1958), 47-59; Hudson, p. 445.

[64]Hudson, pp. 450-1; Pray, 236, 249-51. For a sketch of Bennett on the *Sirius* trip see Henry Wikoff, *Reminiscences of an Idler* (NY 1880), pp. 464-6, 473-4, 486-90.

[65]Hudson, p. 434. They became regular from 13 June 1835.

[66]Hudson, p. 436, for the controversy over the authorship.

[67]Pray, p. 321. Bennett always denied speculating in the money market, a claim in which Pray, p. 187, and Hudson, p. 436, supported him. See also *NYH* 21 Feb 1857 where Bennett characterised one such accusation as an 'unblushing falsehood'.

[68]James Parton, 'The New York Herald'; see also 'John Smith's brother' to Bennett 3 Feb 1844 in Bennett Papers, New York Public Library.

In many spheres of business the *Herald* showed that its boast of appealing to the merchant, principal and employer as well as to the mechanic, clerk and journeyman was not an idle one. The paper put itself close to the commercial pulse of the city and competed with the sixpennies in its shipping news and concern for the maritime matters by which New York lived.[69] The general competence of the *Herald* in discussing the business life of the community foreshadowed the day when it would surpass the sixpennies in its economic analyses, just as it would in its political news.[70] In 1857 the *Herald* predicted the financial panic so accurately as to be accused of fomenting it.[71]

Economic acumen was useful to Bennett in more ways than one. Journalistic skill was one thing – and he proved that he had it in abundance – but the ability to manage a newspaper business successfully was a rarer commodity. Bennett knew from his own experience that newspapers in the city had a high mortality rate[72] and that some of the commercial dailies lost something like a quarter of their profits through bad debts from yearly subscribers.[73] The *Herald* followed the example of the *Sun* in being sold on the streets by newsboys, whereas previously the casual buyer of one of the commercial dailies had to call at its office. The *Herald* was sold in lots of one hundred to newsboys – 'a gang of troublesome ragged boys' – at a discount for sale to the public. Yearly subscribers were obliged to pay cash in advance.[74]

With the advent of the railroad in the 1840s, the *Herald* established a regular system of carriers so that the people of Newark, Patterson, Albany, Troy, Poughkeepsie and Philadelphia could have their *Herald* delivered in the early morning. Bennett may not have originated the practice of delivering the paper so that it could be read

[69]Note the extensive use of the *Herald* as a source in Robert G. Albion, *The Rise of New York Port, 1815-60* (NY 1939) and Philip S. Foner, *Business and Slavery* (Chapel Hill 1941).

[70]For comment see Crouthamel, 'The Newspaper Revolution'.

[71]*NYH* 4, 11, Feb; 18 Mar; 16, 26, 30 Sept; 7, 16, 18, 22, Oct; 6, 7, 8 Nov 1857; 23 Jan 1858. Bennett blamed the crash on reckless and excessive speculation. Even Parton in 'The New York Herald', p. 382, noticed 'among the nonsense which he daily poured forth, some gleams of a superior understanding of the fundamental laws of finance. He appears to have understood 1837 and 1857 better than most of his contemporaries.'

[72]Between 1820 and 1861 no fewer than thirty-five newspapers were discontinued in New York City — Kenny, *Newspaper Directory*. Bennett's *Globe* was one of the these.

[73]Alfred M. Lee, *The Daily Newspaper in America* (NY 1937), p. 261.

[74]James Melvin Lee, *History of American Journalism*, p. 201: Hudson, pp. 441-2; Hone, *Diary*, p. 195.

at the breakfast table or on the way to work, but he made it widespread and regular.[75]

He extended the policy of cash in advance from sales to advertising. It was said that after the destructive fire of 1835 only an advertising contract from Dr Brandreth, manufacturer of quack pills, enabled Bennett to resume publication of the *Herald*.[76] When complaints were received at the number of quack advertisements which appeared in the *Herald* and which even Bennett's biographer admitted were a 'heartless imposition' on the public,[77] Bennett replied blandly: 'Send us more advertisements than Dr Brandreth does – give us higher prices – we'll cut Dr Brandreth dead – or at least curtail his space. Business is business – money is money.'[78] So the *Herald* kept its reputation for advertising the wares of charlatans in the medical, spiritualist and astrological lines: a policy which provided a stick for its enemies to beat it with.[79] Rival editors also professed disgust at the dubious nature of some of the *Herald*'s 'personal' advertisements. Although lawyers failed to make much profit out of pressing indecency charges, prostitutes habitually made assignations through the *Herald*.[80]

From 1836 the *Herald* required cash in advance from its advertisers. From 1847 advertisements had to be inserted and renewed daily. Each one was limited to small print and woodcut illustrations disappeared, which meant that the small retailer or individual received the same treatment as the large manufacturer. If an advertiser wanted more space he just had to buy up more units, but the size of the type used remained the same. There were no full page advertising spreads – in this respect the *Herald* practised commercial democracy.[81] This paid so handsomely that in the 1850s the *Herald*

[75]Hudson, p. 438.

[76]A.M. Lee, p. 317.

[77]Pray, p. 201.

[78]*NYH* 26 June 1836. In 1837 Bennett quarrelled with Brandreth and warned the public 'from being any longer deceived and cheated by the quackeries of this most impudent charlatan' *NYH* 29 Mar 1837. See also James Harvey Young, *The Toadstool Millionaires* (Princeton 1961), pp. 81, 84-9.

[79]Bennett customarily denounced spiritualism as a cover for immorality in his editorial column while printing stories about it on his front page. William H. Russell was struck by this peculiarity of the New York press when he visited America in 1861, see *My Diary North and South* (London 1863), vol 1, pp. 38-9.

[80]*NYH* 12, 15 Jan 1862; 23 Oct 1864; Hudson, pp. 472-8. The *Herald*'s personal column became a legal Achilles' heel during the proprietorship of Bennett's son, and through it William Randolph Hearst was able to deal the paper a severe blow – see Richard O'Connor, *The Scandalous Mr. Bennett* (NY 1962), ch XI.

[81]Hudson, pp. 468-76, deals with *Herald* advertising policy. On mid-century advertising in general, with reference to the *Herald*, see Mott, pp. 298-302.

began to appear in 'double sheets' of eight pages and then in 'triple sheets' of twelve pages to accommodate the volume of advertising.[82] In 1856 the *Herald* received $186,258 in advertising revenue alone. In 1866 it made $196,366 in a three month period.[83]

As a result of this successful management Bennett not only won independence from politicians and advertising patrons alike – which in the 1820s would have been an undreamed of achievement– he also made his personal fortune. Two years after its founding he estimated the *Herald* as already worth $100,000,[84] and it was certainly worth that by the mid 1840s. In 1852 Bennett confided to President Pierce that his personal net income was between forty and fifty thousand dollars annually, 'and every year this revenue is increasing with the increase of the country'.[85] He was able to live in luxury and still plough back large profits into the newspaper which was his passion. More investment in news coverage and technical improvement brought in more revenue from circulation, and so on. In 1869 Bennett was offered and refused $2 million for the *Herald*, musing 'What shall I do with the money. More important yet, what shall I do with myself?'[86] That same year the editor who had landed in America with nothing and who started the *Herald* with a capital of $500 was able to donate $10,000 towards the establishment of a Pension and Annuity Fund Association and a Social Club for the numerous band of *Herald* workers.[87] Bennett was never in the same wealthy league as the great merchant princes of the city but his son was seldom called on to think in sums of less than five figures.[88] Small wonder that the *Herald* paid better salaries than other papers.[89] A despiser of the press, writing in 1859, ascribed 'to the genius of Bennett . . . the origin of that infernal system which has enabled many newspaper proprietors to become

[82]The first double sheet edition appeared on 1 Apr 1850. The *Herald* went into quadruple sheets in 1869. It also increased in size. It started in 1835 at 10½ x 14½ inches and grew until in 1869 it measured 23 x 34, see Hudson, p. 469; A.M. Lee, p. 260.

[83]*NYH* 5 Jan 1857; 31 July 1856. *NYH* 12, 16, Sept 1859.

[84]*NYH* 28 Feb 1837. It cost Henry J. Raymond and his associates that sum to set up the *Times* in 1851.

[85]Bennett to Pierce 15 Dec 1852, Pierce Papers, LC. Compare Bennett to Thomas Ritchie 10 Nov 1845, Bennett Papers, LC, at which time he put his personal income at over $20,000.

[86]Hudson, p. 538.

[87]*Ibid.*, p. 489.

[88]Seitz, p. 377, estimates that the younger Bennett drew $30 million from the *Herald* and spent it during his lifetime.

[89]Parton, 'The New York Herald'.

nabobs in wealth and despots in power'.[90] For a man to make so much money out of a newspaper was unprecedented in America or anywhere else.

This is to run on. There was, it has been said, a third factor in the *Herald*'s early success. Bennett decided that the best way to launch his paper was to make it notorious.[91] His biographer wrote that 'he could attract no public attention till he caricatured himself'.[92] This he did with tasteless abandon. 'I know and feel I shall succeed. Nothing can prevent . . . success but God Almighty, and he happens to be entirely on my side. Get out of my way, ye drivelling editors and drivelling politicians . . .'[93] Every morning he made the *Herald* 'a bundle of detonating fire crackers' on the streets of the city.[94] Alongside his flamboyant proclamations of the *Herald*'s civilizing mission were continual hits and insults to fellow editors, ranging from the wryly humorous to the downright vicious. Bennett was wont to give the impression that he had invented journalism and to contrast his own virtue and energy with that of the 'dull, ignorant, miserable, barbarian papers around me', which according to him were incapable of expressing the spirit of the age.[95]

The other papers, penny and sixpenny alike, were soon forced to take notice of Bennett to defend themselves from his charges, so providing publicity for the *Herald*. Benjamin H. Day inveighed in the *Sun* against 'the notorious vagabond Bennett; the veriest reptile that ever defiled the paths of decency' whose 'only chance of dying an upright man will be that of hanging perpendicularly upon a rope'.[96] Bennett accused James Watson Webb of stock jobbing on Wall Street, and goaded him to the point where the furious colonel attacked him in the street early in 1836. Although the 'respectable' portion of society felt that Bennett had got his just deserts[97] the irrepressible

[90]Lambert A. Wilmer, *Our Press Gang* (Philadelphia 1859), p. 82.

[91]Very possibly he remembered the popularity of Joseph T. Buckingham's *New England Galaxy* when he was in Boston in 1820. Pray says that Buckingham's style was 'extravagant and severe' (pp. 44-5). A.M. Lee, p. 383, thinks that Buckingham's example taught Bennett 'that the American reader consumes most avidly that which he detests most blatantly'.

[92]Pray, p. 225.

[93]*NYH* 20 July 1836.

[94]Paul Peebles, 'James Gordon Bennett's Scintillations', *Galaxy,* 14 (Aug 1872), 258 ff., reprinted in E.H. Ford and E. Emery eds., *Highlights in the History of the American Press* (Minneapolis 1954), pp. 150-9.

[95]Quoted in Pray, p. 228.

[96]Quoted in O'Brien, *Story of the Sun,* pp. 62, 63.

[97]Hone, *Diary,* p. 195.

"Blow, Herald, blow!"

Bennett blows his own trumpet.
(From *Vanity Fair*, 18 February 1860).

editor managed to make capital out of the beating he received. His jaunty account of the affair appeared in the next day's *Herald*. Webb, he related, 'cut a slash in my head about one and a half inches in length, and through the integuments of the skull. The fellow, no doubt, wanted to let out the never failing supply of good humour and wit, which has created such a reputation for the *Herald*, and appropriate the contents to supply the emptiness of his own thick skull.'[98] The *Herald* sold 9,000 copies that day.

This tactic was so obviously successful that Bennett continued his galling verbal flings at Webb, which though often unfair and tasteless, could also be very funny. Not surprisingly, a second assault occurred in May 1836. Although Bennett again got the worst of the brawl, he won the war of words in the next day's *Herald*:

> As I was leisurely pursuing my business yesterday, in Wall Street, collecting the information which is daily disseminated in the *Herald*, James Watson Webb came up to me ... said something which I could not hear distinctly, then pushed me down the stone steps, leading to one of the broker's offices, and commenced fighting with a species of brutal and demoniac desperation characteristic of a fury.
>
> My damage is a scratch, about three quarters of an inch in length, on the third finger of the left hand, which I received from the iron railing I was forced against, and three buttons torn from my vest, which any tailor will reinstate for a sixpence. His loss is a rent from top to bottom of a very beautiful black coat, which cost the ruffian $40, and a blow in the face, which may have knocked down his throat some of his infernal teeth for anything I know. Balance in my favor $39.94.[99]

The various thrashings which Bennett received in 1836 seemed to make him 'a common flogging property' but could not quell him.[100] Twenty years later Bennett's biographer, considering these editorial feuds, marvelled 'how gentlemen of talent, taste and education could carry on so absurd a warfare, for the mere purpose of an ephemeral notoriety. ... Yet it was done, till every vestige of character seemed lost to each assailant ... the public treated them only as they do tragedians, who die at night upon the stage, to live the next day and so on, from year to year'.[101] It was the vulgarity of this epoch of the New York press that Charles Dickens caricatured so savagely in *Martin Chuzzlewit*.

[98]*NYH* 21 Jan 1836; Pray, p. 205.

[99]*NYH* 10 May 1836. See also Crouthamel, *Webb*, pp. 72-3.

[100]NY *Sun* 10 May; 19 July 1836; Pray, p. 214; Carlson, p. 172.

[101]Pray, p. 201.

Criticism notwithstanding, by 1836 the *Herald* was successful even beyond the sanguine hopes of its editor.[102] In that year its price was raised to two cents (at which it sold for the next twenty-six years) yet its circulation was closing on that of the *Sun*. Bennett claimed a circulation of 17,000 in 1840.[103] The basic cause of this popularity, and one which endured through the next thirty years, may have been as one writer tried to put it, 'We do not so much know that we have had the *Herald* as that we have Bennett'.[104]

The Moral War of 1840

Bennett's aggressive techniques for selling his newspaper were proving a huge commercial success by 1840, but they produced a backlash in that year which left its mark on the *Herald* and its editor.

It is doubtful whether the mass of *Herald* readers were so much offended as amused by the 'shocking' things that they read in the paper, but the articulate classes of the city, including many clergy (both Protestant and Catholic), politicians, business people and reformers, were sufficiently outraged to mount a concerted attack to drive the *Herald* out of existence. Bennett always claimed that the 'Moral War' against him was nothing but a scheme by jealous rival editors for eliminating a dangerous competitor, and it is true that among the charges levelled at him incompetence in running a newspaper was not included. It was true, too, that some of the opposition to him was motivated by sheer snobbery and prudishness, as Bennett recognised in his contemptuous challenge: 'Petticoats-petticoats-petticoats-petticoats – there – you fastidious fools, vent your mawkishness on that.'[105]

The strength and passion of the onslaught, however, bespoke something more serious than a business struggle. When in May 1840

[102]*Ibid.*, p. 228.

[103]*NYH* 30 May 1840.

[104]NY *Standard* 14 June 1872.

[105]Quoted in Pray, p. 266. Pray did not attempt a complete defence of Bennett's conduct of the 'War' but he did point out the vindictiveness of the attack (pp. 263-79). A contemporary pamphlet, *The War of the Giants Against James Gordon Bennett and other recent matters* by 'Three Lookers-on in Venice' (NY 1840) likewise found Bennett culpable but questioned the motives and purity of his attackers. Hudson defended Bennett and claimed a victory for him — pp. 456 ff. In his *History of Journalism in the United States* (NY 1924), G.H. Payne stressed the snobbery and anti-democratic sentiment of Bennett's foes and Seitz, p. 84, tends to agree. Carlson, pp. 184-90, considering the volume of the *Herald's* salaciousness and blasphemy, thinks that after all Bennett was more sinning than sinned against. Circulation wars among the New York papers were intermittent. The *Herald* itself joined in one on the *Tribune* in the 1840s and on Pulitzer's *World* in the 1880s.

Bennett suggested that the physical deformity of Park Benjamin, editor of the *Evening Signal*, was a divine punishment he touched off a pre-arranged salvo of abuse against himself and the bad taste of his paper.[106] Webb of the *Courier and Enquirer*[107] and Noah of the *Evening Star* led off against their old associate and were followed not only by the other New York papers but by those in other cities. They exhausted the vocabulary of defamation on Bennett,[108] but the war was not confined to the editorial columns. Committees made energetic efforts to have the *Herald* removed from public reading rooms and put pressure on advertisers to withdraw their subscriptions. They sought to make Bennett a social pariah.

Bennett gained from the excesses of his enemies by his stance of impudence. 'These blockheads are determined to make me the greatest man of the age' he declared.[109] Nor did the 'Holy Allies' as he dubbed them, succeed in undermining to any critical degree the *Herald*'s value as an advertising medium,[110] and the paper proved too firmly established to be dislodged by even the most virulent assaults. But, though Bennett survived the 'Moral War', the publicity this time had not been wholly beneficial. The *Herald*'s own figures indicate that it lost perhaps one third of its readership at this time, and that it took five years to return to the pre-1840 circulation level.[111] If they failed to destroy him, the 'Holy Allies' did force Bennett to a public promise that the tone of the *Herald* would be improved in future. Never again was the paper quite so impishly egotistical, so crudely defiant of good taste: as Greeley later sneered, it gained some decency if not principle.[112]

Bennett's talent for publicising himself, culminating in a flamboyant declaration[113] of his forthcoming marriage to Henrietta Agnes Crean[114] at the height of the 'Moral War', also backfired on his family. An attempt was made to have the honeymoon couple excluded from

[106]See Merle M. Hoover, *Park Benjamin* (NY 1948) pp. 103-9.

[107]For Webb's role in the 'Moral War' see Crouthamel, *Webb* pp. 84-6.

[108]Hudson amused himself and his readers by compiling a list of adjectives, pp. 459-60.

[109]Pray, p. 275.

[110]Hudson cites instances of important advertisers who refused to yield to the pressure of the committees, pp. 457-8.

[111]Bleyer, p. 194; but see Hudson, pp. 460-1.

[112]NY *Daily Tribune* 3 June 1872.

[113]NYH 1 June 1840.

[114]Bennett's brother-in-law, Robert Crean, became manager of the *Herald*'s business department.

the Astor Hotel. Mrs Bennett was subjected to slanders of the lowest kind which Bennett's success in a libel suit against Noah could not still.[115] From 1840 Bennett was more than ever isolated and embittered.[116] Perhaps to escape the consequences of her husband's disrepute, Mrs Bennett began to spend increasing periods in Europe. Even when he was famous and powerful and his paper was the most successful in the world he was never acceptable at the tables of 'good society' in New York. At a public dinner in 1866 Bennett 'seemed quite lost and ill at ease. He did not appear to know anyone, nor anyone to know him'.[117] His success and singular notoriety made him a whipping boy for a rising generation of journalists in the 1840s and '50s, long after the *Herald* had relinquished any claim to being the most scurrilous sheet in the country.

With some justice Bennett pondered, 'what would become of the Sunday and country papers without the HERALD to steal from and Bennett to abuse we really cannot imagine'.[118]

He was able to see the humour of the situation however, as instanced by this reply he made to some press rumours about himself:

> An exceedingly desperate fellow this editor of the HERALD...
> If he goes abroad for his health, he is a villain who cares nothing
> for his country. If he comes home, he is sent by a committee of
> conspirators to consummate a scheme against the interests of the
> United States. If he leads a quiet life, he is an outcast shunned by
> mankind. If he goes into society, he is steeped in 'Parisian
> infamies'. We are sure that the public at large will be delighted by
> this imitation of European manners, in the shape of a Court
> journal to chronicle the doings and movements of such important
> personages as the Editor of the HERALD. It is sure to thrive in
> this country; and we may soon expect to see the *Union* noting in
> double leads that 'the Editor of the HERALD rose at seven this
> morning and shaved himself': or 'Mr. Bennett took his usual walk
> in Broadway on Thursday', or 'James Gordon Bennett had the
> audacity to dine at two yesterday, doubtless for some sinister
> purpose. When we add that he supped at nine and ate part of a
> lobster the villainy of the hoary miscreant can no longer be
> questioned.'[119]

[115]Pray, p. 274; Hone, *Diary,* p. 484-5; Anon, *Life and Writings of James Gordon Bennett,* pp. 58-62.

[116]NY *Daily Tribune* 3 June 1872.

[117]See sketch of Bennett in Junius H. Browne, *The Great Metropolis* (NY 1869), pp. 491-8. On JGB's social ostracism see also Parton, 'The New York Herald' and Dicey, I, p. 27 ff.

[118]*NYH* 11May 1857; also 8 Sept 1859; 30 Mar 1860.

[119]*NYH* 25 Nov 1854.

The irony of Bennett's situation was that his rivals found it fashionable alternately to decry and belittle his influence then make him the bogey behind every social and political development of the day which they found distasteful. The loss of elections, the Panic of 1857, declining moral standards, the Civil War itself, were all laid at his door. (It was irritating to his enemies that Bennett was free of all the conventional personal vices). It was characteristic that when his biography appeared in 1855 it took the form of a cautious apology and the author preferred to be known simply as 'A journalist'. In the same year Bennett was anonymously presented with a fine silver tea service which bore a number of laudatory inscriptions including 'The most abused editor in America'. Such was his reputation that he was immediately suspected of having arranged the whole thing himself.[120]

Near the end of his active career, in an editorial entitled 'The New York *Herald* Agitating the Whole World', Bennett dismissed all abuse of himself as 'the proofs and price of our popularity', but he said of his accusers, 'our sound and healthy conscience, our pure and virtuous life, and our Christian and consistent career, enable us to laugh at them and their ridiculous stories'.[121]

Co-operation and Rivalry in the 1840s and '50s

Meanwhile, in the wake of the 'Moral War', the *Herald* forged ahead as the foremost newsgatherer and Bennett was ever adding to his reputation for being first with the most news.[122] Having failed to destroy it, the opponents of the *Herald* were pressed to match its news enterprise in the 1840s even when they formed combinations for the purpose.[123] Steamboats ventured further and further out to meet ships arriving from Europe.[124] When the Cunard line opened its Liverpool-Boston run in 1840 the *Herald* chartered special express trains to bring the news from Boston. (Bennett had considered establishing another daily in Boston to print early foreign news but did not press the idea for want of a suitable partner.)[125] Later the race for European

---

[120]*NYH* 5, 14 Jan 1855.

[121]*NYH* 8 Nov 1865.

[122]Carlson, p. 204, quotes a contemporary as saying 'Always at work, always finding new ways of building his paper — that is Bennett'.

[123]Pray, pp. 372-7. On these combinations (and for what follows generally) see Victor Rosewater, *History of Co-operative Newsgathering in the United States* (NY 1930), esp. pp. 27-8. See also Giddings, 'Rushing the Transatlantic News'; Crouthamel, 'The Newspaper Revolution'; Emery, *The Press and America,* ch 12, 'The Race for News'.

[124]Hudson, pp. 451-2, relates a 'beat' by the *Fanny Elssler,* a *Herald* boat.

[125]*Ibid.,* p. 560.

news was focused on Halifax, Nova Scotia, the Cunarders' first port of call.

Exploitation of modern technology was paired with the use of such traditional methods as horse expresses and even carrier pigeons. Then in the late 1840s the spread of the 'magnetic' telegraph began to compete with even the steam engine as the most rapid means of getting domestic news.[126] Bennett was among the first to realise the commercial value to the press of the new invention, and his enthusiasm led him to become a heavy patron of the telegraph– quite possibly the heaviest in the country.[127]

The telegraph enabled the *Herald* to get prompt reports of speeches in Congress, so dealing a heavy blow to the prestige of the Washington papers. Bennett had already embarrassed them in the late 1830s by exposing Congressional printing jobs.[128] Now they could no longer retain their lead in reporting national affairs and Bennett boasted with satisfaction that Washington had become merely a place where the ideas of the New York press were discussed. (The *Herald* experienced some difficulty in getting its corps of reporters into the Senate, however. Bennett claimed to be breaking down archaic and illiberal restrictions on free reporting for the benefit of the whole press. The truth seems to have been rather that in 1841 the Senate deliberately proscribed the *Herald* for political reasons. A *Herald* correspondent was supposed to have undue influence with President Tyler and the paper's partisan devotion to the executive was on that account unacceptable to his opponents in the upper house.)[129]

[126]The telegraph was first extended from Washington to Baltimore and the wires reached New York in 1946. At the beginning of that year there were 40 miles of wire in the US, six years later there were 23,283 miles – see Robert L. Thompson, *Wiring a Continent* (Princeton 1947); Rosewater, pp. 27-8.

[127]Rosewater, pp. 41-2; Hudson, p. 480.

[128]Pray, pp. 289-90. Bennett revealed the extent of the federal subsidisation of the Washington organs, claiming that the *Congressional Globe,* the *National Intelligencer* and the *Madisonian* had been receiving between $90,000 and $33,000 each for printing, advertising and reporting. On the decline of the administration 'organs' see Frederick B. Marbut, 'Decline of the Official Press in Washington', *Journalism Quarterly,* 33 (1956) 335-41, and on the beginnings of telegraphic reports from Washington his *News from the Capital,* ch 7.

[129]In this connection see S. Beman to Bennett, 7 June 1843, New York Historical Society MSS collection. Beman reported that President Tyler 'felt under great obligations to Mr. Bennett. . . the Administration would be very glad of the *Herald's* influence and pay in diplomatic promises'. See further Pray, p. 289; Poore, *Perley's Reminiscences* I, p. 260; Pollard, *The Presidents and the Press,* pp. 217-18; F.B. Marbut, 'The United States Senate and the Press, 1838-41', *Journalism Quarterly,* 28 (1951), 342-50 and his *News from the Capital,* ch 5. Even the *Foreign Quarterly Review* of London denounced the *Herald's* partisanship for Tyler – see vol 30 (1843), pp. 197-222.

By gradual stages the breakneck rivalry of individual papers to cut hours and minutes off the publication of fresh news gave way to a measure of co-operation. Expense was the prime consideration. Although the *Herald*'s coverage of the Mexican war of 1846-8 was outstanding (it was considered remarkable that it sent its own correspondent to the front), it worked in close liaison with a New Orleans paper, the *Crescent City*.[130] The celebrated transmission of a speech by Henry Clay from Lexington, Kentucky in 1847 was shared by the *Herald* with other New York and Philadelphia papers to help defray costs.[131] By May 1848 Frederic Hudson, Office Manager of the *Herald*, and Henry J. Raymond of the *Courier and Enquirer* were acting as the representatives of the six largest New York papers in trying to secure cheaper telegraph rates.[132] An agreement between the *Journal of Commerce*, the *Herald*, the *Sun*, the *Express*, the *Courier and Enquirer* and the *Tribune*, signed by Bennett and the other editors or their representatives on 11 January 1849 formed the New York Harbor News Association. Henceforth the papers collected their ship news in common and divided expenses equally. This has been seen as the formal origin of the Associated Press.[133]

Hudson remained on the executive committe of the AP until after the Civil War, and co-operation in the business of newsgathering became routine. Nevertheless the *Herald* continued to spend large sums on its own exclusive 'beats' and Bennett occasionally complained of the inefficiency of the Associated Press representatives. More than once he threatened to take the *Herald* out.[134]

On the editorial plane the New York papers continued as distinct and mutually hostile as ever. Partly in reaction to the 'Moral War', Horace Greeley founded his *Daily Tribune* in 1841 as a cheap paper with Whig principles. Although the *Herald* sometimes supported Whig candidates, Greeley found its diffusion of Democratic attitudes

---

[130]Rosewater, pp. 41-2: Hudson, pp. 476-7. The *Herald* also co-operated with the Baltimore *Sun* and the Philadelphia *Public Ledger*.

[131]Rosewater, pp. 47-8.

[132]*Ibid.*, ch IX.

[133]Richard A. Schwarzlose, 'Harbor News Association: The Formal Origin of the A.P.', *Journalism Quarterly*, 45 (1968), 253-60, and 'Early Telegraphic News Dispatches: Forerunner of the A.P.', *ibid.*, 51 (1974), 595-601. Among the Bennett letters in the New York Historical Society is a document dated 9 Apr 1849 signed by Bennett, the owners of the *Express, Journal of Commerce, Sun* and Raymond for the *Courier and Enquirer* concerning the repair of the steamboat *Newsboy*.

[134]Augustus Maverick, *Henry J. Raymond and the New York Press for Thirty Years* (Hartford 1870), p. 327.

the more insidiously effective for being unavowed.[135] The *Herald* and the *Tribune* became opposed on virtually all the major and minor issues of the day. Ten years later, in 1851, Henry J. Raymond founded the *New York Times* in an effort to find a way of conservative moderation between the eccentric idealism of Greeley and the cynicism of Bennett. He immediately found a market and in three years the *Times* had a circulation of 42,000.[136]

Raymond's journal, with its deliberately high-toned style, appealed to the 'respectable' professional people of New York. If its prudish motto of 'all the news that's fit to print' excited Bennett's derision, Raymond replied that Bennett's journalism was 'cheap, filthy, false and extravagant'.[137] The *Times* was at first Whig, then Republican in politics and its editor achieved a success which made Greeley jealous. Raymond became Speaker of the New York House of Representatives (1851), Lieutenant Governor of the State (1855-6) and later Republican national party chairman and congressman (1864).

Progressive, competitive and ably managed, the *Herald, Tribune* and *Times* began to leave their rivals far behind in circulation. Small circulation religious papers like the *World* were increasingly in financial difficulties. While the staid *Journal of Commerce* continued to be the voice of the merchant community and the bullish Webb conducted his *Courier & Enquirer* as if the 'newspaper revolution' of the 1830s had never happened, by 1855 the trio of Bennett, Greeley and Raymond were the acknowledged titans of American journalism, each opposing and somehow balancing the others. A contemporary defined the differences between them by saying that 'Greeley spoke to the school house and the lyceum, Bennett to the masses of hurried men and Raymond to the family'.[138]

If Greeley and Raymond used their papers as mouthpieces for party principles, nothing was ever certain of the *Herald* save that it would oppose its two rivals — just how, one had to buy the paper to find out. Manton Marble, who became editor of the New York *World* during the Civil War, once wrote in private envy that 'half the singular

[135]Horace Greeley, *Recollections of a Busy Life* (NY 1869), p. 136. The best studies of Greeley are Glyndon G. Van Deusen, *Horace Greeley* (Philadelphia 1953) and Jeter A. Isley, *Horace Greeley and the Republican Party 1855-61* (Princeton 1947).

[136]W.T. Coggeshall, *Newspaper Record,* pp. 149-50. A satisfying biography is Francis Brown, *Raymond of the Times* (NY 1951), though the older work by Maverick cited above is still useful. See also Meyer Berger, *The Story of the New York Times, 1851-1951* (NY 1951) and Elmer Davis, *History of the New York Times, 1851-1921* (NY 1921).

[137]NY *Times* 26 Aug 1859.

[138]NY *Standard* 31 May 1872.

power of Bennett with the people comes from this, that they judge him with no ambition save what the *Herald* embodies. . . '[139]

If editorial invective never again quite reached the pitch of 1840, personal abuse in print was still common in the 1850s. Each editor would profess self-righteous horror for personal insult in one line while serving it out with interest in the next. To Greeley, Raymond was a 'little villain' and Bennett complained that 'no man has used fouler language towards his opponents than Greeley has done in the course of his career. . . . Every man who differs with him in opinion is instantly put down as a liar, a villain, a rascal, a vagabond or a thief, only fit for the gallows'.[140] Yet when Bennett called Greeley a 'big liar' he tried to excuse himself by saying 'we say big liar, because the qualification of this charge in dainty phraseology with Greeley would be like "casting pearls before swine" '.[141] The institution of the Associated Press did not prevent him from habitually referring to its president, the editor of the *Journal of Commerce,* as 'Jerry Sneak' Hallock.[142] Raymond christened Bennett himself 'Old Satanic', which was the most common nickname among a number bestowed on him. Bennett liked to claim that the *Herald* had successfully followed a plan for raising the tone of public morals over the years, a piece of impudence which, as the *Sun* admitted, everybody enjoyed.[143]

At least the duels were mostly verbal in the 1850s. Bennett was beaten up for the last time by a disappointed Tammany office seeker who battered him in the street in front of his wife in 1850.[144] A bomb

[139]Manton Marble to S.L.M. Barlow, Sept 1867, in Barlow MSS., quoted in George T. McJimsey, *Genteel Partisan* (Iowa 1971), p. 86.

[140]*NYH* 24 Oct 1863. Charles Francis Adams Jr wrote to Henry Adams, 17 Sept 1861, 'did you notice a few days ago an article in the N.Y. *Times* about the *Herald,* in which Bennett was called "the old liar", "a skunk", "a stinkpot" etc. How would the two read if the editorial of the celebrated Potts in the Eatanswill Gazette about the "buff-ball in a buff neighbourhood" and that were put side by side? Which would be the caricature?' — W.C. Ford ed., *A Cycle of Adams Letters, 1861-5* (London 1921), vol I. p. 46. On libel laws at this period see Hudson, ch LIII. Some miscellaneous items on the subject may be found in box 84 of the Manton Marble Collection in the University of London Library.

[141]*NYH* 24 May 1861.

[142]On Hallock see W.H. Hallock, *Life of Gerard Hallock* (NY 1869) and *Dictionary of American Biography.*

[143]NY *Sun* 28 May 1861.

[144]Philip Hone, condescendingly noting John A. Graham's assault in his *Diary* (p. 928) wrote 'I should be well pleased to hear of this fellow [Bennett] punished in this way, and once a week for the remainder of his life, so that new wounds might be inflicted before the old ones were healed, or until he left off lying: but I fear the editorial miscreant in this case will be more benefited than injured by this attack. The public sympathy will be on Bennett's side; the provocation was not sufficient, the motive was a

was delivered to Bennett in 1852, but was discovered before it could explode.[145] Two young Republican zealots conspired at Bennett's elimination during the Civil War, but their plot did not materalise.[146]

In the 1850s Bennett's editorial style was less crudely aggressive than in the early days of the *Herald,* but it was recognisably the same in its vigour, incisiveness and facetiousness. With biblical simplicity a contemporary wrote that Bennett's 'pen burns at the nib, and its strokes are like the stings of scorpions'.[147] He achieved his effect by alternating between erudition, dogma, indignation, slang,[148] sarcasm and sardonic wit which bordered on black humour. Mixing humour with editorials and even news was a more notable trait of nineteenth than twentieth-century journalism.[149] The *Herald* never went to the lengths of the *Sun,* which made money out of its famous 'Moon Hoax' in 1835,[150] but in its early days it contained many news items which were at least semi-humorous. By the 1850s such features were less usual and the separation of news and comment more marked. Bennett's editorial page, though, always had something of the flavour of the London *Punch.* If a cold analysis of some of his political and moral views reveals them as cynical and at times bizarre it must be remembered that Bennett could put his arguments over in such a way as to have his readers laughing with him. He stands comparison with the best of American literary humorists. Recalling his personal acquaintance with Bennett, John Russell Young wrote that the spirit of Voltaire seemed to breathe through him: 'His mind teemed with ideas, which streamed into his talk — saucy phrases, invectives, nicknames, keen bits of narrative charged with cynical pessimism, which remained, one might fancy, as a legacy of early days of disappointment and trial.'[151]

The priggish E. L. Godkin feared that Bennett's method of 'treating everything and everybody as somewhat of a joke' had given

bad one and the character of the assailant not much better than that of the defendant.' See also Carlson, p. 232. For Bennett's lasting grudge against Graham see Henry Wikoff to James Buchanan 14 May 1857 in James Buchanan Papers, Historical Society of Pennsylvania.

[145]Hudson, pp. 465-6, narrates the circumstances.

[146]Parton, 'The New York Herald'.

[147]George W. Bungay, *Off-Hand Takings* (NY 1854), p. 390.

[148]For comment see Francis McCullagh, 'The James Gordon Bennetts and American Journalism', *Studies: An Irish Quarterly Review,* 18 (1929), 394-42.

[149]Frank L. Mott,' Facetious News Writing 1833-53', *Mississippi Valley Historical Review,* 29 (1900), 35-54.

[150]O'Brien, *Story of the Sun* has a chapter on this episode. The *Herald* helped to expose the hoax.

[151]John Russell Young, *Men and Memories* (NY 1901) pp. 208-10.

'an air of flippancy to the American character, and a certain fondness for things which elsewhere are regarded as childish, which every foreign visitor now notices'.[152] The 'serious' editors were completely at Bennett's mercy in this respect. He had the ability to cut to the core of an opponent's argument and extend it to a point where it looked utterly ridiculous.[153] A high sounding profession of political principle would be mercilessly exposed in the *Herald* as a cynical cover for a lobby scheme or an electoral trick. The *Herald* was no respecter of persons. Bennett's shrewd predictions and formidable capacity for destructive criticism understandably infuriated his rivals. Greeley's indignant biographer exclaimed that it would be incorrect to call the editor of the *Herald* a liar 'because he is wanting in that sense of truth by violating which a man makes himself a liar'.[154] The 'respectable' affected to despise the *Herald*, yet somehow everybody knew what it said.[155]

Making the 'Herald'

A typical day for Bennett in the 1850s and '60s began early. For sheer industry Greeley was his only rival.[156] Thoroughly professional and dedicated, Bennett boasted that 'we do not, as the Wall Street lazy editors do, come down to our office about ten or twelve o'clock, pull out a Spanish cigar, take up a pair of scissors, puff and cut, cut and puff for a couple of hours, and then adjourn to Delmonico's to eat, drink, gourmandize, and blow up our contemporaries'. Hudson said that: 'Mr. Bennett devoted his whole time and thought to journalism. He was a walking newspaper'.[157]

He would drive downtown and be in his office on the first floor of the *Herald* building by 7.00 a.m., studying the day's correspondence. After an hour examining items in the other papers marked for his attention by assistants Bennett, having taken a light breakfast, would began to dictate his editorials:

[152]NY *Evening Post* 30 Dec 1899.

[153]Parton says: 'The whole of his power as a writer consists in his detection of the evil in things that are good, and of the falsehood in things that are true, and of the ridiculous in things that are important.'

[154]Parton, 'The New York Herald'.

[155]*Ibid.*, for the comment that the *Herald* 'is generally read and its proprietor universally disapproved'. See also Dicey, ch 3.

[156]Parton, 'The New York Herald'.

[157]Hudson, p. 482.

> He. . . begins to talk: first giving the caption of the leading article. He speaks with some rapidity, making his points with effect, and sometimes smiling, as he raps one of his dear political friends over the knuckles. Having concluded his article with 'that will do', he gives the head of another article and dictates it in a similar way, and then, perhaps, another and another, till the reporter sighs at the amount of work he has before him, and he is told that that will be enough for 'today'.[158]

If an assistant editor suggested an idea of his own, so gossip in Printing House Square had it, Bennett might order him to write an article expressing a directly contrary opinion.[159]

While the editorials were being written up 'the Emperor', as his staff knew Bennett,[160] would confer with the heads of the various news departments in turn — financial, commercial, foreign, theatre, city or whatever, constantly supervising every detail.

Between mid-day and 2.00 p.m., while these articles were being prepared, Bennett would receive callers. 'Visit him', wrote an unfriendly one, 'you see before you a quiet-mannered, courteous and good natured old gentleman, who is on excellent terms with himself and the world'.[161]

In the afternoon Bennett would read proofs, mark them for insertion and send them to the printers upstairs, then walk around the office, chatting, observing, dictating to the editorial writers partitioned off in their separate stalls. Reputedly Bennett was apt on these occasions to make 'some very pithy speeches' or to exhort a writer to 'Pitch into Greeley' or 'Give Raymond Hell'.[162]

Before returning home after 3.00 p.m. Bennett would confer with Frederic Hudson, who in modern terms would be called the *Herald's* 'Managing Editor' though he himself ridiculed the term. Completely

[158]This quotation and the bulk of the account given here come from Pray, pp. 461 ff. Other details from Hudson, *passim* and NY press obituaries 2-15 June 1872. Another interesting and little known account of Bennett at work, drawn from the author's observation, is embodied in the novel *Marion* by 'Manhattan' (pseudonym of Joseph Alfred Scoville) (London 1864) – see vol II, chs XII, XIX; vol III, chs VIII, XIII, XVII. The novel is dedicated to Bennett for having encouraged the author to write. There are some letters from Scoville to Bennett amongst the editor's papers in the New York Public Library.

[159]So alleged the *Tribune* of 3 June 1872.

[160]Barnum, *Struggles and Triumphs,* ch XLI. Bennett was fond of referring to himself as 'the Napoleon of the Press'.

[161]Parton, 'The New York Herald'. For a warmer appreciation see William M. Bobo, *Glimpses of New York City* (Charleston 1852), pp. 67-70.

[162]Pray, p. 462; *Evening Post* 30 Dec 1899.

loyal and self-effacing,[163] Hudson was Bennett's right hand man, overseeing many of the business details of the *Herald*. The day-to-day running of the office was in his charge and he ran the paper when foreign news arrangements (as during the Crimean War in 1854), or health and family reasons took Bennett to Europe. His salary of $10,000 per year was the highest paid to any non-proprietor journalist on the eve of the Civil War. He had joined the *Herald* in 1836, when he was seventeen, and his association with Bennett was one of the most successful in newspaper history. Samuel Bowles of the *Springfield Republican* judged Hudson 'the greatest organiser of a mere newspaper that this country has ever seen'.[164] A reporter remembered that 'much as Bennett was the *Herald* and the *Herald* Bennett, we who know understand very distinctly that Hudson was the *Herald* too, yet he will go down unhonored in the next generation as he was unsung in this'.[165] Hudson was apolitical – he never voted and never controlled the *Herald*'s editorial policy. Unlike latter day proprietors, Bennett refused himself the luxury of being a mere figurehead, asserting that 'the proprietor of this paper is alone responsible for its views and opinions'. He ridiculed as superfluous Greeley's and Raymond's habit of signing some of their editorials. Greeley paid Bennett the grudging tribute of saying 'He alone made it; it was personal journalism in all senses of the word'.[166]

In the evening, after looking in at the theatre or opera for a few minutes, Bennett would call at the office for another hour to deal with late news stories. While he returned home to sleep, the work of actually printing, folding and distributing the *Herald* would proceed on the second and third floors of the building. Here in 1859 the *Herald* had installed one six-cylinder and two ten-cylinder Hoe printing presses of the most modern kind, the latter costing $60,000 each and running off 15,000 copies per hour.[167]

---

[163]In addition to the outline of his career in the first supplement to the *Dictionary of American Biography,* a sketch of Hudson (1819-75) may be found in Louis M. Starr, *Bohemian Brigade: Civil War Newsmen in Action* (NY 1954), pp. 22-3, 335, together with a photographic portrait. See also Pray, pp. 228-9. Fragments of Hudson's Diary are in the Concord, Mass., Free Public Library.

[164]Quoted in J.M. Lee, p. 200.

[165]Quoted in Starr, pp. 22-3

[166]NY *Daily Tribune* 3 June 1872.

[167]*NYH* 27 Mar 1859. Some contracts dated 1841 and 1861 between Bennett and R. Hoe and Company for installing and maintaining new presses with data, costs etc. are in the Bennett Papers, New York Public Library. By contrast there is in the New York Historical Society a receipt for just $199.11 for type and cases purchased by Bennett in 1836.

Next morning readers of the *Herald* could see the product of all this activity — a tolerably well printed sheet on good paper, each page divided into six columns of small type. The *Herald* of the 1850s was the recognisable heir of the sheet of 1835, but it was bigger and better produced in every way. It had much more advertising but the amount and proportion of news had grown even more dramatically. The headline was of single column width (although headlines grew bigger in the Civil War, banner headlines spread across the whole page were impossible for technical reasons) and led the reader to the story through multiple 'subheads'. 'Study the telegraphic arrangement of the *Herald*', complained a *Tribune* correspondent to his manager, 'See how *always*, not casually, but invariably the important items are placed first and the minor gradually go last.'[168]

Though no day was typical for a newspaper, the *Herald* reader might find 'Highly Important and Exciting' telegraphic news from Washington on the front page with columns of speeches from the capital interspersed with narrative and gossip. Or, if a ship were arriving, the latest affairs from Europe might take the lead unless some murder, divorce case, execution or election monopolised the space. Inside would be more of the robberies, fires, shootings and political meetings taking place in the Union. Important bills pending in Congress or the State legislature might be printed in full inside together with a remarkable range of local news from the police and coroners courts and the money market to the society column, prices current, city trade, mining, marine intelligence including clearances, arrivals and movements of ocean steamers and clippers, marriages and deaths etc., and whatever was of topical interest in the city. There might be samplings of political feeling on the issues of the day from other parts of the country.

Then there were the advertisements — at least three solid pages with more than forty advertisements to each column, conveniently arranged under classified headings. There were goods for sale at auction or privately, dry goods and clothes for marketing, horses and carriages for sale, rooms wanted and to let, corporation notices, ships departing, train times, political meetings, amusements, concerts, lectures, new publications, lost and found, rewards, vacancies and positions wanted by clerks and 'respectable' housemaids, the services of dentists, astrologers and doctors offered, and potions aplenty: 'Whiskers and Moustaches — My Onguent will force them to grow strong and thick in six weeks: $1 per bottle'. There were also the famous personals:

[168]S. Wilkeson to Sidney H. Gay, Gay Papers, quoted in Starr, p. 69.

Leone:- I have received your note of yesterday and this morning. The answer is in the Post Office.

Information wanted — of Martin Horan, from Castle Red, County Roscommon, Ireland, who has been in the country for the last four years. Any tidings of him will be received by M. WALSH, Office Commissioners of Emigration, Chambers Street.

If Louisa wishes to hear from a friend she may send a note, appointing a time and place to OPAL.[169]

In all, it must be admitted that Bennett had gone far towards making the *Herald* an almanac guide to each day of the city's life, fulfilling his boast that 'the test of a good newspaper is its ability to photograph the events of the day fully and clearly. . . Twenty-five years ago such a newspaper as the HERALD of today would have been as great a curiosity to the public as a steam engine to Adam.'[170]

For a one column summary of the news the reader might turn to the centre page. There too could be found the *Herald*'s heart and the familiar heading:

NEW YORK HERALD
JAMES GORDON BENNETT
EDITOR AND PROPRIETOR

Below, Bennett would hold forth on the main stories of the day, devoting perhaps three quarters of a column to comment on each of the major stories and a paragraph or squib to anything else which caught his eye. Would he be attacking the President, or Greeley, or exposing a lobby trick, or calling an indignation meeting about the abominable state of the streets? He was sure, anyway, to have a ready interpretation of the day's events and a suggested course of action for those who would make tomorrow's news.

[169]These examples taken at random from *NYH* 4 Mar 1854.
[170]*NYH* 7 May 1863.

2

'VERILY, WE ARE A GREAT PEOPLE' –
THE *HERALD* SPEAKS FOR ITS AMERICA

> I have always felt it to be a singularly weak line of argument
> when I have heard either Americans or Englishmen trying to
> explain away any offensive remark in the newspaper organs of
> their respective countries by the common remark, 'It is only the
> press says so;' it is only the utterance of the *Times* or the *New
> York Herald.* It is all very true, but the question still remains –
> why is it that the readers of the *Times,* or the *Herald*, like such
> remarks to be made ? You have proved that the elephant stands
> upon the tortoise, but what does the tortoise stand upon? Take it
> all in all, then, I admit freely that the American press, *if* you
> judge it correctly, is a tolerably fair – probably *the* fairest –
> exponent of American opinion. – Edward Dicey, *Six Months in
> the Federal States.*

Supposing there is some truth in Bennett's claim that the *Herald*
spoke the feelings of the 'conservative masses' of America, what did it
stand for? Clearly we shall not find out if we allow ourselves to be
distracted by the occasional changes of course which so infuriated its
critics. We must look instead for the themes which recur and the
attitudes which persist over a long period of years. It would be
pointless to follow the *Herald* through the political upheavals of
1854-67 without first understanding its characteristic ideas on
contemporary questions such as foreign relations, expansion,
immigration, religion, slavery, abolition, reform and government. If
the word 'principles' was rarely used in connection with the *Herald,*
the paper did have very definite and coherent views on these issues
which are quite as historically revealing as its turn-abouts.

Militant Republicanism and Anglophobia

In 1852 Bennett wrote to President Pierce that it had been his
ambition throughout life to establish an independent journal which
would 'speak strongly the living sentiments of the United States to the
old world'.[1] True to his word, he earned the *Herald* a reputation as
the most belligerently American of all newspapers. It defended and

---

[1]Bennett to Pierce 15 Dec 1852, Pierce Papers, Library of Congress.

asserted American national pride so fiercely that educated observers on both sides of the Atlantic were fearful of its truculent, jingoistic tone. Their sober apprehensions reflected the paper's evident popularity.[2]

Bennett's republicanism (small *r*) had all the zeal of a convert. When he first came to America, by his own account, his youthful head was full of the inspiration of Benjamin Franklin's *Autobiography* and he had tramped the revolutionary battlefields around Boston contemplating the ideals of 1776. As a Catholic Scot, and therefore something of a second-class citizen in his own land, Bennett emigrated with a keen sense of the inequalities of British society and a strong resentment of the British aristocracy.[3] As late as 1831, when he felt depressed about his prospects in America, he seriously contemplated returning to Europe and devoting himself to the 'furtherance of liberty in my native country'.[4] However cynical the *Herald's* anglophobia later became, it had its roots in Bennett's youthful romantic idealism.

One recipe for the *Herald's* success was its continual flattery of its readers by its assertion of the superiority of American ways. Writing letters for the *Herald* from Europe in the late 1830s and '40s, Bennett

[2] Samuel Bowles, the staunchly Republican editor of the *Springfield Republican* complained (*ibid.,* 7 June 1872) that 'the *Herald* though fickle in politics and worthless in editorial judgement . . . became the symbol of newspaper enterprise all over the world. This was at times unfortunate for us as a nation, for the English in the days of the *Herald's* greatness used to think that its sentiments represented the American people. Even now they are not weaned from that delusion, and the vagaries in the tone of that journal, at which we smile, throw an Englishman into fits.' See also remarks to the same effect in James Parton, 'The New York Herald', *North American Review,* 102 (Apr 1866), 373-419, and in Dicey, *Six Months in the Federal States* (London 1863), vol I, pp. 272-3. Bennett's rival, Webb of the *Courier & Enquirer,* acknowledged that 'Wherever I happened to be in Europe, and asked for an American newspaper, the *Herald* was invariably brought to me — never my own paper'. — quoted in Hudson, *Journalism in the United States from 1690 to 1872* (NY 1873), p. 462. The *Herald's* European edition sold an average of 2,000 copies daily in 1856, which figure, though small by modern standards, exceeded the average daily sales of its nearest rival, the *Tribune,* by 1,250 according to sworn statements submitted to the Post Office by both papers in that year (W.Coggeshall, The *Newspaper Record,* Philadelphia 1856, pp. 149-50). Of course most copies of the Herald sold in Europe were probably sold to travelling Americans, who also account for the market of the *Herald's* modern descendant, the *International Herald-Tribune.* Nevertheless the frequency with which European papers, e.g. the London *Times,* singled out the *Herald* for attack bear out Bowles' remarks on its influence there. For an early British attack on the *Herald* see *Foreign Quarterly Review,* 30 (1843), 197-222. We shall see in a later chapter that President Lincoln was sufficiently disturbed about the possible effects of the *Herald's* impact across the Atlantic to raise the subject in Cabinet discussions and to send Thurlow Weed to try and influence Bennett's course.

[3] I.C. Pray, *Memoirs of J.G. Bennett* (NY 1855), pp. 32, 36-7:

[4] Bennett's MS. *Diary* of a journey through New York State, 1831, in New York Public Library, entry for 18 July.

sent back trenchant descriptions of a society dominated by and deferring to its upper classes. Always contrasting old world subserviency and protocol with American popular energy and simplicity in manners, his attitude to Europe is amply contained in this passage about its art:

> Many of the very old paintings which I have seen, are very much like the old wines that old connoisseurs talk of – old humbugs, got up by old humbugs to humbug young humbugs. I am a very unbeliever – a perfect infidel, in the superiority of ancient art. Man and man's works are progressive – monkeys and monkeys' works are the same yesterday, today and for ever. . . . Europe looks backward – America looks forward.[5]

It was quite characteristic that in matters of art the *Herald* invariably encouraged native artists painting native subjects in preference to European trained artists who chose the classical models favoured by the academies. Like many American writers the *Herald* expressed the desire of a young country to assert its own cultural identity against old world domination. Its brash and outspoken style itself became a part of American culture.

The *Herald* led more than a cultural crusade. America had won her national independence only two generations previously and sealed it recently in the War of 1812. The *Herald* jealously proclaimed that Europe must no longer regard the fast growing United States as a 'former colony'. The dominant theme of *Herald* editorials was that the great powers must begin to treat the USA as an equal and learn respect instead of condescension towards her.

If the *Herald's* paranoia may seem to have more to do with sensationalism than idealism, neither Bennett nor his readers lost sight of the fact that republicanism was still very much a minority creed, crushed in Europe in 1848 and regarded with contempt by monarchical governments everywhere. During the 1850s the European edition of the *Herald* was in difficulties with the French imperial authorities for its publication of the proceedings of republican political meetings. In England Benjamin Disraeli thought it necessary as late as 1856 to remind the House of Commons that 'it would be wise if Britain would at last recognize that the United States, like all the great countries of Europe, have a policy, and that they have a right to have a policy'. This echoed Bennett's complaint that the United States was 'recognized as a nation, but given no voice in the councils

---

[5] Pray, p. 390 and generally pp. 380-403. This passage might almost belong in Mark Twain's *Innocents Abroad,* which was based, incidentally, on letters Twain wrote as a *Herald* correspondent in 1867.

of nations – exercising the functions of an independent State, but denied the character of solid nationality'.[6] The truculence of the *Herald*'s opinions on foreign affairs was partly defensive in nature. William H. Russell, sometime American correspondent of the London *Times,* wrote that America in her foreign relations resembled 'a growing lad who is constantly testing his powers in competition with his elders . . . calling . . . to all comers to look at his muscle, to run against or to fight him. It is a sign of youth, not a proof of weakness, though it does offend the old hands and vex the veterans.'[7] It would be difficult to describe the *Herald*'s editorial policy more aptly.

Believing that in the modern age diplomacy was better conducted by the popular press than through the secret channels of diplomats, Bennett realised the commercial value of a war scare. Forty years before the heyday of the 'Yellow Press' proper, he knew the value of 'twisting the lion's tail' as a means of selling newspapers, both at home and in Europe – for the European edition of the *Herald* sold more copies than any other American newspaper. He also believed that there was nothing like naked power for commanding respect in the world of nations.

Throughout the 1850s and '60s the *Herald* seemed bent on provoking hostilities with Britain. It was ready, for instance, to confront her if she dared challenge the United States' right to seize Cuba. During the Crimean War it dared Britain to interfere with neutral US shipping by exercising the right of search, on pain of a Russo-American alliance. Expressing sympathy with Russia and proposing American mediation in the conflict, Bennett found it 'not surprising that many Americans should feel more bitterly towards a power which has injured, fought, bullied, interfered with and thwarted us, than towards one with which we never had any intimate relations whatsoever'.[8]

Conversely the *Herald* led the clamour of the 'hawks' during the Anglo-American war scare over the *Trent* affair in 1861, when Britain was aggrieved at interference with her own neutral shipping.[9]

[6]Speech by Disraeli 16 June 1856, quoted in Ivor D. Spencer, *The Victor and the Spoils* (Providence 1959), p. 276. *NYH* 12 Jan 1856.

[7]William Howard Russell, *My Diary North and South* (London 1863), vol I, p. 141.

[8]*NYH* 31 Dec 1854, also 28 Mar to 17 Apr 1854. For a later stout defence of neutral rights see *NYH* 21 May 1859.

[9]*NYH* 17 Nov 1861 to 7 Jan 1862. For a satire on the *Herald*'s course see the editorial entitled 'How it was Done – Splendid Zampillaerostation' in NY *Times* 31 Dec 1861. A recent account of the *Trent* crisis which makes excellent use of the *Herald* files is D.P. Crook, *The North, The South and the Powers, 1861-1865* (NY 1974), ch 5. See also chapter 9 below.

At that time relations between the two countries became so exacerbated that John Bright wrote to Senator Charles Sumner that 'it is unfortunate that nothing is done to change the reckless tone of your *New York Herald*'.[10]

In the sensitive issues arising out of European neutrality during the Civil War the *Herald* found every opportunity for issuing its own ultimatums to Britain and France. The two chief bones of contention became the French expedition in Mexico and the building of Confederate commerce raiders[11] and rams in British shipyards. New York's vulnerability to a possible attack by ironclad rams and the very heavy losses of her merchant marine to the Confederate cruisers[12] made the *Herald* hypersensitive on this point, and it warned that England would be forced to pay the cost of the lost American shipping plus Canada and an indemnity of several million dollars for 'insolence' to the United States.[13]

In 1864, when the notorious *CSS Alabama* was sunk and its survivors found refuge in Britain, the *Herald* called for war unless they were yielded up. That the celebrated 'Alabama claims' became such an emotive post-war issue and a focus for diplomatic dispute owed much to the *Herald*'s stirring of popular feelings on the subject.[14] When Vermont and New York suffered from Confederate raids launched from Canadian soil in the autumn of 1864 the *Herald*'s bitterness against Britain overflowed in the declaration that 'it is England we are fighting'. It began to refer to the Confederacy as the 'Anglo-Rebel' cause and favoured pursuing the Confederate guerrillas into Canada at the risk of war.[15] With increasing ill temper, the *Herald* elaborated its pet theory that the Civil War had been caused by the British aristocracy's jealousy of American prosperity. Pre-war British interest in American abolition societies was evidence, Bennett

[10]Bright to Sumner 20 Nov 1861, Sumner Papers, quoted in J.F. Rhodes, *History of the United States from the Compromise of 1850* (London 1893) vol 3, p. 516.

[11]These ships were commissioned in the Confederate Navy, but Bennett always implied their illegality by calling them 'privateers'.

[12]Losses not only by direct enemy action but through the transferral of the registry of American ships to foreign flags. In 1860 two thirds of New York City's trade was done by US merchant vessels, but by 1863 only one quarter — see D.M. Ellis *et al.*, *A History of New York State* (Ithaca 1975), p. 339.

[13]*NYH* 25 Aug 1863.

[14]*NYH* 6, 9 July 1864; 24-7 Oct 1865. See also Adrian Cook, *The Alabama Claims* (Ithaca 1975), especially pp. 87-88.

[15]*NYH* 7 Nov 1864 and generally 20 Oct 1864 to 11 Jan 1865. For the raids see Robin W. Winks, *Canada and the United States: The Civil War Years* (Baltimore 1960), ch 14.

proclaimed, that the anti-slavery movement was merely the tool of an anarchic British conspiracy to destroy the Union. Yet British slavers had first saddled America with the Negro and now, with typical duplicity, 'perfidious Albion' was doing everything in its power to aid the Confederacy. *Herald* readers were assured that British gold was the sinister root of all America's troubles. For the last two years of the conflict the *Herald* boasted almost daily of the punishment which would be visited on the English at the end of the war, and of what the French might expect if they did not evacuate Mexico voluntarily.

To say that the *Herald* contributed to poor Anglo-American and Canadian-American relations during and after the war is a mild understatement.[16] Probably only the rabidly pro-Southern views of the London *Times* (called 'The Thunderer' in England, nicknamed 'The Blunderer' by Bennett) worked more mischief than the *Herald* in this respect.[17]

We could dismiss Bennett without further comment as a demagogue and warmonger, as educated Americans preferred to do. That abuse of Britain was pleasing to the *Herald*'s substantial number of Irish born readers is obvious. Yet, besides general ideological hostility to British society, there are a number of distinct elements in the *Herald*'s anglophobia which suggest the American outlook at mid-century.

The *Herald*'s attitude can hardly be explained away as the product of provincial ignorance and isolation. The popular excitement which greeted the arrival of the iron *Great Eastern* from England in June 1860 climaxed an era in which the clipper ship and the steamship had shrunk the time needed to cross the Atlantic. As the forest of masts along its busy waterfront testified, New York City thrived on trade with Europe and its commerce benefitted from British investment. Its membership of an Atlantic economic and cultural community was reflected in the fact that the *Herald* always carried far more European news and comment than it did of the affairs of the states of the Mississippi Valley. It maintained a testy dialogue with the London *Times* as well as leading Canadian journals. No one had been more active or enthusiastic than Bennett for improved transatlantic com-

---

[16]By the autumn of 1861 there was a marked cooling of Canada's original sympathy for the North for which Seward and Bennett jointly were much to blame. For instances of reaction in the Canadian press see the early chapters of Winks, especially pp. 20-1, 222-8, but consult also John C. Kendall, 'The New York City Press and Anti-Canadianism: A New Perspective on the Civil War Years', *Journalism Quarterly,* 52 (Autumn 1975), 522-30.

[17]For a comparison of the incendiary roles of the *Times* and the *Herald* see Arnold Whitridge, 'Anglo-American Troublemakers — J.G. Bennett and J.T. Delane', *History Today,* 6 (1956), 88-95.

munications, and when the transatlantic telegraph was successfully put into operation in 1866 (after a false start in 1858) the *Herald* became a hungry seeker for increased European news. There is no reason to suppose that the *Herald*'s bullish tone would have been improved by greater contact.

In large part of course the *Herald*'s sabre-rattling against Britain was a desperate if crude ploy to divert attention from the sectional crisis. Just as the *Herald* called for the seizure of Cuba from Spain throughout the 1850s in the vain hope that the squabbling Democrats might thus be diverted from the slavery issue, so it counted on the unifying power of hostility to Britain to hold Americans back from civil war. In the spring and summer of 1861 the *Herald* advocated a foreign war as a remedy for domestic ills with a breezy cynicism which seems incredible – except that identical views were held by Lincoln's Secretary of State, Seward, and submitted to the President in all seriousness on 1 April 1861.[18]

Bitterly hostile to Seward on domestic issues (a fact not likely to be appreciated by foreigners) the *Herald* was at one with him in its approach to foreign policy, believing that threats rather than persuasion were the best means to forestall intervention in the Civil War. Europe's distrust of Seward's diplomacy (or in the wider sense his lack of it) in the early days of the war is better understood in context with the *New York Herald*.[19] Charles Sumner, Republican chairman of the Senate Foreign Relations Committee during the war, who was poles apart from Bennett on the slavery question, could nevertheless utter a speech in 1863 which for its anglophobia won the *Herald*'s strong approbation.[20]

If the circumspect Lincoln preferred 'one war at a time', the *Herald*'s faith in a foreign war as a short cut to reunion never faltered throughout the Civil War. If the slaughter of 1861-5 revolted Greeley's humanity it merely made Bennett impatient to see American might turned on an external foe. When the South surrendered in the spring of 1865 the *Herald* was exultant not only because the tories of

[18]The notorious memorandum 'Some Thoughts for the President's Consideration' in Roy P. Basler ed., *The Complete Works of Abraham Lincoln* (New Brunswick 1953-5), vol. IV, pp. 317-18.

[19]For studies sympathetic to Seward's handling of diplomatic affairs see Glyndon Van Deusen, *William Henry Seward* (NY 1967) and the enthusiastically defensive Norman B. Ferris, *Desperate Diplomacy* (Knoxville 1976). Winks, *Canada and the United States,* considering the evidence from the Canadian viewpoint, is less charitable to Seward; likewise Brian Jenkins in his *Britain and the War for the Union* (Montreal 1974).

[20]*NYH* 15 Sept 1863.

Europe had been foiled in their hope for the demise of the Union but because America's formidable military and naval might was now displayed for the world to see – and respect. Bennett's imagination had been whetted by the powerful siege guns which had reduced Charleston and the ironclad fleet which the United States had developed for the war. He had long prophesied with bravado that once the civil strife was over these weapons would be well employed against foreign powers. In early 1865 he was editorialising eagerly about

> The Greatness of this Country and the
> Prospects of a Foreign War[21]

primarily to cement reunion and also as a means of averting the financial collapse which he declared would follow too rapid demobilisation. Now that America's strength had been proven the *Herald* wanted to see it put to vigorous use, and one part of its prophecy was fulfilled when a United States army was sent to the Rio Grande as a caution to the French. In agitating for this move there can be little doubt that the paper had spoken the sentiments of the average American citizen.

Though in the twentieth century it is a basic fact of life that the United States is a world power, that truth was only beginning to emerge in the 1850s and '60s and the *Herald* devoted its energies to asserting it. If in doing so it was brash, vulgar, jingoistic and strident, it was partly because Bennett believed that this was the only kind of language which would be effective in a diplomatic world where stronger powers automatically encroached on weaker ones – above all in a world dominated by the likes of Lord Palmerston and Napoleon III. After the *Trent* crisis Bennett made a significant boast. He claimed that:

> Had not the HERALD threatened England with the confiscation of all the British property in this country in the event of war the Southern Confederacy would have been recognized by Russell and Palmerston many months since. That threat, uttered at a critical crisis, did more for the preservation of peace with England than all the diplomacy of the Administration.

When due allowance has been made for journalistic bombast, there remains a core of truth in his words.[22]

[21]*NYH* 29 Jan 1865.

[22]*NYH* 15 Sept 1863. See also *NYH* 31 Dec 1861 and NY *Times* of same date. One may agree with a recent student of the international aspects of the Civil War who concludes that 'the *Herald,* so often dismissed in the commentaries as an unrepresentative and irresponsible troublemaker in the international arena, in fact offered some of the

The *Herald*'s concerns did not extend only to the vindication of American national integrity. French eagerness to invade Mexico while the United States was battling domestic foes emphasised that the *Herald*'s expressions of chronic insecurity about European designs on the American continent were not entirely fanciful bluster. If we seek the other major theme in the paper's anti-British tirades it is imperial rivalry.

The *Herald*'s consistent demand for great power status for the USA included a broad interpretation of the Monroe Doctrine which called for European powers to leave the American continent altogether.

The *Herald* considered it a simple decree of 'Manifest Destiny' that Canada was ripe for annexation to the United States. It frequently expounded the economic 'necessities' which would bring Canada into the Union, whether or not America had to fight Britain for possession. Bennett's advocacy of invasion from 1861 onwards and his complete insensitivity to Canadian feelings and rights helped to produce a new depth of distrust between the two countries in the 1860s. Moreover Bennett sought to balance any British inclination to aid the Confederacy by quite deliberately exciting her fears for her remaining North American possessions.

While Britain blocked America's path to the north and her fleet remained the most powerful strategic force on the high seas, the *Herald* also saw her in the path of 'Manifest Destiny' to the south. Bennett's frustration and annoyance with sectional politics in the 1850s arose largely from his insistent belief that America's main business ought to lie in southward expansion, and that her mission was to civilise – by annexing – Mexico, Cuba and Central America. British interests in Central America and the Caribbean made her watchful and jealous of American designs, and Bennett complained that the 1850 Anglo-American Treaty was a one sided affair which chained the US to the status quo. He chafed to take advantage of the commercial possibilities which American exploitation of these regions could secure. Hence the *Herald*'s agitation at inefficient and corrupt Spanish rule in Cuba, at political instability in Mexico (which it attributed to the 'debasing' mixture of Spanish and Indian blood), and at outrages on American citizens in Central America. When Northerners protested against American expansion for the benefit of slaveowners and merchants Bennett accused them of being in British pay. At every point the *Herald* saw a menacing British encirclement of America's sphere of ambition.

more perceptive analyses of power realities in the new world. . . . Its attitudes were probably more symptomatic of embedded American values than civilized Americans would like to admit.' — Crook, *The North, The South and the Powers*, p. 282.

Thus when the paper criticised the deficiencies of British imperial rule in the 1850s and moralised at British expense about the Indian Mutiny it was not being anti-imperialistic. On the contrary it was arguing that American vigour could confer the benefits of empire on subject peoples far more quickly and efficiently than Britain had managed. Bennett insisted that Britain should accept and welcome America in an imperial role instead of treating her with distrust and that the two countries should be partners in an Anglo-Saxon mission to civilise the world. To rub in the point the *Herald* spoke of Mexico and Cuba as America's potential 'Indian Empire'[23] and when encouraging filibuster expeditions in Central America in the '50s (escapades that made splendid copy) the *Herald* was sure to draw close parallels with the 'filibuster' methods by which Britain had gained her own empire. If Britain had interests in Turkey, the 'sick man of Europe', why should not the USA intervene with her chronically disordered neighbour Mexico, the 'sick man of America'? Bennett resented British criticism of American expansionism which he felt was founded on a double standard of judgement.

This makes it easier to understand why the *Herald* led the cordial reception which the American press gave to Edward, Prince of Wales, when he visited the country in the autumn of 1860. We mistake the case if we dismiss the *Herald*'s gushing welcome as just a glaring inconsistency. Doubtless republican principles seemed to waver when America encountered royalty in the flesh, and Bennett was very proud to conduct members of the royal entourage around his establishment. But the *Herald*'s enthusiasm was of a piece with its warmongering. It took the visit of a future king of England (the first since independence) as a compliment to the republic. Bennett wanted to show the British that America, successful in her independence, could afford to give a generous welcome, and for this reason was anxious that Edward's reception on republican soil should outshine that given him in Canada. He even had hopes of marrying Edward off to an American lady and hoped that a lasting Anglo-American alliance might result.[24] Forgetting its own stance during the Crimean War, the *Herald* professed a bitter sense of betrayal when the British government denied encouragement to the Union cause in the Civil War and adopted at best a 'wait and see' attitude.

The close of the war gave Americans confidence that republicanism was no longer on trial, and if we have seen the *Herald* in the moment

[23]*NYH* 17 Feb 1857.
[24]*NYH* 11 June; 28 July; 12, 13, 14, 15, 16, 17, 18 Oct 1860.

of victory eager to challenge the world in arms, its tone soon moderated. By the summer of 1865 Bennett was publicly and privately pressing President Johnson to propose an international peace conference, or congress, at which Britain would pay reparations for her alleged breaches of neutrality and, most important, at which the American interpretation of the 'Monroe Doctrine' would be accepted. The European powers must acknowledge the USA as 'sole arbiter' between the Atlantic and Pacific and understand that 'their pigmy pretences here are simply impertinent'.[25] More soberly Bennett declared that 'we want France, England and Spain to leave America. Their institutions and policy are different and inimical to ours. We want no other relations than the most extended commerce and perpetual friendship with them.'[26] Although President Johnson promised to confer 'freely and fully' with Bennett on the subject, nothing materialised. Yet in time the French did withdraw from Mexico and Britain did pay for the *Alabama*'s exploits, and the day was undeniably closer when Europe would treat the USA as a world power.

That America had great prospects in the Far East as well as in the western hemisphere had been symbolised by the visit of a Japanese embassy in the summer of 1860. American imaginations were captured by the meeting of two alien cultures and the occasion gave rise to much moralising about the state of American civilisation. Gawping crowds of New Yorkers followed the Japanese around the city and a fascinated Bennett entertained two oriental princes in his Fort Washington home. The real purpose of the embassy was to discuss trade, and regarding relations between the two countries the *Herald* could confidently declare that 'the ice may now be said to be fairly broken'.[27] The opportunities open to American commercial expansion seemed endless.

As to the future, Bennett was supremely confident that America's commercial, financial, industrial and military strength would one day dominate the whole western hemisphere. The visit of a Russian fleet to New York harbour in the autumn of 1863 led him to wax enthusiastic at the prospect of a Russo-American alliance against

[25]*NYH* 6 Aug 1865.

[26]*NYH* 30 Aug 1865. Stressing the importance of foreign policy to the new administration, Bennett wrote privately to the President, 'The U.S. came out of the recent war as one of the great powers of the world. . . . It seems to me that we ought to settle our foreign questions with Europe without war, and the best means to do so would be in a Congress of all the great princes. . . ' — see Bennett to Andrew Johnson 26 Aug 1865; Johnson to Bennett 6 Oct 1865, Johnson Papers, Library of Congress.

[27]*NYH* 17 June 1860 and generally 12-18 June 1860.

Western Europe.[28]   Even after his first ardour had cooled at the prospect of America being 'cheek by jowl with such a despotism' (for he assured his readers that the Southern cause was in no way comparable to that of oppressed Poland) he fondly mulled over Napoleon's prediction that the future lay with the two countries: 'It is now evident that the world will be divided between the Cossacks and the republicans within the next half century.'[29]   Furthermore he thught that in a hundred years they might be fighting each other for possession of it. 'Verily, we are a great people', declared Bennett, never doubting that 'our mission is to rule the world'.[30]

Foreigners in America

Bennett's view of the United States as a great power exerting friction against nations like Mexico whose 'mongrel' races made them politically and morally weak[31]   was reflected in his attitude to the immigrant in the United States. Not that he proscribed foreigners: he was after all an immigrant himself and retained a thick Scots accent all his days. His wife was of Irish Catholic extraction and he was well used to being abused as 'foreign scum' by his newspaper rivals.[32] Yet this, it has been suggested, only served to make his own identification with his adopted country more assertive and self-conscious. He took no special pride in his Scottish birth[33]   and spoke in large terms of the 'Anglo-Saxon' destiny of America. Bennett expected other foreigners to become thoroughly Americanised as he himself had done.

[28]*NYH* 31 Aug; 26 Sept; 7 Oct; 12, 18 Nov; 10 Dec 1863. The *Herald* guessed correctly that the Russians had come in order to avoid being iced in their own harbours in the event of a war with France over Poland. This fact was not generally known for another half century after the war — see F.A. Golder, 'The Russian Fleet and the Civil War', *American Historical Review,* XX (1915), 803-4.

[29]*NYH* 31 Aug 1863.

[30]*NYH* 26 July 1864; 4 Nov 1864.

[31]*NYH* e.g. 28 May 1854; 23, 25 Dec 1855; 4 Jan 1856.

[32]Lambert A. Wilmer, in his indictment of Bennett in *Our Press Gang* (Philadelphia 1856), seemed most exercised about the editor's foreign birth, and the strongest terms he could find to condemn the editorial corps of the *Herald* was to call it 'a band of foreigners' — p. 84.

[33]When rebuked for being untrue to the land of his birth Bennett rejoined that 'it is the fate of Scotland, as it is that of all other countries, to give birth to its natural portion of barren, heartless, empty blockheads. . . I am indeed a native of Scotland — But what of that?. . . The introduction, or perpetuation of these ridiculous castes of Scotchmen, Irishmen, Englishmen, & c., & c., & c., in the social habits of this land is utterly preposterous and absurd. The classification of men according to nativity is unfit for a civilized and intelligent age. . . . ' — Pray, pp. 219-20.

For he lived in a polyglot community. In 1855 just over one half of Manhattan Island's population of 622,924 were of foreign birth. Over twenty-eight per cent of the total population were Irish born and nearly sixteen per cent German.[34] The *Herald* was for many of these a first contact with American culture and the medium through which they learned about the politics of their new country once they felt bold enough to leave the familiar circle of their own churches, schools and press.

The *Herald* extended a warm welcome to immigrants. There was plenty of work for them to do in developing the nation and in Bennett's view they could only be a source of strength. This was especially true during the Civil War when potential soldiers were at a premium. Bennett came to see the immigrant working with 'either the musket or spade' as the means by which the USA could remain a first class military power without slackening its rate of industrial growth.[35] The *Herald* therefore took great pride in immigration statistics (for instance, over 5,000 immigrants arrived at New York Port in the first week of June, 1863)[36] and it frequently exposed the frauds and abuses to which the hapless new arrivals too often succumbed.[37] In later chapters we will see how the *Herald* championed the Germans and Irish on occasions when it considered them the objects of undeserved censure by portions of the community.

It would be quite mistaken however to portray the *Herald* as a paper with a mission as regards the immigrants. It paid no undue attention to any ethnic group, a daily paper having a vested interest in appealing to all citizens. The exception to this rule was at election times of course when the *Herald* vied with other papers in its appeals to Irish voters.[38] At other times evidence of resistance to assimilation drew acid comments from Bennett. Normally good humoured about the characteristics of the German community, he did not temper his language in denouncing those Germans who were actively working to promote socialist doctrines both in America and in their native land.[39] Similarly Bennett was furious when during the visit of the

[34]Robert Ernst, *Immigrant Life in New York City,* 1825-63 (NY 1949), Table 14.

[35]*NYH* e.g. 11 Sept; 28 Dec 1863. Consult also Ellis, *History of New York,* pp. 340-1 and the early chapters of John Higham, *Strangers in the Land 1860-1925* (New Brunswick 1955).

[36]*NYH* 7 June 1863.

[37]*NYH* e.g. 30 Apr 1854; 10 Mar; 26 June 1859; 7 Aug; 4 Sept 1864.

[38]For Irish opinion on political matters, as expressed through the *Irish American* newspaper see Florence H. Gibson, *Attitudes of the New York Irish* (NY 1951).

[39]*NYH* 8 Jan 1854.

Prince of Wales in 1860 the 69th New York (Irish) regiment marred the occasion by its refusal to parade. The *Herald* demanded that they should be disbanded for disobeying orders and suggested that their boorish manners rendered them fit only for a despotism.[40] These instances seemed to Bennett abuses of American hospitality, betraying a failure to grasp the essential promise of American citizenship.

Whereas European revolutionaries visiting America were customarily feted extravagantly by civic dignitaries and the press, the *Herald* scorned them. When Kossuth, the Hungarian 'patriot', became the object of a rapturous popular reception in 1851 the *Herald*'s voice was one of the minority which denounced him as a humbug.[41] So it was with a string of Irish 'patriots' who visited New York during the '50s.[42] If these men had come to settle as American citizens in good faith, said the *Herald*, they were welcome. If, as it seemed, they came only to raise funds from the gullible for non-existent revolutions, then they were charlatans who should return whence they came; the Irish must learn, Bennett lectured, that they could be citizens of only one country.[43] Certainly he supported famine relief for Ireland and was trenchantly critical of British rule there but unlike Greeley, who was passionate for Irish freedom, Bennett was unsentimental on the subject. Bennett enjoyed 'stirring the pot' by predicting liberal revolutions in European countries, but he stopped short of advocating direct American intervention in them. For America to become a sort of supply depot for European revolutionary interests would be contrary to his avowed aim of 'Europe for the Europeans, America for the Americans'. The new world, he wanted it understood, would be at nobody's calling. Only because of the deterioration of Anglo-American relations during the

[40]*NYH* 18 Oct 1860 and see 16 Jan 1859, for the argument that the Irish were a 'naturally' undemocratic race. The Civil War made all well again though; on 28 Aug 1862 the *Herald* appeared with headlines in Gaelic to celebrate the departure to the front of the 'Glorious Sixty Ninth'. See *NYH* 21 June 1863 for an argument on racial grounds for the good fighting qualities of the Irish. Amongst the Bennett Papers in the Library of Congress is an invitation to Bennett to celebrate St Patrick's Day, 1863, at the headquarters of General Thomas F. Meagher, leader of the Irish Brigade.

[41]Bennett expressed concern at irregularities in selling Hungarian bonds, though cynics said he was disgruntled at not being invited to the dinner given for Kossuth by the press. See 'Arguments of John Graham Esq.', printed as *New York County: Court of General Sessions. The People ex. rel. Daniel Sickles vs James Gordon Bennett, Complaint for Libel,* (NY October 1857); Pray, p. 451; Carlson, pp. 245-6, 260; Donald S. Spencer, *Louis Kossuth and Young America, 1848-52* (Columbia 1977), p. 170.

[42]Bennett's reservations concerning Irish Home Rule had caused him to clash publicly with Irish leader Daniel O'Connell in 1843. No doubt this incident coloured his later thinking. It is described and documented in Pray, pp. 329-45.

[43]*NYH* 2, 7 Apr 1854; 11 Apr 1856; 27 June 1858; 16 Jan; 22 Feb; 24 June 1859.

Civil War was the *Herald* sufficiently aroused in 1865 to encourage a Fenian attack on Canada in order that the United States should have the chance to give Britain a taste of her own 'neutrality'. With a nice sense of justice, the paper advocated selling these Irish Americans a captured Confederate privateer for use against English shipping.[44]

The *Herald*'s treatment of the Roman Catholic Church paralleled its attitude to the ethnic groups which so largely formed its membership. Born a Catholic in a predominantly Protestant region of Scotland and educated in a seminary, Bennett as a youth had conceived a dislike of religious intolerance. He did not take holy orders and became a renegade to the authority of the Church.[45] He is reputed to have born a grudge because of the death of his brother Cosmo under the harsh regime of monastic training and vowed: 'For the negligence that led to his death, my holy mother, the Church, must suffer some, and by my hands. See if she don't.'[46] The early *Herald* was irreverent and scoffing in tone, and it has been seen that this was one cause of the 'Moral War'. Bennett virulently attacked New York's bishop John Hughes in personal terms for trying to form a Catholic political party during the public schools controversy of 1840-1, and the *Herald* ridiculed the doctrine of transubstantiation in its usual forthright language. In return Hughes denounced Bennett publicly as '*decidedly* the most *dangerous man*, to the peace and safety of a community, that I have ever known'.[47]

Although the feud with Hughes, who became Archbishop in 1850, smouldered on in its columns for a decade, the tone of the *Herald* became much softer on religious matters generally in the 1850s. The boisterous anti-clericalism of the 1830s was apparently no longer acceptable fifteen years later – perhaps because of the increasing proportion of Irish Catholics in the city or because of Mrs Bennett's influence. The *Herald* in its latter days discussed doctrinal questions with patience and knowledge and was notably free of that Protestant bigotry which characterised some other papers. It was consistent

---

[44]*NYH* 1, 21 Oct; 2 Dec 1865. For background see Brian Jenkins, *Fenians and Anglo-American Relations During Reconstruction* (Ithaca 1969).

[45] This apparently led to a disagreement with his parents which was a major reason for his emigration to America. Bennett's early religious experiences and attitudes are treated in Pray, pp. 25-37, and Carlson pp. 3-26.

[46]Pray, p. 246. On his later religious attitudes see *ibid.*, pp. 276-9.

[47]See John Hughes, *A Letter on the Moral Causes that have produced The Evil Spirit of the Times* (NY 1844). For details and examples of Bennett's invective see Pray, pp. 346-9. On the public school issue see John W. Pratt, 'Governor Seward and the New York City School Controversy, 1840-2', *New York History* 42 (1961), 351-63 and Vincent P. Lannie, *Public Money and Parochial Education* (Cleveland 1968).

though in arguing that the true policy of the Church was to renounce all secular claims; 'What the clergy have lost in real estate, the church has gained in doctrine'[48] was a typical Bennett dictum which he applied to international as well as municipal affairs. So in 1859-60 the *Herald* welcomed the Italian Risorgimento as being in the best interests of the Church, and always opposed the clerical party in Mexico. Similarly it denounced the Protestant clergy for the prominent part it took in the anti-slavery controversy. So long as the churches observed his own distinction between religion and politics Bennett was happy to support them. Indeed, one of the editor's favourite hobbies was to advocate that the papacy, as a strictly spiritual concern, should be established in America, and he publicly extended to the Pope the hospitality of his Fort Washington home.[49]

The religious and racial disturbances which flared up in a number of cities during the 1840s and '50s were not, the *Herald* stressed, the result of democracy but an inheritance from the intolerant prejudices and passions of the old world, and should be deplored by true Americans.[50]

Yet characteristically an important exception must be recorded against the *Herald*'s generally liberal acceptance of the foreigner. For a while in 1854-5 it lent its support to the American or Know-Nothing party, which was founded on hostility to the immigrant.[51]

The reason for this departure is not far to seek. The *Herald*'s support of the Know-Nothings was a matter of political opportunism. Before the New York State elections of 1854 Bennett had dismissed the secretive Nativists as a basically un-American organisation whose appearance on the scene would be only temporary.[52] At that time there was a confusion of party tickets in the state and the Know-Nothings seemed to be a 'mere effervescence' on the surface of political life like half a dozen others doomed to rapid extinction.[53]

[48]*NYH* 25 Jan 1855. See also 19 Jan; 20 Nov 1854; 4 Mar 1855.

[49]*NYH* 23 Feb; 21 Mar 1854; 4 May 1855; 1 Feb; 31 Mar; 27 May; 22 June; 2 July 1859; 3 July 1863; 14 Jan 1865; 25 Aug; 13 Sept; 5 Oct 1866.

[50]*NYH* 30 Jan 1854.

[51]On the Know-Nothing movement see Michael F. Holt, 'The Anti-Masonic and Know-Nothing Parties', in A.M. Schlesinger Jr, ed., *History of U.S. Political Parties* (NY 1973), vol. 1, pp. 575-620; David M. Potter, *The Impending Crisis, 1848-61* (NY 1976), ch X; Ray Allen Billington, *The Protestant Crusade 1800-60* (NY 1938); Louis D. Scisco, *Political Nativism in New York State* (NY 1901).

[52]*NYH* 3 Apr; 10, 20 June; 1 July, 19 Oct 1854.

[53]*NYH* 2 Sept 1854. A particularly detailed study of state politics at this time is Mark L. Berger, *The Revolution in the New York Party Systems* (Port Washington 1973).

'Every fresh expression of illiberal opinion which comes from the Know-Nothings', wrote Bennett, 'alienates them from the sympathies of honest right minded men'.[54] In the contest for the governorship however the Know-Nothings showed a remarkable and unsuspected strength in the state.[55] Their candidate, Ullman, ran well ahead of Bronson, the 'Hardshell' Democrat who had the *Herald*'s support.[56] The *Herald* thereupon jumped on the bandwagon and began speculating freely about the chances of a Know-Nothing President in 1856, pushing forward New York capitalist George Law as a possible candidate. Law, promoter of the United States Mail Steamship Company, had leapt to popularity by his dramatic support of a *Herald* correspondent. One Smith, purser on Law's ship *Crescent City,* had sent material to the *Herald* whose publication enraged the Captain-General of Cuba, who forbade the man ever to enter Havana again. Nothing daunted by this or the disapproval of his own government, Law defiantly ran his ships into Havana with Smith on board time and again.[57]

Other papers dismissed Bennett's 'Live Oak George' as a 'live hoax', and the *Herald*'s motive was obviously to ride with the popular political movement in the hope that it would be the means of defeating the Whigs and the nascent Republican party within New York. The Know-Nothings became a weapon in the *Herald*'s campaign against the Seward-Weed machine during a period of Democratic weakness.[58] If the Know-Nothings could repeat their local success nationally by capturing the Southern Whig vote, Bennett saw a party with the potential to drive the slavery issue out of national politics – so he declared.[59]

Portraying the Americans as 'national' and 'conservative', Bennett chose to play down their nativist principles and to stress that they were the party to purify 'grogshop politics'. In fact he strove to supply plausible arguments designed to show that the Know-Nothings were not anti-foreign at all[60] and undertook to persuade the German

[54]*NYH* 25 June 1854.

[55]*NYH* 9, 10, 13, 14 Nov 1854.

[56]The vote was:

Clark	(Whig)	156,804
Seymour	('Soft' Democrat)	156,495
Ullman	(Know-Nothing)	122,282
Bronson	('Hard' Democrat)	33,850

[57]On Law see *NYH* 2 June 1855; *Dictionary of American Biography,* and Scisco, p. 147.

[58]See next chapter on Democratic divisions.

[59]*NYH* 26, 28, 30 Dec 1854; 3, 8, 14, 19, 24 Jan; 12 Mar; 7, 8, 10, 18, 21 May 1855.

[60]e.g. *NYH* 20 Feb 1854.

community to give the party its support. He did go so far as to attribute the rise of the Know-Nothings to the 'base and grovelling' election pledges made by American politicians to foreigners during the campaign of 1852.[61] The *Herald* also approved the proposal that a longer period of residence should be required of immigrants before naturalisation papers were granted, for it had always viewed askance the means by which Democratic ward bosses customarily led recent Irish immigrants literally in droves to be naturalised immediately prior to any election. The paper grumbled at the high proportion of the city's crime which was justly attributable to the city's immigrants,[62] and warned the Irish that: 'No cause in the world was ever helped by thick sticks or paving stones. Every man who is knocked down by the Irish, augments the popular prejudice against the race.' But equally Bennett found it 'neither necessary nor wise, nor manly, nor honorable for twenty three million Protestants to hunt down two million Roman Catholics in their midst'.[63]

The *Herald* would say no word against law abiding immigrants. Bennett's dalliance with the Know-Nothings was as insincere as it was unscrupulous. When the party failed to make decisive electoral progress nationally during 1855 and showed divisions on the slavery issue the *Herald* became disenchanted. Most important, the Nativists showed themselves without leadership or purpose in the New York legislature and failed in the crucial task the *Herald* had set for them: to defeat W. H. Seward in his bid for re-election to the US Senate.[64] Whig control of the state remained unshaken in that respect. Further, serious outbreaks involving the Know-Nothings in Baltimore, Philadelphia, Louisville, Cincinnati and New York itself made the Nativists indefensible as a respectable political party.[65] In the summer of 1855 the *Herald* dropped them as rapidly as Bennett would a reporter who failed in an assignment.

[61]*NYH* 30 Nov 1854.

[62]*NYH* 1 Jan 1855, and for statistics Ernst, *Immigrant Life,* appendix VI.

[63]*NYH* 9 July 1855.

[64]*NYH* 5, 21, Dec 1854; 12 Jan; 1, 7 Feb 1855. It seems that Weed bartered Whig support of a prohibition law in return for Nativist votes for Seward's re-election — see Thomas J. Curran's 'Seward and the Know-Nothings', *New York Historical Society Quarterly,* 51 (1967), 141-59.

[65]*NYH* 11 Apr; 26 May; 2, 3-22 June; 8 Aug; 9 Nov 1855. In later years the *Herald* often referred to the 'detestable' Know-Nothing spirit.

Black men and white men: The 'Almighty Nigger' and the 'Beastly Radicals'

Whatever his aberrations in regard to the immigrant Bennett proved himself a typical Celtic American in his racial prejudice against the Negro. As far as the black race was concerned he held that the promises of the Declaration of Independence were a mere 'figure of speech'.[66] Erratic and devious in its support of every other party or cause of the day, the *Herald* was thoroughly consistent throughout the period in its outspoken antipathy to Negroes and in its belief that America was and always should be a white man's country.

Since the status and future of the Negro, or as Bennett customarily referred to him, 'the eternal', 'the everlasting', 'the infernal' or just 'the Almighty Nigger', was the focus of all the political struggles of the period, the development of the *Herald*'s position on these questions will be described in later chapters. Here it is only necessary to mention some of Bennett's basic propositions regarding the Negro and slavery. He declared plainly: 'We have been true to our principles on slavery from the first: we have opposed, at no small cost of popularity to ourselves, every anti-slavery movement that has originated in the North during the last thirty years, and intend to die in that belief and that course.'[67]

It may seem paradoxical that a man who was the embodiment of Northern enterprise and progress should also be a standard bearer of the pro-slavery cause in New York, but such he was. The editor avowed that his early residence in Charleston, South Carolina, had caused him to form an opinion of the Negro which four decades of reflection only confirmed. It was not merely that Bennett had mixed with Southerners and imbibed their ideas; he had also arrived in Charleston in 1823 in the wake of an attempted slave insurrection which had badly scared white citizens there.[68] The memory of this stayed with him. If the abolitionist saw in the black man a white liberal struggling to get out, the *Herald* saw only a bloodthirsty savage whose primal passions must be restrained by the discipline of slavery. Nor could the nature of the Negro be changed. According to Bennett's racial stereotype he was afflicted with the curse of Ham, his black skin was a divine stigma of inferiority, and therefore the Negro could never be the intellectual or social equal of the white man and education was

[66]*NYH* 14 Apr 1857.

[67]*NYH* 13 Mar 1854.

[68]This was the insurrection plotted by the Negro Denmark Vesey — see Herbert Aptheker, *American Negro Slave Revolts* (NY 1969), ch XI.

simply wasted on him. By nature 'the negro' (always singular) was described in the *Herald* as so lazy that he would not possibly work unless driven, or alternately as so violently excitable and criminal in his tendencies as to require severe restraint. He was physically repulsive and the 'pollution' of the 'pure' Caucasian race by amalgamation with blacks was a horror to be shunned.

To support his views from history, as well as from the Bible and racial theory, Bennett was continually lecturing his readers on the history of slave rebellions, especially in Santo Domingo, describing atrocities committed on whites by blacks in blood curdling detail. The history of emancipation in the British West Indies proved to him that free negro labour was ruinous to whites and blacks alike. He accused the British of having saddled America with the Negro in the first place, but having brought him it appeared that the worst evil which Britain could inflict on America would be the ruin of her prosperity by fostering the emancipation movement. In other words the *Herald* presented the Negro as having an essential role in American economic life as a labourer and a clearly defined social position as a slave.[69]

Believing slavery right, Bennett could see no conflict in its existence in a free society. The Constitution sanctioned it, the system was beneficial to white men and the greatest kindness to the Negro, so why should not a 'House Divided' stand for ever, he demanded? There were cruel slave drivers, he admitted, only to rejoin that they could no more be blamed on the system than could a cruel employer in the North. He conceded also that the slave trade was an evil, but discussed it only to argue that Northern fears of its revival were baseless or, worse, fabricated (they were neither), or else to accuse Northern abolitionists of owning the ships which were employed in it. Rather disingenuously Bennett advocated the seizure of Cuba as the best means to strangle the African slave trade, yet frankly wanted the island for fear that emancipation by the Spanish authorities would make it a magnet for fugitive slaves from the USA and hence a base for negro insurrectionists. Cuba would also provide an additional slave state which the South could put into the sectional balance in the Senate.

Believing in slavery, Bennett also believed in the right of the South to protect it against the hostility of the growing Northern majority. For

---

[69]A presentation of these views may be found in virtually any copy of the *Herald* during the 1850s. On the contemporary background to Bennett's racism see Leon F. Litwack, *North of Slavery* (Chicago 1961); Forrest G. Wood, *Black Scare* (Berkeley 1970); Thomas F. Gossett, *Race: the History of an Idea in America* (Dallas 1963).

this reason he thought that the safety of the Union depended on maintaining equal numbers of slave and free states. So he championed the Kansas-Nebraska Act of 1854 which opened the possibility of those free territories being admitted as slave states. At first the *Herald* was not dogmatic about the westward expansion of slavery; it upheld 'popular sovereignty' until it was proved incompatible with law and order, and prior to 1857 would have accepted the admission of Kansas as a free state if it were made so by a majority of settlers. In that year the *Herald* vigorously agreed with the Supreme Court's Dred Scott decision which declared that Negroes could not be US citizens, that the Missouri Compromise of 1820 had been unconstitutional and that a slaveowner's property right in slaves was inviolable in the territories. Nevertheless it dismissed extreme Southern demands for slavery extension and for the re-opening of the slave trade as justifiable but impolitic and impractical.

The *Herald* laid much stress on this matter of practicality – 'practical' men realised the necessity of respecting slavery for its value to the Union and as the keystone to the Southern social system; 'practical' men recognised the danger of criticising it and the necessity of enforcing the fugitive slave law; 'practical' men understood that even if Kansas were admitted as a slave state it would effectively become free; 'practical' men realised that the North had given up slavery only because it did not pay. The *Herald*'s hatred of the Negro and belief in the right of slavery remained unchanging, yet on the *political* issue of slavery in the sectional contest the paper became steadily more extreme during the decade of the 1850s, keeping only one pace in the rear of ever mounting Southern demands until, as we shall see, by 1860 it had taken the position that 'practical' men should concede anything to slavery in order to conciliate the South and save the Union.

The *Herald* therefore opposed the anti-slavery men in the North because they believed slavery wrong and because in wanting to prevent its extension and/or by interfering with it they threatened to alienate the South and destroy the Union, and because their agitation could only end in an upheaval of the relations between blacks and whites to the detriment of the latter. The message that the *Herald* preached throughout the '50s was that continued Northern hostility to slavery must clash with the South's desire to defend it and produce civil war.

Yet these statements perhaps do not tell the whole truth about Bennett's motivation. From the files of the *Herald* for the '50s and '60s the first impression is that the fate of the Negro was of supreme importance to New Yorkers, although only a few thousand freemen of the despised race actually lived in their midst.[70] The fashion of hating blacks was real enough, and one must assume that the *Herald*'s expression of it was at least acceptable to the majority of people who bought the paper, but beyond the Negro in the South was the white man at home who favoured changing his status, and here Bennett found his real enemy. More detestable to him than the 'nigger' was the 'nigger worshipper', the 'mental negro' who was a slave to ideas. Was not Satan the first abolitionist, who freed man from the bondage of God?[71] Bennett stated his beliefs about the Negro and the sectional problem 'in a nutshell', as he would have put it, when he claimed that the majority of voters of the North dismissed 'the nigger' as 'a bore and a humbug' – 'the whole country, depend upon it, is sick of this everlasting dish of niggers. . . . It is clear that slavery is not the cause of the trouble, but the fanatical disposition at the North to meddle with it'.[72]

The year 1854 saw the birth of the anti-slavery Republican party in New York and throughout the Northern states in response to the passing of the Kansas-Nebraska Act. The party was composed of ex-Democrats as well as former Whigs, but it was the Whig hierarchy which assumed leadership of the new state organisation in 1855.[73] The leading figure of the Republicans was William H. Seward, a former governor of New York and now a propounder of anti-slavery doctrines in the US Senate. Bennett had no personal feud with him but opposed his policies throughout the 1850s, declaring that 'Seward richly deserves to be broken upon the wheel'.[74] If any political label describes the *Herald* during this time it is that of 'Anti-Seward Organ'. Seward's party manager within the state – his 'Man Friday' as

[70]Although the coloured population was increasing, in 1860 there were only 12,472 Negroes in New York City as against 793,181 whites — *American Annual Cyclopedia* for 1861, p. 525: on their condition see Rhoda G. Freeman, 'The Free Negro in New York City' (Columbia Univ. thesis, 1966).

[71]*NYH* 20 July 1855; 4 Dec 1861.

[72]*NYH* 11 June 1859; 6 Dec 1854; 20 Sept 1861.

[73]On the political history of pre-war New York State see D.A.S. Alexander, *A Political History of the State of New York* (3 vols. 1906-9), vol. 2 for this period; A.C. Flick, ed., *History of the State of New York* (10 vols. NY 1933) — vols 6 and 7; D.M. Ellis (cited in note 12); for the political transformation of 1854-6 see particularly Berger (cited in note 53) and the more compact account by Judah B. Ginsberg, 'Barnburners, Free Soilers and the New York Republican Party', *New York History*, 57 (1976), 475-500.

[74]*NYH* 12 Jan 1855. On another occasion (6 Feb 1855) Bennett spoke of Seward as 'the personification of the evils which threaten the dissolution of this Union'. Their political rivalry went back to 1826, when Seward had been active for John Quincy Adams — Pray, p. 78.

Bennett always referred to him– was Thurlow Weed, veteran editor of the Albany *Evening Journal.* Weed was without peer as a lobby manager, and as Whig and Democrat he and Bennett had conducted a war of words for thirty years.[75] Weed's lobby techniques had a regular and frank exposure in the columns of the *Herald.* Bennett knew and understood the methods by which Weed worked, and was endlessly indignant that ex-Whigs chose to promote their ascendancy in the state by championing the anti-slavery sentiments of the upstate area. He could see no sincerity in it– to him the slavery issue was only a 'dodge', a 'pretext', a 'criminal humbuggery' by which artful politicians could rise to power, a vehicle for Seward's presidential ambition: 'In the North and West, the Almighty Nigger is worshipped as representing so much political capital. Without him the underground railway stock would not be worth a cent. . . . Where, in point of fact, would the whole republican party be without the Almighty Nigger?'[76] Wrath that the Union was being endangered by such 'scheming' for office was sharpened in Bennett by the Republicans' success. Despite his dogged predictions of their imminent collapse, the Whig-Republican-Temperance alliance which gained control of the state in 1854 preceded a long period of Republican domination interrupted only in 1863-4. The *Herald* could claim to be the voice of New York City, but as a result of Democratic divisions it was mostly a voice of opposition within its own state during the period under study. Yet while the *Herald* affected to believe that anti-slavery was nothing more than a political ramp (a view which found some colour in the venality of the Weed machine and in the participation of many Republicans in racist attitudes) the paper found its living in attacking abolitionists.

Bennett despised the 'radical' mind which wanted to change society in acordance with a belief and gave priority to aims other than maintaining the Union and the Constitution. A reader of the *Herald*, on any day during the dozen years here under consideration, could open the paper and find streams of more or less virulent abuse of 'radicals', 'fanatics', 'agitators', 'schemers', 'traitors', 'jacobins'. The arch bogeymen of Bennett's world picture were Wendell Phillips, William Lloyd Garrison, Henry Ward Beecher, Charles Sumner, 'that silly, miscellaneous jumble of odds, ends and isms which is covered with a white hat, lays claim to manhood and calls itself Greeley',[77] and other abolition lights who wanted to upset the

---

[75] Glyndon Van Deusen's *Thurlow Weed, Wizard of the Lobby* (Boston 1947) contains some information on their feud; see also Carlson, p. 102 on its origin.

[76] *NYH* 11 June 1859. The 'underground railway' of course referred to the smuggling of fugitive slaves to freedom.

[77] *NYH* 1 Aug 1862.

established relations of society. These were 'monomaniacs on the negro question. They are men of but two ideas: one idea being the almighty nigger and the other referring to the best mode of riding into office on the almighty nigger's back.'[78]

To understand the full importance of this clash of 'radical' and 'conservative' temperaments it must be seen in a wider context than the confines of the slavery question, which was to some extent merely its focus. The conflict extended to all spheres of social life. It is interesting that Bennett defined the differences between the *Herald* and the *Tribune* as those between a 'practical' and an 'abstract' or 'theoretical' paper. Greeley in his time had dabbled with nearly every progressive movement and idea of the age;[79] Bennett saw in them only 'immorality'. Greeley was a sometime pacifist; Bennett desired a large defence establishment and honoured the disciplined virtues of military life, being 'happy to acknowledge that this journal has had for many years the credit of being a staunch supporter of the army and navy'.[80] At a time when voices were raised against maintaining a national military academy at West Point, the *Herald* defended it.[81] Greeley opposed capital punishment; Bennett defended it as necessary in a society where random violence was all too common and was appalled by the number of pardons which some of New York's governors were inclined to grant. He favoured anything which made punishment sure, inevitable and close after the crime.[82] The *Herald* published prurient details of divorce and rape cases, yet editorially was properly aghast at them and disapproved of divorce thoroughly. In the exhibition of a painting of a nude Bennett found a moral outrage which was the 'high road to universal license and infidelity'.[83]

[78]*NYH* 12 Feb 1865.

[79]It should be said that Greeley regarded himself as a practical reformer. The best study of his pre-war political thought is Jeter A. Isely, *Horace Greeley and the Republican Party, 1853-61* (Princeton 1947); see also Vernon L. Parrington, *Main Currents in American Thoughts* (NY 1958), vol. 2, pp. 247-58. For some comparisons and contrasts in the careers of Greeley and Bennett see Harvey Saalberg, 'Bennett and Greeley, Professional Rivals, Had Much in Common', *Journalism Quarterly,* 49 (1972), 538-46, 550.

[80]*NYH* 29, 30 June 1860.

[81]An investigation of civilian hostility to West Point is Marcus Cunliffe, *Soldiers and Civilians* (Boston 1968).

[82]*NYH* 6 Apr 1860.

[83]*NYH* 10 Feb; 11 Oct 1859. The *Herald*'s forays into the world of art on behalf of 'non-establishment' artists would form a chapter in themselves. Bennett incurred odium amongst upper class art lovers and patrons when he destroyed the American Art Union by a law suit in 1851. (The Union was closely identified with the *Times*). See E. Maurice Bloch, 'The American Art Union's Downfall', *New York Historical Society Quarterly,* 37 (1953), 331-59.

Greeley championed the women's rights movement, which Bennett found merely ludicrous – the *Herald* expressed very definite views that the proper place of 'crinoline' was in the kitchen and in the nursery.

Greeley might descant on the virtues of agriculture and exhort young men to go west; Bennett, though an apostle of 'Manifest Destiny', scoffed at the idea that superior virtue was to be found outside the city and to him the countryside seemed devoid of opportunity. It was pleasant of course to drive out to Washington heights in the evening or to walk in Central Park, but nobody seeking their fortune or improvement should leave the city, counselled the *Herald*. Greeley favoured protection for industry and cheap public land for farmers. Bennett opposed protective tariffs as detrimental to commerce, was wary of paper inflation and saw the public lands as a government trust which should be used to pay off the public debt to bondholders rather than given to 'mendicant settlers'.

Greeley had a vision of what American society might become and of the millenium which would follow certain reforms. America was to Bennett a land whose promise had largely been achieved. He took pride and satisfaction in American institutions, believing that the only serpents in the American garden of Eden were the malignant reformers themselves. The *Herald* exposed vice and crime in Northern society continually, yet the paper disseminated a philosophy of contentment with the rules of the existing order. Bennett accused the 'philosophers' of the *Tribune* of:

> eternally declaiming about the universal misery and crime which exists on all hands. Everything is wrong in their eyes. Everybody is suffering. The world is in their eyes one vast lazar house. . . . They are oppressed with a moral nightmare. They can only see the dark side of the picture. . . . But the world of these gloomy enthusiasts has no existence in reality. The great mass of mankind, living in civilized society, are happy. The suffering and misery are only exceptions to the general condition. The world is an excellent world. It is a happy world.[84]

The *Herald* exulted in technical progress and material growth. In fact according to Bennett the material progress of the United States had for thirty years been endangered by a 'moral cholera' which manifested itself in all the reform movements and freakish 'isms' of the day – Fourierism, Mormonism,[85] abolitionism, atheism and the

[84]Pray, pp. 359-60.

[85]On Bennett's semi-farcical connections with Mormonism see D.C. Seitz, *The James Gordon Bennetts* (NY 1928), pp. 102 ff.

free love movement. The *Herald* always discussed these ideas (or rather caricatures of them) as being of one piece, a single threat to the set of values which it upheld as normal. Horror of subversion was always coupled with ridicule of the manners and personal characteristics of reformers. Here is a typical *Herald* comment on the annual meeting of religious and charitable societies in the city;

> One of the most peculiar traits of metropolitan society is the heterogeneous assemblage of pharisees, enthusiasts, pious old ladies and strong minded women of an uncertain age, who flock to this city from the rural districts and from New England to the May anniversaries . . . the amount of stupendous lying, pharisaical cant, infidel profanity and abolitionist treason that has been given utterance to during the week, in the churches and public places where these societies have held their reunion, has been perfectly appalling.[86]

To the *Herald* radical ideas merely constituted 'anarchy' which would pass into a 'reign of terror' if implemented. In America as in Europe, nineteenth century conservatives found no ghosts so terrifying as those of Robespierre and Saint-Just.

It is beyond the province of this study to enquire why the sensational press sold, and still sells, newspapers by assuring the reader of his normality while titillating his sense of insecurity, but the *Herald* was decidedly of this mould. It assured the white working men and women of New York that their aspirations were legitimate. It upheld their values and self esteem while catering for their vices. Racial prejudice was just one aspect of this flattery. Having to live by their own labour and savings, white workers could at least treasure the status which their skin conferred on them. The *Herald* also reflected the resentment of whites at 'negro philanthropy'. Although it was forward in proposing public works schemes during periods of unemployment such as followed the Panic of 1857, and encouraged charity (as opposed to 'morbid philanthropy') to the poor during hard winters, the *Herald* championed a philosophy of 'no free rides'. Why should the Negro be helped, asked the *Herald* time and again, when nobody helps the white man? Republican concern for the Southern Negro caused the editor to grumble that the day would come when white men would be treated as pariahs 'and when one must be a nigger to be respectable'.[87] The following is a typical *Herald* leader on the theme:

[86]*NYH* 16 May 1863.
[87]*NYH* 12 Feb 1865.

> More Black Benevolence – We see by the *Journal of Commerce*
> of yesterday morning that it has succeeded in raising $100 for
> another black family. Did anybody ever hear of the *Journal*
> raising a single cent for a case of distress where the parties were
> white? Is it absolutely necessary to have thick lips, wooly hair
> and ebony skin to move our contemporary's bowels of compassion?
> We begin to think it is.[88]

The very men who would help the Negro, Bennett re-iterated,
were those who would assume the power to curtail the rights and
liberty of whites. It is highly revealing that Bennett referred to the anti-
slavery orators and politicians as the 'Holy Alliance' – the selfsame
nickname which he had applied to the 'pharisaical' journals which had
attacked him in the Moral War of 1840. The probability that this war
of ideas had at least as much to do with his opposition to anti-slavery
as his early residence in the South cannot be too much stressed. In
some cases the men who had attacked him in 1840 were the same who
bore the Republican standard in the 1850s.

Bennett maintained that moral reform should not come within the
sphere of political discussion or legislation. Even though intemperance
was an admittedly fearful evil in New York and gave rise to the
Temperance Party, Bennett opposed the passage of a Maine style
liquor law in 1855 on the grounds that it would lead to violence,
besides favouring the private drinking of the rich. As a result he was
accused of condoning drunkennes and vice by Greeley whose abuse
was, the *Herald* noted wryly, shockingly intemperate. Nevertheless
the new state law of 'pains and penalties' was effectively nullified in
the city, as the *Herald* had hoped and predicted.[89]

The obverse of Bennett's traditionally Democratic contempt for
moral legislation was his belief in economic freedom from monopoly.[90]
The *Herald* was most conspicuously a crusading paper in this respect.

[88]*NYH* 20 Jan 1854.

[89]*NYH* 8 Jan, 11, 26 Mar, 2, 10 Apr; 22 Sept; 30, 31 Oct; 7, 19, 30 Nov; 14 Dec
1854; 22 Jan; 2 Feb; 10, 13, 14, 15, 16, 17, 18, 19, 21, 23, 26, 28, 29 Apr; 4 May; 2, 3,
20, 21 June; 3, 6, 10, 14 July; 14, 28, 30 Aug 1855. The importance of the temperance
issue in city politics has been stressed by W.J. Rorabaugh, 'Rising Democratic Spirits;
Immigrants, Temperance and Tammany Hall. 1854-60', *Civil War History,* 22
(1976), 138-7. This theme is examined further in chapter 4 below.

[90]Understandably, Democratic politics in the 1850s have always been 'explained'
either in terms of pro-slavery commitment, or patronage and personal ambition. While
not denying the importance of these elements, arguably there is yet room for an
'ideological' treatment of the post-Jacksonian Democratic party comparable to Eric
Foner's work on the Republicans, *Free Soil, Free Labor, Free Men* (NY 1970). A
pioneering article is Bruce Collins, 'The Ideology of the Ante-Bellum Northern
Democrats', *Journal of American Studies,* 11 (1977), 103-21. For the war period the
gap has been partly filled by Joel H. Silbey, *A Respectable Minority* (NY 1977).

It was the scourge of the flagrant abuses of the railroad, ferry and gas companies in New York, which very often operated with brazen disregard for the public interest and for individual safety. Railroad and steamboat accidents were alarmingly frequent at this period and 'Another Railroad Slaughter – Anybody to Blame?' was a familiar headline. Between 1854 and 1865 there were 1,413 railroad and 324 steamboat accidents in New York, as a result of which 7,576 people were killed and 9,935 were injured[91] – the equivalent of a Civil War battle. Yet in nearly every case the companies involved were cleared of all responsibility by the courts, which made Bennett furious. That his withering editorials had little positive result was due to the tight control which the railroad and ferry lobbies exercised in the state legislature at Albany, but he did foster a climate of opinion increasingly intolerant of these transgressions on the rights of travellers. In this case he urged congressional action to regulate the monopolists and make them accountable, since clearly no relief could be had from the state.

In other ways the *Herald*'s tirades against unfettered capitalism have a modern ring. During the Civil War coal monopolists got a sustained blasting from the *Herald* for their extortionate prices, and the paper encouraged shoppers to refuse to buy certain groceries in order to force prices down. Bennett boasted that he ran a 'live' newspaper which looked after the community of New York City. The kinds of reform which the *Herald* championed were measures of immediate value to the life of the metropolis. Let the abolitionists use their energies on the cause of the Negro, but Bennett questioned: 'We should really like to know what possible consequence it is to us whether or not the black man is held in bonds a thousand miles away from us, compared with the evils that misrule and corruption have brought upon the white man within our own borders.'[92] By contrast the *Herald* would campaign day in and day out for such humdrum objects as the cleaning of the notorious filth of the city's streets to remove the danger of further epidemics such as the cholera outbreak of 1854. (The *Herald* realised the connection between filth and disease and was advanced in its advocacy of a board of public health controlled by doctors rather than politicians.) Other causes championed by the *Herald* ranged from improving quarantine facilities, better building regulations and fire precautions down to the placing of a drinking fountain. The paper battled for the creation of Central Park for the recreation of the working classes; it was the scourge of insolent

[91]*NYH* 31 Dec 1865. By sad irony Frederic Hudson was the victim of a railroad accident in 1875.
[92]*NYH* 5 Jan 1859.

omnibus drivers, negligent contractors and of butcher boys who drove their carts so recklessly as to imperil life and limb.

City and State

For all its complaints, the *Herald* took immense pride in New York City and kept up a running campaign to have it made not only the state capital instead of Albany but the federal capital instead of Washington D.C. Typically, when the Prince of Wales arrived in the USA in 1860 Bennett urged him to come straight to New York, because New York was America. Not only were the editors of the Philadelphia, Boston and Chicago papers 'scurvy nincompoops' in the *Herald*'s view, but their cities were mere villages in comparison with the great metropolis.[93]

The *Herald* frequently expressed New York's traditional antipathy for New England. Although much of the city's business remained in the hands of native New Englanders, New Yorkers took satisfaction from the fact that in the preceding half century their city's commercial vigour had surpassed Boston's and gained the economic leadership of the eastern seaboard. Yet there was more than trade rivalry behind the *Herald*'s animus against the 'codfish aristocracy'. Bennett's disillusioning youthful failure to find fortune in New England and his unsympathetic treatment by people there rankled with him, sharpening his detestation of the puritan and anti-slavery views with which the region was identified. These the *Herald* eternally denounced. As we shall see Bennett never left any doubt that in his view the Union would be happier if New England were excluded. In the midst of the Civil War the *Herald* denounced 'Yankee tyranny' as fiercely as any southerner, and complained that in fighting for emancipation the Central and Western states had become mere 'helots of a Yankee oligarchy'.[94] This was an indirect admission that, for all its size and

[93] One can get an idea of the physical appearance of Bennett's New York from I.N. Phelps Stokes, *The Iconography of Manhattan* (NY 1915-28), vol. 3, and from H.C. Brown, *Glimpses of Old New York* (NY 1917). A number of older histories have material of value: Junius H. Browne provided a full and lively portrait of the city in *The Great Metropolis* (NY 1869), which may supplement the more formal essays in James G. Wilson ed., *The Memorial History of the City of New York* (NY 1893), vol. 3, ch XI; Martha J. Lamb, *History of the City of New York* (NY 1877-80), ch XX; Mary L. Booth, *History of the City of New York* (NY 1859), ch XXII. Among modern works Robert G. Albion, *The Rise of New York Port, 1815-60* (NY 1939), is outstanding on commercial and maritime aspects while Bayrd Still, *Mirror for Gotham* (NY 1956), is a compilation of accounts by perceptive travellers. Lloyd Morris, *Incredible New York* (NY 1951) treats the social life of the city. Profitable to an understanding of conditions in the city also are Seymour J. Mandelbaum, *Boss Tweed's New York* (NY 1965), Leo Hershkowitz, *Tweed's New York: Another Look* (NY 1977), and the early chapters of Adrian Cook, *Armies of the Streets* (Univ. Kentucky 1974).

[94] *NYH* 18, 25 Aug 1864. For his youthful disillusionment with Boston see Pray, pp. 39-40. On the 'Yankee Invasion' of New York see Albion, pp. 241 ff.; Ellis, ch 16, and

boasted economic success, New York had somehow failed to make its political influence count for as much as New England's in federal politics.

In so much of its economic and political life the city was not so much badly governed as simply ungoverned. The daily press was one of the few forces making for cohesion in society. Although the city was long established, its rapid and inchoate expansion gave rise to many of the symptoms of lawlessness that characterised the newer western towns which had sprouted up in a generation.[95] The sheer size of New York made it unmanageable; despite northward expansion half of its population of three quarters of a million was crammed into squalid tenement houses on the southern end of Manhattan Island. Charity work barely made an impression on the housing conditions which existed in the worst areas of the city.[96] Rack renting was common. As yet nothing came of the *Herald*'s occasional suggestions that overcrowding could be eased by the upward building of well ventilated apartment flats or else by a series of new towns upstate. Bennett complained that employers could not be induced to invest in housing for their workers so long as railroad stocks and Wall Street speculations were so profitable.[97] Street cleaning was not the only function that was inadequately performed. The city's relatively high mortality rate testified that sanitation was not even elementary;[98] fires not infrequently started through acts of arson by one of the unruly volunteer fire companies who occasionally fought each other with clubs, knives, axes and pistols for the honour of putting out a blaze.[99] The police force was pathetically inadequate to cope with crime. It was quite normal for the *Herald* to exclaim that the city was going to 'perdition and pestilence'.[100]

Bennett frequently posed the question of why the city was the most heavily taxed yet most miserably governed of any in the western

on the rivalry between the sections Dixon R. Fox, *Yankees and Yorkers* (NY 1940). The novelist 'Manhattan' recounted that at a dinner party Bennett told how he had been refused a teaching job by a Connecticut school board because of his Catholicism – see *Marion*, vol. 2, ch 6 (pp. 92-6).

[95] *NYH* 12 July 1859.

[96] See M.J. Heale, 'Harbingers of Progressivism: Responses to the Urban Crisis in New York, c. 1845-60', *Journal of American Studies*, 10 (1976), 17-36, and Ernst, *Immigrant Life, passim.*

[97] *NYH* 13, 18 May 1854; 20 July 1859.

[98] John Duffy, *A History of Public Health in New York City, 1625-1866* (NY 1968), part III, is a comprehensive treatment of the subject.

[99] On the rivalry of the 'fire laddies' and low life in the city generally see Herbert Asbury, *The Gangs of New York* (NY 1928).

[100] *NYH* 23 Nov 1864.

world. He saw the answer in the general apathy of taxpayers, especially of those whose wealth gave them the opportunity to become leaders of the community. The city was a victim of its own prosperity and growth. New Yorkers were so immersed in the pursuit of wealth that they were apparently prepared to tolerate irrational and corrupt government. Power passed by default into the hands of ward politicians whose chief interest proved to be plundering the city's revenue. Street cleaning contracts for instance were regarded as a financial reward for political service to the Democratic party.

The *Herald* campaigned against the division of authority between the heads of municipal departments, the common council and the board of aldermen. Throughout the period the paper called for a new charter embodying the establishment of an executive system for the city similar to that by which the nation itself was governed. In other words the mayor should have full power over and responsibility for the municipal departments. Further, all officials should be properly salaried to discourage peculation. This rational reform was not forthcoming because too many vested interests favoured the municipal spoils system, and when the Republicans held power in the state they were distrustful of enlarging the power of a Democratic mayor.

The most controversial figure in the municipal politics of the era was Fernando Wood, mayor in 1855-7 and again in 1860-1. Wood was the doyen of the ward politicians – master of all the techniques of vote catching by hook or crook and of carrying elections with gangs of toughs.[101] He broke away from Tammany Hall in 1858 and formed his own Democratic organisation in the city at Mozart Hall. Wood was always portrayed by his enemies as the incarnation of corrupt government, and abused as though he were a gallows bird with every epithet the Republican press could lay upon him. He was certainly a rogue, and the Republican view of him has been generally accepted, but he had one staunch defender in the *New York Herald*. Wood admitted that 'I attach great importance to the support of the *Herald*. It is the most influential paper north of Washington . . . . under its constant and dreadful fire no public man of this day is sufficiently strong to maintain himself.'[102] Furthermore he boasted of his friendship

[101]The only biography of Wood is Samuel A. Pleasants' scholarly but brief *Fernando Wood of New York* (NY 1948). He deserves a more extensive treatment. There are also two articles of value by Leonard Chalmers, 'Fernando Wood and Tammany Hall: The First Phase', *New York Historical Society Quarterly,* 52 (1968), 379-402, and 'Tammany Hall, Fernando Wood and the Struggle to Control New York City, 1857-9', *idem,* 53 (1969), 7-33.

[102]Fernando Wood to James Buchanan 28 Nov 1856, Buchanan Papers, Historical Society of Pennsylvania.

with Bennett and of the fact that 'I am the only public man in the nation who has *always* been supported by him'.[103] In pleading for greater executive power for the mayor the *Herald* was endorsing Wood's views. It palliated or ignored his transgressions in the hope that he would prove an effective mayor, and for a while in 1855 he won even Republican support for his strong measures to enforce law in the city.

The reform honeymoon lasted until Wood refused to enforce the new state prohibition law: the political influence of several thousand liquor retailers was not to be taken lightly.[104] In 1857 there was outright war between Wood and the Republican legislature, which passed a law creating a new Metropolitan police force for the city. Wood refused to recognise the validity of the act, considering it a usurpation of his power, and the *Herald* supported him in strong language, arousing public indignation by beating the drum of civic liberty against 'Legislative Tyranny'. The *Herald* tried to outbid the Republican warcry of 'bleeding Kansas' with pictures of the alleged victimisation of 'bleeding New York'.

The Republicans claimed that the new force was required because the Municipal Police were merely a political tool at Wood's disposal. Although its own files contained heavy indictments of Municipal inefficiency, the *Herald* opposed the Metropolitan for exactly the opposite reasons – that it would not be accountable to the elected city authority and that it would become a political weapon for upstate Republicans trying to increase their patronage and influence in the predominantly Democratic city. The two police forces collided, the Metropolitans attempted to arrest Wood, and eventually the mayor yielded and the Municipal force was disbanded. (The notorious gangs of New York had a field day in the meanwhile and troops had to be used to restore order.)[105] By way of compromise Wood became one of the five commissioners for the new force, and the *Herald* accepted this arrangement with the best grace possible. At the next charter election the city repudiated Wood.[106]

[103]Wood to Buchanan 26 Dec 1856, *ibid.* We shall see later on that Wood spoke too soon. Even at this time Bennett reproved Wood 'with emphasis' privately when he suspected him of trying to dictate the *Herald*'s course. See Henry Wikoff to Buchanan 29, 31 Dec 1856; 3, 9 Jan 1857, *ibid.,*

[104]Bennett estimated that there were 10,000 private liquor dealers in the city — probably an exaggerated estimate. Another contemporary put the figure at 6,000 but pointed out even so that if each dealer influenced only five voters it made 36,000 votes to be reckoned with — see Rorabaugh, 'Rising Democratic Spirits'.

[105]Asbury, pp. 112 ff.; Joel T. Headley, *The Great Riots of New York* (NY 1971 ed.), ch IX.

[106]*NYH* 2, 6, 12 Feb; 10, 23, 24, 27, 28, 29, 30 Apr; 1, 2, 4, 20, 23, 24 May; 17 June; 4, 7, 12, 15, 21, 23 July; 27, 30 Aug; 17 Oct; 3, 7, 13, 22, 24 Nov; 1 Dec 1857.

This episode illustrates the difficulties standing in the way of reform, even though the *Herald* itself bore witness to the crying need for it. Party politics and the fierce jealousy between city and state stood in the way. The local Democrats were apparently incapable of giving the city good government but would countenance no interference from upstate. The *Herald* declared that 'we regard our republican reformers at Albany somewhat as the fox regarded the offer of the swallow to drive away the swarms of flies that had fastened upon Renard's head while swimming the stream:- "If you drive these away" said he, "they will be succeeded by a hungrier swarm, that will suck every drop of blood from my veins."'[107]

The whole question of corruption is an elusive one. To raise the cry was good journalism, and the *Herald* was raising it continually. As we have seen it was part of Bennett's religion that politics could not be otherwise than dirty. The *Herald*'s strictures were directed against city officials, against its rivals in the newspaper field and against the politicians of both parties in the state legislature. It was easy to make extravagant accusations without naming names or giving facts. Yet not all its accusations were groundless, for jobbery and fraud were undoubtedly rife. Little transpired in the state capital at Albany or in the city departments that the *Herald* did not get to hear about. The *Herald* had a habit of asking awkward questions and chastising the negligent. 'It is not merely that he impudently pulls your nose,' it was said of Bennett, 'but that he pulls it in the view of a million people'.[108] As early as 1865 the *Herald* was advertising publicly for anyone who could produce sufficient evidence to convict William M. Tweed and his associates.[109]

In his turn Bennett was constantly being accused of accepting bribes, of using the threat of exposure in the *Herald* for blackmail, and using his money column for speculative purposes. Although it was difficult to prove there were always some who believed Bennett to be the ruthless operator of a 'hush money' system. Said Webb, 'this pest of society holds a poisoned dagger at the throats of certain government officials in this city, who have been compelled to subsidize him into silence. They have been forced by fear of exposure to throw a crust to

The Metropolitan-Municipal conflict is examined in James F. Richárdson, 'Mayor Fernando Wood and the New York Police Force, 1855-7', *New York Historical Society Quarterly,* 50 (1966), 5-40.

[107]*NYH* 14 Apr 1859.

[108]Parton, 'The New York Herald'.

[109]*NYH* 28 May 1865. It was the *Times* though which later headed the campaign to expose the 'Boss' and in his *Diary* (vol. IV, p. 383) for 8 Sept 1871, George T. Strong sourly accused the *Herald* of having been subsidised into silence.

this troublesome dog.'[110] Many of these charges of venality were probably as far fetched as those which Bennett levelled against Greeley, Raymond and Webb, but certainly the *Herald* did sometimes champion notorious rogues such as Madame Restell the abortionist and corruptionists like Tammany politician Francis I. A. Boole. In 1860 Boole brazenly syphoned $75,000 of taxpayers' money into aldermanic pockets on the pretext of 'expenses' for the reception of the Japanese embassy. Bennett denounced this accurately as 'one of the grossest swindles ever perpetrated by the Corporation'. Yet the *Herald* ardently and mysteriously supported Boole for mayor in 1863.[111] In at least two other cases there is some evidence that the *Herald* was not always quite so fiercely independent as Bennett protested. One journalist reported that in conversation in 1856 Bennett had remarked that 'he had only supported Mayor Wood in order to procure the nomination of "Abe" Russell, a relative of his wife's, for City Judge of New York. . . .'[112]

Now the *Herald* did show a remarkable partiality for Abraham D. Russell, who was elected City Judge that year. It puffed him at every possible opportunity as the nonpareil of all jurists and defended him when Republicans tried to have him removed for incompetence. In return the complainant in an 1857 libel hearing accused Russell of unduly favouring Bennett.[113] After the local elections of 1860, however, Raymond gloated in the *Times* that:

> the most curious vote of all is that for Recorder, in which Mozart Hall, the special pet and protegé of the *Herald,* allows the *Herald*'s candidate for the Recordership to run about fourteen thousand votes behind the balance of the ticket. ABRAHAM D. RUSSELL was made City Judge four years ago by a bargain driven with FERNANDO WOOD, by the *Herald*'s editor; and the support of that paper in the last contest was pretty publicly stated to be at the disposal of whatever organization would promise to secure Judge RUSSELL's election to the higher office which he sought. This bait, rejected by Tammany Hall,

[110]Quoted in Wilmer, *Our Press Gang,* p. 192. The blackmail charges feature prominently in the anonymous 1844 pamphlet *The Life and Writings of James Gordon Bennett.* For a contemporary defence of Bennett from these charges see William M. Bobo, *Glimpses of New York by a South Carolinian* (Charleston 1852), pp. 67-70.

[111]*NYH* 25, 28 July 1860; Oct-Nov 1863. On Boole's record see Gustavus Myers, *History of Tammany Hall* (NY 1917), pp. 199, 203, 205; and Duffy, *History of Public Health in New York,* part III, pp. 323-6, 372-3, 530, 551-2, 556-8, 569.

[112]Malcolm Ives to James Buchanan 7 Sept 1856, Buchanan Papers, HSP.

[113]*New York County. . . the People ex. rel. Daniel E. Sickles vs. James Gordon Bennett* (NY 1857).

78

was eagerly clutched at by the Mozart people, and the result is that we find them, having used the *Herald* for many years as the special organ of their billingsgate against Tammany, now quietly 'cheating the eye teeth' out of the only candidate in whose success the *Herald*'s editor took deep personal interest.[114]

Thereafter Bennett petitioned both President Lincoln and Governor Seymour on Russell's behalf, though apparently without effect.[115]

On a broader scale, there is some correlation between the *Herald*'s attitude to the municipal authorities and its enjoyment of the Corporation advertising. To wit, charges of corruption were apt to fly thick when the *Herald* was excluded from this source of revenue, as in 1858, 1862 and 1865. Bennett of course affected great indifference as to whether he received this perquisite, but his protestations were laboured and he was pleased enough when he obtained the contract.[116] He claimed that the *Herald* ought by law to receive the advertising as the paper with the largest circulation in the city, and that he was justified in asking a higher price than other papers because advertisements in the *Herald* reached a larger readership. (This was the *Herald*'s normal advertising policy. Bennett argued that it was unfair that chambermaids and clerks should have to pay more for advertisements than the Corporation or the Federal Post Office.)[117] Whether from straight politics or because they genuinely balked at Bennett's prices, some municipal administrations distributed the advertising amongst several smaller circulation newspapers, including the *Times*. The *Herald* was left out in the cold sourly criticising the 'corporation organs'; in 1865 it was so out of humour with the Democratic regime that it called on Radical Republican Governor Fenton to remove arbitrarily all the city officials, from mayor down, to save the city from misgovernment. The battle for 'municipal liberty' against 'Albany despotism' which the paper had fought under Wood in the 1850s seemed to be quite forgotten.[118]

[114]New York *Times* 9 Nov 1860.

[115]Bennett to Abraham Lincoln 22 Oct 1861, Lincoln Papers, Library of Congress, item 12602. Lincoln forwarded the request to Seward, see Basler, *The Complete Works of Abraham Lincoln*, vol. 5, p. 5. Also Stewart Mitchell, *Horatio Seymour* (Cambridge, Mass., 1936), p. 305 and note.

[116]See *NYH* e.g. 30 Nov 1861; 18 June 1862. Henry J. Raymond thought that Bennett was actively working to get the Common Council of the City to give him the job — NY *Times* 6 Dec 1861. A typical Corporation invitation for advertising tenders, dated 1850, is in the Bennett Papers, New York Public Library.

[117]Hudson, pp. 468-9.

[118]*NYH* 12, 15, 19, 29 July; 2, 11 Aug 1865.

To these instances where personal or financial interest shaped the *Herald*'s editorial course must be added another of greater significance and more fully documented. This, as the following chapters will reveal, was Bennett's long standing but carefully concealed desire for a diplomatic post.

PART TWO

THE *HERALD* IN POLITICS AND WAR

3

VANITY PRICKED: PIERCE, BUCHANAN AND THE 'AUTOCRAT OF NEW YORK'

Bennett is the vainest mortal that has lived since the days of Boswell, and his vanity makes his friendship or his enmity equally injurious. I do not know which I would prefer — his inordinate praise or his stinging tongue. He is also anxious through his weakness and his wife to figure as a diplomat, aspiring to the mission to France [:] nor does he suppose his chance hopeless for that position. He will return [from Europe] therefore, hopeful that his services will have this reward, believing as he does that he alone can decide the next election. — Albert C. Ramsey to James Buchanan, 2 July 1856

I hav no pollertics. Nary a one. I'm not in the bisniss. If I was I spose I should holler versiffrusly in the streets at nite and. . . go to the Poles arly. I should stay there all day. I should see to it that my nabers was thar. I should git carriges to take the kripples, the infirm and the indignant thar. I should be on guard agin frauds and sich. I should be on the look out for the infamus lise of the enemy, got up jest be4 elecshun for perlitical effeck. When all was over and my candydate was elected, I should move heving & arth — so to speak — until I got orfice, which if I didn't get orfice I should turn round and abooze the Administration with all my mite and maine. But I'm not in the bisniss. — Artemus Ward

In 1852 Franklin Pierce of New Hampshire was elected President by the victorious Democrats. New York's *Democratic Review,* clarion of the expansionist 'Young America' wing of the party, was enthusiastic in crediting the triumph to Bennett,[1] and in his restrained way Pierce himself felt bound to tell a political friend that: 'It is quite unnecessary for me to say that I have not been insensible to the vast influence of the *Herald* throughout the late canvass. Will you assure Mr. B. when you write him that I appreciate the motive and the ability, and at the same time present him my sincere acknowledgements.'[2]

Pierce was never to prove very adept in his handling of press relations, as the lack of real warmth in his indirect message to Bennett

[1]'The *Herald* — Onward!', *Democratic Review,* 31 (Nov 1852), 409-19.

[2]Text in F. Hudson, *Journalism in the United States from 1690 to 1872* (NY 1873), p. 485

suggests.[3] Yet the President-elect had reason to be cautious. The *Herald* had indeed poured damaging broadsides into the Whigs and had very effectively ridiculed their candidate, General Winfield Scott, but it had shown little positive enthusiasm for the virtually unknown Pierce. In fact its editorial on election day had omitted to mention his name at all. It was well known that the *Herald* had championed the Whigs in 1848, when they ran Mexican War hero Zachary Taylor. The paper's avowed and essentially negative reason for opposing Scott was its claim that if elected he would be dominated by William Seward and his anti-slavery clique, who would re-open the sectional quarrels so recently papered over in Congress by what Bennett sceptically but accurately called 'The Armistice of 1850'.[4]

Bennett himself felt that the quality of his support admitted of no quibble and had been worth more to Pierce than a passing acknowledgement could repay. In the past the editor had paid court to Presidents Tyler[5] and Taylor and now, while delighting the public daily with livid denunciations of spoils hunters and office seekers, he made bold to approach Pierce directly. Little more than a month after the election, Bennett solicited appointment as US minister to France, in whose capital his wife and family resided much of the time and where he had established a permanent *Herald* bureau for the collection of European news. In his curious and revealing private letter to the President-elect he begged the appointment for a short time only, as it would not suit him to stay abroad longer than one year. Moreover he confided to Pierce a singular reason for coveting such a high position. Personally, said Bennett, he believed himself to be far from ambitious — indeed he had been 'conscious from infancy in [*sic*] the purity and integrity of my intentions and aspirations'. His private income from the *Herald* was such that he declared himself beyond any financial necessity for government patronage. Rather, he hoped that Pierce's own experience would help him to understand his motive:

> For four or five months last summer, a certain portion of the press and public poured calumny on calumny over your own devoted head. The generous votes of the American people have wiped out those stains, and covered with merited disgrace the calumniators. For more than twenty years, worse and more bitter calumnies have been poured not only over my name and

[3]On Pierce's press relations generally see James E. Pollard, *The Presidents and the Press* (NY 1947), pp. 282-91 and *NYH* 8 Dec 1856.

[4]e.g. *NYH* 24 Jan 1854. This term has recently regained favour as a description of the political situation, see D.M. Potter, *The Impending Crisis 1848-61* (NY 1976), ch 5.

[5]See note 129 to chapter 1.

reputation but also over that of my family, my friends and my all
. . . an act of confidence extended by your administration towards
me personally, such as I have indicated, might perhaps put the
cap on the pyramid — the keystone in the arch, and place my
calumniators where yours now are and where all such ought to be
placed.[6]

Bennett's pleas were in vain. Eventually, in October 1853, Pierce
gave the Paris mission to a Southern Democratic politician, John Y.
Mason of Virginia. From that time forward the *Herald* was the Pierce
administration's most vengeful critic. Between 1854 and 1856 the full
editorial invective of the nation's largest selling journal was directed
against the harrassed and annoyed occupant of the White House, who
had only the relatively feeble defence of the *Washington Union*.
Pierce henceforward was invariably presented to *Herald* readers as
'imbecile', 'blundering', 'treacherous', 'weak', 'cowardly', 'wicked',
'corrupt', 'reprobate', 'degraded', 'too mean to hate, too pitiable even
to despise'.[7] The *Herald* never found a shortage of things to criticise
and the resourcefulness, if not the subtlety and consistency of its
attacks was truly remarkable.

The major event of domestic politics was the Kansas-Nebraska
Act of 1854, which received Pierce's assent. Throughout the North
the President was denounced furiously for complying with extreme
Southern demands and sanctioning the spread of slavery into western
territories where it had been assumed prohibited. Aroused Whigs and
'Free Soil' Democrats began to organise the Republican party,
dedicated to arrest the spread of slavery. The *Herald,* however,
attacked Pierce on opposite grounds. Unlike the rest of the New York
City papers (except the conservative *Journal of Commerce*) Bennett
was not indignant about the spread of slavery at all. He approved the
bill as 'constitutional' and belaboured Pierce precisely for having
been half-hearted in support of it. The *Herald* alleged that the
President was playing his Southern allies false and sought to damn
him in the eyes of true Democrats by continually hinting at the
existence of a'Scarlet Letter' revealing free soil leanings, supposedly
written by Pierce some years before. (The name play arose from
Pierce's friendship with Nathaniel Hawthorne, who had written his
campaign biography.) For Bennett, of course, to show that a man had

---

[6]Bennett to Pierce 15 Dec 1852, Pierce Papers, Library of Congress. Bennett publicly
denied that the had sought the post, e.g. *NYH* 22 Jan 1854 — a lie which was
swallowed by both Pray, *Memoirs of J.G. Bennett* (NY 1855), p. 454 and Hudson, p.
485, and has gone unchallenged by later writers.

[7]This last comment *NYH* 13 Mar 1854. That Pierce was nettled by these attacks see
Roy F. Nichols, *Franklin Pierce* (Philadelphia 1931), p. 318.

dabbled even mildly with free soil ideas or politics was to expose his utter moral depravity.[8]

When in 1855 Kansas became a battleground between free soil and pro-slavery settlers the *Herald* took care not to overplay the disorders there, protesting vigorously that most of the trouble was merely exaggerated propaganda by the Republican press. Yet in condoning Southern provocations the paper could hardly resist the temptation to lash Pierce's 'malign imbecility' in failing to prevent disorder. In strong contrast to the *Tribune* and *Times,* to whom Pierce was simply a tool of Southern border ruffians, the *Herald* asserted that such trouble as existed was the result of Pierce being soft on what it labelled an illegal free soil organisation of the territory. When Pierce did prove himself a partisan of Southern 'rights' and took measures against the free soilers, the suspicious *Herald* insisted that, like Senator Douglas who had sponsored the bill, he was merely trying to ingratiate himself with extreme Democrats to further his ambitions for another presidential term.[9]

Pierce's patronage policy provided another stick for the *Herald* to beat him with. The President could hardly hope to please both factions of the badly divided New York Democratic Party, whose chronic and damaging disunity dated back to the banking issues of the 1830s. In so far as these squabbles had involved only a clash of personalities and ambitions and the desire of rival factions to monopolise the limited number of federal jobs in the state, they seemed as meaningless as the struggles of blues and greens in ancient Constantinople. But they had greater import. In 1847 the party had split into 'Hunkers' and 'Barnburners' over the slavery issue. (The former put party ascendancy before opposition to slavery, and so were said to 'hunker' after office. The latter's willingness to break up the state party over slavery led them to be likened to the farmer who burned his barn to get rid of the rats.) The following year the Barnburners in large numbers deserted to the new Free Soil Party, returning again in 1849 after that party had failed to gain the presidency or secure them political rewards.[10]

[8]*NYH* 19, 21, 27, 29, 30 Jan; 1, 9, 16, 22, 23, 28 Feb; 2, 24 Mar; 8, 12, 15, 24, 25 May 1854. Hawthorne's *The Scarlet Letter* had been published in 1850.

[9]Sample leads on Kansas affairs *NYH* 1, 18 June; 9 July; 29 Aug; 3 Sept 1854; 3, 4, 8, 13, 15 May; 10 Nov; 5, 7, 21 Dec 1855; 26 Jan; 19 Feb; 8 Mar; 29 Apr; 31 May; 7 June etc. 1856. For events in Kansas see Allan Nevins, *The Ordeal of the Union,* vol. 2 – *A House Dividing 1852-57* (NY 1947).

[10]The intricacies of Democratic politics in New York can be followed in H.D.A. Donovan, *The Barnburners* (NY 1925) and Walter L. Ferree, 'The New York Democracy: Division and Reunion 1847-52' (unpublished thesis, University of Pennsylvania, 1953). Also helpful are the political histories of New York State cited in

This transformed the nature of the party schism into those who favoured the reunion of the Barnburners on easy terms ('Softshells' or 'Softs') and those known as 'Hardshells' or 'Hards' who believed that they ought to be received, if at all, as heretics who had forfeited their claims to preferment within the party. Thus the 'Softs' were more receptive, albeit guardedly, to free soil aims than the 'Hards', who either approved of or were indifferent to the expansion of slavery in the western territories. Indeed, large numbers of Barnburners and Softs were later to join the Republican party.

Bennett's sympathies were generally with the Hards. He was at one with their 'conservative' or pro-slavery attitude and detested the free soil proclivities of the erstwhile Barnburners or 'nigger worshipping' Democrats as he was wont to call them. Also the Barnburners had been the adherents of Martin Van Buren, whose nomination for the presidency as the Free Soil candidate they had secured in 1848. As we have seen, Bennett had a long standing grudge against Van Buren, and extended it to cover all his political followers. To him the 'defection' of 1848 had been a shameful manoeuvre by a set of spoils hunters and 'vile disorganisers'.

The *Herald* therefore shared the indignation of the Hards that Pierce did not award them exclusive enjoyment of the federal patronage within the state. In fact, after a wrangle, the Barnburners and Softs did rather well in securing jobs in the Federal Custom House for New York Port — the richest source of patronage in the state for office seekers. Pierce had sought to create party harmony by favouring those Democrats, North and South, who had opposed the Compromise of 1850. In doing so, the *Herald* complained, he insulted those who had supported it.[11]

On the national level, Bennett found one of Pierce's appointments unforgivable. This was the President's choice of New Yorker William L. Marcy to be his Secretary of State. Bennett had a feud with Marcy that went back to 1832. In that year Bennett, then Washington correspondent for the *Courier and Enquirer,* had intrigued with Marcy to make the latter Governor of New York State. Marcy had

note 73 to chapter 2 above. A study which gives full weight to the role of the New York Democrats within the Free Soil movement is Frederick J. Blue, *The Free Soilers* (Chicago 1973).

[11]*NYH* 2, 16 Feb; 28 Mar; 24, 27 May; 4, 9, 14 July; 24 Aug; 8 Sept 1854. Roy F. Nichols, *The Democratic Machine, 1850-54* (NY 1923), pp. 202-15 details Pierce's patronage measures. On the political importance of the Customs House see William Hartman, 'The New York Customs House: Seat of Spoils Politics', *New York History,* 34 (1953), 149-63. On the relative popularity of Hards and Softs in the 1854 gubernatorial contest see note 56 to chapter 2 above.

been elected and in return for his support Bennett had expected some help in securing a position on the *Washington Globe*. When this was not forthcoming Bennett was keenly resentful of the slight. Said Hudson, who was in a position to know: 'Mr. Bennett never forgave Mr. Marcy for his conduct to him in this affair. He held him as a Scotch terrier would a rat through the remainder of his political life.'[12] Bennett himself was later to boast of the satisfaction he had taken of the 'utterly selfish' Marcy and Van Buren by attacking them in the *Herald* over the years as a return for their manipulation of him.[13] Pierce had selected a Secretary of State who could do no right in the *Herald*'s eyes, and its onslaughts on his foreign policy were fierce and slashing throughout the course of the administration.

The *Herald* soon found an opportunity to embarrass the government. It secured and published a copy of the secret Gadsden Treaty, by which Mexico sold the United States territory along the Gila River. The Senate was outraged by the *Herald*'s leak and Senator Slidell of Louisiana called for Bennett's arrest for contempt. Not to be outdone, the indignant editor informed the public that the United States had been saddled with a strip of 'useless desert' inhabited only by 'a few bloodthirsty Apaches'. It was not enough that $20 million was to be 'burgled' from the US Treasury to finance Santa Anna's suppression of liberty in Mexico; the *Herald* further alleged that much of the money would go into the pockets of the sycophants, jobbers and railroad speculators who surrounded the President and who were destroying national morality. Even when the Senate cut the appropriation to $10 million Bennett was not appeased — $10 million for speculators yet 'Lord save us!' cried the editor, the President could veto a grant of land to lunatic asylums because it was an 'extravagant' and 'unconstitutional' internal improvement.[14]

The *Herald* clamoured that the money wasted on the Gadsden Treaty should have been used to finance a war against Spain for Cuba. The opportunity for annexing the island seemed glittering while Britain was preoccupied in the Crimea, yet Pierce did not fulfil Bennett's bellicose ambitions. For this, and for failing to give overt aid

[12]Hudson, p. 359. Bennett's letter to Marcy, 15 Mar 1833, William L. Marcy Papers, vol. 2, Library of Congress. On the feud see also Pray, pp. 136-7; Henry Wikoff, *The Adventures of Roving Diplomatist* (NY 1857), pp. 291-3; and Ivor D. Spencer, *The Victor and the Spoils* (Providence 1959), pp. 65-75.

[13]*NYH* 28 Apr 1857.

[14]*NYH* 1, 12, 23 Feb; 27 Mar; 6, 14, 18 Apr; 23, 30 June; 9 July 1854. See also P.N. Garber, *The Gadsden Treaty* (Philadelphia 1924), p. 117. The *Herald* had been in trouble with the Senate in 1848 over its early publication of the Treaty of Gaudelope-Hidalgo — see F. Marbut, *News from the Capital* (Carbondale 1971), ch 8.

to American filibuster expeditions in Central America, the *Herald* poured scorn on him.[15] Yet when an American captain bombarded Greytown on the Mosquito Coast because the inhabitants had failed to make compensation for a fancied insult, and received administration sanction for his act, the *Herald* was roused to a passion. Bennett joined the opposition press in denouncing the high handed act as a 'humiliating, criminal and imbecile bombardment and burning of a helpless village'.[16] He wanted Pierce impeached for abusing the war power by this bullying affair, but outstripped the other papers in claiming that Greytown was not an independent colony but under the authority of the United States; *ergo* Pierce was guilty of making war on Americans. Thus Bennett got the best out of the imperialist and anti-imperialist clamour at the same time. Similarly the *Herald* could flay Pierce and Marcy for truckling to England in Central American and Caribbean diplomacy, or alternately for trying to drag the country into war with England as an electioneering ramp.[17]

The *Herald* scored another scoop by publishing the notorious 'Ostend Manifesto' drawn up by American diplomats in Europe to justify future American seizure of Cuba. Opposition papers were aghast. For the *Herald* though the great cause for regret was that the President was too pusillanimous to put the manifesto into operation.[18]

While Bennett might sympathise with the expansionist and filibustering ideals of the 'Young America' movement, the behaviour of some hot headed politicians of this school gave him fuel for his attacks on Pierce. The *Herald* made a feast of the scandalously undiplomatic activities of envoys Pierce Soulé in Spain and Daniel Sickles in London, blaming the President for such disreputable appointments. In advocating a professional diplomatic service which would improve national prestige abroad Bennett produced some irrefutable arguments, and his words were doubtless sharpened by the disappointment of his own diplomatic pretensions.[19]

---

[15]*NYH* 20 Mar; 7, 10 Apr; 3, 10, 13, 15, 16, 27 May; 4, 11, 23 June; 2 Aug; 29 Dec 1854; 26 Mar; 9, 10, 30 Apr; 8 Sept 1855; 1, 9, 12, 26 Jan 1856. For a general picture of Pierce's foreign policy the reader is again referred to Nevins, *Ordeal of the Union,* vol. 2. See also Basil Rauch, *American Interest in Cuba 1848-55* (NY 1948), ch X. Bennett himself had visited Cuba and been entertained by the Captain-General in 1850 — Pray, p. 444.

[16]*NYH* 28 July; 6 Dec 1854.

[17]*NYH* 26, 27 July; 8, 12 Aug 1854; 23 Jan; 6, 13 May 1856.

[18]*NYH* 7 Nov 1854; 7 Mar 1855.

[19]*NYH* 18, 23 June; 16 Nov; 1, 3 Dec 1854; A.A. Ettinger, *The Mission to Spain of Pierre Soulé* (Newhaven 1932), especially pp. 157-8, 219-20, 375, 405, 443; and on how Sickles retaliated on Bennett see W.A. Swanberg, *Sickles the Incredible* (NY 1956), p. 92.

Pierce was no doubt genuinely surprised and disappointed when in 1856 his party failed to renominate him at the Cincinnati Convention for a second term.[20] The reason most commonly alleged for this is his alienation of the politicians of his own party. The pro-compromise Democrats had been offended by his patronage of the free soil and secessionist extremes of the party; yet the free soilers were outraged by the Kansas-Nebraska Act and the Southern Rights men were less than content with his failure to take Cuba. This political ineptitude, combined with the powerful rival ambitions of James Buchanan and Senator Stephen A. Douglas, were perhaps sufficient to account for his failure. The point that needs stressing here though is the importance of Bennett's enmity as a factor in Pierce's downfall. It was natural that the anti-slavery press of the North was in full cry after the blood of the administration, but it is scarcely an exaggeration to say that no newspaper did more than the *Herald* to bring low the President's name during the two and a half years prior to the Cincinnati Convention.[21] Never widely popular, Pierce in 1856 had no personal prestige whatever with which his rivals had to contend. Politically he was a dead cock in the pit, and the *Herald* was a principal murderer. With damning condescension Bennett had adopted the habit of referring to the President as 'Poor Pierce', and that simple epithet may well been more ruinous to the political career of New Hampshire's favourite son than the resentments of a hundred other disappointed office seekers.

With Pierce effectively discredited by early 1856 it seemed certain that the *Herald* would campaign for a Democratic candidate on a 'clear up Pierce's corruption' programme, for it had now abandoned its dabbling with the American or Know-Nothing Party as a likely victor. By the spring of 1856 the paper was tuning up against the Republicans or 'NIGGER WORSHIPPERS' as it began to refer to them as a matter of course. Bennett relied chiefly on racist appeals ('Can there be anything more disgusting than NIGGER WORSHIPPING?')[22] as the best means of combating the Republican technique of making political capital out of 'bleeding Kansas'. In the Kansas excitement the *Tribune* clearly had the lead in sensationalism over the *Herald*, whose political views prevented it from playing the story up to the full. To offset this unaccustomed disadvantage Bennett could only continue to insist that all the trouble was either 'artificial'

[20]Nicholas, *Franklin Pierce*, p. 468.

[21]For retrospective comment on the *Herald's* course see *Charleston Mercury* 16 May 1860.

[22]*NYH* 6 Mar 1856.

or the work of the free state men themselves.[23] He accused Greeley and Raymond of having a professional interest in bloodshed, hinting besides that the pacifist Greeley had a pecuniary interest in the shipment of arms to Kansas. He also tried to match eye-catching Republican headlines with his own brand of satire. With pointed reference to the 1826 state election in which Thurlow Weed had notoriously used anti-masonic excitement over a murder victim to win votes, Bennett headed one of his editorials 'Kansas and the Nigger Worshippers — Their Devices to Keep up the Excitement — Another Morgan Wanted. . . Who will consent to sacrifice himself for the deliverance of Kansas? Almost anybody will be "good enough Morgan till after the election". Inquire of Thurlow Weed.'[24] With prophetic irony these remarks came only a few weeks before the caning of Senator Sumner by South Carolina congressman Brooks, an event which greatly added to sectional excitement.[25]

The Republican press in turn girded for the expected battle with the *Herald*. The Buffalo (NY) *Express* sneered at the *Herald* as a 'slave driver's organ'. Bennett thought this cruel, 'and yet as far as the charge relates to the driving of Seward and his seditious gang of mouthing conspirators and silly slaves out of the councils of the government, local and national, we plead guilty. Anything more?'[26]

Then a metamorphosis took place. On 23 April 1856, James Buchanan returned to New York from England, where as ambassador he had escaped the obloquy attaching to the Pierce administration. His reception made it plain that as Pennsylvania's favourite son he was a prominent contender for the Democratic nomination. Intriguingly enough, when passing through Paris en route home almost the first visit Buchanan had made was to Mrs. Bennett, with whom he evidently discussed his campaign plan at length.[27] The Bennetts had been acquainted with Buchanan for years, and had last met him a few months previously while travelling in Europe.[28] Buchanan had

[23]Press coverage of the Kansas troubles is considered by Bernard A. Weisberger, 'The Newspaper Reporter and the Kansas Imbroglio', *Mississippi Valley Historical Review,* 36 (1949-50), 633-56, and *Reporters for the Union* (Boston 1953).

[24]*NYH* 18 Mar 1856.

[25]Bennett disapproved equally of Sumner's intemperate speech which provoked the assault and of Brooks's violent action — a position which won him abuse from partisans in both sections. See *NYH* 23, 24 May 1856.

[26]*NYH* 4 Apr 1856.

[27]NY *Evening Post* 22, 23, 24 Apr 1856.

[28]On one occasion in the 1840s Bennett had carried some official despatches to Europe for Buchanan. Seitz, *The James Gordon Bennetts* (NY 1928), pp. 157-9, has some material on their early connections.

probably not needed the urging of Bennett's attorney Daniel Sickles to realise the political importance of a little civility to the editor's family.[29]

Yet for several weeks after Buchanan's return the *Herald* was virtually silent on the question of the Democratic succession, confining itself to strictures on Pierce and the Republicans. In fact Bennett had decided to keep his paper non-committal for the present.[30] When the Democrats nominated Buchanan for the Presidency at their Cincinnati Convention in June, the *Herald's* reaction was surprisingly cool. Bennett admitted that Buchanan was 'respectable' and 'amiable' but cautioned that he was 'cold' and 'timid'.[31] Two weeks later, on 20 June Buchanan received a brief telegram from a political friend. It told him that the Republicans had nominated John C. Fremont at their Philadelphia Convention and added '*Herald* endorses Republican ticket and platform'.[32]

Actually the *Herald* had been warming to Fremont for several days before his official nomination, although only a short while previously it had dismissed him as a mere adventurer and speculator. Now it professed to find in him the popular choice — the only safe, national and conservative man.[33] In the summer of 1856 readers were treated to the unique spectacle of the *Herald* asserting that the Democrats were the dangerously sectional party and denying that Fremont's election would cause a dissolution of the Union. On the contrary, Fremont would be a second Jackson whereas Buchanan would be a weak man controlled by unscrupulous advisers who did not falter at using the threat of secession as a political lever even though it was 'threadbare nonsense'.[34]

Though speaking of the 'Fremont Revolution' sweeping the North, the *Herald* paid almost no attention editorially to the campaign being made for Fremont by his party. In fact not only did the term 'nigger worshipper' decline in the *Herald* after June but the word 'Republican' hardly ever appeared in its leaders. The *Herald* always

[29]Daniel E. Sickles to James Buchanan 3 Feb 1856, Buchanan Papers, Historical Society of Pennsylvania. See also same to same 24 May 1856. Sickles was at this time retained by Bennett to fight libel suits against the *Herald,* particularly the Fry case (see chapter 1).

[30]Albert C. Ramsey to James Buchanan 2 July 1856, Buchanan Papers.

[31]*NYH* 7, 8 June 1856.

[32]George N. Sanders to Buchanan 20 June 1856, Buchanan Papers.

[33]Compare *NYH* 26 May with same 12 June 1856.

[34]*NYH* 15, 22 July; 13, 20 Aug; 18, 30 Sept 1856.

referred to the 'Fremont Party' or the 'popular fusion' forces. Glossing over the Philadelphia platform with sublime independence, Bennett averred that slavery would be quite safe in Fremont's hands, that he would observe the Fugitive Slave Act and in all would be a good friend to the South.[35] Indeed, the *Herald* laid great stress on the fact that Northern abolitionist groups opposed Fremont. Bennett conceded that it would be well if a popular majority brought Kansas in as a free state, but he would desire to see the South compensated with another slave state elsewhere — perhaps by dividing Texas into two.[36] If in this the *Herald* was directly at odds with the Republican platform and with Fremont's own professed principles it did not worry Bennett, who explained blandly:

> We feel justified. . . in passing over in silence that portion of Col. Fremont's letter [i.e. accepting the Philadelphia platform] which refers to slavery. We regard it as unimportant, and as irrelevant. . . In our view Colonel Fremont stands before the people on a much higher ground than he would occupy as the champion of a sectarian school of economists. He appears to us to be the leader of a great sweeping and radical revolution against the wickedness and corruption and the profligacy of. . . the present federal administration.[37]

The Democratic reaction to Bennett's abrupt championship of Fremont was a mixture of bafflement and outrage.[38] In the South the Democratic press could find no terms too harsh to apply to Bennett. Charges that the *Herald* had been bought for Fremont were rife and they afforded Bennett some amusement in their widely varying estimates of the sums involved.[39] Buchanan, finding himself described in the *Herald* as an 'old fogy', a 'superannuated dotard' and a bachelor with an 'utter want of human sympathy',[40] became enraged. When the paper's gossip columns made cruel sport of his social activities he reputedly asked why none of his supporters went to New York to slit Bennett's ears.[41]

---

[35]See especially *NYH* 13 June 1856.

[36]*NYH* 2, 3, July 1856.

[37]*NYH* 10 July 1856.

[38]See for instance Washington *Daily Union* 13 June 1856, which spoke as the official party organ.

[39]*NYH* 30 June; 13 July 1856; Gideon G. Westcott to Buchanan 8 July 1856, Buchanan Papers.

[40]*NYH* 6 July; 25 Sept 1856.

[41]Lambert A. Wilmer, *Our Press Gang* (Philadelphia 1856), p. 214.

Buchanan pondered the possible cause of Bennett's defection and what, if anything, he should do about it.[42] He received varying advice on both points from his political correspondents. One thought that Bennett really wanted the mission to France and could be induced back to the Democratic camp with a little flattery.[43] New York politicians Daniel Sickles and John Cochrane made their own efforts to placate Bennett, but apparently succeeded only in antagonising him.[44] Pennsylvania congressman J. Glancy Jones thought that the *Herald*'s 'fiendish assaults' must receive direct refutation, and some Buchanan men in New York toyed with the financially daunting idea of funding a Democratic daily in the city to combat the *Herald*.[45] Only Buchanan's confidant, Philadelphia editor John Forney, consistently advised that the *Herald*'s attacks would benefit the Democratic nominee.[46]

Buchanan was soon informed that Forney himself was one cause of Bennett's pique. Bennett and Forney disliked each other intensely, each holding the other's professional, political and personal morality in low esteem. The *Herald* played up accusations that if elected Buchanan would be Forney's tool, and privately Bennett vowed that he had 'a long account to settle with Forney'.[47] But something more

---

[42]Philip G. Auchampaugh looked at the situation from Buchanan's viewpoint in 'Political Techniques 1856 — Or Why the *Herald* went for Fremont', *Western Political Quarterly*, 1 (1948), 243-51.

[43]Albert C. Ramsey to Buchanan 2 June; 2 July 1856, Buchanan Papers. The Washington *Daily Union* 12 Aug 1856, also jeered that Bennett was in vain pursuit of the French mission.

[44]John Forney to Buchanan, 25 July 1856, Buchanan Papers; Sickles to Buchanan 26 July 1856; 'W.H.' to Buchanan 22 Sept 1856, *ibid.* After this Sickles and Bennett became estranged, the editor denouncing his former lawyer in 'unlimited terms'. The next year, when Sickles supported the brother of John A. Graham (who had cowhided Bennett in 1850) for local office, the *Herald* assailed Sickles. Sickles thereupon brought suit against Bennett for libel, employing to represent him none other than John A. Graham. Bennett was furious, but the case was settled out of court and in time he and Sickles were reconciled. See *NYH* 28 Sept; 7 Oct 1857, and Graham's denunciation of Bennett in *New York County, the People ex. rel. Daniel E. Sickles vs. James Gordon Bennett* (NY 1857); also Carlson, *The Man Who Made News* (NY 1942), p. 260; Swanberg, *Sickles the Incredible,* pp. 85, 103-4.

[45]J. Glancy Jones to Buchanan, 3 Aug 1856; Christopher L. Ward to Buchanan 20 July 1856, Buchanan Papers. Meanwhile the Washington *Daily Union* continued to attack the *Herald* regularly — see 24 June; 17, 28 July; 2, 12 Aug; 17, 23, 30 Sept; 15, 17 Oct 1856.

[46]Forney to Buchanan 29 June; 7, 25 July; 18 Oct 1856, Buchanan Papers. Forney's *Daily Pennsylvanian* took every opportunity to pillory the *Herald*'s inconsistency – see 20, 25 June; 7, 11, 16, 17, 18, 19, 26, 29, 31 July; 2, 6, 9, 13, 19 Aug; 2, 9, 12, 19, 25, 29 Sept; 7, 16, 18, 21 Oct 1856.

[47]Henry Wikoff to Buchanan 8 Aug 1856, Buchanan Papers. On Forney see the sketch by Roy F. Nichols in the *Dictionary of American Biographhy*. Nichols'

than this must have provoked Bennett to take up the Repubublicans. Buchanan sought an emissary to try and soothe Bennett, and eventually found one in New York journalist Malcolm Ives.[48] On 7 September Ives reported the result of a two hour interview with Bennett:

> I stated to him, *unauthoritatively,* the substance of your remarks, concerning your relations with himself and his family. He was much affected. . . and admitted that he had deemed himself purposely led astray by you while in Europe in relation to your being a candidate for the Presidency. He made no pledges, but said that my assurances had convinced him that he had done you injustice. There was a warmth in his language, when speaking of you, which convinced me that, notwithstanding the decided position he had taken of late, he might, by prudent management, still be gained. . . He said he had never seen Mr. Fremont but once, and that he was but a 'poor shotie' to put up for the Chief Magistracy of the country.[49]

From another source too Buchanan learned that Bennett had taken deep offence because in Europe in July 1855 and again early in 1856 the editor had understood Buchanan to confide that he would not be a condidate: 'He thinks you intended to be a candidate at the very time you informed him in Europe you would not, and says you intended to deceive and humbug him when you ought to place confidence in him as a friend.'[50] Bennett also let it be known that he was in dudgeon over some petty matter of letters which he accused the candidate of having failed to forward to him, 'from indifference or contempt'. For, as the bearer of this message intimated, Bennett was 'morbidly alive to what he considered a slight'.[51]

Moreover it seemed that Bennett could not be calmed by the assurances of an intermediary, for as late as 11 October Ives had to report that:

Disruption of American Democracy (NY 1948) also contains interesting material on Forney, as does William Dusinberre, *Civil War Issues in Philadelphia, 1856-65* (Philadelphia 1965). His later career is dealt with by Elwyn B. Robinson. 'The Press: President Lincoln's Philadelphia Organ', *Pennsylvania Magazine of History and Biography,* 65 (1941), 157-70. Bennett seldom let a week pass without some editorial attack on Forney, who reciprocated in kind.

[48]Ives came to Buchanan with a letter of introduction from L.R. Shepherd dated 3 Sept 1856, in Buchanan Papers. We shall meet Ives again in chapter 9. Previously Buchanan had tried to enlist one Simeon N. Johnson, but Johnson had declined the dubious honour — see his letter to Buchanan of 6 Aug 1856, Buchanan Papers.

[49]Malcolm Ives to Buchanan 7 Sept 1856, Buchanan Papers.

[50]Albert G. Ramsey to Buchanan 27 Sept; 18 Oct 1856, *ibid.*

[51]Henry Wikoff to Buchanan 18 Oct 1856, *ibid.*

Bennett continues his reckless, mendacious career, but with constantly decreasing influence in the city. As late as a day before yesterday, he assigned to some gentlemen the same motive for opposition to you. . . viz. that you had misled him in Europe concerning which he confessed, four weeks since, that he had done you an injustice.[52]

Clearly Bennett was playing a political game with the Democratic candidate. Not that the importance of Bennett's personal vanity should be underrated for its effect on the *Herald*'s course; but it is remarkable how his caprices could be tempered to the winds of political fortune. If Bennett had really discounted Buchanan's candidacy since 1855, why was the *Herald* still playing with his name up until April 1856?[53] As Bennett's henchman, the rather disreputable international intriguer Henry Wikoff,[54] observed, the editor of the *Herald* was first and foremost a journalist and when it suited him he deliberately misled Buchanan's agents.[55] These politicians judged Bennett 'very uncertain' and 'very impulsive',[56] but as a newspaper man he held that 'a journal in the position of the *Herald* can no more stand still than the sun in its orbit. It must move onward. . . '[57]

The *Herald*'s switch to Fremont was undeniably sensational, and for Bennett that may have been the objective of the exercise. He had opted for the controversial rather than the expected course and claimed that the *Herald*'s circulation actually increased in the South as a result.[58] Moreover at the time of the *Herald*'s change of heart in June the Democrats in New York were in a more than usually divided

---

[52]Ives to Buchanan 11 Oct 1856, *ibid.*

[53]See e.g. *NYH* 2, 21 Feb 1856; Washington *Daily Union* 9 Feb 1856.

[54]Wikoff, as we shall see again in chapter 9, is an important figure in the *Herald*'s secret political history. There is an account of his unconventional and slightly incredible career in the *Dictionary of American Biography*, and a sketch of him with some information on his connection with Bennett in John Forney, *Anecdotes of Public Men* (NY 1873), vol. 1, pp. 366-71. See also Frank Maloy Anderson, *The Mystery of 'A Public Man'* (Minneapolis 1948), pp. 126-9. Wikoff sets forth portions of his own story in *The Adventures of a Roving Diplomatist* (NY 1857) and *Reminiscences of an Idler* (NY 1880). A modern biography is Duncan Crow, *Henry Wikoff, the American Chevalier* (London 1963) which deals with his theatrical and European involvements but has little to say of his role as an intermediary and intriguer in American politics, although there are many of his letters in the Buchanan Papers which could be used for that purpose. The *Herald* itself provided occasional if sometimes cryptic comments on the 'Chevalier's' exploits.

[55]Wikoff to Buchanan 21 Oct 1856, Buchanan Papers.

[56]Sickles to Buchanan 24 May 1856; A.C. Ramsey to Buchanan 18 Oct 1856, Buchanan Papers.

[57]Bennett to Buchanan 22 Oct 1856, *ibid.*

[58]*NYH* 2, 6, 18 Aug 1856.

condition, which may have induced Bennett to believe that in backing Fremont he was backing the national winner. That the *Herald's* conversion resulted from calculation rather than conviction is further indicated by the respectful rather than really enthusiastic terms in which it spoke of Fremont, and most of all by the anomaly that in the state and city elections Bennett clung to a through and through Democratic ticket. Without the slightest air of embarrassment and perhaps to relieve the discomfort of making his political bed with Greeley and Raymond (an 'unholy alliance' which provoked much derision from the Democratic press) he denounced John A. King, the Republican candidate for Governor of New York, as a corrupt abolitionist.[59]

The evidence suggests that Bennett fobbed off Buchanan's advances so long as the Fremont movement looked strong, playing up his sense of personal injury as a pretext. By mid October Bennett had begun to have disagreements with the leaders of the Fremont party in New York and was apparently surprised by Republican defeats in Pennsylvania and Indiana.[60] He therefore rapidly became much more receptive than formerly to Buchanan, whose agents urged the candidate to write a conciliatory letter to the editor and gave assurances that Bennett was eager to become a firm friend of the Democrats. One wrote:

> So nearly balanced are the parties in. . . [New York, New Jersey and Connecticut]. . . that a change of front on the part of the *Herald* might secure all three. . . the moral effect in more distant parts of the Union would be sensibly felt, and I know how anxious all our friends are to secure the co-operation of that influential journal.[61]

Another added: 'The moment your letter arrives, down goes the Fremont flag for ever.'[62] Upon these promptings Buchanan, though probably galled,[63] wrote one of his few letters during the campaign in

[59] See e.g. *NYH* 20 Sept; 3 Nov 1856. For comments see particularly the files of the Washington *Daily Union*, Philadelphia *Daily Pennsylvanian* and Richmond *Enquirer*. Nothing could better illustrate the *Herald's* opportunism at this juncture than the consent Bennett gave to one of his Democratic editional writers, troubled by his employer's course, that 'I might write an article against the black republicans and abuse them as much as I pleased so that (*sic*) I did not abuse Fremont personally he would print it' – Alexander Jones to Buchanan 28 Sept 1856, Buchanan Papers.

[60] A.C. Ramsey to Buchanan 18 Oct 1856, *ibid*. Ramsey thought that at this stage Bennett was 'at open war with the leaders of the Fremont party'.

[61] *Ibid.*

[62] Wikoff to Buchanan 18 Oct 1856; see also Sickles to Buchanan 21 Oct 1856, *ibid*.

[63] See draft letter Buchanan to Ives 10 Sept 1856, *ibid*. In it Buchanan bemoaned the *Herald's* failure to become 'a great public benefactor' by coming voluntarily to his support.

an attempt to win over or at least muzzle the *Herald* in the remaining fortnight before the election.

> I rejoice that our former friendly relations are about to be restored. I can assure you that I am truly sorry they were ever interrupted; and this not only for my own sake but that of the country. The New York *Herald* exercising the influence which signal ability and past triumphs always command, can contribute much to prostrate the Sectional party which now so seriously endangers the Union & to restore the ancient friendly relations between the North and the South. . .
>
> The truth is that when I parted from you in Paris I had neither the purpose nor the desire again to become a candidate for the Presidency. A ground swell, however, in this State [i.e. Pennsylvania] among a noble people who had sustained me for more than thirty years forced me reluctantly into the field.
>
> I confess that I had calculated with the most perfect confidence you would be as you had been my friend. It has been throughout between us a Comedy of Errors, in which I have been the sufferer. But let by-gones be by-gones; & when we again get together, I feel that we shall never seperate.[64]

Bennett, thanking Buchanan for 'your very kind letter — indeed your very very kind letter', still insisted that Buchanan had misled him and recanted nothing but expressed hope that now the 'Comedy of Errors' was over, 'All's Well that Ends Well'.[65]

Simultaneously the *Herald* began to back away from the Republicans. It suddenly declared that the campaign for Fremont was losing steam, that his managers had served him badly, that Seward was against him and that, in all, true friends of Fremont should begin to think of him as a suitable candidate for 1860 in the likely event of his present failure.[66]

Republican leaders, knowing nothing of Bennett's negotiations with Buchanan, were naturally disconcerted, while relieved Democrats spoke of the 'tremendous' effect and 'great talk' produced in New York by the *Herald*'s new course.[67] During the week before the election Fremont visited Bennett to plead with him, but without result.[68] Yet the *Herald* tacked carefully and avoided extreme

[64]Buchanan to Bennett 20 Oct 1856, *ibid.*

[65]Bennett to Buchanan 22 Oct 1856, *ibid.*

[66]*NYH* 20 Oct – 4 Nov 1856.

[67]A.C. Ramsey to Buchanan 20 Oct; Henry Wikoff to Buchanan 22 Oct 1856, Buchanan Papers. For sarcastic comment see NY *Times* 22 Oct 1856.

[68]Wikoff to Buchanan 29 Oct 1856, Buchanan Papers.

statements. Bennett's friend Wikoff assured Buchanan that the editor was merely using proper circumspection in disengaging himself from the Republicans.[69] A franker explanation might have been that Bennett was still hedging his bets in order to curry favour with the eventual winner. On election day the *Herald* adopted the same kind of Delphic straddle it would repeat in 1864. Bennett continued to praise Fremont personally and to defend him from attacks, but had nothing good to say about his party. The *Herald* displayed none of its wonted bravado and urgency. Absent were the customary repeated injunctions to vote early for the right man; nor was there any suggestion that any important or even distinguishable issue was at stake. In fact the *Herald* declared that the Union was safe whichever party won, and a dispassionate discussion of Fremont's chances for 1860 was hardly likely to arouse an avalanche of enthusiasm for him amongst doubtful voters.[70]

Fremont carried New York and ten other Northern states, but it was not enough. The failure of the Republicans and Know-Nothings to combine elected Buchanan although he received a minority of the popular vote.[71] Bennett lost no time in mending his fences with the President-elect. Privately he let it be known how gratified he had been by Buchanan's letter and that he 'was now as friendly to Buchanan as ever, and . . . will always come to the aid of Buck in any tight pinch'.[72] In the *Herald* he earnestly warned Buchanan against taking Jefferson Davis ('the Mephistopheles of the South') or any of the extreme states' rights group into his cabinet. The demands of these men would be insatiable, he warned, urging Buchanan to imitate Jackson rather than Pierce in facing up to disunion agitators.[73]

Southern Democrats were of course enraged that Bennett should presume to dictate policy to the party faithful. Henry A. Wise of

---

[69]Wikoff to Buchanan 22, 23 Oct; 1 Nov 1856, *ibid.*

[70]*NYH* 4 Nov 1856.

[71]The result was:

	Nation	New York
Buchanan	1,838,169	198,878
Fremont	1,347,264	276,007
Fillmore	874,534	124,604

Judah Ginsberg in 'Barnburners, Free Soilers and the New York Republican Party', *New York History*, 57 (1976), 475-500, emphasises that Fremont carried the state by attracting many formerly Democratic voters.

[72]A.C. Ramsey to Buchanan 8 Nov 1856; Wikoff to Buchanan 10 Nov 1856, Buchanan Papers. In his *Anecdotes of Public Men,* vol. I, p. 367, Forney says that after the election Buchanan's friends were jubilant over what they considered the 'annihilation' of Bennett.

[73]*NYH* 6, 7, 8, 9, 12, 13, 19 Nov 1856.

Virginia, long a bitter foe of the *Herald,* denounced Bennett both on the stump and through his Richmond newspaper.[74] But Bennett was unrepentantly bold in offering advice to the new administration. He sent his kinsman, Judge A.D. Russell, to Buchanan's home at Wheatland to assure Buchanan again that he too regarded their past misunderstandings as a comedy of errors and that the President-elect was sure of his support.[75] On 23 December he wrote again to Buchanan, jocularly wishing him a happy Christmas and dropping a hint:

> I suppose you see how I am sailing my ship day by day. Perhaps you may find things in the *Herald* that don't exactly square with your notions — but never mind, it will all come out right in the end — When your mind is made up on any particular point of your policy. . . then I should like to know through some suitable channel, in order to help you along.[76]

Buchanan replied promptly that he had 'no doubt we shall get along well together and better because each will pursue an independent course. I know that I intend to do right and have no desire but to leave a name behind me at the end of my term which shall be honored and respected by my countrymen.'[77]

In effect, an 'entente cordiale' had been established between the two men by which Buchanan would receive support and Bennett news.[78] Friends meanwhile arranged a truce in the war of words between Bennett and Forney.[79] In addition, at Bennett's request, Buchanan appointed Gabriel G. Fleurot, a friend and former employee of Bennett's, to the US consulship at Bordeaux.[80] Before

[74]*NYH* 4 Dec 1856. Bennett got his revenge in August 1859 by publishing correspondence which seriously damaged Wise's chances for the Presidency — see Richmond *Enquirer* 9, 12, 30 Aug 1859; Albany *Atlas & Argus* 5, 9, 10, 12, 15, 16, 17, 24 Aug 1859.

[75]Bennett to Buchanan 2 Dec 1856, Buchanan Papers. See also Buchanan to Fernando Wood 1 Dec 1856, *ibid.*

[76]Bennett to Buchanan 23 Dec 1856, *ibid.*

[77]Buchanan to Bennett 29 Dec 1856, *ibid.* Perhaps it was significant that on the same day Buchanan wrote to John Y. Mason, US minister to France, that 'I have determined that you shall not be disturbed during the next year, no matter what may be the pressure upon me. . . ' — *ibid.*

[78]See also Wikoff to Buchanan 21 Oct; 18 Nov; A.C. Ramsey to Buchanan 8 Nov; John Cochrane to Buchanan 15 Nov 1856, *ibid.*

[79]Wikoff to Buchanan 23 Oct; 18 Nov; 31 Dec 1856; 11 Jan 1857, *ibid.*

[80]Bennett to Buchanan 7 Feb 1857; 6 May 1858; 18 Apr 1859, *ibid.; NYH* 16 Jan 1858. For a brief autobiographical note see Fleurot to Bennett 15 Mar 1865, enclosed with W.O. Bartlett to A. Lincoln 22 Mar 1865, Abraham Lincoln Papers, Library of Congress, item 41390 — and see below chapter 13.

long Bennett was exchanging friendly letters with the new President as if nothing had happened.[81]

So it was that the *Herald* had no peer in its loyalty to Buchanan throughout his term. It praised his every speech and official action from the time of his inauguration onwards in such terms as 'wise', 'patriotic', 'prudent', 'able', 'cautious', 'sagacious', 'statesmanlike', 'eminently sensible' etc., and in general the paper went to great pains to build up that 'honored and respected' name which the new President so hankered after. During 1858 the *Herald* loyally supported Buchanan in his desire to have Kansas admitted speedily as a slave state in the hope that this would somehow settle the sectional controversy, and in his proscription of Senator Douglas and those Democrats who refused to accept Presidential dictation on this matter. This pro-Southern position was unpopular throughout the North outside New York City, but by this time Bennett's temporary dabbling with Republicanism in 1856 was long forgotten and the *Herald* had unapologetically resumed its accustomed occupation of denouncing 'negro worship' and all its works daily. Yet Bennett had no patience with secessionists; he had hard words for Southern extremists in Congress who showed impatience with the President, and throughout the deepening sectional crisis he laboured to prove that Buchanan alone was the 'sound' and 'conservative' statesman able to unite the diverging northern and southern wings of the Democratic party and the nation itself. His favourite recipe for Democratic renaissance, expounded often during 1859, was for the party to rally around Buchanan on the platform of acquiring Cuba. But to Bennett's disgust Congress would not vote funds for the purpose.[82]

At the beginning of his term the *Herald* had rejoiced at Buchanan's announcement that he would not be seeking renomination in 1860 because, it said, he was thus freed from the necessity of paying servile court to party spoilsmen in the manner of Pierce.[83] It is interesting though that in September 1859 Bennett was a visitor at the White House on some undisclosed business, and that in January 1860 the *Herald* came out strongly in favour of Buchanan's renomination by the Democratic party.[84] Although it cannot be known whether this move was Bennett's own — made either from conviction or from the desire to sell newspapers — or whether it was inspired from the White

[81]e.g. Bennett to Buchanan 23, 26 Feb 1857, Buchanan Papers.

[82]See particularly *NYH* Jan-Mar 1859.

[83]*NYH* 20 Dec 1856.

[84]*NYH* 20 Sept; 11 Nov 1859; 24, 25, 30, 31 Jan 1860.

House, plausible direct and indirect evidence has been produced to suggest that Buchanan privately hoped for renomination despite his public denials of any such ambition.[85] Anyway, the floating of this trial balloon in the *Herald* drew such reaction as to underline the fact that Buchanan was totally unacceptable to those Northern Democrats led by Douglas who had opposed the administration's attempt to force the pro-slavery Lecompton constitution on Kansas, and equally to extreme Southerners who regarded him as a man of straw.[86] Early in February 1860 the *Herald* announced that Buchanan positively refused to stand for renomination — public men in those days customarily accepted the inevitable with a great show of self-sacrifice.[87]

A later chapter will treat the *Herald*'s role during the final stages of the sectional crisis in some detail. Suffice it for the moment to say that Buchanan had secured in the support of the *Herald* an advantage which Pierce had signally lacked, namely the favour of a major national daily newspaper. For this support he paid something more than fair words to the editor: during the period of his administration (to the annoyance of the rest of the New York press)[88] the *Herald* received advance copies of state papers from the White House and spoke with confidence of presidential policy and intentions to the extent that it was widely regarded as the 'administration organ' at this time.[89] Bennett and his wife received invitations to Washington social functions and in 1860 *Vanity Fair* printed a cartoon strongly suggesting that Bennett was receiving payments from the White House secret service funds.[90] Perhaps Buchanan considered that he had done enough to keep the editor loyal and that he owed him no more, although even the hostile *Tribune* observed that 'President Buchanan owes more to Mr. Bennett than all his partisan journalists

[85]R.R. Stenberg, 'An Unnoted Factor in the Buchanan-Douglas Feud', *Illinois State Historical Society Journal*, 25 (1933), 271-84.

[86]The *Richmond Enquirer* had long suspected that the *Herald* was putting out feelers on Buchanan's renomination and had rebuffed the idea — see *ibid.*, 10 Aug 1858; 5 Aug 1859.

[87]*NYH* 3 Feb 1860.

[88]A.C. Ramsey to Buchanan 10 Dec 1858, with enclosure James W. Simonton to Ramsey 9 Dec 1858, Buchanan Papers.

[89]Seitz, p. 163, reprints a covering letter from Buchanan to Bennett dated 7 Dec 1857, enclosing an advance copy of his first annual message. See also Buchanan to James J. Roosevelt 22 June 1860, Buchanan Papers. That the *Herald* was widely regarded as Buchanan's semi-official organ see e.g. NY *Courier and Enquirer* 22 Aug 1860; *Richmond Enquirer* 5 Aug 1859; Albany *Atlas & Argus* 20 July 1859.

[90]*Vanity Fair* 3 Nov 1860.

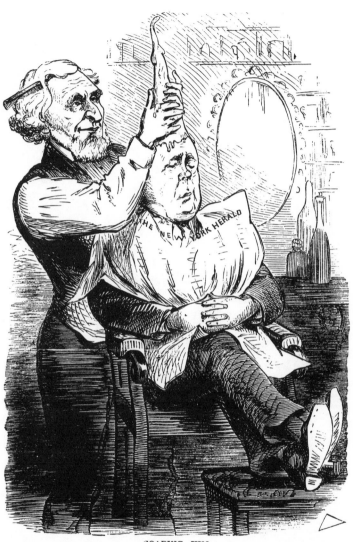

SOAPING HIM.

"The man for Charleston is Mr. Buchanan. His administration has been so firmly and wisely conducted as to win the applause of the whole country. The conservative Union men of the great Central States will demand a man whose election will allay the foolish slavery agitation, restore confidence between the North and the South, insure the permanence of his institutions, and promote the material prosperity of the repblic. Mr. Buchanan is the man. He will call out the full strength of his own party and the independent reserve vote. Mr Buchanan, then, should receive the Charleston nomination by all means."—*N,Y. Herald*, Feb., 1860.

Bennett grooms Buchanan for a second term.
(From *Vanity Fair*, 3 March 1860).

Reproduced by permission of the British Library

and fulsome flatterers put together. For all this, Mr. Buchanan, with his well known coldness of heart, makes no return.'[91]

Apparently the same thought nagged Bennett sometimes, for word occasionally reached the President that Bennett wanted reassurance that his devotion was appreciated and a little more advance news into the bargain.[92] But it was left to Mrs. Bennett to put her husband's case forthrightly.

Although she confessed that politics were a foreign language to her and indeed that 'Mr. B. thinks me such a blab that he is afraid to talk politics before me',[93] Henrietta Bennett had apparently favoured Buchanan in 1856. In fact Bennett had joked with the President about his 'better half' as he called her, saying that 'I ought to be glad that you were elected. . . for my wife now promises to return to New York [from Europe] next spring in order that she may have the pleasure of seeing you . . . and thus spare[s] me the trouble and expense of going so often to Europe to meet and enjoy my family. . . '[94] When the Bennetts' younger son Cosmo died in 1859 Buchanan wrote a letter of condolence to the afflicted mother, to which she made a touching reply.[95] Later, in May 1860, Mrs. Bennett in her grief stricken state decided to return to Europe and asked Buchanan for a foreign mission for her deserving husband on the simple ground that Bennett would thus have a strong business reason for accompanying her.[96]

Buchanan replied apologetically, intimating that although he had thought of posting Bennett to Turin he dared not remove the present incumbent at the Sardinian court, who was a protegé of Secretary of War John B. Floyd.[97]

In the very last weeks of the administration, after Floyd had left the cabinet, it seems that Buchanan took a fresh initiative to get Bennett appointed to Turin. Certainly in February 1861 the President received warnings (or threats) from Henry Wikoff and Daniel Sickles

[91]NY *Daily Tribune* 25 Aug 1859.

[92]A.C. Ramsey to Buchanan 13 Feb; 6 Apr 1857; 11 Feb 1858; Wikoff to Buchanan 22 Apr; 22 July 1857; John Cochrane to Buchanan 7 May 1859, Buchanan Papers.

[93]Mrs J.G. Bennett to Buchanan 20 Nov 1859, *ibid.*

[94]Bennett to Buchanan 7 Feb 1857, *ibid.*

[95]Buchanan's letter, 1 Apr 1859, is reprinted in Seitz, p. 164: Mrs Bennett's reply 20 Nov 1859, Buchanan Papers.

[96]Mrs J. G. Bennett to Buchanan 8 May 1860, *ibid.*

[97]Buchanan to Mrs Bennett 12 May 1860, *ibid.* The US minister to Turin at this time was the sometime fiery secessionist editor of the *Richmond Examiner,* John Moncure Daniel.

that failure to give Bennett a foreign mission would cause the *Herald* to turn on him savagely.[98] But in cabinet discussions John A. Dix, the former New York 'Barnburner' who had become Secretary of the Treasury, vigorously opposed the appointment, and Postmaster General Joseph Holt was also 'bitter and intensely hostile'.[99] Nothing came of the matter, and when Buchanan left office in March on the eve of the Civil War all Bennett got from him was a cheery letter thanking him for his 'able and powerful support'. The ex-President asked the editor to redirect his daily copy of the *Herald* to his new address, declaring that he would be 'quite lost without it'.[100]

Bennett was evidently neither placated nor amused by his failure to be offered a foreign appointment. Moreover on the outbreak of war in April 1861 he had pressing reasons for showing off the patriotism of the *Herald*[101] and the paper rapidly became the chief journalistic persecutor of the ex-President. The *Herald* so vilified Buchanan for having dallied with the encouraged treason that by mid-May he was fearful that these attacks would endanger not only his character but his life, and he complained to a friend in anger that

> The *Herald*. . . from a spirit of malignity. . . takes every occasion to blame me for my supineness. It will very soon arrive at the point of denouncing me for not crushing the rebellion at once, & thus try to make me the author of the war. Whenever it reaches that point, it is my purpose to indict Bennett for libel. . . '[102]

It very soon did reach that point, but the irate Sage of Wheatland was dissuaded from publishing an immediate defence by ex-members of his cabinet. Edwin M. Stanton wrote that it would be better to weather Bennett's attacks, and offered the hope that the editor's day as a powerful influence was passing.[103] So Buchanan endured in silence and Bennett, who had so recently been praising him to the skies and

[98]Henry Wikoff to Buchanan 19 Jan; 28 Feb 1861; Sickles to Buchanan Feb 1861. See also Buchanan's angry annotation on the envelope of Wikoff's 28 Feb letter.

[99]See Edwin M. Stanton to Buchanan 26 July 1861, and Buchanan to 'Mr King' 2 May 1867, in J.B. Moore ed., *The Works of James Buchanan* (NY 1960), vol. XI, pp. 213, 444-5. Dix's opposition must place the discussion in early 1861, for he was a late entrant to the cabinet.

[100]Buchanan to Bennett, Wheatland, 11 Mar 1861 in Moore, vol. X, pp. 165-6.

[101]See below chapter 7.

[102]Buchanan to James Henry 17 May 1861, in Moore, vol. XI, pp. 192-3. Buchanan saw Bennett's onslaught as 'one of those great national prosecutions, such as have occurred in this and other countries, necessary to vindicate the character of the Government'. See further Pollard, *Presidents and the Press,* pp. 301-2. For a just comment on the *Herald*'s abuse of Buchanan see NY *Daily Tribune* 9 June 1862.

[103]Stanton to Buchanan 16 July 1861 in Moore, vol. XI, p. 210.

comparing him with Andrew Jackson, did a demolition job on his reputation from which it never really recovered in the popular mind. Perhaps Buchanan recalled his own observation to Mrs. Bennett in 1857 that her husband 'makes his mark when he strikes and his blows fall so fast and heavy it is difficult to sustain them'.[104]

Bennett's influence had proved inadequate to obtain his heart's desire — a foreign mission. But in retaliation he was able to damage severely the reputations of Presidents Pierce and Buchanan — the former while the was in office, the latter after he quitted it. Buchanan's letters to Bennett reveal him as most vulnerable in his obsessive desire to stand right with posterity and leave an 'honored and respected' name. Bennett took satisfaction in stabbing him in precisely that sensitive spot, his cherished claims to statesmanship.

A comedy of errors, perhaps?

[104]Buchanan to Mrs J.G. Bennett 14 Apr 1857, quoted in Seitz, p. 162.

4

LOOMINGS OF THE SECTIONAL CRISIS:
A FOCUS ON NEW YORK DURING AND AFTER
THE ELECTIONS OF 1859

> You are a prophet who can materially aid in accomplishing your
> own prediction – James Buchanan to Bennett, 29 December
> 1856
>
> After you will come the Deluge . . . the future has a fearful and
> frightful struggle in its bosom, the end of which I cannot discern
> at all – Bennett to Buchanan, 7 February 1857

We have now seen evidence that the self-styled 'independent' course
of the *Herald* could be shaped by Bennett's personal aspirations as
well as by his sense of the market, even though few of his readers were
aware of this. Yet it would certainly be a mistake to assume that
Bennett's desire for recognition 'explains' all there is to know about
the *Herald*'s coverage of the sectional crisis which rose to fever pitch
during Buchanan's term. Because most Americans saw the events of
their political world almost exclusively through the medium of the
press we must now look at that coverage in some detail, analysing the
particular view of the North-South rift which the *Herald* presented to
its readers, and what it claimed were the issues. In order to
understand how continuous election excitements in New York added
to the dramatic momentum which produced disunion and civil war it is
illuminating to turn back the *Herald* files to the autumn of 1859.
Through them it is possible to appreciate the surprising and even
decisive extent to which local questions, personalities, and events
affected the national struggle.

The Democratic Plight and John Brown

Startling atmospheric freaks appeared to New Yorkers in the first
week of September 1859. The Aurora Borealis made an appearance
and the city and harbour were wracked by sudden squalls and
unseasonable hail and snow storms. The *Herald* noted that these
occurrences revived ancient superstitions about impending disaster.[1]

[1]*NYH* 5 Sept 1859.

Politics seemed to be taking their usual course and the state party conventions were about to convene, but Bennett was sounding ominous warnings that the state election in November would be no ordinary contest. The Republican party, said he, represented sectionalism in its most dangerous and repugnant form. If it triumphed in New York it would be a long stride nearer winning the presidency in 1860, and it seemed certain that in that case William H. Seward would be the first Republican President. To endorse Seward, said Bennett, was to endorse his Rochester doctrine of 'irrepressible conflict' which could logically mean nothing less than 'bloody and treasonable' civil war on the South and the destruction of the federal Union.[2]

Was this just the usual extravagantly partisan abuse which attended local elections? Was Bennett trying to make up in vivid rhetoric what the Democratic party lacked in unity and strength? Certainly the state party was in poor shape. Only if it were united could it hope to defeat the Republicans and reverse the national trend of Democratic defeats, but the prospect of achieving unity looked remote in the summer and became progressively worse. Ironically, although the *Herald* was loud in its calls for party harmony, it was the leading journalistic opponent of the established party leadership at Albany – the 'Regency'. Bennett did not believe that the party could prosper under Dean Richmond, Peter Cagger and William 'Confidence' Cassidy, the triumvirate which now ruled the political machine originally created by the supporters of Van Buren.[3] Throughout the August dog days the *Herald* had campaigned against their management of the funds of the New York Central Railroad and the 'Regency' returned volleys through its organ, the Albany *Atlas and Argus*.[4] Behind the mud-slinging lay differences of opinion which looked beyond the state election to the Democratic National Convention, scheduled to meet in Charleston in April 1860.

The quarrel was an extension of the old Hard-Soft feud within the state and of the Buchanan-Douglas cold war nationally, and was given spice by the political ambitions of Fernando Wood. The Regency,

[2]e.g. *NYH* 30 July; 2, 24, 26 Aug; 7, 10, 16 Sept; 5, 6, 11 Oct 1859.

[3]On the Regency in its early days, see Robert V. Remini, 'The Albany Regency', *New York History*, 39 (1958), 341-55. There are sketches of Dean Richmond and William Cassidy in the *Dictionary of American Biography*. The memory of his rejection in 1834 evidently cut very deep with Bennett, for if anything exceeded his animus against anti-slavery it was his hatred of the 'traitors' of the Albany Regency who 'lent anti-slavery fanaticism, in 1848, the only strength it ever possessed' — *NYH* 1 Oct 1861.

[4]*NYH* 2, 4, 10, 17, 18, 25, 30 Aug 1859; Albany *Atlas & Argus* 5, 9, 10, 12, 15, 16, 17, 24, 26 Aug; 6 Sept 1859.

leading the 'Softs', hoped to appoint the state's delegation to Charleston directly at the state convention at Syracuse in mid-September. Bennett made it clear where he stood by railing against this policy as 'selfish and besotted'[5] – an undemocratic attempt to dictate the party programme. If the Regency was intent on treating the 'Hardshells' so cavalierly Bennett foresaw a schism at Syracuse which would result in two delegations from New York to Charleston, the consequent neutralisation of the state's proper influence in choosing a presidential candidate, and the loss of the state to the Republicans. He therefore supported the claims of the 'Hards' and of Fernando Wood their acknowledged leader in the city. The 'Hards', having the bulk of their strength in the metropolis, were the weaker faction in the state as a whole. They therefore wished the party to choose its delegates to Charleston by holding direct elections based on congressional districts. This would give them a fair proportional representation at Charleston, and Bennett pressed this more democratic procedure strongly.[6]

Being in control of the state machinery, however, the Regency refused all concessions and nominated the state's delegation to Charleston as a unit at Syracuse on 14 September.[7] The 'Softs' could not be made any softer by Bennett's accusations that they were conceited oligarchs, treating the rank and file of the party like slaves in order to monopolise the state and federal spoils. The desire for plunder, charged the *Herald*, was their only motivation, and they wished to keep themselves a small and exclusive clique for this purpose. It was almost superfluous for it to add that this scheme of 'divide and rule' would be self-defeating since it would simply hand victory to the Republicans in 1859 and 1860.[8]

It could not be pretended that the question of patronage did not figure heavily on both sides, just as it did between the opposing Democratic factions within the city. But the division between 'Hards' and 'Softs' was rather more than a childish squabble over jobs or whether Horatio Seymour ('Soft') or Daniel S. Dickinson ('Hard') should receive the state's vote for the presidency at Charleston. The factious quarrels of the Empire State might vitally affect the fate of the Union. For Seymour or Dickinson, as a favourite son, would

[5]*NYH* 14 Sept 1859.

[6]*NYH* 31 May; 1, 16, 27 June; 1 July; 2, 4, Aug; 5, 7, 9, 13, 14 Sept 1859. The Regency's view of the delegate question is argued in the *Atlas & Argus* 3 Aug onwards, especially 25, 26 Aug; 2 Sept 1859.

[7]*NYH* 15 Sept 1859; *Atlas & Argus* 15-17 Sept 1859.

[8]*NYH* 16, 17 Sept 1859.

probably have to be dropped after a courtesy vote by whichever delegation was admitted to Charleston. The 'Softs' were not unfavourable to Douglas while the 'Hards' were identified with the policy of the Buchanan administration and would support the nomination of a Southern candidate as the Democratic choice for the Presidency. The winner of the local dog fight in New York might therefore be in a position to dictate the national party ticket.

The difference between the factions on the slavery question was important within New York, because by upholding Douglas's popular sovereignty doctrine and denying the right of congress to make laws for or against slavery in the territories the 'Softs' were bidding for the freesoil vote in the rural areas of the state.[9] It was only natural that they should try to win back the voting strength upstate on which Van Buren had led the Free Soil Party in 1848 and which had gone to Fremont in 1856. Only thus could they hope to prevent the drift of anti-slavery Democrats into the Republican camp. Taking the hard pro-slavery line against Sewardism which Bennett advocated[10] would doubtless have had the opposite effect. The Regency apparently did not think that 'firm principles' as the *Herald* used the term would do anything to stop party erosion. On the other hand Bennett claimed that their political methods would keep thousands away from the polls.[11]

The Syracuse Convention did the Democrats enormous harm in the state not only because of the substance of the quarrels which were aired there but because of the brutal ruffianism which was on display.[12] It really seemed that the violence of Democratic politics as practised in New York was making a mockery of popular government, and it certainly provided material for the foreign critics of democracy. The *Herald* argued that the thuggery had been the work of the Albany Regency, who countered with the accusation that Wood had caused all the trouble in an effort to get his own way or have vengeance. With the weight of truth on their side they charged him with having hired famous prize fighters and gangs from the slums of the city to come and stir things up at Syracuse.[13]

[9]*NYH* 17 Sept 1859 for Bennett's critique of the Regency platform.

[10]e.g. *NYH* 21 Sept 1859.

[11]*NYH* 15 Sept; 17 Oct 1859.

[12]*NYH* 16, 17 Sept 1859. For the Syracuse Convention see R.F. Nichols, *Disruption of American Democracy* (NY 1948), pp. 259-61; S. Pleasants, *Fernando Wood* (NY 1948), pp. 93-8 and Sidney D. Brummer, *Political History of New York State during the Civil War* (NY 1911), pp. 27-30.

[13]*NYH* 17, 20 Sept 1859. Daniel S. Dickinson, upstate leader of the New York 'Hards' (popularly known as 'Scripture Dick' — see *Dictionary of American*

The *Herald* declared that the Regency must never again be allowed to run its vile system of politics out of the purses of decent men.[14] Whether agreeing or not as to exactly where the blame lay, the Democratic merchants and businessmen of New York decided that they had had quite enough of contributing party funds to be used in such a disgraceful way.

In a short while the reaction against rowdyism had become an issue in itself in the political campaign. The men of 'honor, intellect and wealth', as Bennett called them, started a movement to withold funds from the party organisation until it mended its ways. Nearly every New York City Democrat of prominence signed a pledge to this effect and the movement snowballed. Soon the 'Democratic Reform Association' had set up its executive committee in the Fifth Avenue Hotel and Bennett was following its progress with excited interest.[15] 'In every democratic community', he reflected, 'the neglect of duty by the respectable majority . . . and the transfer of power to the hands of the base and vile, is the signal for decay', and he looked to working people to join with capitalists against 'the tyranny of the shoulder hitters, gamblers, gongers, keepers and owners of dens of prostitution, pothouse loafers, criminals from Blackwell's Island and from Sing-Sing – the very offscouring of the community' who considered that they had a 'divine right to power'.[16]

The difficulty was that despite the *Herald*'s intonations against Sewardism and rowdyism in the same breath,[17] it was very hard to link the two convincingly and to persuade the electorate that after the exhibition at Syracuse the Democrats had suddenly seen the light. By 17 October it was clear that the Democratic campaign was in the toils and that the Republicans were going to win the state in November just as they were sweeping the other Northern states. How could the fight against them pick up momentum? Some incident, some issue, was urgently needed to breathe new fire into the Democratic effort.

Almost providentially, an enterprising *Herald* man was at that very hour tapping onto the wires from the South the biggest domestic

Biography) publicly dissociated himself from Wood's rough-house tactics and started mending his fences with the Regency. For his Syracuse speech see John R. Dickinson, *Speeches, Correspondence etc. of. . . Daniel S. Dickinson of New York* (2 vols, NY 1867), vol. 1, pp. 623-8; see also his campaign speech of 20 Oct, *ibid.,* pp. 654-66.

[14]*NYH* 1 Oct 1859. Regency's reply in *Atlas & Argus* 3 Oct.

[15]*NYH* 28 Sept 1859 for a list of the Democrats involved. See also 30 Sept; 1, 2, 3, 5, 16, 17, 18 Oct.

[16]*NYH* 19, 24 Oct 1859.

[17]e.g. *NYH* 3 Oct 1859.

news story of 1859. The first reports appearing on 18 October indicated a Negro insurrection in Virginia led by whites. Then in the next few days the whole sensation was unfolded as the most dramatic piece of anti-Republican propaganda that any Democrat could have devised. John Brown, sometime resident of New York state and abolitionist marauder of Kansas fame, had descended upon the Virginian village of Harper's Ferry with the aim of seizing the government arsenal there. With the weapons obtained he intended to arm the slaves in the surrounding counties and to organise a general slave revolt or guerrilla war from the Appalachian mountains. The attack which he and his handful of supporters made was poorly planned and proved a fiasco. It was ended within thirty-six hours by the charge of a squad of US marines hurried to the scene by the order of the Washington government. Seventeen people died in the insurrection and the wounded Brown was taken prisoner and held for trial by the Virginia state authorities.[18]

The *Herald* led the anti-Republican press of the North in condemning without qualification both Brown's aims and his method. The raid was given the fullest coverage in its columns and its headlines proclaimed unmistakably that Brown was but the instrument of Seward's irrepressible conflict doctrine. The Senator's Rochester speech of the previous year was printed as the practical manifesto of the insurrectionists and the casual or gullible reader of the *Herald* would have believed that there was substantial evidence implicating Seward in Brown's plan, for Bennett openly asserted that Seward had criminal foreknowledge of the conspiracy. It was an unmissable opportunity for ruining Seward's electoral prospects and his career. To Bennett, who wrote on the assumption that every abolitionist was guilty of treason until proved innocent, Seward was now indisputably unveiled as the 'Catiline of America', a 'traitorous demagogue . . . ready at any time to teach evil if it will help his own political advancement', and he called on New Yorkers to show proper abhorrence of his doctrines at the polls: 'Mr. Seward's friends defend him, by asserting that he wants to carry out these destructive tendencies [i.e. an anti-slavery programme] only through constitutional means; but they might as well argue that a murderer does not wish to kill a man, but only to cut his jugular vein.'[19]

A number of prominent abolitionists had been involved with Brown to a greater or lesser degree, notably wealthy New Yorker

[18]The raid is described in Stephen B. Oates's biography of Brown, *To Purge this Land with Blood* (NY 1970), pp. 229-306.

[19]*NYH* 18-22 Oct 1859.

Gerrit Smith and the free Negro leader Frederick Douglass. The *Herald* hunted up and published whatever correspondence it could find to incriminate these men and tried to stir up a witch hunt against them. It suggested that Governor Wise of Virginia should demand their extradition from New York, or else that the federal authorities should take over the trial of Brown and his band. Bennett was full of praise for Buchanan's promptness in sending federal troops to Harper's Ferry, and he wanted to see the affair turned into a sort of grand inquisition against the anti-slavery movement and that 'league of Treason', the Republican party. He suggested that nearly every prominent political anti-slavery man should be put on trial for complicity with Brown, including besides Seward, Smith and Fred Douglass such leading names as Chase, Sumner, Giddings, Wilson, Hale and Beecher, not forgetting Greeley of course. Nor did the *Herald* refrain from demanding that all these should be hanged.[20]

Republican leaders were certainly alarmed and shaken by the first news of Brown's escapade and hastened to disclaim all connection with acts of violence against the slave states.[21] Their sensitivity on the subject would be reflected in the Chicago Platform of 1860, which denounced 'the lawless invasion by armed force of the soil of any State or Territory, no matter under what pretext, as among the gravest of crimes'.[22] Bennett hit back at their 'sophistries', contending that the abolitionist hierarchy differed from Brown only in lacking the courage of their convictions.

Nor was Bennett receptive to the plea of some of Brown's friends that their champion was 'mad' and should be put in a lunatic asylum rather than hanged. A *Herald* man travelled to Charlestown, Virginia where Brown was in jail and, in company with a party of congressmen, questioned him about his actions and motives in detail. The interview appeared verbatim in the *Herald* of 21 October. The country was thus able to judge the man by his own words even before he turned his trial into an occasion for self-justification. It goes without saying that Bennett sought to impress upon the public from this time until the firing on Fort Sumter the view that Republicanism was synonymous with

[20]*NYH* 20-22, 24, 27-31 Oct; 1-3 Nov, 1859. Besides printing an incriminating letter from Smith to Brown , the *Herald* scooped other papers by publishing the story of Hugh Forbes, one of the Conspirators. In reply to Bennett's accusations Greeley charged that Bennett himself had paid a mysterious visit to Harper's Ferry in August or September — NY *Daily Tribune* 12 Nov 1859. If this was true then like Greeley one can only ponder the motive.

[21]For reaction to the raid see Oates, pp. 310-18.

[22]See the fourth resolution of the Chicago Platform, conveniently reprinted in H.S. Commager, *Documents of American History* (NY 1968), vol. 1, pp. 363-5. This wording condemned equally the pro-slavery 'border ruffians' in Kansas.

abolitionism and that Brown, 'a notorious Kansas shrieker – one whose hands had more than once been dipped in human blood',[23] was the sane instrument of a quite deliberate policy of murder and treason. In order to discredit the opposition party he always portrayed it as the instrument of its most extreme and unpopular wing.

During the excitement over Harper's Ferry a number of forthright citizens of Gotham took pen in hand to write to the *Herald*. These exasperated worthies agreed in wishing for Brown to be hanged quickly, for they avowed themselves utterly 'tired to death with niggers and politicians'. Replying editorially, Bennett sympathised with them but warned that Brown's destiny was now the plaything of ruthless politicians, and that the question would not lie down until after the election.[24] He spoke as one who should know, for the *Herald* was at full stretch to create a popular reaction that would send the Republican party into a decline from which it would never recover. Might not the anti-slavery party prove as transient as the anti-foreigner party? For the American party in the state was now clearly decomposing, and as the *Herald* put it was 'auctioning itself off' between the Democrats and the Republicans.[25]

News arrived of the almost hysterical reaction to Brown's raid in the South and of military preparations in Virginia which even Bennett thought 'extravagant'.[26] So intense was the emotional atmosphere that on 5 November, three days before the election, the *Herald* spoke of civil war as having effectively begun, and looked forward to secession and a general struggle commencing before the end of the next session of Congress. On the 8th, election day, it had no special candidates to recommend for the state offices; indeed it frankly admitted that the 'dirty democracy' needed a wholesome scrub and that hardly any of its nominees were honest or worthy of public confidence. Bennett foresaw that whether Republicans or Democrats got in the revenue of the state canals would be plundered and the public debt would soar. But, he told voters, 'If the black republican revolutionary ticket should be elected in New York and New Jersey, the news will fall on the ear of the South like the knell of a departed

[23]*NYH* 20 Oct; 10, 22 Dec 1859.

[24]*NYH* 3, 6 Nov 1859.

[25]On the American Party in the State at this time see *NYH* 27 Aug; 23 Sept; 28 Oct 1859 and Louis D. Scisco, *Political Nativism in New York* (NY 1901), pp. 235-8. The extent of their abdication is shown by the fact that the Know-Nothings endorsed a mixed ticket, part Republican and part Democrat. Bennett approved this ticket as the best possible in the circumstances: an electoral victory which would be a rebuff for both major parties could not but fascinate him.

[26]*NYH* 7 Nov 1859.

Union, and the excitement will reach a crisis and assume a political shape which will appal and astound the people of the North'. Therefore, 'it is the duty of the conservative classes to come forward, one and all, and rally around the Union and the Constitution, that they may no longer lay themselves open to the imputation of the Richmond journal, that "they are cowed and trampled under foot by abolitionism". . . . A small effort will extinguish a fire in the beginning. It is hard to quench when it gains the ascendant.'[27]

All this was of no avail, and if Republican leaders had been worried that a popular revulsion against them might reach serious proportions their fears were put at rest by the results of the New York poll. They retained their hold on the state legislature, having a two thirds majority of both houses and three out of five of the important state offices below Republican Governor Morgan. New York had followed Iowa, Indiana, Minnesota, Ohio and Pennsylvania which had voted solidly Republican in October. Although Bennett insisted archly that it was a defeat for the Democratic party but not for the Buchanan administration, even he had to admit that the chances of Seward winning the next presidency were now very good, because if the Democrats lost New York again in 1860 they would lose the whole election.

But he had some interesting arithmetic for his readers to reflect on. The turn out on election day had been very poor – of 600,000 qualified voters in New York State nearly one third did not bother to vote. Throughout the Northern States in the recent elections he reckoned that at least 800,000 voters had stayed away from the polls either from disgust with politicians or from sheer apathy. Bennett assumed that apathy was next to conservatism and that if these people could be induced to take their heads out of the sand the Republicans might yet be defeated and the nation saved from civil war.[28] This appeal to the 'reserved vote' was to be the key to the *Herald*'s political editorials down to November 1860, although Bennett doubtless suspected that if the violent act at Harper's Ferry had proved insufficient to redeem Democratic fortunes then little short of a miracle would be required.

Fernando Wood again

There was no respite from electioneering at this juncture. The municipal elections, due to be held on 6 December, became the chief

[27]*NYH* 8 Nov 1859.
[28]*NYH* 10, 20 Nov 1859.

point of interest as soon as the result of the state election had been analysed and digested. To an unusual degree, national issues figured prominently in city politics.

While urging taxpayers to take an interest in the choice of evils among common councillors, Bennett freely spoke of the election as a 'farce' in its municipal aspect, since all the candidates for the 168 offices and $12 million worth of patronage involved were to a greater or lesser extent corrupt. He feared that whichever set of rum-shop nominated politicians got in, the city would be mulcted for higher taxes: 'There is no use trying to stem the tide of corruption, fraud and misgovernment; we have only to submit to be robbed and plundered, unresistingly.' Similarly he complained that whoever was elected mayor would be fettered by controls imposed from Albany.[29]

Why then did it matter who became mayor? The essence of Bennett's answer was that the recent state victories for the Republicans were a virtual declaration of war by the North against the South. Hence the importance of demonstrating to that aggrieved and alarmed section that the Empire City was still the conservative citadel of the Union, a firm link holding the sections together. He reasoned that if New York were to take an anti-slavery mayor her trade with the South would be ruined, and therefore he paid special court to the merchants of the city, warning them to beware of any 'infatuation' with the anti-slavery issue which might reduce New York to the status of a provincial town.[30]

To the *Herald* the situation looked especially alarming because Tammany Hall had decided to match like with like. The Republican candidate, merchant George Opdyke, was running very strongly, and to combat him Tammany ran William F. Havemeyer, a freesoiler who might appeal both to reform minded moderates and anti-slavery men. This was a promising ticket, as may be judged by the fact that the *Times,* the *Evening Post*[31] and the *Journal of Commerce* lent it their support as the one most likely to succeed in the traditionally Democratic city. The *Herald* had for months been out of sorts with the Tammany 'coal hole', as Bennett now delighted to call it, because Tammany was in effective alliance with the Regency organisation

[29]*NYH* 5, 8, 25, Aug; 1, 16, 19, 20, 21, 22, 28, 29 Nov; 6 Dec 1859.

[30]*NYH* 28 Nov; 2, 5 Dec 1859.

[31]Incidentally, Bennett always referred patronisingly to William Cullen Bryant, editor of the *Evening Post* as 'the Poet of the Post'. The paper has been the subject of Allen Nevins, *The Evening Post* (NY 1922), a classic in the history of journalism and one which contains a memorable treatment of Bennett, pp. 156 ff. A recent biography is Charles H. Browne, *William Cullen Bryant* (NY 1971).

upstate and therefore favourable to Douglas and freesoil nationally. To Bennett the election of either Opdyke or Havemeyer[32] would have been anathema, as he made clear by attacking Havemeyer as a 'puritan fanatic' who had supported the Wilmot Proviso, and by throwing in a few corruption charges for good measure. Just as the *Herald* called on the Republican masses to 'disenthrall' themselves from the fanaticism of their leaders, so on the other hand it called on the foreign rank and file of the city Democracy, the Irish, to desert the 'abolitionized' Tammany Hall and vote against all 'nigger worshippers'.[33]

Who then was to be Bennett's candidate for mayor and the standard bearer of the national (i.e. pro-Administration and pro-Southern) Democrats? As a matter of fact Bennett himself had been suggested as a suitable Democratic candidate back in August. The idea had actually come from the *Tribune*, blandly offering impartial advice to its opponents. (The lapse may be explained by the fact that Greeley himself was absent in the Far West at this time, giving Bennett an opportunity to enjoy himself by portraying the meeting between Greeley and Mormon leader Brigham Young as a ludicrous encounter of fanatics.)[34] The *Tribune* article suggested that Bennett, although 'sometimes wilful and obstinate, is never lacking in brains ... the *Herald* has done for the Democratic party what none of its busy intriguing spoils hunters or shallow theorists and plotters could do for it. It has indicated policy, furnished ideas, carried elections and defended Administrations. . . .' Furthermore if a man had enough business capacity to run the *Herald* then he was easily fit to be mayor of the city.[35]

Commendation from such a quarter must have been warming, but in response came a sedate announcement in the *Herald* that the party nominating Bennett 'will have to elect him at its own expense, as we know that Mr. Bennett would not bleed to the extent of five dollars for an election to any office in the gift of the people. On these conditions

---

[32]Sketches of both in *Dictionary of American Biography*. On Havemeyer in the election of 1859 see also Howard Furer, 'The Public Career of William Frederick Havemeyer' (Unpublished thesis, New York University 1963), ch 3. I dissent however from the description of the *Herald's* course given *ibid.*, pp. 207-8.

[33]*NYH* 28 Nov – 5 Dec 1859.

[34]*NYH* 24 Aug 1859.

[35]NY *Daily Tribune* 24, 25 Aug 1859. The *Tribune* added, 'though should Mr. Bennett be nominated for Mayor, it would be our duty to oppose his election, and support his Republican opponent, we should do so with the consciousness that in Mr. Bennett was put forward a competent and truly congenial representative of the Democratic party of New York, its principles and its aims'. For a sarcastic reaction see NY *Times* 26 Aug.

we have no doubt he would accept the position; and we are convinced that he would conduct the municipal affairs of this city in a manner very unlike that to which our citizens have been accustomed for some years past.'[36] Although the *Tribune* reported that its suggestion had been favourably received by some Democrats, Bennett protested that he was quite happy in his present occupation of exposing silly newspapers and politicians. About the time of the Syracuse bear garden in September he snapped that 'we repudiate the rotten democratic party, especially the ruffian democracy of Tammany Hall'.[37]

Bennett was slow in coming out directly for Fernando Wood for mayor even when it became clear at the beginning of November that he would be in the running.[38] Of course the *Herald* had supported Wood in the struggle at the Democratic State Convention and signs of its preference for him were not lacking. Caution was necessary though. Wood had been written off as politically dead after his defeat in the mayoralty contest two years previously. Out against him was the Democratic Vigilant Association, the municipal heir of the Fifth Avenue reform movement. Although Bennett admired Wood's political vigour and enthusiastically called him 'the master spirit of the times' it was difficult to write off his record of organised rowdyism and public plunder, especially considering all that Bennett had had to say on those subjects recently. If Wood could lend his abilities to a genuine reform movement, mused Bennett, what a boon it would be to the city. The *Herald* hinted that if Wood came out squarely for ending peculation he might get more votes than he expected. The contest still looked a very close one, but Wood was making prodigious efforts to mobilize support and prove that he was still very much politically alive. With Sickles in temporary exile from public life,[39] Tammany had no head who could match Wood's vigorously personal style of leadership. The Irish element, disgruntled at Tammany's alliance with freesoil, began to desert to the Wood organisation.[40]

Forced to choose between anti-slavery candidates and the king of the rowdies, the *Herald* finally switched openly to Wood by a deft

[36]*NYH* 26 Aug 1859.

[37]*NYH* 17, 24 Sept 1859.

[38]*NYH* 1 Nov 1859. For Bennett's changing attitude to Wood cf. *NYH* 2, 17 Sept; 20 Oct.

[39]Congressman Sickles had shot his wife's lover earlier in the year – see *NYH* 1, 4 Mar; 27 Apr 1859; W.A. Swanberg, *Sickles the Incredible* (NY 1956), pp. 1–76.

[40]*NYH* 26, 27 Oct; 8, 9, 18, 27, 30 Nov 1859. See also articles on Wood by Leonard Chalmers cited in note 102 to chapter 2 above.

flanking manoeuvre. A week before the election it was still concentrating on attacking Opdyke and Havemeyer, without explicitly coming out for the ineluctable alternative.[41] Readers were left to draw their own conclusions from the ineligibility of the anti-slavery candidates. Then the *Herald* focused attention on the Sabbatarian issue and demonstrated that Wood was the only acceptable candidate on this platform.

The Sunday question, as it may conveniently be called, was put to good electoral service for Wood, but this does not alter the fact that it was a cause dear to Bennett's heart and not something which he suddenly conjured up. In fact he had called for the Sunday laws to be made an issue in the mayoralty contest as far back as July.[42] It may even be said that the *Herald* was devoted to few causes so constantly as this one. An edition of the *Herald* during 1859 which did not contain some arguments about the wrongs of Sabbatarian legislation was exceptional, and next to national issues the importance of this matter in New York City can hardly be overrated. It is probable that resentment against Sunday blue laws has never been sufficiently emphasised as an element in the medley of attitudes which might grandly be called 'Democratic ideology'.

The trouble arose out of the efforts of the Republican controlled Metropolitan police to enforce the laws against retailing alcohol and opening theatres on Sundays. The city's grogshops were notorious dens of vice, besides being Democratic strongholds, and the connection of drinking with violence was so obvious that an enforcement of the temperance laws seemed the quickest and most logical way of safe-guarding law and order on Sundays. This policy offended the Irish community, who were apt not to see any sin in drinking. It also deeply antagonised the Germans. Although the *Herald* described the New York Germans as generally more thrifty and industrious than the Irish, they too were fond of enjoying themselves on Sundays by drinking beer and going to the theatre. Indeed Bennett noted that they had made lager beer an institution in a very short time, and that several theatre owners who objected to being closed down on Sundays were themselves Germans.[43] The *Herald* became their champion.

Bennett never denied the serious proportions of drunkenness and disorder, but he disagreed with the temperance and Sabbatarian reformers on the proper remedy for the evil. He stated his case

[41]*NYH* 1 Dec 1859.
[42]*NYH* 26 July 1859.
[43]*NYH* 25 Apr; 10 June; 25 Nov 1859.

succinctly: 'two thirds of the crime in this city proceeds from drunkenness and more than two thirds of the drunkenness proceeds from the Sunday laws and the Puritanical observance of the Sabbath.' His remedy was not to clamp down on the grogshops, for repression merely encouraged vice, but to open theatres, fairs and other places of entertainment and to encourage the use of Central Park to attract the young away from drink. The problem arose, he said, in trying to force people to spend their one day of leisure in sepulchural gloom and boredom, which simply encouraged them to get into mischief. He found fault with the reforming 'Protestant popes' because, said he, they were narrow minded fanatics whose ignorance of human nature blinded them to this simple truth. He also deprecated the tendency in some Republican quarters to use alarming crime statistics against the Irish as a group[44] and was suspicious that the Metropolitan police were anxious to please the reformers in an attempt to divert attention from corruption in their own ranks.[45]

Though expressed with characteristic verve, Bennett's sustained campaign for Sunday recreation for New York's labouring classes was at bottom enlightened, and argued from humane principles. His views, however, were greeted with barrages of abuse from the *Times*, the *Courier and Enquirer*, the *Journal of Commerce* and other bastions of respectability, and by the religious press. Bennett was denounced as a blasphemer, an infidel, an advocate of drink and a defender of vice. This only served to incite him, for the situation smacked of the 1840 'holy alliance' against the *Herald*. He boiled over when the *Journal of Commerce* denounced him for producing the *Herald* on Sundays. Everybody knew this was rank hypocrisy, said Bennett, for the Sunday editions of the *Herald* were produced on the preceding Saturday, and the Monday edition of the *Journal of Commerce* was produced on a Sunday just as the *Herald* was. Worse, the Metropolitan police took to arresting news boys for selling the *Herald* on a Sunday, which Bennett naturally thought was a pretty poor way of suppressing vice. The issue of religious liberty became mixed up with a slanging campaign which had reached white heat by mid-summer.

Bennett countered the religious arguments by campaigning for a Sabbath made for man, not vice-versa, and claimed 'for each the right to observe the day of rest from labor as his religion may teach or his necessities demand, and for all that every one shall respect the right of

[44]*NYH* 16 Jan; 13, 20 Feb 1859.

[45]*NYH* 19 Mar; 1 Apr 1859. With his usual facility for choosing nicknames that stuck Bennett dubbed the offending police superintendent 'Pious Pilsbury'.

his neighbour to do so'.[46] But primarily he treated the issue as a social one, launching into the 'sanctimonious black coats who seek to tyrannize' over the labouring classes and 'would put people to death for violating the Sabbath as was done under the law of Moses'. He attacked the injustice of 'Black Republican popes' who lived in comfort themselves yet sought to 'conspire against the Sunday enjoyment of the poor mechanic and artisan, shut up in the heated workshop or factory by day, and stowed at night into crowded tenement houses in filthy alleys'.[47] It was only natural that when the Germans of the city organised a mass demonstration against the Sunday laws in July that they should marshal themselves outside the *Herald* building, for Tammany Hall and at this time Mozart as well were against them on the Sunday question. Bennett took pride in regarding his paper as the embattled defender of common sense and progress.[48]

Here then was an emotive issue which was ready to become political tinder. On 27 November the *Herald* called on the three mayoral candidates to declare themselves on the Sunday issue. The anti-slavery men were predictably for the enforcement of the blue laws. Said Bennett of Havemeyer: 'He is in favor of keeping the Sabbath day holy, which means that he is in favor of shutting up the working classes in their houses on that day, so that they may not disturb the Sabbath amusements of our pious aristocracy.'[49] The *Herald*'s choice was now made plain: 'We advise all friends of rational legislation, for Sunday as well as every other day in the week. . . to see that they vote for the only man who is in favor of equal rights for every day of the week, and for the laboring man as well as the rich one, and that man is Fernando Wood.'[50]

Apart from the *Herald*, Wood had only the *Daily News* supporting him. (It would have been surprising indeed if the *Daily News* had not supported him, since he had purchased it earlier in the year and his brother Ben was the editor.)[51] Ranged against him were twelve city papers supporting Havemeyer and four supporting Opdyke. From the

[46]*NYH* 17 July 1859.

[47]*Ibid.,*

[48]*NYH* 4, 19, 26 June; 3, 17, 20, 23, 26, 29, 31 July; 1, 10, 14, 20, 21 Aug; 4, 16, 18, 25, 27 Sept; 2, 13, 19 Oct 1859.

[49]*NYH* 30 Nov 1859.

[50]*NYH* 4 Dec 1859.

[51]Ben Wood and the *News* have their historian in David F. Long, 'The New York News, 1855-1906; Spokesman for the Underprivileged' (Unpublished thesis, Columbia University, 1950).

point of view of daily circulation, though, Wood's chances were much better, for the combined sales of the Havemeyer journals roughly equalled that of the *Herald* and *Daily News* together, or so the *Herald* claimed.[52]

After an exciting contest Wood won with a plurality of 3,000 over his opponents. Bennett described the victory as a popular victory of conservatism and a rebuke to anti-slavery treason, sabbatarian cant and Tammany rottenness.[53] The defeated parties ascribed their misfortune to brazen rowdyism and wholesale ballot stuffing by the Wood forces. However gained, Wood's return to political ascendancy after two years in the wilderness of defeat was a truly remarkable personal triumph,[54] and one in which the *Herald* shared. Bennett promised the *Herald*'s continuing support for Wood in his stand for a return of executive powers to the mayor from the state if he kept his electoral pledges to fight corruption.[55] For instance, when Wood early in his term got into conflict with some of the city departments, Bennett said 'He may be called a despot; but that is just the kind of person that is required for a city government like ours'.[56] Later it will be told how far Bennett supported Wood's manoeuvres at the Democratic Convention at Charleston.

For the Democrats the animosities of the contest had widened the breach made at Syracuse and would be another element making for discord in April 1860; and one which would make a material difference to the fate of the Democrats nationally. After the election the *Herald* advised President Buchanan to cut off the Tammany 'traitors' from government patronage root and branch.[57]

Bennett claimed that a Republican victory in the city would have been a tragedy, because it would have been a final decree of separation between the Northern and Southern States. That had not yet happened but the chances of avoiding it were looking slimmer daily. Having experienced the excitement of political campaigns in the state and in the city, New Yorkers were now, in December 1859,

[52]*NYH* 10 Dec 1859.

[53]*NYH* 7 Dec 1859.

[54]See John A. Dix to Buchanan 7 Dec 1859, Buchanan Papers, Historical Society of Pennsylvania.

[55]*NYH* 8 Dec 1859; 4, 6 Jan 1860.

[56]*NYH* 18 July 1860. However, Bennett branded as 'vulgar and mendacious' the accusation by the Albany *Atlas & Argus* that the *Herald* was merely Wood's mouthpiece — *NYH* 4 Apr 1860.

[57]*NYH* 8, 9, Dec 1860.

treated to further sensations. To judge by what was happening in congress the sectional confrontation could not get much more intense before reaching breaking point.

Girding for the Presidential Battle

We are now standing upon a mine, which may explode and scatter the confederacy in fragments at any moment. –*Herald*, 5 December 1859

On 2 December, 1859, John Brown was hanged at Charlestown, Virginia, leaving as his last message his certainty that the crimes of this 'guilty land' could never be purged away but with blood.

Once it had become clear that Brown was to be tried by the state authorities of Virginia, rather than by a federal court, Bennett desired his rapid execution. The man was nothing more than a cold blooded murderer, said the *Herald*, and hanging was exactly what he deserved.[58] The reaction elsewhere in the North on the day of the hanging was far different. To Bennett's disgust church bells tolled for one who was felt to be, if not spotless, at least a martyr in a noble cause. Brown's conduct and eloquence at his trial had won widespread admiration, and he died a sworn enemy of slavery.[59]

Bennett, who had counted on working the Harper's Ferry raid to the detriment of the Republicans, had obviously failed to take a majority of public opinion with him. He confessed it; the times seemed out of joint. Now it seemed to him that the rank and file of the Republican party were being 'abolitionised' at a 'fearful speed'.[60]

In this highly charged atmosphere, three days after the execution, the 36th congress assembled at Washington. The *Herald* had anticipated that a sectional row of fearful proportions would break out there because in one way or another this congress would be mostly concerned with President-making. Perhaps a sectional confrontation would develop out of a Democratic attempt to investigate the John Brown business from bottom to top (that was the strategy Bennett favoured), which would clash with the Republican desire to expose Democratic corruption publicly.[61] The *Herald* picked up rumours too

[58]*NYH* 27 Oct; 1, 6, 11, 22 Nov; 2 Dec 1859.

[59]For Brown's trial and execution and the reaction to it see Oates, pp. 307-61.

[60]*NYH* 3, 4, 5, 21, 25 Nov; 5, 12 Dec 1859. On 'Treason in the Pulpit' and 'sanctimonious scoundrels' see *NYH* 19 Nov.

[61] *NYH* 11 Nov 1859.

that Southerners might organise their own presidential party, seeking guarantees of slavery within the Union. Bennett thought that such demands were amply justified by recent events and that the movement should be encouraged in order to bring the 'lower North' to its senses as to the value of the Union. If the demands of the South were not met in congress then the *Herald* speculated that Southern members might adjourn to Richmond and set up their own independent government.[62]

Whatever happened in this congress would be relayed to the public in greater detail than ever before in the *Herald*, which announced plans to extend its telegraphic coverage of events at the capital. This development was to be of more than passing significance because the ensuing session of congress was probably the most disorderly in American history. Fists, knives and even pistols were on display and the language which honourable gentlemen used to each other was on occasions decidely impolite. People could read all the details of these uproars in the *Herald*, and it is likely that some congressmen were aware that they were playing to an ever wider audience. Bennett professed the hope that wider publicity would give the House a sharper sense of accountability and raise the standard of conduct in the national councils, but the reverse seemed to be the truth.[63]

Trouble started in congress over the very organisation of the House. This was forseeable because the Republicans, though the largest single party, were not in an overall majority. The election of a speaker proved a bone of contention as in vote after vote the anti-Republican groups blocked the candidacy of John Sherman of Ohio, who had made his reputation by attacking Democratic corruption. Sectional animosities, already sharp after the Brown affair, were made sharper by the publication of *The Impending Crisis* by Hinton R. Helper. Sherman, among other leading Republicans, had endorsed the book with his signature, little suspecting the furore it would cause. Irate southerners resolved that nobody who had approved doctrines deemed so offensive to their section was fit to be Speaker of the national legislature, and as a result public business was at a standstill for weeks.

[62] *NYH* 2, 3, 4 Dec 1859. In an article for the *Springfield Republican* of 9 Dec 1859. Samuel Bowles wrote from Washington: 'It is amusing to see the greed with which the *Herald* is snatched up and devoured on its earliest arrival here in the evening; and what is worse, to see the simplicity of these Southern fellows who seem to pin their whole faith upon it. Where Northern men look at it only for amusement, as they look at *Punch* or *Frank Leslie's*. Southern men swallow it gravely with a sigh and a knowing shake of the head.'

[63] *NYH* 17, 20, 21 Sept; 20 Dec 1859.

Bennett was wholeheartedly behind the Southerners in their action and virulent in condemnation of Helper's book. Though he tutted at violent behaviour of congressmen from both sections his attitude to Sherman's candidacy was unbending: 'If the house cannot be organised otherwise than by the election of such a fanatic endorser, let it never organise.'[64] Those who complained at the delay involved in the fight against Sherman were dismissed by Bennett as mere cormorants after the spoils.[65]

This was oddly obstructive language for an avowed 'conservative'. The Republicans had hoped to use the Helper book as campaign publicity but it had backfired against them. By giving it maximum publicity Bennett hoped to drive moderate voters away from the Republican camp.[66] The *Times* complained that Helper's book had passed 'almost wholly out of the public knowledge, when the *Herald* hit upon it, in one of its mousing hunts after a sensation'.[67]

Helper himself was a Southern white who was suggesting that socially and economically slavery was a blight on the white men of the South, and in fact was a greater curse to them than to the Negro. Bennett was at first sceptical about the authorship, suspecting that the theme smelled strongly of having been composed in the *Tribune* office.[68] (The *Tribune* was serialising the book.) To him the message it proclaimed was but a treasonable abolitionist plan to raise an insurrection of blacks and agrarian whites in the South against the slaveowners.[69] Seward, Brown, Helper; revolution, emancipation, confiscation – how many times were these names and ideas linked in the *Herald* columns. Bennett answered Helper's arguments with barrages of statistics aimed at showing that far from being crippled by slavery the South and the nation were flourishing because of it.[70]

In parts of the South lynch law was in force, so great was the terror of further abolitionist infiltrations. In New York City during December

[64]*NYH* 5 Jan 1860. Be it noted that Bennett suggested the tactic of blocking the Republican organisation of Congress on 24 Oct 1859, long before the House met. See also 10 Dec 1859; 1-9, 15, 21 Jan 1860. Ollinger Crenshaw, 'The Speakership Contest of 1859-60', *Mississippi Valley Historical Review,* 29 (1942-3), 323-38, suggested that some Southerners were quite prepared to push the matter to bloodshed and disruption.

[65]*NYH* 24 Dec 1859.

[66]*NYH* 23, 30 Dec 1859.

[67]NY *Times* 5 Jan 1861. See also NY *Daily Tribune* 7 Dec 1859.

[68]*NYH* 26 Nov 1859.

[69]*NYH* 3, 5, 7, 8, 10, 11 Dec 1859; 16 Jan 1860.

[70]See especially *NYH* 26 Dec 1859.

and January there was considerable alarm at the prospect of disunion and the *Herald* cautioned all men of property who had publicly approved *The Impending Crisis* to disown their rash action, for they were cutting their own throats.[71] It at first encouraged the efforts of alarmed businessmen to get up Union meetings as a way of applying pressure against the Republicans in congress. Bennett's enthusiasm for these mass gatherings of anxious men was strongly tempered however by his desire to see them under the right political control, as he made clear by lecturing in the *Herald* about 'The Conservative Movements in the North – The True and The False'.[72] He warned that a 'mere assemblage of old fossil whigs, or disbanded Know Nothings, or tainted Tammany Hall fugitives, or frightened republicans doing business "in the cotton trade and sugar line" will not answer'.[73] To be successful a Union rally ought to be held with Mayor Fernando Wood as leader of the popular movement, for he was now established as the city's foremost national and Union man, said the *Herald*.

President-making was the game which everybody was now playing and the struggle to win votes was on in earnest. Union meetings, to Bennett, were useless unless they proposed a Presidential candidate,[74] and it boded ill for the Democracy that the *Herald* would evidently favour a third party movement rather than see a freesoil, anti-Administration Democrat nominated.

---

[71]*NYH* 26 Nov; 25, 30 Dec 1859; 4, 6, 12 Jan 1860.

[72]*NYH* 14 Dec 1859. For a rejoinder see Albany *Atlas & Argus* 29 Dec 1859.

[73]*NYH* 9 Dec 1859.

[74]*NYH* 14 Dec 1859.

5

PROPHET AND PARTISAN:
THE *HERALD* IN THE PRESIDENTIAL CAMPAIGN
OF 1860

> To the brink of. . . [disunion]. . . we are brought by the miserabl intrigues of demagogues and spoils politicians, of fanatical declaimers of sophistries and absurd abstractions and forgetfulness on the part of the people of the true rights of others and the holy compacts of our common bond of union. – *Herald* 10 January 1860

> Whatever the *Herald* praised, sickened, drooped, and if the *Herald* persisted in praising it, finally died; while whatever the *Herald* attacked prospered, and all the more, the more it was abused. – P. T. Barnum

Democratic Fission: A 'Four Cornered Political Scrub Race' Develops

At the approach of the long anticipated Charleston Convention Bennett mused that the Democracy was a very 'imperfect instrument' with which to defend the Constitution against Republican assault. Nevertheless it appeared the only viable one, and he hopefully referred to it as the 'Conservative Party'.[1] Which candidate would fulfil the requirements of the time?

After the failure of its Buchanan 'boom' in February,[2] the *Herald* favoured some 'conservative' pro-slavery man for the Democratic nomination. It played with the names of Sam Houston of Texas, Senators Hunter of Virginia and Lane of Oregon, and Mexican War hero John E. Wool of New York. Bennett was also keeping Fernando Wood's name to the fore as at least a Vice-Presidential possible, for the situation seemed to favour a 'dark horse' contender.[3] In a more normal contest than that of 1860 the *Herald*'s choices might have proved admirably suited to harmonise the sectional quarrels of the Democracy; in retrospect they were to appear almost sadly eccentric.

[1] *NYH* 6-13, 21-3 Apr 1860.
[2] See above, chapter 3.
[3] *NYH* 3, 8 Feb; 8-13 Apr 1860.

The Democratic Convention assembled in Charleston on 23 April and the reports which came clicking over the wires brought apprehension that the will to party harmony was woefully lacking. The 'fire-eaters' from the cotton states insisted on a party platform which explicitly defended the right of slavery to go into the territories as a national institution. The Northern delegates, adhering to Douglas as the only man who could carry the Northwestern States, would not admit such a principle. They could compete with the Republicans at home only with the popular sovereignty argument.

The deadlock was absolute. Bennett demanded that the Northern Democrats should cease to evade the issue and strongly support the pro-slavery demands of the South: they must realise, he warned, that the slavery issue could not be wrapped up in words and that the Republicans must be squarely confronted with it.

At bottom, though, Bennett could hardly believe that the Convention would be rent by a quarrel over the platform, and held that Southern threats to bolt the Convention were mere brag. Similarly, once it was obvious that Douglas's supporters could not realistically hope to get the two-thirds majority of votes necessary to nominate their man, Bennett remained confident that the party would compose its differences for the sake of $80 million worth of federal offices. It all seemed like the normal quadrennial Convention huckstering which prefaced compromise.[4] The nation was prosperous under the federal system – surely the 'cohesive power of public plunder' would work its magic on the politicians even if they could not grasp this truth as clearly as the editor of the *Herald*? For the moment New York took more interest in an international prize fight which boosted *Herald* sales to a record 104,160.

Perhaps some of the Charleston delegates imagined themselves engaged in a game of bluff, but if so both sides underestimated the determination of the other. The Southern delegates bolted the Convention when it became obvious that the Northern men would not desert their popular sovereignty platform for an unequivocally pro-slavery one. The Northern men were disinclined to beg the malcontents to return or to yield up the chance of nominating Douglas. They adjourned the rump Convention until 18 June at Baltimore.

Bennett's view of the matter was amply expressed in his editorial headline 'Gigantic Cheat Upon the Administration by Northern Officeholders'.[5] He began predictably by damning politicians in

[4]*NYH* 23-9 Apr 1860.
[5]*NYH* 1 May 1860.

general, then got down to cases, laying the blame for the débâcle on the Douglas supporters, whom he described as the 'freesoil faction'. They were guilty, he proclaimed, of trying to force Douglas and his 'fine drawn abstractions' regarding slavery onto the South merely to pander to fanaticism: for so he regarded Democratic attempts to win the freesoil vote. Incensed also by the news that another fugitive slave had been rescued at Troy, New York, in 'shameless disrespect' of Southern rights, Bennett groaned that 'the whole country. . . is revolting at this continued agitation of the nigger question' by the North. He could not regard the action of the cotton state delegates at Charleston as anything other than a justifiable defence of their legitimate interests.

Simultaneously, the *Herald* demanded that Buchanan oust the 'traitors' who had enjoyed federal patronage while working against the President, so indirectly betraying the interest felt at the White House in defeating Douglas.[6] The supporters of the 'Little Giant' actually had no reason to be grateful, because Buchanan had been trying to strangle their enjoyment of government offices ever since they had rejected the fraudulent pro-slavery Lecompton constitution for Kansas. The *Herald* however insisted that a benign executive had been basely stabbed in the back by ungrateful politicians.[7]

Nor was Bennett's wrath directed mainly at supporters of Douglas in the distant Northwest. For him perhaps the most outrageous of the events at Charleston had been the acceptance of the Albany Regency's delegation by the Convention. Fernando Wood's claim to lead New York's delegation had been rejected and he had not secured even half and half representation with the Albany men.

Ostensibly Bennett had been neutral on the question of which of the two New York delegations should be admitted, declaring that 'New York has been the bane, curse and scourge of the democratic party for nearly fourteen years'. In fact though his suggestion that the Charleston Convention should refuse admittance to both New York factions until they had composed their differences and then accept or reject both together was less impartial than it seemed. The Albany Regency led the stronger of the two groups in the state as a whole, and

[6]*NYH* 2, 3, 4 May 1860.

[7]On the patronage question see Philip G. Auchampaugh, 'The Buchanan-Douglas Feud', *Illinois State Historical Society Journal*, 25 (1932-3), 5-48; R.R. Stenberg, 'An Unnoticed Factor in the Buchanan-Douglas Feud', *ibid.*, 271-4, and David E. Meerse, 'Origins of the Buchanan-Douglas Feud Reconsidered', *ibid.*, 67 (1974), 154-74. See also Philip S. Klein, *President James Buchanan* (University Park, Pa., 1962) and chapter XXII ff. of Robert W. Johannsen, *Stephen A. Douglas* (NY 1973).

under the unit rule of the Convention the whole of New York's decisive vote went against the Southern pro-slavery platform. To ask for equal representation was in reality to beg a place for Wood and for at least half of the delegation's vote. It was an appeal to the national party to overrule the Regency's exclusion of Wood at Syracuse the previous September.

Those Southerners who had voted against Wood's admission at Charleston, said the *Herald*, had sacrificed their true friend. When the Albany delegation voted with the Douglas men Bennett could hardly express himself strongly enough against their 'treachery' and urged the President, who shared his bitterness, to lose no time in replacing Albany office holders in New York with Wood men.[8] The cause for bitterness was deep. Had Wood been admitted the New York vote would probably have been decisive against the Douglas platform and the cotton state men might at least have hesitated before withdrawing.[9] In time, when it transpired that the Charleston bolt had

[8]*NYH* 27 Apr; 1-6, 17 May 1860. Buchanan's resentment against the New York delegation is expressed in his autobiographical *Mr. Buchanan's Administration on the Eve of the Rebellion* (NY 1866), p. 78.

[9]Wood's movement had looked formidable when organised in February 1860. On 18 February the *Charleston Mercury* took care to puff him as a 'sound' Democrat. In hoping to share the state's seats at the party convention Wood had precedent on his side, for the New York delegation had been divided both in 1852 and 1856. Working against him was his reputation for rowdyism and the fact that the Regency delegation were seated at the convention prior to the struggle over credentials. One authority (Brummer) finds it surprising that Wood's appeal to the South was not more effective. In the event only a minority of the Committee on Credentials (mostly from the cotton states) favoured admitting an equally divided New York delegation and the Convention adopted the majority report that only the Regency delegation should be admitted by 210½ votes to 55. There is a likelihood that Dean Richmond secured this assent by making promises to the Southern delegates which he did not fulfil. Not all of the Regency delegation were former 'Softs'; supporters of 'Hard' Daniel S. Dickinson were included, and in caucus the delegation voted for Douglas 37, Dickinson 20, Guthrie 10, Hunter 2 and Breckinridge 1. The whole of the state's vote of 35 in the Convention therefore went to Douglas under the unit rule. Dickinson and his supporters felt cheated by Richmond and fought against the Regency during the election campaign. Dickinson had disavowed Wood and his tactics after the Syracuse Convention and had allowed himself to be wooed by Richmond. Now he swung back and was to support the Breckinridge party in opposition to fusion with the Douglas ticket in New York during August. After the bolt of the Southern delegates from Charleston, the Regency delegation voted that any candidate must be nominated by two thirds of the entire (i.e. pre-bolt) Convention. This made Douglas's nomination at Charleston impossible, and caused the *Herald* to charge that the devious Regency had played both sides false in the hope of nominating Seymour as a compromise candidate. See *NYH* 17 May 1860; Brummer, *History of New York State during the period of the Civil War* (NY 1911), pp. 48-56; S. Pleasants, *Fernando Wood* (NY 1948), pp. 104-10; Milledge L.Bonham, 'New York in the election of 1860', *New York History*, 15 (1934), 124-43; Nichols, *Disruption of American Democracy* (NY 1948), ch 16. Dwight L. Dummond, *The Secession Movement, 1860-61* (NY 1963), pp. 42-3, states flatly; 'Had the New York delegation been uninstructed or the Wood delegation seated, the Southern-rights platform would have been adopted by the convention.'

been the direct prelude to secession and civil war, the *Herald*'s animus against the Regency for the 'perfidy' of 1860 eclipsed even the deep resentment which Bennett nurtured against freesoil disruption of the party by the Barnburners back in 1848.

With the Democrats in disarray, would the *Herald* swing its support to the Constitutional Union party? Having sung summer and winter long of the paradise which would attend the formation of a national conservative party, and having recently spoken of the Constitutional Union movement as the refuge of conservatives in the event of Democratic failure, Bennett might have been expected to show at least some enthusiasm when John Bell, a border state man, was nominated for the Presidency on 9 May on the simple and ambiguous platform of the constitution and the law. But the *Herald* was at first cold. The public were dissatisfied, Bennett pontificated, with a platform which did not face up squarely to combating the evil of abolitionism. (Some conservative platforms were evidently more conservative than others in his eyes.) To add insult to injury, he dismissed Bell and Edward Everett of Massachusetts, the Vice-Presidential candidate, as 'estimable men but fossils with no sympathies in common with the present generation'.[10]

Then from Chicago came news which Bennett declared should rouse the Democrats from their confusion and inspire them with fresh hopes of victory. On 19 May the front page of the *Herald* announced that the Republicans, having adopted a platform which condemned slavery in the Territories and endorsed the Declaration of Independence, had chosen 'Abram' Lincoln of Illinois as their Presidential candidate.

As the mis-spelling of his name suggests, Lincoln was relatively little known in the east before 1860. His debates with Douglas in Illinois in 1858 had received scant comment in the *Herald*, save as further proof of Douglas's freesoil 'treachery' to Buchanan on the Kansas issue. Lincoln had visited New York City in February and in a speech at the Cooper Union had argued powerfully against the extension of slavery. The *Herald* had deigned to refute him but had regarded the westerner merely as another of Seward's lieutenants.[11]

Bennett had taken it for granted that Seward would be the Republican candidate (so had Seward) and with such headlines as 'W. H. SEWARD AN INCENDIARY OR A HUMBUG'[12] had raked him without pause since the John Brown raid. He had frankly

[10]*NYH* 11 May 1860 and cf. 12, 17 May. On the Constitutional Union Party in New York see Brummer, pp. 60-2, 71-3.

[11]*NYH* 27, 29 Feb 1860.

written: 'Let Seward by all means be nominated. There is no man the national and conservative element in this State so ardently desires to have for an opponent in the great contest of next November as the apostle of "higher law" and the champion of the "irrepressible conflict".'[13] With his favourite bogey man suddenly out of the running Bennett had to adapt rapidly for an assault on the new candidate.

For a spontaneous effort it lacked nothing in vigour. Bennett introduced Lincoln as 'a third rate Western Lawyer, poorer than even poor Pierce'. He wept crocodile tears that such able men as Seward and Chase had been passed over by their party for 'a fourth rate lecturer, who cannot speak good grammar, and who, to raise the wind, delivers his hackneyed, illiterate compositions at $200 apiece. Our readers will recollect that this peripatetic politician visited New York two or three months ago on his financial tour, when, in return for the most unmitigated trash, inter-larded with coarse and clumsy jokes, he filled his empty pockets with dollars coined out of Republican fanaticism.'[14] (The charge that Lincoln had accepted more than the normal expenses for his speeches was not new in the columns of the *Herald*. It nettled Lincoln, who denied it.)[15]

Bennett exerted himself to prove that Lincoln was a rabid and implacable abolitionist. Voters must be doubly watchful against Republican attempts to soothe them with professions of unionism and peace, for all such were 'hollow and false' said the *Herald*.[16] Although Lincoln was described as an 'illiterate Western boor' and the weakest nomination which the Republicans could have made, the *Herald* was soon able to announce to its readers that it had discovered him to be the real author of the 'irrepressible conflict' idea. Indeed, examination of his speeches showed that he had preceded Seward in expounding it and was aptly called 'Honest Abe' because he was sincere in his desire to put his revolutionary doctrine into practice and invade the South to overthrow slavery by force or fraud.[17]

Later on in the summer Bennett found another ramp to annoy the Republican candidate. Unlike Douglas, Lincoln did not campaign actively for the Presidency but stayed at home in Springfield.

[12]*NYH* 22 Dec 1859.

[13]*NYH* 2 Feb 1860.

[14]*NYH* 19 May 1860.

[15]*NYH* 12, 14 Mar; 17 Apr 1860; Lincoln to C.F. McNeil, Springfield 6 Apr 1860 in Roy P. Basler, *The Collected Works of Abraham Lincoln* (New Brunswick 1953-5), vol. IV, p. 38.

[16]*NYH* 19, 21, 30 May 1860.

[17]*NYH* 22, 23, 26, 30 May; 1, 2, 7 June 1860.

Although it was not the custom for candidates to stump and Lincoln would have risked personal violence had he ventured into a Southern state, Bennett taunted him for lacking moral courage. The *Herald* had it that Lincoln was fearful of a 'trap' to 'inveigle' him into a slave state, and poked fun at his timorousness while mixing ridicule with self-righteous indignation at such cowardice in a candidate.[18]

The story annoyed Lincoln, as its basis was one of his playfully told anecdotes. He wrote out a correction and sent it to a party contact, George C. Fogg, asking him to have it inserted in the *Herald*. Fogg called on Bennett, who was apparently so urbane that he gave the impression of being well disposed to Lincoln personally. However, Bennett was not prepared to admit editorially that the *Herald* had been wrong, though he was quite willing to print the correction over the signature of Lincoln or his representative. Fogg would not agree to that condition and so reported to Springfield. Lincoln replied: 'You have done precisely right in that matter with the *Herald*. Do nothing further about it. Although it wrongs me and annoys me some, I prefer letting it run its course, to getting into the papers over my own name. . .'[19]

At the time and since, Lincoln has been censured for remaining silent about his policies during a national crisis. But when he declined to add anything to his published speeches, referring to the distortions which 'bad men' might make of any remark of his, he may well have had a certain New York editor in mind, and his fears were not unjustifiable.

Before this episode Lincoln's friends had made an effort to win Bennett over. Joseph Medill, editor of the staunchly Republican Chicago *Tribune,* wrote to Lincoln of the attempt:

> A fortnight ago we cautiously opened correspondence with a reliable, discreet, influential Republican in New York City suggesting to him to sound Bennett of the *Herald*, and if he found him open to conviction to ascertain his terms. He has seen B. and finds him not unwilling to 'dicker', terms moderate, and 'no cure no pay'. . . I'll have a preliminary interview with his 'Satanic Majesty'. . . and ascertain his state of mind etc. etc. We deem it highly important to spike that gun; his affirmative help is of no great consequence, but he is powerful for mischief. He can do us much harm if hostile. If neutralized a *point* is gained. We think his terms will not be immoderate. He is too rich to want money.

[18]*NYH* 13, 14 Aug 1860.

[19]Lincoln to Fogg 16 Aug; Fogg to Lincoln 23 Aug; Lincoln to Fogg 29 Aug 1860 in Basler, vol. IV, pp. 96-7.

Social position we suspect is what he wants. He wants to be in a position to be invited with his wife and son to dinner or tea at the White house occasionally and to be 'made of', by the big men of the party. I think we can afford to agree to that much. It is not only the damage he can do us in the canvas in the close Eastern States, but the blows he can inflict on a Republican Administration during all its term. He has a vaste corps of writers and correspondents at home and abroad and a universal circulation North, South, East, West, Europe, Asia, Africa and the Isles of the Sea. . .

When our confidential friend at N.Y. conversed with him about you, he (B) spoke quite handsòmely of you, said you were the strongest man Reps could have nominated, were honest, capable, not dangerously ultra, thought you would make a good president, and stated that if your campaign was properly fought you could be elected, etc. dide'nt know what he would do etc. . .[20]

It is not known whether Medill did meet Bennett or what the result was. Although the *Herald* did soften its tone towards Lincoln a little later, it will be suggested that ulterior motives were involved, and in Bennett's defence he did not jump aboard the Republican train even when their victory became reasonably certain. It seems that Bennett was adept at playing his visitors along. Medill's estimate of his man may have been too glib by far.[21]

Meanwhile Greeley's opposition to Seward's nomination at Chicago produced a hot feud in the Republican camp as Weed, Webb and Raymond attacked him through their journals. Bennett played this theme for all its worth and presented a dark picture of Republican disintegration and demoralisation. He was particularly amused when Greeley, attempting to vindicate the purity of his own motives in the *Tribune*, produced as an argument in his own defence the fact that Seward had been rendered unavailable by the attacks of the *Herald*. Bennett enquired with irreverent cynicism whether the Republicans

---

[20]Medill to Lincoln, Chicago, 19 June 1860 — full text in David C. Mearns ed., *The Lincoln Papers* (NY 1948), vol. 1, pp. 261-2. One suspects that Bennett rather enjoyed giving visitors to his office exactly the impression they wished to receive. In the novel *Marion* (London 1864), 'Manhattan' wrote that 'one of the most prominent traits in the character of Mr Bennett, and which is only known to those who know him as well as he knows himself, is his perfect editorial closeness. He does not let his left hand know what his right hand writes. He will appear to be communicative and frank, and yet what he says is the very frankness of hypocrisy. His hearer gains nothing, obtains nothing from him.' — vol. III, pp. 118-19.

[21]In the same letter, incidentally, Medill claimed to have confidential information that Bennett was 'at heart' a freesoiler. If true this was the best kept secret of the age and Bennett's propensity for publicly mortifying his private feelings approached the grandly masochistic.

would try improving their propaganda campaign by hiring someone to give Senator Sumner another caning.[22]

Democratic Fusion and Confusion

Better vote for any ticket than let Lincoln be elected. - *Herald*
18 September 1860

Bennett hoped in midsummer that the organisation of the opposition would stimulate the Democrats to see reason and act to prevent the Republicans riding to victory over the divisions of their opponents. The rival factions, however, showed few signs of composing their 'insane quarrels'. Encouraged by the decision of the cotton state delegations, meeting at Richmond, to adjourn until the result of the Baltimore Convention was known, Bennett entered a plea for the Democracy not to throw away what remained of its prestige and Tradition as the only truly national party. He suggested that Daniel S. Dickinson or Joseph Lane would be acceptable as national candidates if nominated by acclamation North and South.[23]

These insubstantial hopes were quickly dispelled at Baltimore. The Regency-controlled New York delegation, anxious to foster Horatio Seymour's claims to run on the Presidential ticket, voted with the Douglas men against the readmission of the Charleston bolters. Disgusted by this exclusion, the delegations of the states of the upper South and Far West withdrew and joined with the cotton state delegates to nominate John C. Breckinridge, currently Buchanan's Vice-President, with Joseph Lane as his running mate. Meanwhile the Northern rump proceeded to nominate Douglas.[24]

There were now two Democratic parties, each unlikely to carry any states outside its own section. Bennett interpreted the party's demise as due not to slavery but to Douglas's obstinate desire to imitate Van Buren's action in 1848 which, according to the *Herald,* had been to split the party for personal revenge. The paper ran an obituary on the Democratic party on 24 June, tracing its history from the battle of New Orleans to what seemed now its final expiration. Sourly Bennett consoled himself by assuring his readers that 'We have no regrets . . . to express over the broken down democracy. We

[22]*NYH* 21-6 May; 1, 15, 16 June; 10 July 1860.

[23]*NYH* 20-5 May; 5, 8, 10, 11, 14 June 1860.

[24]*NYH* 22 June 1860. The Regency delegation's vote was once again decisive. For discussions of Dean Richmond's controversial role at Baltimore see Brummer, pp. 56-9 and Bonham, 'New York in the Election of 1860'.

congratulate the American people that this corrupt and demoralized party of juggling and swindling spoilsmen, with political vagabonds and vagrants as its managers, has at last broken to pieces from their quarrels over the spoils.' Soon he was preaching that the republic could only be stronger for the destruction of this party tyranny and was referring to the event as 'the present happy revolution'.[25] However morally wholesome this might be, the disintegration of the Democracy appeared ill-calculated to keep Lincoln out of the White House.

Faced with the looming possibility of a Republican President, at the end of June and the beginning of July the *Herald* perceptibly modified its tone towards Lincoln. Bennett began to make light of the disunion bugbear because Douglas supporters were using the 'disunionist' cry to smear all Breckinridge adherents. The *Herald* retracted its alarmist predictions of the previous winter, chirping that 'nobody threatens disunion, nobody fears it any longer', and that the Union was now perfectly safe from the threats of agitators. With unconscious irony Bennett admitted that 'the truth is at last discovered that the Union and the gaunt and ghastly spectre of disunion have been charlatan tricks by which our democratic politicians have retained their hold upon the public plunder'. Furthermore he conjectured that the election of a Republican President would recreate and unify the opposition, especially by discrediting the extremists in the South, and in this context he said that Lincoln 'would be an excellent dose for the fire-eaters who threaten secession. They may have to swallow him, bitter as he is; but they will not secede. On the contrary, Old Abe will cure them of secession.'[26]

This was a mere lull in the storm, probably designed to render the Breckinridge ticket acceptable in New York, because by the middle of August the *Herald* was back on the old soap box, cursing anyone for a fool who did not believe that Lincoln's election would mean irretrievable disaster.[27] It cannot be known to what extent such inconsistencies in strategy affected those readers of the *Herald* whose memories stretched back to the day before yesterday, but understandably the Democratic *Journal of Commerce* warned its readers that the *Herald* was a wolf in sheep's clothing to their cause.[28]

[25]*NYH* 30 June; 3, 4, July 1860.
[26]*NYH* 23, 26, 30 June; 3, 7 July 1860.
[27]*NYH* 14 Aug 1860.
[28]NY *Journal of Commerce* 25 July; 2 Nov 1860.

Actually Bennett freely admitted that his attitude to the various factions opposing Lincoln was now opportunistic.[29] He threw the support of the *Herald* in turn to whichever faction he thought could best lead the way to a successful local fusion ticket. In the immediate aftermath of the Democratic smash up he switched his allegiance to the Constitutional Union party but during July concluded that the rupture at Baltimore had not weakened Democratic loyalties in the South after all. The Breckinridge wing of the party moreover enjoyed the favours of Administration support.[30] Well then, since Breckinridge was entrenched in the South and Douglas was the unyielding champion of the North, why should they not agree to withdraw from each other's respective section? While remaining split the Democratic party might thus maximise its strength at the polls. Then if Lincoln were defeated by an electoral majority against him, surely the warring factions might do a deal and make up? A compromise might be arranged which would lead to the election of Joseph Lane to the Presidency by congress.

Bennett first came out with this suggestion in definite form on 11 July. Significantly it was also Fernando Wood's hobby of the moment. Two days later the *Herald* announced in an authoritative tone that Buchanan would approve such a bargain, with a split ticket in New York.[31] Bennett sensed a ruffling of Republican confidence at this suggestion and gave a cool estimate that $50,000 contributed by wealthy Democrats ought to suffice to carry the fusion ticket in the state and 'overthrow the Almighty Nigger with the Almighty Dollar'.[32]

But Douglas had by no means so despaired of his prospects in the Upper South that he would voluntarily cede them to Breckinridge, who was unlikely to steal much of his thunder in New York and certainly nowhere else in the North. Douglas men distrusted such a proposition endorsed by Buchanan. By agreeing to it they would in their view simply allow themselves to be duped into being the work

[29]*NYH* 18 Aug 1860.

[30]Buchanan made a speech in Washington on 10 July in which he openly declared his preference for Breckinridge; see Nichols, *Disruption,* pp. 336-7.

[31]*NYH* 13 July 1860. For Wood's efforts at fusion see Pleasants, pp. 110-12; Brummer, pp. 71-2.

[32]*NYH* 15 July 1860. The financing and organisation of the campaign may be profitably studied through the biographies of the opposing national party chairmen, both New Yorkers: on the Republican side James A. Rawley, *Edwin D. Morgan 1811-1883* (NY 1955), ch IV, and for the Democrats Irving Katz, *August Belmont* (NY 1969), ch 6. Besides the studies by Brummer and Bonham there are good treatments of the campaign of 1860 in New York in the histories of the state by Alexander (vol. 2, chs XX-XXIV); Flick (vol. VII, pp. 61-95); and D.M. Ellis (ch 19) – see note 73 to chapter 2 above.

horses of the Southern section of the party. Had they fought their battles against such a fate only to succumb to fair words of compromise?

So the *Herald* proposal and the efforts of Mayor Wood in the same direction were snubbed for the time anyway, with the consequence that on 19 July the paper came out four square for Breckinridge against Lincoln. A Breckinridge meeting held in New York City the night before was portrayed as the authentic expression of the popular will. The *Herald* called on Douglas and Bell to withdraw and laboured to prove that Breckinridge had a good chance to win the Presidency by carrying both New York and Pennsylvania, and that their failure to support him would result simply in the Kentuckian becoming President of the Southern half of the Republic and Lincoln President of the North.[33] A Douglas organ, the Cincinnati *Enquirer* replied by accusing Bennett of accepting $25,000 to support Breckinridge.[34]

There ensued a further period of confusion and demoralisation in the anti-Republican camp. It was a summer of intense heat and excitement and the Republicans seemed to be having things all their own way.[35] Bennett swung back to the view that Breckinridge could not after all carry New York on his own. With the danger of defeat growing daily more imminent, the *Herald* in mid-August was arguing for a fusion ticket in every state with agreed proportions of Bell, Breckinridge and Douglas electors:

> That the conservative masses are ready to effect this union there can be no doubt, and the only obstacle in the way is the selfish claims of the professional politicans and party wire pullers. If these remain obstinate in disunion they will merely defeat their own aims, for it is evident that no one party clique among them can succeed by itself. Should they not unite for the common good they consign themselves to oblivion, and a scattered and divided people will remember them with a just indignation when the bitter fruits of their insane bickerings in this time of danger ripen for the country.[36]

Such arguments, combined with threats from various wealthy merchants to withold political funds unless fusion were effected, at last helped produce a result, for two days later the *Herald* reported that within the city itself the Tammany and Mozart Democratic

[33]*NYH* 27 July; 2 Aug 1860.
[34]*NYH* 29, 30 July; 3 Aug 1860.
[35]*NYH* 4 Aug 1860.
[36]*NYH* 16 Aug 1860.

factions had agreed a joint ticket.[37] At Syracuse Douglas and Bell men came together and the prospects for a statewide fusion suddenly seemed much brighter. It was announced that a state electoral ticket would be drawn up with twenty-three Douglas electors and ten for Bell on it. Bennett enthusiastically predicted that the state would give a 50,000 majority against Lincoln in November and hoped that the fusion movement would now become infectious across the Northern states. To cement the political marriage of convenience the *Herald* called for a great Union meeting to be held in the city: 'A long pull and a strong pull, a pull altogether, and away goes Old Abe clear up to the head waters of Salt river.'[38]

The mass meeting was held under the promotion of several wealthy merchants on 17 September with a crowd of 30,000 attending. But for all the *Herald*'s ponderous enthusiasm the Breckinridge men stayed stubbornly aloof from the Bell-Douglas fusion arrangements and the local Democratic politicians continued to abuse each other as 'traitors', 'bolters' and other choice terms.[39] On the national scene the two halves of the Democracy remained as far apart as ever. Douglas came to New York on 12 September as part of his wide ranging and vigorous campaign against disunionists. Bennett was unimpressed. To him every speech against Breckinridge was neither more nor less than a speech for Lincoln, and he persisted in blaming Douglas for playing dog in the manger by rejecting a truly national fusion.[40]

Finally in early October the efforts of the committee set up at the 17 September Union meeting bore fruit and the Breckinridge men did come into the fusion scheme. It was agreed between the supporters of each faction that in the event of an anti-Republican victory New York would give nineteen electoral votes to Douglas, ten to Bell and six to Breckinridge, estimated as representing their proportionate strengths in the state.[41] 'Union for the sake of the Union' was the slogan which

[37]*NYH* 18 Aug 1860. On the use of financial pressure to force fusion see Philip S. Foner, *Business and Slavery* (Chapel Hill 1941), ch 8.

[38]*NYH* 18, 21, 24 Aug; 1, 6, 11 Sept 1860. Bennett may lay some claim to having popularised the sobriquet 'Old Abe', though originally it seems to have been intended in a disparaging rather than affectionate sense.

[39]*NYH* 11, 16, 17, 18 Sept 1860. On the rancour between Breckinridge and Douglas men see Brummer, pp. 73-5.

[40]*NYH* 12, 13 Sept; 1 Oct 1860. To follow Douglas through the campaign of 1860 see R.W. Johannsen, *Stephen A. Douglas* (NY 1973), pp. 749-807.

[41]*NYH* 4 Oct 1860. Later the ratio was changed to 18 Douglas, 10 Bell and 7 Breckinridge electors. On the problems of negotiating the fusion see also Brummer, pp. 60-86, and Foner, ch 8.

the *Herald* suggested for this combined movement, in reply to Republican jeers that it was bound together by no consistent principle.[42] Greeley dubbed it the 'Confusion Ticket'.

This shell of unity contrasted sadly with the march through New York of a solid column of 'Wide Awakes' – young Republicans parading in ominously military dress and style. Even while trying to write down this demonstration Bennett had to admit its impressive appearance.[43] The disarray of their opponents was a gift the like of which the Republicans had scarcely dared hope for. One of their strongest campaign appeals was simply their claim to be the only organised party. And if the chance of Republican defeat looked slim in early September after they won the Maine elections, it became minute when they took Pennsylvania by a 32,000 majority in October.

In New Orleans the *Daily Crescent* gave the anxious warning to Southerners that 'New York is now our only reliance. . . . We must now look to . . .[NY] whose electoral vote is sufficient of itself to turn the scale, to throw herself into the breach, and avert the dire calamity to the South and the Union of the triumph of a party justly obnoxious to the people of one half of the Confederacy'.[44] Five days later, on 17 October, the *Herald* proclaimed 'Outside Calculations Exhausted – New York to the Rescue'. But Bennett could see that the hopes of 'conservative' Southerners were doomed to disappointment. He was becoming weary with the squabbles of the contending cliques and their failure to heed his warnings, and despaired of any grander scheme than the election of as many anti-Republican congressmen as possible.[45] Aspiring to a height worthy of Pontius Pilate he announced on 19 October that the rascalities and intrigues of the politicians 'stink in the nostrils of the country. . . . We abandon the vain effort to kindle a spark of patriotism among such materials. They are doomed. They are beyond reformation till thoroughly thrashed.'

For the remaining fortnight of the election campaign the *Herald* attacked Republicanism without remission, but its arguments were predominantly negative. It exhausted its rhetoric in trying to prove why Lincoln and his party should be defeated, but beyond that it could but hope that its own particular vision of 'Unionism' would be

[42]*NYH* 10, 15 Oct 1860.

[43]*NYH* 18, 27 Sept; 2, 4, Oct 1860. The *Herald* complained that in arresting counter-demonstrators the Metropolitan Police were actively aiding the Republican compaign.

[44]New Orleans *Daily Crescent* 13 Oct 1860.

[45]*NYH* 18, 19, 22 Oct 1860.

persuasive enough alone to swell the vote in New York State to victorious proportions despite the failure of the political leaders to offer anything more definite by way of a candidate. Would voters see in the fusion schemes a lofty submission of interest to principle or would they accept the Republican view that they were just the cynical products of bargain and sale politics? Paradoxically the *Herald* had pursued a policy of 'principles, not men' with such frankness and vehemence as to damage friend almost as much as foe.

'Much Ado About the Nigger'[46]: The Ideas and Arguments of the Campaign

We call heaven and earth to witness that if this Union perishes through the conduct of fanatics and fools, we at least are innocent. – *Herald* 29 January 1860

The political events of 1860 lost none of their excitement as relayed to the public by the press. It may have been crude and quaint by modern standards, but the press of 1860 was exploiting technological advances to the full in narrowing the interval between the occurence of any event and news of it getting to the public. The telegraph was busier than in any previous campaign in relaying reports and speeches. Bennett maintained his reputation as the foremost of newsgatherers, spending sums which other papers could only goggle at enviously. For instance he boasted that in one week of August 1860 the *Herald* spent a record $1,275 on special telegraphic despatches, exclusive of Associated Press reports which it paid for jointly with other papers. This was a good investment and one which Bennett could well afford since the sale of around 29 million copies of the *Herald* in 1859 had brought in receipts of $750,000. During 1860 the *Herald*'s estimated average daily circulation of 70,000 was often surpassed and in periods of intense excitement daily printings of over 90,000 and 100,000 became more common. Even if only three people read each copy of the *Herald* (a conservative estimate) Bennett's opinions were reaching perhaps a third of a million Americans daily.[47]

Early in 1860 Bennett despatched a team of newsmen to the different regions of the Union to report on conditions throughout the country. The avowed object of these enterprises was chiefly to counteract the image of the South popularised by the *Tribune* (whose

[46]*NYH* 10 May 1860.
[47]*NYH* 4 Jan; 16, 21, 30 Apr; 31 May; 17, 27 Sept; 12 Oct 1860.

editor had never been there).[48] The *Herald*'s picture of conditions as they 'really' were presented the South as prosperous and happy, with none of the slave-burnings, auctions and Uncle Tom sob stories beloved by the Republican press. As a result *Herald* reporters were generally persona grata in the South while *Tribune* reporters ventured into that region at their peril. Bennett was accused of favouring the South in order to safeguard the circulation of the *Herald* there. He indignantly denied this and was probably telling no less than the truth when he said that the *Herald* relied for its profits on its circulation in New York City and its hinterland alone and only broke even on Southern sales. That Bennett sympathised with the South in part out of a desire to gain access to news is rather more plausible. On the other side too Bennett did not allow politics to interfere too much with newsgathering. The *Herald* employed Republican reporters who might prove useful in tapping prominent politicians of their own party for information.[49] In all, the public had no lack of information (or misinformation) about the sectional quarrel.

The extremist speech was always more newsworthy than a duller but perhaps more representative one. While counselling moderation, the *Herald* gave full coverage to the speeches of abolitionists and fire-eaters and interpreted them editorially as even more extreme than the texts sometimes warranted in the interest of 'exposing' them to the public.[50] On at least one occasion it seems that Bennett deliberately falsified the date of a speech in order to enhance its sensational value.[51] A speech by a prominent anti-slavery man such as Seward, Sumner, Beecher, Garrison or Phillips would be reported in full in the *Herald*, and the editorial exegesis instructed the public on the satanic and revolutionary import thereof. It was small wonder that the *Herald* occasionally received praise or blame for being an 'abolition rag' because of the amount of anti-slavery material it disseminated in order to assail.[52] Bennett's view that 'anti-slavery harangues are synonomous with cant and drivel' apparently had no effect on his willingness to print them.[53]

In general, the tactical arguments which Bennett employed against the Republicans in 1860 were elaborations of those he had

[48]*NYH* 9 Mar 1860.
[49]*NYH* 18 Dec 1859; 27 Jan 1860.
[50]Bennett's defence of this policy *NYH* 9 Sept 1860.
[51]See NY *Journal of Commerce* 30 July 1860.
[52]*NYH* 7, 11 Jan; 11 Feb 1860.
[53]*NYH* 28 May 1860.

used in the fall election of 1859. Local questions such as the Sunday laws, for instance, continued to be bones of contention, and Bennett issued regular reminders that the Republican party was the party of Sabbath repression.[54] On the federal and state scenes the perennial cries of corruption sounded their familiar note.

Bennett was rarely happier than when inveighing against the venality of politicians of all parties, and in the spring a case of rank legislative corruption occured which the *Herald* called 'monstrous' and 'vile and unblushing' even by the standards of the day. The railroad interest at Albany, under the adept parliamentary captaincy of Thurlow Weed, 'bought' the legislature on a scale sufficient to pass a series of bills benefiting themselves at the public expense. The 'Gridiron bills' were so called because they aimed to criss-cross New York City with street railways. Bennett was livid that the leases for the railways, which rightly belonged to the city, had not been sold to the highest bidder on conditions that should have ensured the public the cheapest and most efficient service possible. On the contrary, some of them were of doubtful utility to the city and were parcelled out by what Bennett called with scant exaggeration 'wholesale robbery' to benefit a few interested parties on conditions which they wrote themselves. About $20 million was involved. The swindles were so brazen that Republican Governor Morgan used his veto power.[55] So well organised was the railroad lobby however that the bills were repassed over his objection. The gridiron scheme was legal despite the concentrated fury of the *Herald* against it.

Actually it was difficult to make a purely party issue out of the gridiron business. The chief culprits were Republicans (and the taint of his local party's corruption certainly did Seward no good at the Chicago Convention) but Democrats had also been involved. On the local level therefore the *Herald*'s electoral fight was for 'pure men' to conduct New York's affairs and against the re-election of all those state representatives who had accepted money in connection with the gridiron deals and with similar omnibus and ferry schemes.[56] The effect of the gridiron scandal was soon counterbalanced when in May Tammany Democrat Isaac V. Fowler absconded with $150,000 of Post Office funds and Republicans charged that Buchanan had set the

[54]*NYH* 16 Mar; 5, 8, 10, 13, 20, 30 June; 21, 22, 23, 28, 30 Sept; 5, 6 Oct 1860.

[55] See further Rawley, *Edwin D. Morgan,* pp. 98-101.

[56]*NYH* 9, 10, 12, 13, 15, 16, 19, 24, 27, 29, 31 Mar; 2, 9, 11, 12, 13, 15, 18, 29 Apr; 5, 9 May 1860. See also Brummer, pp. 32-6, 41-5. The Republicans in this legislature attacked the franchises of the New York Central Railroad, the chief source of Democratic party funds.

auditors on his trail as part of the general proscription against Douglas men.

On the national level the Chicago platform specifically denounced Democratic corruption, and the nomination of 'Honest Abe' was a powerful prop to the Republican claim to be the party of clean government. During 1860 the Administration was badly damaged by the exposure of a number of jobbing contracts in congress, chiefly involving government printing and army and naval supplies.[57] Obviously this was a godsend to the Republican campaign effort and they went to work in congress to improve the opportunity. The Covode Committee was set up to give administrative scandals a public airing. Bennett took up the gauntlet immediately and rushed to defend Buchanan's integrity, deeming the President 'above all praise' for his forbearance under the 'disgraceful' attacks of his opponents.

Bennett toiled to convince the public that the Committee's findings amounted to nothing, but the worst he could find to say about the Republicans was in effect that they were as corrupt as the Democrats and that their charges, even if true, were 'ill timed'. It might have been easier for Bennett to convince the public that the Covode Committee was wasting public time and lowering the country's prestige abroad if he had devoted less space in the *Herald* to slanging the Republicans for corruption.

The testimony heard by the Committee became embarrassing. In June Congress passed a vote of censure on Buchanan. The *Herald* claimed that this was done from base motives and was constitutionally absurd. Nevertheless the Republicans realised the effect their vote could produce on the popular mind, and Bennett complained that the President needed more alert advisers to fight Republican fire with fire.[58] Buchanan simultaneously came to the same conclusion and in his hour of need took up his pen to appeal to Bennett:

> Private and Confidential
> Washington 18 June 1860
>
> My dear Sir,
>
>   I thought I never should have occasion to appeal to you on any public subject and knew if I did I could not swerve you from your independent course. I therefore now only ask you as a personal

[57]For background see Nichols, *Disruption,* pp. 182-201; and David E. Meerse, 'Buchanan, Corruption and the Election of 1860', *Civil War History,* XII (1966), 116-31, which stresses the importance of corruption as a campaign issue.

[58]*NYH* 5, 7, 9, 21 Feb; 31 Mar; 9, 14, 20, 30 Apr; 29 May; 1, 3, 16, 19, 26, 28 June 1860.

friend to take the trouble of examining yourself the proceedings of the Covode Committee and the reports of the majority and minority, and then to do me what you may deem to be justice. That Committee were engaged in secret conclave for nearly three months in examining every man, ex parte, who from disappointment or personal malignity would cast a shade upon the character of the Executive. If this dragooning can exist, the Presidential office would be unworthy of the acceptance of a gentleman.

In performing my duties I have endeavoured to be not only pure but unsuspected. I have never had any concern with awarding contracts . . . I have ever detested all jobs and no man at any period of my life has ever approached me on such a subject. .

I shall send a message to the House in a few days on the violation of the Constitution involved in the vote of censure and in the appointment and proceedings of the Covode Committee. I am glad to perceive from the *Herald* that you agree with me on the Constitutional question. I shall endeavour to send you a copy in advance.[59]

The *Herald* hardly needed encouragement and continued its course of sturdily defending Buchanan against Republican anger, which was doubly concentrated when the President vetoed their Pacific Railroad and Homestead bills. It came as a great relief to the friends of the Administration when Congress dispersed late in June and Buchanan was left, in Bennett's euphemistic phrase, 'above party'.[60]

The Union and slavery were of course the main issues in the campaign and Bennett addressed himself to them not simply as political problems but as questions embracing the whole of American social philosophy. Crude, partisan, contradictory his editorials often were, but they cleverly wove a myriad of issues into the one overriding cause of defeating Republican political control of the Union.

The *Herald*'s dominant theme was that Republican victory at the polls in November would mean not just a change of government but the destruction of the conservative federal experiment begun in 1787 and based on a community of interests between the states. In February, while the Democracy was yet an entity, Bennett advised its leaders that disputes over the legalities of popular sovereignty were a waste of time and exhorted them to face the issues as he saw them:

[59]*The Works of James Buchanan,* ed. J.B. Moore, vol. X, p. 431.

[60]For Bennett's view of the 'disgraceful record' of the first session of the 36th Congress see *NYH* 27 June 1860. The *Herald* dismissed the Railroad bill as a stockjobbing operation and the Homestead bill as a piece of 'red republican socialism'. Neither had much appeal in the metropolis.

WONDERFUL SURGICAL OPERATION,
PERFORMED BY DOCT. LINCOLN ON THE POLITICAL CHANG AND ENG.

POLITICAL CHANG, J. B———N.
POLITICAL ENG, J. G. B———TT.

A few days before the election of 1860 this cartoon suggested that
Lincoln, wielding the sword 'vox populi', would discomfit the unholy
alliance of Bennett and Buchanan. (Note Bennett's talons).
(From *Vanity Fair*, November 1860).

This is revolution. This is civil war... This is the inauguration of the reign of fanaticism and frenzy. It will sweep over this Union like a whirlwind over a prairie on fire, scattering flames and bloodshed in every quarter, destroying property in the North as well as the South, and breaking up every bond of the Union, every family tie, every hope of leaving our present inheritance to our children. Let the democratic Senators and the party look the evil and the danger square in the face, and throwing overboard such foolish hairsplitters as Douglas and [Jefferson] Davis, take up the defence of the conservative cause and save the country from the ruin in which the revolutionary black republicans would involve it.[61]

Bennett did not rely on generalised pictures of ruin alone. Priding the *Herald* as guardian and mouthpiece of American material progress, he unceasingly appealed to New Yorkers in the way he judged most effective; namely to their pockets.

The files of the *Herald* for 1860 constitute a sustained appeal to the patriotism and self interest of the merchants and manufacturers of the North-East to exert themselves to 'suppress' the Republican anti-slavery 'fanaticism'. Urgency was given to these appeals by the fact that Southern purchasers were already blacklisting and boycotting Northern firms who endorsed or were suspected of endorsing anti-slavery views. Bennett hopefully declared in March that New England was 'almost ruined' by this non-intercourse policy, and predicted the same sad fate for New York unless her prominent men became active in the fight against Sewardism. Bennett did not write one word in rebuke of Southern threats and refusals to honour debts to Northern firms, but regarded such occurrences as the 'legitimate fruits' of anti-slavery agitation, and found assaults on Northerners in the South 'understandable' and sorely provoked. Towards the climax of the contest Bennett was talking about Southern secession causing an immediate financial panic which would prelude the whole North becoming a 'waste, howling wilderness'. As for the metropolis itself 'the shipping of New York would rot in the docks and the grass would grow in its streets. Real estate, now so valuable, would be reduced to ten per cent of its value.'[62] Unemployment and rioting would finish the city as a financial centre.

Bennett's premise for predicting this anarchic twilight was his belief in the economic superiority of the South. His view of the situation, which he argued at length and with a mass of impressive sounding

[61]*NYH* 14 Feb 1860.
[62]*NYH* 30 Oct 1860.

statistics, was basically as follows: the South, with its beneficial labour system, was the producer of the nation's 'real wealth' in the form of raw cotton. The North lived only by monopolising the carrying trade for that commodity and providing the entrepreneurial services involved in shipping and marketing cotton. It also depended on the South for the sale of its manufactures. Wedded to the concept of 'irrepressible harmony' between the sectional economies, Bennett did not see how the North could prosper if the South became closed and hostile territory. (By 'the South' he meant all fifteen slave states and assumed that a Southern nation would possess Washington D.C. with the apparatus and prestige of the old government.) He accepted implicitly the argument that only the existence of the stable Southern market had enabled the North to recover from the panic of 1857. That lifeline would no longer be available in the event of secession.

Moreover, Bennett argued that the South could easily adapt itself to independence and in fact flourish, for the industrial nations of Europe had an insatiable demand for cotton and would rally to protect their source of supply. The people of the North, Bennett was convinced, had come to take economic growth for granted as the natural order of things. Their faith might be rudely shattered if the Union were sundered and they would receive a lesson in the suicidal folly of sacrificing one's own best interests for the satisfaction of interfering in somebody else's business.[63]

Arguing thus, Bennett was crossing swords with the Republican journals which with their own statistics held up the South to their readers as an economically contemptible region whose chief product was political brag and bluster. At worst Bennett's views were a deliberately incendiary device to defeat the Republicans by threatening financial panic and civil war if they won. At best they were a reminder that the Union was an economic whole in which all ought to be mindful of each other's interest and prosperity. Interlaced with the *Herald*'s assertions that trade and prosperity could not be reconciled with a government hostile to the labour system of one half of the Union were arguments that ideologically and socially, as well as materially, the old Union could not survive Republican victory.

For instance when a poorly constructed factory collapsed at Lawrence, Massachusetts, in January 1860 killing 200 operatives,

[63]*NYH* 4, 6, 9, 9, 10, 12, 16, 18, 19, 21, 22, 23, 27-30 Jan; 2, 4, 8, 13, 14, 15, 18, 25, 28 Feb; 9, 13, 14, 23, 24, 26, 27, 28, 29, 31 Mar; 1, 2, 3, 4, 6, 7, 10, 12, 14, 25, 27, 29 Apr; 5, 6, 7, 9, 12, 26, 28 May; 2, 5, 11, 14, 26 June; 27, 29 July; 1, 14, 20, 21, 22, 24, 27, 28, 29, 30, 31 Aug; 3, 6, 13, 15, 16, 18, 19, 24, 25, 28, 29 Sept; 1, 3, 4, 6, 7, 8, 11, 16, 17, 18, 19, 23-31 Oct; 1, 3, 4, 5, 6 Nov 1860.

Bennett immediately dubbed it the 'Lawrence Massacre', the name given by the Republican press to the sacking of the Free State capital of Kansas by border ruffians in 1856. To improve the counterpoint he laid responsibility for the 'appalling and reckless loss of lives' involved on the same men who had financed the freesoil emigration to Kansas, to prove that the obverse of Boston philanthropy was a callous disregard for not only the jobs but the very lives of white working people. The well cared for Negroes of the South, Bennett reminded readers, were not subject to being massacred by their employers in this way. 'Northern White Slaves and Southern Black Ones' was a familiar theme of *Herald* homilies, and white labourers were told that Republicans 'deify the nigger and oppose both the interests and the liberties of the poor working man with a skin coloured like their own'. White workers should realise that Republican doctrines degraded them and that their exploitation at the hands of capitalists was far worse than that suffered by the Southern Negro. (Perhaps the *Herald*'s argument would have had more persuasive power had it omitted the fatuous contention that the South suffered fewer strikes than the North because of the better understanding between capital and labour there.)[64]

Yet with a dexterous shift of emphasis from Republican practice to principle Bennett could appeal to capitalists and employers in demonstrating that the revolutionary tendencies implicit in the party doctrine would not be confined to one region. If Negroes were entitled to social equality could not the argument be applied equally to labour and women? 'The moment the dogma that all men are equal is diverted from a political to a social application, from that moment the descent to anarchy begins. . . other wrongs take it up and the tide of sophistry runs its course of riot and ruin.'[65]

With similar versatility he presented the Republicans as the party not only of atheism, infidelity and free love[66] but of religious extremism as well.

'Ignorance and fanaticism', by which Bennett meant anti-slavery sentiment, he regarded as an atavism confined mostly to rural areas; a relic of New England puritanism, 'characterized with all the self sanctification, the idiosyncrasy and the intolerance of that peculiar sect'. In the towns, where the New York *Herald* was read, said the editor, error could be combated with truth. This fact, together with the

[64]*NYH* 12, 16, 18 Jan; 2, 4, 7, 29 Mar 1860.
[65]*NYH* 18 Feb 1860.
[66]*NYH* 12 Oct 1860.

influence of trade with the South, made urban opinion more 'progressive', i.e. tolerant and even sympathetic towards slavery.[67] He often treated his readers to potted histories of the New England settlements, stressing that bigotry and persecution were things that the rest of America had outgrown. Announcing the 'Demoralizing Effect of Abolitionism upon the Clergy' he strove to show that by preaching against slavery New England ministers were creating an unchristian hostility to Southern white men and shamefully neglecting the spiritual needs of their own flocks. With so much vice in the metropolis, why was it necessary to go denouncing the supposed sins of people hundreds of miles away? Against Republican allegations of the barbarism of the South Bennett set down the delights of free society as reported in the columns of his newspaper; freedom to murder, rob, defraud, commit adultery and perpetuate every kind of social evil coincident with urban life. He found more 'true religion' on the Southern plantations than among the 'New England Pharisees' who in his view 'believing in the Almighty Nigger. . . cease to believe in Almighty God'.[68]

Bennett's hostility to Republicanism as a disruptive creed is comparable to the revulsion which conservatives of a later generation manifested towards communism. The *Herald* filled many editorial columns with elaborate historical arguments from sixteenth and seventeenth century European history, aiming to show that the Republicans were bent on introducing into America an essentially foreign attitude to the relationship of religion and government. No abolitionist could have exceeded Bennett's enthusiasm for depicting the Republicans as a 'one idea party'. Their victory, he asserted, would create a state church under which opinions would be persecuted.[69] He identified 'tolerance' with the freedom to express pro-slavery sentiments and 'intolerance' with any criticism of a man's right to own a slave.

In his seductive logic the issue of the campaign resolved itself into one of self-government (for white men):

> If we today strike a blow at the rights of the Southern States, because we believe to be a moral and social evil what they sustain as the scheme of society best adapted to the happiness and welfare of all, the next step will be to apply the same pride of opinion to some among ourselves, and by insisting upon

[67]*NYH* 4 Apr 1860.
[68]*NYH* 1, 25, 29 Apr; 6, 9, 10 May; 26 Sept; 14 Oct 1860.
[69]*NYH* 1, 27 Aug; 21, 23, 25, 27,30 Sept 1860.

subjecting them to the rule of some other dogma, consummate forever the ruin of the institutions our fathers established in the spirit of fraternity, and which we shall have converted into instruments of tyranny. It is the weakness and the misfortune of humanity that no tyrant is so terrible as the one that is convinced that he alone is acting from motives of the highest morality. . . hence the greater danger of black republican rule.[70]

Bennett believed, as did Lincoln, that at bottom of all the legal arguments lay the single issue of whether slavery was right or wrong.[71] All else flowed from the initial assumption on this point. Bennett of course took the opposite view from Lincoln, for his ground was that 'the South hold, and hold rightly, that the institution of domestic servitude for the African race among them is neither an evil nor a crime'.[72]

The editor saw clearly that the sectional quarrel could only be finally 'settled' if the South were to concede that slavery was wrong and ought to be abolished, or preferably when the North was persuaded that slavery was right and good. Regarding slavery as constitutionally justified and morally beneficial, he made no concessions whatever to anti-slavery opinion. He could not find in it any principle worthy of respect and would not believe otherwise than that material interests alone had dictated the original abolition of slavery within the Northern states. There could be no mistaking the fact that he looked hopefully toward the time when slavery would be legal in all the states, arguing that humanity would compel the North to cast off its eccentric attachment to the anti-slavery cause and re-enslave the degraded and criminal free blacks in their midst.[73]

Free Negroes were the subjects of an important debate in New York this election year, because at the same time that citizens balloted for the Presidency they would be asked to decide on the question of franchise extension. Specifically they were to be asked whether the $250 property qualification for free black voters under the state constitution should be abolished. Bennett could not believe that enough white men could be found in the state, even Republicans, who would willingly commit an act of 'self degradation' by voting for the

[70]*NYH* 18 Sept 1860.

[71]See Lincoln to A.H. Stephens in Basler, *Collected Works of Abraham Lincoln*, vol. IV, pp. 146-60.

[72]*NYH* 19 Oct 1860.

[73]*NYH* 2, 6, 9, 13, 16, 19, 21, 24, 26, 27, 28, 29 Jan; 6, 7, 8, 12, 16, 18, 24, 29 Feb; 1, 2, 4, 7, 9, 12, 26, 28, 29 Mar; 1, 3, 4, 12, 27 Apr; 2 May; 13, 31 July; 1 Aug; 3, 8, 9, 10, 14, 19 Sept; 1, 18, 28, 31 Oct; 1, 3, 5, 6 Nov 1860.

amendment. The Republican authors of the bill, he said, were pursuing 'an exaggerated notion of individual rights' in seeking racial equality, which could only be disastrous in its practical results. This was not the full extent of Republican sins either: 'The revolutionists blasphemously set themselves up as the vicegerents of God upon earth, and proclaim the intention of doing what the Creator, in his infinite wisdom, failed to do — and that is, to make the blacks and whites equals.'[74]

Bennett argued that blacks with the right to vote would become tools in the hands of Republican politicians (just as immigrants in the city were to Democratic ward heelers). Anyone who read the *Herald* knew by rote that to be a free Negro was to be by definition thriftless, brutal and demoralised. Virtually any day's edition could be relied upon to demonstrate the murderous and criminal nature of fugitive slaves, the ignorance and squalor of free Negroes in the North, or else to carry a long discourse on how emancipation had ruined both the economy of the British West Indies and the blacks for work. Of more immediate service were editorials threatening that servile insurrection and civil war in the South, such as Republicanism must inevitably produce, would spill over into the North, which would become infested with bands of vicious and predatory Negroes. Did the Republicans realise what they were starting if they tampered with a system which imposed some kind of order on four million blacks? 'Would the liberation of a horde of ignorant and lawless negroes benefit the North, or increase its prosperity and contentment?' What did they propose to do with them once free? Were they such hypocrites as to advocate the gift to Southern Negroes of civil rights which were denied free blacks in the Northern states?[75]

There was no haggling about the legal niceties of slavery in the territories to be found in the *Herald* during 1860.[76] Bennett was under no illusions that Republican rule would not mean an end to slavery sooner or later, and his warning against Republican beliefs cut straight to the heart:

> If slavery must be excluded from the Territories because it is an evil and a crime, the same reasons will apply to its exclusion from the states. If the moral sentiment of men must make war upon it in one place, it must do so in all places. Time and place make no excuse for palliating war against a moral evil or a social

[74]*NYH* 8, 19 Sept; 31 Oct 1860.

[75]*NYH* 9 Jan 1860.

[76]*NYH* 28 Aug 1860, for a condemnation of politicians for talking too much about the subject.

crime. If it is right at one time and in one place, it is right in all. This is the only logical result of the black republican creed, and to this it must come at last.[77]

Hence his contempt for Republican professions of conservatism. How, he asked, could a revolutionary object be pursued by conservative means? To accept that slavery should be put 'in the course of ultimate extinction' was to accept its condemnation as an evil by a hostile federal government. To yield this principle was for the South to yield everything. The *Herald* made it clear that the issue between the Republicans and the South was no imaginary misunderstanding. The irrepressible conflict would inevitably mean bloodshed.[78]

Suppose Lincoln were personally kindly disposed towards Southerners. This could not alter the fact, in Bennett's view, that Republican party rule would mean an assault on their property. The Republicans would no doubt fill vacancies in the Supreme Court with their own men, which would be but the prelude to a reversal of the Dred Scott decision and the prohibition of slavery in the western territories by congress.

The Supreme Court might also tamper with the inter-state slave trade. Where would the South be if the federal armed forces patrolled the borders of the slave states and tried to suppress free commerce in Negroes? Federal custom houses, forts, navy yards and arsenals manned by Republican appointees would be anti-slavery cells in the very bowels of the cotton kingdom. With impunity they would become main line terminals on the underground railroad for fugitive slaves. An anti-slavery regime in the District of Columbia would infect Virginia and Maryland. Most of all, too, there were the federal post offices in the Southern states. No slaveholder could be so fond as not to believe that Republican control of the post offices would mean at least the toleration of abolitionist literature, perhaps its active encouragement. If a slave insurrection occurred in the South as a result of this activity (as readers of the *Herald* knew inevitably it would), would a Republican government be in haste to send federal troops to suppress it? On the contrary, Bennett was confident that a Lincoln administration would encourage the non-slaveholding whites to active hostility against the slaveowners.[79]

These were the bogeys which Bennett conjured up to scare the conservative into voting against the Republicans. Where these

[77]*NYH* 19 Oct 1860.

[78]*NYH* 14 Aug; 18 Oct 1860.

[79]*NYH* 1 Aug; 17, 19 Sept; 28 Oct 1860.

editorials were read in the South they served to excite passions and strengthen the impression that the existence of slavery in the Southern states and Republican rule at Washington were incompatible. In South Carolina the disunionist Charleston *Mercury* jubilantly reprinted *Herald* leaders on its front page as evidence of Northern impotency to resist secession.[80] They helped create a situation (if Southerners needed any help) in which the South would look extremely foolish if it were to 'climb down' and accept Lincoln's election calmly. On the other hand Bennett's occasional changes of mind, previously observed, on how much harm Lincoln could do in practice, had the tendency to discredit all his arguments as mere partisan contrivances intended to frighten the nervous.[81] If the Republicans were such a menace to slavery and the Union, why were they at the same time so contemptibly weak that they were about to break up? Bennett was too fertile in arguments against the opposition for the good of his own consistency.

This anomaly comes out clearly in Bennett's attitude to the disunion issue. The *Herald* claimed to be the staunchest of Union papers, and none was more active in trying to arouse the North from its apparent apathy, even levity, regarding Southern threats of disunion. Nobody could accuse the *Herald* of not heeding earnest Southern warnings that secession would follow a Republican victory or of failing to alert its readers to the seriousness of the situation. It was willing and eager to do so.[82] Yet by treating the secession of the Southern states as a foregone conclusion if Lincoln were elected, the *Herald* helped to give the idea currency and respectability. While piously deprecating the more violent utterances of the fire-eaters Bennett always argued from the assumption that the South would be quite justified in refusing to accept tamely an 'abolition victory' at the polls.[83]

Bennett took no part in the debate on the legality of secession. To him the question of theoretical right was extremely barren, 'but the fact of the Southern States believing it is sufficient for their action, and practically amounts to the same thing as if it were a principle of our

---

[80]*Charleston Mercury* 28, 30 July; 15, 17, 20 Aug; 8, 13, 19, 28 Sept; 12 Oct; 12, 21 Nov 1860.

[81] See e.g. NY *Courier & Enquirer* 31 July 1860: 'The *Herald's* disunion thunder is ... powerless to frighten the people of the North.' For Webb's angry protests at the *Herald's* persistent misrepresentation of the Republicans see *ibid.*, 31 May; 18, 22, 24 Aug; 20 Sept; 24, 27 Oct; 1 Nov 1860.

[82]*NYH* 23, 31 Oct are representative samples. The *Herald* habitually carried headlines like 'The Progress of the Revolution'.

[83]*NYH* 9 Aug; 11 Oct 1860 are fair samples.

government and beyond dispute. For no power on earth can keep the Southern States in the Union against their will, and when it ceases to be their interest to remain the Union is but a rope of sand. . . As for coercion, it is madness to think of it.'[84]

Bennett was to be proved right about the shape of events and the Republicans who ignored or laughed at the possibility of secession and civil war wrong. For these predictions Bennett could (and did) claim credit as a superior prophet. The trouble was that the *Herald*'s 'conservatism' tended to be dangerously intemperate. So often did Bennett reveal to his readers the jack-in-the-box of horrors that would follow Lincoln's election that it seems possible that his words of doom had a numbing effect. Like an old man wearing sandwich boards proclaiming the end of the world, the *Herald* was noticed by everybody but heeded only by the already converted: it seemed to be using the bugbear of disunion to stampede voters into another four years of inept and turbulent Democratic rule. Though this rule might be essentially negative, it carried in its belly the threat of conceding every demand of the South by making slavery national. There was no mistaking that this was what the *Herald* would regard as a 'settlement' of the question.

Bennett relied on trying to threaten and bully Northerners out of their anti-slavery feelings. He warned them that the South would not accept the Union unconditionally, yet this is exactly what he was asking Northerners themselves to do. Like the true cynic he put much faith in rational appeals to the material interests of the North. It was not so much, perhaps, that he underestimated the popularity of anti-slavery, but that he did not understand the power of threats to make people stiffen in defensive attitudes. Many Northerners, not abolitionists, nevertheless disliked slavery and may have resented the *Herald*'s opinion that they had not as much constitutional right to express that dislike as Southerners had to own slaves.

It is questionable how far people in the North enjoyed being told constantly that their jobs and livelihood depended on the good will of the slaveholding South, or that *they* must give over opposition to slavery or suffer for it economically, or that an end to Democratic rule must mean resistance and bloodshed. All Bennett's lurid portrayals of

[84]*NYH* 11, 28 Oct 1860. Interestingly, this very phrase about the Union becoming 'a rope of sand' occurs in Buchanan's fourth annual message of December 1860. Yet when Yancey, the 'Prince of fire-eaters' came to New York and defended the right of secession at the Cooper Institute, the *Herald* commented that 'were this principle recognized and acted on, we might soon fall into the disorganized condition of Mexico'. — *NYH* 11 Oct 1860.

servile insurrection and universal mayhem could easily sound like the inflated rhetorical bluster of a graceless loser. Perhaps the worst weakness of sensationalist journalism is that it lives on crises as its daily bread and deals in superlatives as a matter of course. It has no reserve vocabulary when a real emergency arises. One may speculate that Bennett's psychologically crude fulminations may have produced an effect quite the opposite of what he intended, namely to make Northerners refuse to be browbeaten into accepting Southern political domination of the Union under intimidation. It would be very interesting to know, as a historical curiosity, how many Northern voters were strengthened in their Republicanism or even converted to it by reading the *New York Herald.*

The Issue Joined

On the day before the election Bennett told voters in effect: if you believe slavery and freedom cannot coexist, if you favour race war, revolution, and treating free Negroes in the North on terms of equality, then vote Republican.[85] On election day, 6 November, the *Herald* carried nearly two pages of captions and editorials, summed up by the exhortation 'New York to the Rescue – One Day for the Union and the Constitution'. The message was repeated in every column: vote for the Union by voting against Lincoln and bringing white men down to a level with Negroes. Special appeals, brief and trenchant, were made to women to influence their husbands, to labourers, mechanics, frequenters of the watering places, builders and shoemakers, soldiers and sailors, tailors; carriage makers, immigrants, and to almost every trade, class and interest in the metropolis to preserve the prosperity which depended on the maintenance of the old Union. Every individual was asked to ponder what he had to gain by the destruction of the Southern labour system, and what to lose. Even if he had realised defeat was inevitable, Bennett was going to go down with the flag flying.

Meanwhile on the Republican side Greeley announced jubilantly to *Tribune* readers that 'The battle of Freedom is to be won or lost in our City and its suburbs. . . Unless Fusion can go out of this City and Brooklyn Forty Thousand ahead, it is dead as Julius Caesar.'[86] More sober was Raymond in the *Times,* who on election day assured voters that the Republican party 'is eminently national and conservative'

[85]*NYH* 5 Nov 1860.
[86]NY *Daily Tribune* 5 Nov 1860.

despite what its enemies might say. What was more, Raymond gave expression to the argument which caught Bennett in his weakest spot, and which the divided state of the anti-Republican forces prevented him from answering: 'If the defeat of LINCOLN would end the contest, or put the matter in the way of a peaceful solution; — if it would elect anybody else or settle the principles and policy of the Administration, there would be some show of excuse for pressing it with so much zeal.'[87]

New York's electoral vote might well be decisive in the election. Without that block of thirty-five votes in the electoral college, Lincoln's chance of gaining a clear right to the Presidency would be dim. If it was cast against him the election might well go into the House. What would happen there? Bennett wouldn't exactly say. Perhaps Bell would be elected, perhaps not. What the *Herald* did not remind its readers of was its own threat, made the previous March, that what had been done over the speakership contest could be repeated for the Presidency.[88] Whether or not voters remembered this promise of blatant obstructionism, the danger was plain that the defeat of Lincoln would lead not to a settlement of the sectional problem but quite the reverse — a protracted, vicious and disturbing quarrel in congress that might easily end in civil war. Working against Bennett's eloquent appeals to the uncommitted was the strong argument that to vote for Lincoln was to vote for something definite, while to vote against him might appear an invitation to more party wrangling and strife.

Next day, 7 November, the *Herald* sold 105,840 copies to readers anxious to get all the results.[89] The *Tribune* by contrast sold 72,000 copies [90] This was a rough indication of the proportionate disparity of Fusion and Republican strength within the city, for the Fusion ticket won there by 62,328 votes against 33,007 for Lincoln.[91] More interesting was the number of people in the city who evidently agreed with Bennett about the Negro suffrage amendment, which if successful would have raised the number of black voters from three or four hundred to nearly 10,000.[92] By a crushing majority of 37,471 to

[87]NY *Times* 6 Nov 1860.

[88]*NYH* 15 Mar 1860.

[89]*NYH* 9 Nov 1860.

[90]NY *Daily Tribune* 8 Nov 1860.

[91]*Ibid.*

[92]*NYH* 18 Sept 1860. The Negro suffrage amendment is discussed in Charles Z. Lincoln, *The Constitutional History of New York* (Rochester 1906), vol. 2, pp. 232-3.

1,640 the proposed amendment to the state constitution was defeated. Bennett claimed that this showed that the Republicans were hypocrites towards the Negro, because over 30,000 of those who voted for Lincoln had not voted for the social elevation of the black man.[93] It certainly did show that more than half the voters of New York City didn't care about the subject at all, and of those who did only a tiny fraction were in favour of Negro manhood suffrage.The story was much the same in the state as a whole. In the nineteen counties where the amendment was approved it was by majorities smaller than those won by the Republican ticket. Overall the amendment was defeated by a 140,000 majority and 30,000 more votes were cast against it than were cast for the Fusion ticket in the state.

At the time this was just a footnote to the presidential result. New York City was safe for the Fusion forces, which was no surprise. It was no surprise either that the election had made Abraham Lincoln President-elect of the United States. The news that New York State had gone Republican by a majority of over 50,000 over all opponents had brought rejoicing to Springfield on election night. Even in the counties where they were in a minority the Republicans had nearly everywhere increased their vote in the state over Fremont's 1856 total. (The size of the Fusion majority in the city should not obscure the fact that this was true there also). The totals in the state were:[94]

Lincoln 353,804
Fusion 303,329

In other words New York had contributed nearly one fifth of Lincoln's share of the popular vote, all of which came from Northern or border states. More important, New York's electoral vote of 35 was Lincoln's and was included in his eventual total of 180, as against a combined national total of 123 for his opponents. If those 35 votes had gone the other way Lincoln would have had only 145 to a total of 158 shared among his opponents and the election would have gone into the House. With New York in his pocket Lincoln's position was clear and unassailable, and made victory look easier than it was.

Bennett could reflect that in a total vote of over 660,000 in New York State it would have needed the change of less than 30,000 votes

[93]*NYH* 9 No 1860. A recent discussion is Phyllis F. Field, 'Republicans and Black Suffrage in New York State: The Grass Roots Response', *Civil War History,* 21 (1975), 136-47.

[94]These figures and those in the paragraphs above are based on the computations of the *Herald* and the *Tribune.* See also Brummer, pp. 97-8, and the *American Annual Cyclopedia for 1861.* For an excellent summary of New York's role in the election see Milledge L. Bonham, 'New York and the Election of 1860'.

to have given the state to the Fusionists and the Presidency to someone other than Lincoln as a consequence. Doubtless the editor would not have agreed with the Douglas party manager, August Belmont, who attributed the Democracy's loss of the crucial votes to the damage caused by the corruption of the Buchanan administration.[95] Bennett did not stop to ponder the 'ifs' of the election, including the 'if' of what his paper might have accomplished to change those 30,000 votes if it had consistently championed Douglas from an early date. Given the editor's pro-slavery views and his venal devotion to Buchanan that had never been a possibility. Now the weakness of the Administration Democrats in the North had been fully revealed and the party defeated as a result. On the day after the election Bennett announced to his readers that 'The great battle has been fought and lost'.[96]

[95]Belmont to John M. Forsyth 22 Nov; 19 Dec 1860, quoted by David E. Meerse, 'Buchanan, Corruption, and the Election of 1860'.

[96]*NYH* 7 Nov 1860.

6

THE SECESSION WINTER, 1860-1

> We do the *Herald* the justice to say, that it has come nearer realizing the present condition of the States, and their future prospects, than any other journal North of the line. —
> Charleston *Mercury,* 18 December 1860

> An editorial ISHMAEL, his hand raised against every man, and every man's hand raised against him. – Utica *Morning Herald and Daily Gazette* on Bennett, 14 December 1860

From the Election to the Secession of South Carolina: November – December 1860

In the five months between Lincoln's election and the outbreak of civil war in April 1861, the *Herald*'s voice was for conciliation of the South to preserve the Union, but finally for disunion rather than bloodshed. Its fluctuating editorial attitudes evidenced the chronic uncertainty which prevailed in the North at this time.[1]

There was a note of humility unusual in the columns of the *Herald* once the election results were in, for it came oddly to hear it advise 'Let us now drop politics'.[2] Was this an admission that all the dire things the paper had been saying about the consequences of Republican victory had been mere campaign nonsense after all, to be forgotten now until the next election? On the face of things it seemed that Bennett and the other Northern foes of the victorious party were going to acquiesce in Republican rule with what grace they could muster. But could the excitement so recently and heedlessly raised be so easily dismissed? What would the reaction be in the South?

Within a few days the *Herald* was reporting that revolutionary excitement was gathering momentum in Dixie in response, as Bennett

---

[1]There is no point in attempting to list here even a significant portion of the vast literature dealing with the secession crisis. Of obvious relevance to this study are the two compendiums of contemporary press opinion in Howard C. Perkins, *Northern Editorials on Secession* (2 vols, NY 1942), and Dwight L. Dumond ed., *Southern Editorials on Secession* (NY 1931). Although they are no substitute for first-hand study of the newspaper files these works do provide the essential context in which the disputes of the big New York dailies were set. Still in many ways the best study available of Northern attitudes is Kenneth M. Stampp, *And the War Came* (Chicago 1950).

[2]*NYH* 7 Nov 1860.

put it, to the revolutionary declaration of hostility to slavery by the North at the polls. The paper also became more outspoken on the 'undeniable right' of the 'gallant and chivalrous South' to secede than it had been before the election.[3] Bennett warned Northern readers that the people of the 'sovereign state' of South Carolina were even more united than during the Nullification crisis of 1832. Federal officials and representatives from the state were already resigning their places, and even the 'conservatives' and non-slaveholders there were ardently in favour of secession.

The *Herald* remained cautiously unionist though. Even if it was obvious that the Palmetto State was bent on leaving the Union, Bennett hoped that it would delay what he regarded as the just exercise of its rights until the North had had the opportunity to show its repentance. He counselled that the Carolinians' best course was to refrain from violent acts and await a conservative reaction in the North which the *Herald* would do its best to encourage. To this end the paper called on the merchants and working men of New York City to hold a meeting to assure the South that they had no intention of taking part in an abolition crusade against it.[4] Meanwhile the *Herald* re-iterated that the federal government must 'do nothing in the way of coercion. That will ruin everything. . . Coercion, if it were possible, is out of the question.'[5]

At this time Greeley's *Daily Tribune* was also dismissing the idea of coercion to compel a state to remain in the Union against its will. On 9 November it declared that 'Whenever a considerable section of our Union shall deliberately resolve to go out, we shall resist all coercive measures designed to keep it in. We hope never to live in a republic whereof one section is pinned to the residue by Bayonets.' This was not quite the cheerful acquiescence in secession that it seemed. Greeley had reserve clauses. To him 'deliberately resolve' meant the due organisation of a thorough plebiscite to test majority opinion on secession in the South, not the rash action of a state legislature called into extra session; and he made it clear that he was not convinced that such a plebiscite would show a majority for disunion in any state except South Carolina: 'The measures now being inaugurated by the Cotton States with a view (apparently) to Secession, seem to us destitute of gravity and legitimate force.'[6]

[3]*NYH* 11-16 Nov 1860.

[4]*NYH* 10, 12, 13, 14, 17, 24 Nov 1860.

[5]*NYH* 8, 9, 15, 23 Nov 1860.

[6]NY *Daily Tribune* 9, 10 Nov 1860. There is a nice little controversy among historians as to whether Greeley meant what he said. It may be followed in Thomas N.

Where Bennett differed from Greeley at this stage was in his taking the Southern threats far more seriously, (it was highly significant that the *Herald* carried more Southern news than any of its Republican contemporaries) and in his opinion that the situation required urgent concessions from the North. Greeley's statement lent itself to misinterpretation, and Bennett himself was largely responsible for propagating the view that the *Tribune* editor was flippantly encouraging dissolution of the Union.[7]

Bennett was confident that some finite measure of appeasement would suffice to satisfy the South within the Union, and that this was a rational game of political bargain. The merchants of New York, to whom he so often appealed, perhaps needed little convincing that secession would be ruinous to their interests, but power did not rest with them.[8] The *Herald* addressed eloquent appeals to Lincoln as President-elect to proclaim a conciliatory programme towards the South. On 8 November it had announced that it would stand by him as President if he would 'harmonize the country' by observing the Fugitive Slave Law and respecting Southern slavery, rebuffing the 'irrepressible conflict' men in his party. Every day the *Herald* implored Lincoln to make some statement to the South and suggested that a Union appeal by Buchanan backed by a conservative letter from Lincoln would suffice to stay the South from precipitate action.[9]

These calls brought angry comments from the Republican press. Greeley wrote tartly in the *Tribune* that 'Some of the Fusion journals, which have been trying for three months to convince the South that as soon as Lincoln is inaugurated he will cross Mason and Dixon's line with fire and sword and liberate all the slaves, are now beseeching him to come out with an address and assure the South that they have been lying. It doesn't appear, however, that he thinks it necessary to do anything so superfluous.'[10] Raymond in the *Times* agreed: 'Of what avail are . . . assurances in the face of the constant and persevering

Bonner, 'Horace Greeley and the Secession Movement, 1860-61', *Mississippi Valley Historical Review,* 38 (1951-2), 425-44, and David M. Potter, 'Horace Greeley and Peaceable Secession' (with postscript) in *The South and the Sectional Conflict* (Baton Rouge 1968), pp. 219-42.

[7]*NYH* 20 Nov; 1, 2 Dec 1860.

[8]On November 19, for example, the *Herald* claimed that in fighting anti-slavery the South was battling 'in behalf of the material interests of society everywhere' for 'objects which should be the common aim of all right-minded and patriotic men, both North and South'.

[9]*NYH* 8-14, 19, 22, 24, 30 Nov; 8, 19 Dec 1860.

[10]NY *Daily Tribune* 12 Nov 1860.

BADGERING HIM.

J. G. B——TT.—Bow! Wow! Come out, Mr. Lincoln!

The Scotch terrier of the *Herald* tries to draw a statement of policy from the President-elect.
(From *Vanity Fair*, February 1861).

Reproduced by permission of the British Library

misrepresentations of the leading Democratic organs?'[11] There was silence from Springfield.

By early December New York City was in the grip of a financial panic prompted by lack of confidence in the stability of the Union and the prospects for the Southern trade. The *Herald,* having now quite forgotten its own recent injunction to 'drop politics', reported the 'revulsion' in the city with earnest intensity, claiming that its prophecies were vindicated and that the country was now going to taste the bitter fruits of 'Black Republican' rule. Predicting 'a condition of anarchy which it is fearful to contemplate;' it warned that distress among the unemployed would cause a revolt of free labour against capital in the North sooner than a slave insurrection would occur in the South.[12] Every business failure in the city and every piece of news from the excited South drew from Bennett ever more bitter denunciations of the abolitionists and their party as the ones directly responsible for the impending disaster to the material interests of the country.[13] The *Times* fiercely resented this logic, and laid into its rival in a leading editorial entitled 'The Panic Makers':

> We have received a great many communications denouncing the *Herald* for its systematic endeavours to aggravate the existing sectional and financial excitements.... That paper is doing now precisely what it had been doing from the first day of its existence. It has lived and prospered by feeding every flame that accident or design might kindle in the community. It has but one rule of conduct, and that is to minister to every excitement that seizes at any time, no matter how much damage it may inflict on individuals or communities.
>
> And it finds its account in so doing. Partly by inspiring fear and partly by stimulating curiosity it makes itself talked about and sought for by the public — and the very men, merchants and others, whom it injures most, strengthen its hand for evil by contributing to its advertising columns. . . . It has done everything in its power to increase the panic. . . . It has exaggerated the facts tending to increase it, — and has utterly suppressed every fact tending to allay it. . : — It fabricates pretended telegraphic dispatches in its own office — and it changes and modifies dispatches which actually reach it from other quarters, for the purpose of stimulating the excitement of the public mind, — but these are the tricks and devices which it always employs in similar emergencies.[14]

[11]NY *Times* 24 Nov 1860.

[12]*NYH* 4 Dec 1860.

[13]On the panic: *NYH* 11-19, 23, 24, 26, 27, 29 Nov; 1, 4, 6, 7, 9, 10, 12, 13, 15, 16 Dec 1860; P.S. Foner, *Business and Slavery* (Chapel Hill 1941), ch 9.

[14]NY *Times* 23 Nov 1860. Bennett's defence in *NYH* 24, 26, 27 Nov; 10 Dec 1860.

The *Times* warned the South that it would be deceived if it believed the overdrawn pictures of panic and violence in the metropolis to be found in the *Herald*.[15] Greeley also referred to the *Herald* as 'The Organ of the Disunionists and Alarmists in this City'.[16] Upstate, the Utica *Morning Herald* charged Bennett with personally conniving at the dissolution of the Union out of sheer diabolic malignancy and concluded that 'the fact that such a man is permitted to grow prosperous in this life, is a tolerably strong argument in favour of future punishment'.[17] Even President Buchanan sought to allay the panic and wrote to Bennett that 'if the merchants of New York would sit down calmly and ask themselves to what extent they would be injured by the withdrawal of three or four cotton States from the Union, they would come to the conclusion that although the evils would be very great, yet they would not destroy the commercial prosperity of our great Western Emporium'.[18]

Bennett, unabashed, continued to write in the same vein which assumed that the crisis must deepen until the Republicans had 'sober second thoughts' about their policies regarding slavery. With a compassion that was doubtless unappreciated, he regarded those who had voted Republican in November as 'honest minded but wickedly misled' and asserted that many of them now repented.[19]

He searched about editorially for concessions which the Republicans must make to satisfy the South, accompanying his sermons with heavy moral imperatives on the duty of that party to bow to the popular will. For one of the *Herald*'s favourite themes was succinctly expressed in the headline 'The Voice of the People Against the Chicago Platform'.[20] Over and over again it underlined to readers that Lincoln had received a minority of the popular vote and was therefore 'morally bound' to make concessions to the South: he must abandon 'the impracticable anti-slavery programme upon which he has been elected'. Indeed the President-elect ought in Bennett's view to seize greatness by declaring himself independent of his party. He pictured to his readers a country facing a clear choice between the Union on

[15]NY *Times* 12, 13 Dec 1860.

[16]NY *Daily Tribune* 15 Dec 1860.

[17]Utica *Morning Herald and Daily Gazette* 14 Dec 1860. Webb heartily endorsed this charge in the *Courier & Enquirer,* see 12, 26 Feb; 4 Apr 1861.

[18]Buchanan to Bennett 20 Dec 1860, in J.B. Moore ed., *The Works of James Buchanan* (NY 1960), vol. XI, pp. 69-70.

[19]*NYH* 13, 22 Nov; 11, 17 Dec 1860.

[20]*NYH* 19 Dec 1860. See also 8, 10, 12, 14-18, 20 Dec 1860.

one hand or Republican principles on the other; and which, he asked, was more important?[21]

Bennett was trying to work on the susceptibilities of what he termed the 'political' wing of the Republican party, as opposed to the 'religious' wing of dedicated anti-slavery men and haters of the South. He played on their fears that intransigence might turn public opinion against them and result in the split in the Union which would make their victory Pyrrhic. If this happened they would not be able to enjoy the full possession of the federal government which they were so proud of having won. There were already signs that Thurlow Weed was seriously worried by such considerations and was ready to contemplate conciliatory measures.[22]

The *Herald*'s own plan for appeasement concentrated in the first instance on the Personal Liberty laws as a major obstacle to compromise.[23] These laws were on the statute books in several Northern states, being designed to protect free Negroes from being seized as fugitive slaves by unscrupulous slave-catchers. They often contained provisions frankly aimed at hindering the operation of the federal Fugitive Slave Law. Bennett had always been an enemy of these bills, characterising an unsuccessful one which came before the New York Assembly early in 1860 as an 'atrocious wrong'.[24] Holding them to be in direct defiance of constitutional obligations, he saw their repeal as a first step — and only a first step – towards preserving the Union. He answered accusations of having misrepresented the Republican party[25] by challenging it to show its good will in this matter, in which, he argued, the South was demanding not concessions but only its legal rights.[26]

As the crisis deepened the *Herald*'s programme of conciliation became more comprehensive and it suggested that a petition be organised in the city in favour of Southern rights in slave property in the Territories. Again it presented this not as a concession but as a 'right' which ought to be cheerfully yielded.[27] It favoured a constitutional guarantee of slavery together with a more rigid enforcement of the

[21]*NYH* 8, 10, 14, 15, 16 Dec 1860.

[22]*NYH* 14 Nov; 4, 19 Dec 1860.

[23]*NYH* 17, 18, 20, 24, 28, 29 Nov; 1, 4 Dec 1860.

[24]*NYH* 29 Jan 1860.

[25]This charge had been forcibly made by Webb in the *Courier & Enquirer;* see *ibid.,* 15, 21, 27, 29 Nov and *NYH* 24, 27 Nov 1860.

[26]*NYH* 4 Dec 1860.

[27]*NYH* 11 Nov; 2, 3, 4, 8 Dec 1860.

Fugitive Slave Law. Also, be it noted, Bennett thought that the right of transit for owners to take their slaves through the free states ought to be enacted. This would mean that Southerners could take their slaves with them anywhere in the Union – bring them to New York and even Boston if they liked. It would mean that no case comparable to that of Dred Scott could ever arise again, and posed the question of whether the inter-state slave trade might be protected by federal law. Bennett made this suggestion as a 'conciliatory' measure of appeasement towards the South. In fact its adoption would have been only next door to making slavery legal throughout the North. For if slaves were protected property under the Constitution, how could a mere state legislature abridge the rights of slaveowners? The right of transit with slaves, put forward as a 'compromise' can only have aroused the worst fears of anti-slavery men that the demands of the advocates of slavery were insatiable. In the wake of the Dred Scott decision, the bogey of slavery being protected in the North may not have seemed so 'absurd' to Northern minds in 1860 as it has done to historians.[28]

Greeley answered Bennett's 'compromise' proposals in the *Tribune:* 'This is tolerably cool, i' faith!. . . Those who have been beaten in the late contest propose to graciously forgive the victors, provided that they will give up all that was at stake and a great deal more.'[29] Greeley could hardly believe that even Bennett could be so hard of heart as to be personally capable of returning a fugitive to slavery. The Fugitive Slave Law had scarcely been palatable to the North in 1850, and to demand its stiffening now as a 'compromise' seemed to Greeley totally unrealistic: 'If a new compact between the North and the South is to be made, let it recognise and respect Human Nature instead of attempting to ride roughshod over it.' In his view it would be more rational to agree a scheme of compensation, rather than rendition, and he advised that the enforcement of the Fugitive Slave Law was simply impractical.[30] As for the Personal Liberty laws, they could be tested in the Supreme Court at any time, if Southerners wished, without the necessity of any initiative from the Northern states. Frankly, said Greeley, he would rather listen to outright secessionists than to the *Herald*'s demands that Republicans

---

[28] Allan Nevins in *The Emergence of Lincoln* (NY 1950), vol. 1, p. 362 reproaches Lincoln for having raised this 'absurd bogey' as a political manoeuvre during his 1858 debates with Douglas. Harry V. Jaffa is less sure that the matter can be so easily dismissed; see 'The Legal Tendency Toward Slavery', ch XI of his *Crisis of the House Divided* (Seattle 1973), especially p. 277.

[29] NY *Daily Tribune* 19 Nov 1860.

[30] *Ibid.*, 23, 29 Nov 1860.

should abandon anti-slavery as the price of Union.[31] Lincoln himself was disinclined to repent, as he put it, of the crime of being elected.[32]

The *Times* was similarly intransigent. On the day after the Presidential election it had predicted that all the talk of disunion in the South would be forgotten within three months, or at least put in storage until 1864.[33] Now it declared that 'what the Democrats mean by compromise is the absolute *surrender* of the Republicans'.[34]

It became more evident that the Republicans were not going to panic at the first alarm after President Buchanan had delivered his last annual message to Congress on 4 December 1860. Buchanan pointed to the material prosperity of the country and condemned the 'long continued and intemperate interference of the Northern people with the question of slavery in the States' which menaced it. He also denounced 'vague notions of freedom' for arousing fears of servile insurrection in the South and the Northern Personal Liberty laws for provoking 'revolutionary resistance to the government of the Union'. All the same he cautioned the South that the election of Lincoln was not in itself a sufficient provocation to disunion and that secession was a revolutionary and unconstitutional act. Buchanan went on to argue nevertheless that a seceding state could not be coerced by the federal government and that the Union could only be restored by conciliation. To this end he recommended a constitutional amendment which would include a specific recognition of slave property and the right of slaveholding in the territories. Finally, the North should show good faith to the South by returning fugitive slaves.[35]

This message, apart from its generally temperate tone, could have done service as a *Herald* editorial, and it was to be expected that Bennett was delighted with it. Labelling it 'eminently satisfactory' and 'patriotic' the *Herald* saw in the President's programme the best hope for peaceful readjustment.[36]

But Bennett's reaction was untypical in the North. The Republican press showered the outgoing President with criticism and abuse.

[31]*Ibid.*, 7 Dec 1860.

[32]Lincoln to John A. Gilmer 15 Dec 1860 in R.P. Basler ed., *The Collected Works of Abraham Lincoln* (New Brunswick 1953-5), vol. IV, pp. 151-3.

[33]NY *Times* 7 Nov 1860.

[34]*Ibid.*, 6 Dec 1860.

[35]For the text of Buchanan's message see J.D. Richardson ed., *Messages and Papers of the Presidents* (NY 1907), vol. V, p. 626 ff.

[36]*NYH* 5 Dec 1860. In fact arguments almost indentical to Buchanan's had appeared in the *Herald* leader for 13 Nov.

Greeley set the keynote with an editorial which began: 'Let us devoutly thank God, that, for the ensuing four years at least, the People of the United States are relieved from the annual visitation of a long Presidential lecture wherein Reason is insulted, Humanity outraged, History travestied and Common Sense defied, in the interest of Human Slavery and for the gratification of its upholders.' The President, said the *Tribune*, was not merely asking Northerners to let slavery alone, but to submit to having it rammed down their throats.[37]

The *Times*, similarly irate, complained that 'True to his partisanship, if true to nothing else, Mr. Buchanan attributes the entire responsibility for existing public evils to the Northern States, – and it is they alone who are to make sacrifices of position and principle for their removal'. Raymond was puzzled by Buchanan's appeal for the safety of Southern matrons living in fear of servile insurrection. If slavery was such a beneficial system for both races as its apologists claimed then why, asked Raymond, should the Negroes want to murder anybody? The *Times* concluded that Buchanan's message was, in its judgement, 'an act of moral and official cowardice. . . an incendiary document. . . It backs up the most extravagant demands which have been made by the South, – indorses their menace of Disunion if those demands are not conceded; – and promises the seceding States that the power of the Federal Government shall not be used for their coercion. . . The country has to struggle through three months more of this disgraceful imbecility and disloyalty to the Constitution.'[38]

Seeing what he called the party of 'negro philanthropy' either 'incredulous or defiant', Bennett declared on 7 December that the Union could not now be preserved intact and that all the cotton states would be out of it by 4 March. His call, in late November, for President Buchanan and then Congress to summon a federal convention of the states had not been implemented.[39] Bennett had specified that the delegates to such a convention should be elected directly and not nominated by current state legislatures, so that they should reflect the present state of popular opinion, which he asserted was now more favourable to compromise than a month previously.[40] At its baldest this was a suggestion that the crisis was sufficiently serious for the

[37]NY *Daily Tribune* 5 Dec 1860.

[38]NY *Times* 5 Dec 1860. The *Charleston Mercury* 6 Dec 1860 argued that Buchanan's speech proved the South need not fear coercion.

[39]*NYH* 18-21 Nov 1860.

[40]*NYH* 24 Nov 1860.

Republicans voluntarily to abdicate their recent victory at the polls. Needless to say a Republican dominated Congress was less easily convinced that such a necessity had arisen than the editor of the *New York Herald*.[41]

A Union meeting in New York City sent delegates to counsel delay on South Carolina, but it was too late.[42] On 20 December the South Carolina Convention sitting in Charleston had declared the state out of the Union, alleging among its reasons that the Northern states had violated their consitutional obligations in respect of the Fugitive Slave Law, and that while observing the forms of the Constitution had elected a man to the Presidency whose 'opinions and purposes are hostile to slavery'. Futhermore: 'Those States have assumed the right of deciding upon the propriety of our domestic institutions; and have denied the rights of property established in fifteen of the States and recognized by the Constitution; they have denounced as sinful the institution of slavery; they have permitted the open establishment among them of societies, whose avowed object is to disturb the peace and eloin the property of the citizens of other States.'[43]

At last then the Union was sundered and the question now was whether secession would be followed by peaceful reconstruction or civil war. The *Herald* was for reconstruction based on Northern conciliation of the South and the abandonment of Republican principles. But the fact of disunion made negotiation more, not less, difficult. South Carolina had acted in good time if an independent government of several Southern states was to be on its feet by 4 March, when Lincoln would be inaugurated. But she had incurred the moral odium, in the eyes of the North, of having broken up the government before any overt act of hostility had been committed against her. She had issued no ultimatum to the President-elect, the government nor anyone else prior to her act. Adjustment of the problem of slavery now had to play a subordinate role to the question of the integrity of American nationality, on which the North was more united. As the *Tribune* put it, 'whatever shall now be done in the way of concession

---

[41]*NYH* 3, 17 Dec 1860. See David M. Potter, *The Impending Crisis* (NY 1976), p. 551.

[42]On the Pine Street meeting and the consternation of the city business community see Foner, *Business and Slavery,* pp. 227, 231-2, and *NYH* 17 Dec 1860.

[43]The South Carolina Ordinance of Secession (20 Dec 1860) and the 'Declaration of the Causes of Secession' (24 Dec 1860) quoted here can be found in H.S. Commager, *Documents of American History* (NY 1968), vol. 1, pp. 372-4. Steven A. Channing, *Crisis of Fear* (NY 1970), reveals how little effect the appeals of Northern conservatives had in that state.

to slavery will be hailed and exulted over as yielded by Northern fears to Southern threats of secession and civil war'.[44]

'This government can never exist by force': December 1860 – February 1861

The news of South Carolina's departure caused Bennett to reaffirm that 'the people of the North will never give their consent to the raising of a standing army which, if successful in subjugating the Southern States, would very soon be turned against their own liberties'.[45] Neverthless the Springfield *Journal*, generally taken to be the mouthpiece of the President-elect, had recently spoken of the impossibility of peaceful secession. If this statement was truly representative and if Lincoln persisted in his 'criminal' silence on the crisis, then the *Herald* saw no alternative to a 'bloody collision' between the Federal authorities and South Carolina.[46]

The *Herald* strongly defended President Buchanan's cautious policy. Was it right, asked Bennett, for Republicans to assail the President as a dotard just because he was anxious not to begin a civil war?[47] On Christmas Eve he approved Buchanan's forbearance in an editorial entitled 'Coercion or Conciliation?', but in the last week of the old year a noticeable change of tone came over the *Herald*. The paper seemingly reflected Buchanan's growing disillusionment with the demands of the Southern extremists. If Northern conservatives were hoping for time to produce a Republican surrender, the South Carolinians seemed inclined to force the issue at once. State militia seized the Custom House, Post Office, Arsenal and several of the forts in Charleston. Major Anderson, commanding the US regular army garrison around the city, withdrew his force on his own initiative to Fort Sumter, an isolated position at the mouth of the harbour. This at once made his troops more secure and ducked the prospect of an immediate collision with state forces in the city. South Carolina's commissioners in Washington demanded that Buchanan order Anderson back to the mainland (i.e. to an indefensible position), which even the distracted President would not do. Their tone in lobbying him was markedly overbearing.[48]

[44]NY *Daily Tribune* 7 Jan 1861.
[45]*NYH* 21 Dec 1861.
[46]*NYH* 17, 18, 20, 21, 22 Dec 1860.
[47]*NYH* 23 Dec 1860.
[48]*NYH* 28, 29 Dec 1860.

The *Herald* accordingly lectured the Carolinians in a way it had never done hitherto. They should not forget, it said, that they had many friends in the North, if they would only given them a chance. To secede as a means of forcing concessions from the opposing party was one thing, and even the act of disunion itself had failed to stir Bennett to a firm stance on the question of loyalty to the Constitution. But he was genuinely affronted by the discovery that the South Carolinians could be so aggressive to a sympathetic administration. It may be added that even *Herald* correspondents were now finding life difficult among the hotheads of South Carolina, which may well have had a bearing on Bennett's attitude.[49]

On 30 December 1860, ten days after secession, the *Herald* gave its opinion that South Carolina was not legally out of the Union. It was still adamant that the federal government had no right of coercion against a state, and that the very idea was 'preposterous', but the force of this was nullified by its assertion that the federal government reserved the right to enforce the law against *individuals* in South Carolina responsible for attacking federal property: 'It will be solely a matter of policy with the federal government whether it will enforce its laws in that and other seceding states.'[50] On no account could Buchanan therefore officially recognise the South Carolinian commissioners or receive them in Washington, and the *Herald* warned that the President would be obliged to execute the laws with regard to the collection of revenue in Charleston harbour unless Congress relieved him of the responsibility by suspending their operation for a limited time. (Lest anybody should think he was being bellicose, Bennett recommended that Congress should hasten to do exactly that.) With a turn of false optimism that he usually left to the Republican press, Bennett claimed that such an initiative from Congress would cause the fires of secession to die out for lack of combustibles.[51] It might not do that, but if the peace could be kept in Charleston harbour there was still hope for compromise.

Civil war seemed imminent in early January 1861. On the first day of the new year Bennett accompanied his diurnal call for slavery to be guaranteed by constitutional amendment with a harsher demand for Congress to call out 60,000 militia from the border states, to be placed under General Scott's command in readiness to protect the national capital. For some of the louder secessionists in Virginia and

[49]*NYH* 27-31 Dec 1860.
[50]*NYH* 27 Dec 1860; 10 Jan 1861.
[51]*NYH* 9 Jan 1861.

Maryland were calling on their states to capture Washington and prevent the inauguration of Lincoln.[52] On 9 January the merchant vessel *Star of the West* was fired upon by the Charleston batteries when it attempted to land supplies at Fort Sumter. The South was a hive of military activity and the *Herald* was pressed to find some variant on 'The Revolution' as the main news heading. During January and early February the other five cotton states of the deep South and Texas followed South Carolina in seceding from the Union.[53]

Deprecating the threats of coercion which began to appear more frequently in the Northern press, the *Herald* nevertheless began to keep pace with the tide of Northern opinion which, it admitted, was being rallied more firmly to the Union by Southern precipitancy.[54] The paper's pre-war hostility to disunionism reached a peak early in January 1861. Bennett, always more aware of the conditional nature of Southern Unionism than many Northern contemporaries, was gradually realising that the now dominant secession leaders in the cotton states had no intention of bargaining for readmission to a Union they detested. Bennett called for 'justice' for the South, but to back his demands there was no apparent desire in the Gulf States themselves for anything save the possession of federal forts and arsenals. The editor was playing self-appointed defence counsel for the South with no brief from his client. Taxing himself to guess the formula for compromise, there was something plaintive in the way Bennett urged Southern 'conservatives' to state their terms with one voice.[55]

Still the *Herald* battled on doggedly for a Union saving compromise, giving encouragement wherever popular feeling could be roused to organise street meetings, conventions or petitions. The paper received over one hundred plans for compromise from readers and offered to forward them to Congress.

The most promising of all the various compromise schemes in Congress was that of Senator Crittenden of Kentucky. Bennett found it very 'reasonable' in that it required a stricter enforcement of the Fugitive Slave Act, repeal of the Personal Liberty Laws, and forbade Congress ever to abolish slavery in the District of Columbia or any

[52]*NYH* 1, 15 Jan 1861.

[53]Mississippi seceded on 9 Jan 1861, Florida on the 10th, Alabama the 11th, Georgia the 19th, Louisiana the 26th and Texas effectively on 1 Feb.

[54]*NYH* 8, 15 Jan 1861.

[55]*NYH* 3, 4, 5 Jan 1861.

other federal property within the slave states or to interfere with the inter-state slave trade.[56] (Ideally the editor of the *Herald* would have liked the right of transit with slaves through the free states included as well and would have added a one term presidency.)[57] The crux of the compromise was the proposal to restore the Missouri Compromise line of 36° 30' in the territories as a dividing line between freedom and slavery. Early in December the *Herald* had dismissed such an idea as 'absurd'[58] because it claimed nature made slavery impractical there, but by the end of the month Bennett's mind had changed.

Doubtless he was largely swayed by a personal letter addressed to him by Buchanan on 20 December, the very day on which South Carolina seceded. In the midst of a characteristically unctuous passage of self-justification, the tired President mooted the idea that the restoration of the Missouri Compromise line would be the most successful peace formula because 'the South can lose no territory north of this line; because no portion of it is adapted to slave labor, whilst they would gain a substantial security within the Union by such a constitutional amendment. The Republicans have for some years manifested indignation at the repeal of the Compromise, and would probably be more willing to accept it than any other measure to guarantee the rights of the South.' Buchanan hoped that Bennett would approve the plan and urged: 'You wield the most powerful organ in the country for the formation of public opinion, and I have no doubt you feel a proportionate responsibility under the present alarming circumstances. . . you could do much by directing your energies to this single point.'[59]

[56]Text of the Crittenden proposals in Commager, pp. 369-71. Here they are summarised in their original form, though they were later considerably amended in their passage through Congress.

[57]*NYH* 25 Dec 1860; 10, 20 Jan 1861.

[58]*NYH* 4 Dec 1860. His hostility may have been due to the proposal having originated with Thurlow Weed.

[59]Buchanan to Bennett 20 Dec 1860; see citation in note 18 above. In this letter Buchanan also complained to Bennett 'I do not know whether the great commercial and social advantages of the telegraph are not counterbalanced by its political evils. No one can judge of this so well as myself. The public mind throughout the interior is kept in a constant state of excitement by what are called "telegrams". They are short and spicy, and can easily be inserted in the country newspapers. . . Many of them are sheer falsehoods, and especially those concerning myself.' The President's anxiety to cultivate Bennett may in part be explained by the fact that he had felt compelled to withdraw his official support from the Washington *Constitution* which was becoming ever more secessionist in tone (see Buchanan to Wm. M. Browne, 25 Dec 1860, Buchanan Papers, Historical Society of Pennsylvania). It is interesting to note that the President's grievance was echoed in the *Herald* of 16 Jan 1861 almost verbatim though transposed to the third person. However Bennett concluded that on balance the telegraph had amply proved its worth in revolutionary times!

Bennett tried, but as usual his arguments were two edged. He could flay the Republicans for trying to limit slavery where it could not exist anyway for merely party ends, while at the same time he made great play of the South's magnanimity in being prepared to give up its 'rights' in the same region north the 36° 30'. He could lecture Republicans that slavery was receding from the Upper South anyway, but never pretended to share the timid belief that slavery was necessarily coterminous with the climatic zones suited to cotton, sugar, rice and tobacco cultivation. Despite his beliefs about the natural capabilities of Negroes, he judged that the existing evidence gave good promise for the successful use of blacks in large scale industry in the future. Most curious of all was the *Herald*'s plea for the expansion of slavery into the Southwest on grounds of humanity to the Negro. It pictured horrific scenes of overcrowding if the growing negro population were 'walled in' in the states where slavery already existed, and asked the Republicans whether they were afraid of allowing slavery into new areas where it would be strangled by competition from free labour.[60] These disingenuous arguments merely testified that arguments about the 'geographical limits' of slavery were little more than party playthings.

In any case Lincoln, though not present during the compromise debates as Bennett had suggested he should be, was obdurate against the Crittenden proposals.[61] Among all the cast iron constitutional guarantees of slavery the only points which favoured the Republicans were the provision for the enforcement of the laws against the international slave trade[62] and the prohibition of slavery in the territories north of 36°30'. The Republicans had fought their electoral campaign on the issue of prohibiting slavery in all the territories. Now they were being asked to establish and protect it in half of them and to agree the possibility of southward exapansion of slave territory, so implicitly recognising slavery as a permanent national institution. This they would not do. In the *Times* Raymond made it clear that Republicans expected Lincoln to 'do all in his power. . . to *arrest* the tendency to make slavery national and perpetual. . . on this point, we take it for granted, he will be firm and immovable. . . A conservative, stand fast policy is all that is now necessary to secure every foot of the

[60]*NYH* 11, 13, 17 Nov; 3, 4, 8, 13, 15, 30 Dec 1860; 5, 7, Jan; 16 Feb 1861. Compare 11 Apr; 1 June 1859 and 1 Oct 1860.

[61]See letters of Lincoln to Lyman Trumbull, William Kellogg and Elihu B. Washbourne in Basler, vol. IV, pp. 149-51.

[62]Bennett would have preferred the 'unanimous consent' of both houses of Congress before the international slave trade could be restored, which was perhaps less grandly impossible than it sounded if 'unanimous consent' could be construed as simple majorities in both chambers – *NYH* 20 Jan 1861.

public domain to free labor.'[63] Greeley was even more direct in urging Lincoln to stand firm on the Chicago platform: 'No Compromise – No Concessions to Traitors.'[64] For Republicans the history of the last decade seemed to point the moral that compromise and appeasement only aggravated rather than settled the slavery and disunion problems. Greeley complained that 'if anyone sees a project of conciliation and compromise submitted, and respectably supported from the Slave States, which does not involve an assumption that even the bare existence of the Republican party is an impertinence and an offense, we will thank him to send us a copy'.[65] He accused Bennett of demanding the suicide of the Republican party. And if the Union was in danger, why not? replied the *Herald*.[66]

Seward came out in mid-January with a compromise scheme of his own which included a repeal of the Personal Liberty Laws, a faithful observance of the Fugitive Slave Law with the important proviso that private citizens should not be obliged to help implement it, a constitutional amendment forbidding Congressional interference with slavery in the states, no slavery in the territories, a national convention after two or three years to review the situation and lastly a southern and a northern Pacific Railroad. Bennett dismissed this angrily as no compromise at all and evidence of complete ignorance of the situation. He characterised the idea of a constitutional guarantee of slavery in the states where it already existed as gratuitously insulting to the South.[67]

Bennett expected little further from a Congress whose proceedings disgusted him. National affairs seemed to be drifting and the prevailing mood in the capital seemed to be one of confusion permeated by suspicion of treason on all sides. George T. Strong wrote in his diary that 'a visit to Washington gives one no special insight into national affairs. People there are eager for New York papers to tell them what the government did or talked about the day before.' In New York City 38,000 signatures were collected in favour of the Crittenden Compromise but it could not be revived, despite the efforts of a border state Convention.[68] (This assembly at first drew rage

[63]NY *Times* 8 Nov; 4 Dec 1860.

[64]NY *Daily Tribune* 17, 30 Jan; 19, 27 Feb 1861.

[65]NY *Daily Tribune* 9 Jan 1861.

[66]*NYH* 12 Jan 1861.

[67]*NYH* 13 Jan 1861; also 13 Feb; 2 Mar. Seward's speech was made in the Senate on 12 Jan. For other reaction to the speech see Stampp, pp. 170-2; D.M. Potter, *Lincoln and his Party in the Secession Crisis* (Yale 1942), pp. 285-7.

[68]*NYH* 22 Jan; 2, 16, 19 Feb; 4 Mar 1861.

from Bennett because its sessions in Washington were held in secret. With his reporters chafing outside locked doors Bennett demanded to know whether these 'fossils' and 'grogshop politicians' realised that 'the country has advanced a whole century since they were alive'.)[69] By February it appeared that concessions by the Republicans could at best only prevent the upper South and border states from joining the seceded 'gulf squadron'. The *Herald* was anxious to achieve even this much and chastised the dominant party for its obstinacy in headings which told their own story: 'Blood! Blood! Blood! – Who will be Responsible?' (29 January); 'Gigantic Conspiracy of the Anti-Slavery School of Massachusetts to Destroy the Union and Establish a Military Despotism' (8 February); 'Civil War Upon Us' (13 February); 'The Bloody Programme of the Radical Republicans' (23 February). This kind of chivying was in a spirit directly contrary to the tolerance which the *Herald* itself had paraded as essential to a peaceful settlement, but was clearly calculated either to rouse a popular revulsion against coercion of the South or, if hostilities did occur, to make sure the blame rested on the Republicans.

The signs of growing militancy in the North were alarming to Bennett. There was an increasing demand for firearms in the metropolis, and he condemned the 'indecent haste' with which Northern state legislatures, including that of New York, were showing their readiness to forward militia to Washington to have matters out with the secessionists. True, he wanted the capital protected from the 'wicked' Southern designs to seize it before the inauguration, but he became fearful that an assembly of Northern troops there might become a pretext for hostile action against the South.[70]

Bennett was furious when New York's Metropolitan Police seized a cargo of arms bound for Georgia from a vessel in the harbour in January. By what right did they do so, he demanded? Ex US Senator Robert Toombs of Georgia telegraphed Mayor Wood for an explanation. Wood replied that he was powerless to prevent the seizure (the state assembly having deprived him of his seat on the Metropolitan Police Board a year previously, despite the *Herald*'s strong protests).[71] Nevertheless he declared that he would have forbidden this 'illegal and unjustifiable seizure of private property' had he been able, and Bennett applauded his stand. He was right in saying that the legal

[69]*NYH* 5, 7 Feb 1861. This Peace Convention had been called on the initiative of Virginia.

[70]*NYH* 27 Nov 1860; 25 Jan; 4, 5, 8 Feb 1861.

[71]*NYH* 12 Apr 1860.

position of the New York police was weak, although everybody knew that the arms were for use against the federal government. Georgia seized some New York shipping in her own harbours by way of retaliation and New York let her vessel go.[72] Bennett was also horrified when Democrat John A. Dix, now a member of Buchanan's cabinet, ordered the shooting on the spot of any secessionist attempting to haul down a United States flag in New Orleans. The very idea of fighting a civil war was characterised by Bennett as 'an absurdity' got up by 'a few small politicians' for the sake of a little 'notoriety which is as cheap as it is contemptible'.[73]

By the latter half of January the danger of a coercive policy being initiated after 4 March seemed so great that the *Herald* again changed direction. It toned down its recent complaints against Southern impatience, accepting the secession of the lower South as something which could not be undone for the moment and concentrating its energies on preaching against the imminent peril of an actual clash of arms. Bennett expressed his conviction thus: 'The Union is broken; to restore it our first necessity is peace; and if we cannot restore it, still our only course of wisdom and safety is peace.'[74] From this time until the firing on Fort Sumter Bennett defied accusations of treason and did not falter in his belief that it was 'far better that the Union should perish forever that that fraternal hands should be turned against one another to deluge the land in blood'.[75] Eight years before the phrase was made famous by Ulysses S. Grant, Bennett pleaded 'Let us have peace',[76] and two months before Seward suggested the same thing privately to Lincoln the *Herald* clamoured for foreign adventure as a means of reuniting the Union.

Bennett assumed that if Lincoln tried to coerce the states of the lower South the other slave states would join them.[77] A contest with fifteen slave states would probably produce no decisive result save to leave a bitterness which would make reunion forever impossible. Faced with the alternatives of peaceful dissolution or civil war with a determined South he now found 'nothing so dreadful in the idea of two great confederacies managed upon the same general plan as the present

[72]*NYH* 24, 26, 29 Jan; 10, 11, 15 Feb; 20 Mar 1861.

[73]*NYH* 25 Jan; 14 Feb 1861. This could account for Dix's hostility to Bennett's appointment to a foreign mission when Buchanan raised the matter in cabinet: see above p 104.

[74]*NYH* 28 Jan 1861.

[75]*NYH* 15 Jan 1861.

[76]*NYH* 8 Feb 1861.

[77]*NYH* 24 Jan 1861.

Union, with trade, commerce, manufactures, friendly intercourse going on the same as in the most peaceable times. If our Southern brethren think they can better themselves by going out, and are resolved to try the experiment, in Heaven's name let them go in peace. We cannot keep them by force.'[78] He pressed the politicians to tackle the task of arranging a peaceful separation of the two republics, entitling his editorial of 25 January 'The Two Great Confederacies – Manifest Destiny of the North and South'. This, it will be noticed, was more than a week before the seceding states formally inaugurated the government of an independent Southern nation. Separation ought to satisfy the abolitionists, he pointed out, since their consciences would no longer be burdened by association with slaveholders. Let Lincoln face the logical consequences of his own dictum that the Union could not survive half slave and half free, and recognise the Southern Confederacy.[79]

The essence of Bennett's plan, as developed in succeeding days, was for each of the twin republics to expand in its own sphere instead of squabbling over the Territories: the Southern Confederacy could annex Mexico, Central America and Cuba, to their inestimable benefit, while 'our brethren' in Canada would naturally wish to rise up and join the Northern United States, and even if they did not 'the annexation of Canada is manifest destiny'.[80] Bennett discoursed at fulsome length on the economic prospects for a united North American Confederation with its capital at New York – Washington would be given to the South. Liberated from the stultifying sectional confrontation, what great things might be achieved by the inhabitants of North America?

There was method in this reckless talk. Even as it stood Bennett's scheme might divert the North from the loss of national face internally if it could be reasserted elsewhere, and if a foreign war developed North and South might be reunited in a common cause. For in the last resort would that not be better than Americans shedding each other's blood? On a more subtle level, Bennett was convinced that Britain would lose no time in recognising the Southern Confederacy. Fear that the North might take her revenge on Canada might restrain her from hasty interference in American affairs. He seems not to have realised the irony of his argument that North and South would one day be reconciled just as Britain was with her former colonies.[81]•

[78]*NYH* 17 Jan 1861.
[79]*NYH* 24 Jan; 1 Feb 1861.
[80]*NYH* 24-7 Jan; 1 Feb 1861.
[81]*NYH* 24 Jan 1861.

By early February the *Herald* was claiming that Canada was on the verge of a mighty revolution in favour of annexation to the United States. Offering his readers on one hand this rosy and supposedly imminent prospect of Northern empire, Bennett simultaneously exuded enthusiasm at the birth of the Southern Confederacy in Montgomery, Alabama. He was impressed by the dignity of the proceedings – a clear refutation of Republican slanders, he claimed – and predicted that they would command respect North and South as well as abroad. He spoke of the 'Great Southern Republic' and of 'President' Davis in deferential terms, reminding Northerners that the Southern Confederacy had the loyalty of millions of people who 'are no more rebels and traitors than were the patriots of the rebel colonies in '76'.[82] Speculating on the bright commercial prospects before the new nation, he found it 'indisputable' that the border states would shortly find it in their best interests to join it, and suggested that if New York and the central states considered their own best interests they might be wise to do so as well, leaving New England to wither on the vine.[83]

In January Fernando Wood had actually suggested the possibility that New York City should secede from New York State and the Union to become a free city, which drew from Greeley the comment that 'Mr. Fernando Wood evidently wants to be a traitor; it is lack of courage only that makes him content with being a blackguard'.[84] Back in the distant days of early 1859 Bennett himself had proposed a similar scheme whereby the city would become the separate state of Manhattan.[85] Now, however, he was disposed to greet Wood's suggestion coldly and dismissed it as impractical. He sympathised with the mayor's grievances against Albany rule, as he always had done, but he made it clear with his usual pungency that he did not relish the prospect of rule by the present City Common Council. Economically it would be 'the secession of the market from the garden' and politically Bennett felt that on the whole the nation had diversions enough.[86]

[82] *NYH* 11, 12, 13, 14 Feb; 8 Mar 1861.

[83] *NYH* 14 Feb 1861.

[84] NY *Daily Tribune* 8 Jan 1861.

[85] *NYH* 14, 15 Feb 1859.

[86] *NYH* 21 Dec 1860; 8 Jan 1861. Text of Wood's recommendation in Commager, vol. I, pp. 374-6. For discussion see S. Pleasants, *Fernando Wood* (NY 1948), ch VII.

February – April 1861; 'Let the American people prepare for a civil war'. – *Herald* 5 April 1861

On 11 February President-elect Lincoln set out from his Illinois home toward Washington amidst a general atmosphere of deep gloom. His first speeches were uninspired. At Columbus, Ohio, Lincoln assured the nation that there was 'nothing going wrong'. Bennett commented that it was hard to see that anything was going right and for once advised Lincoln to keep quiet.[87] Lincoln arrived in New York City on 19 February and was received with few cheers – according to *Herald* reports anyway.[88] Bennett praised Mayor Wood's speech at the reception, in which he spoke of restoring the Union through 'only. . . peaceful and conciliatory means'.[89]

No fewer than eight times on the editorial page of 19 February the *Herald* repeated in italics its own programme for the new chief magistrate:

> If Mr. Lincoln hopes to be the second Washington of this great Confederacy, let him come out emphatically in his inaugural and recommend the Crittenden resolutions as amendments to the constitution, let him call an extra session of the new Congress, and in his first message boldly reiterate this plan and its submission at once to the people throughout the States; let him appoint his Cabinet, but not dispose of another office in his gift until this great and overwhelming question is settled.

Bennett was clutching at straws, still hoping that Lincoln might disavow his principles and his party. He did not rate Lincoln's ability very highly and gloomily foresaw that his seeming policy of 'masterly inactivity' was bound to lead to war unless the Southern Confederacy were recognised. The *Herald* helped propagate the notion that Seward was to be the 'premier' of the administration,[90] and in the weeks before the inauguration even wooed him in the hope that he

---

[87]*NYH* 15 Feb 1861.

[88]Press attitudes to Lincoln at this time and throughout the war period as well as his political relations with the city are admirably dealt with by Joseph F. Ryan, 'Abraham Lincoln and New York City, 1861-5', (unpublished thesis, St. John's University 1969).

[89]*NYH* 19-22 Feb 1861.

[90]*NYH* e.g. 12 Jan 1861. Lincoln had his own wry comment on this supposition; at the Inaugural Ball a *Herald* reporter on being introduced to the President 'was emboldened to ask whether he had any special news that I might send to Mr. Bennett. . . "Yes", he replied looking at me significantly, "you may tell him that Thurlow Weed has found out that Seward was not nominated at Chicago!" ' — quoted in Emmanuel Hertz, *Lincoln Talks: A Biography in Anecdote* (NY 1939), p. 193.

might lead the way in compromise negotiations with the upper South.[91]

The new administration got off to a poor start. To avoid a reported assassination attempt Lincoln slipped unceremoniously through the turbulent city of Baltimore at dead of night en route to Washington. The *Herald* was at first sceptical that such a plot had ever existed, then became certain that it had been a simple Republican propaganda trick worked up to provoke hostility to the South.[92]

Bennett was scathingly discontented with Lincoln's inaugural address, delivered on 4 March. He discussed it under the heading 'The Country No Wiser than it was Before – Is Coercion the Policy?' and concluded that for all he had said, Lincoln might just as well have told one of his jokes. The editor was suspicious of deliberate vagueness and detected Seward's fingermarks in the 'weak, vacillating, unsatisfactory and contradictory' message. He misrepresented Lincoln as having 'attacked' the Supreme Court because of his challenge to the Dred Scott decision, and complained that the new President's mind was hopelessly saturated with the Chicago platform. The crucial point, as Bennett grasped, was that the South would consider the continued federal occupation of forts around the Southern coast, especially Fort Sumter, an act of provocation by a foreign power; only federal withdrawal, not honeyed phrases, could avert war. In plain English, asked Bennett, did Lincoln's declared intention to 'hold, occupy and possess' federal property mean that he would retain what was still held or retake what had been lost? In the absence of a clear definition of policy he concluded that coercion was now a certain consequence of Republican rule.[93]

The story of Bennett's attitude to the Administration during the next month may be summed up as a continuing flow of taunts and abuse of Lincoln and his party either for inactivity or aggressive intentions. W. H. Russell, sent to cover the American crisis by the London *Times,* found such vituperation of the country's chief executive incredible.[94]

---

[91]For the *Herald's* curious dalliance with Seward at this time see *NYH* 2, 9, 18, 20, 27, 28, Feb 1861 and NY *Daily Tribune* 19 Feb; *NYH* 2, 3 Mar 1861.

[92]*NYH* 24, 26 Feb; 6, 11 Mar 1861. Bennett's solicitude for the safety of the new president was far overshadowed by his indignation that the Republican controlled New York Metropolitan Police should have been operating as far afield as Baltimore and Charleston in trying to uncover conspiracies whose existence he denied.

[93]*NYH* 4, 5, 6, Mar 1861.

[94]William Howard Russell, *My Diary North and South* (London 1863), vol. I, pp. 28-9. Discussing this abuse by 'one of the journals' with a New Yorker, Russell was told: 'Oh yes. . . that must strike you as a strange way of mentioning the Chief Magistrate

Bennett totally rejected Lincoln's assertion that the question of peace or war lay with his 'dissatisfied fellow countrymen' rather than with the President himself. In his view Lincoln's choice of policies towards the South was very simple: he could either do as the *Herald* advised and yield to the demands of the Confederates and evacuate forts Sumter and Pickens (on the Florida coast) or reinforce them and provoke war.[95] Actually for a long time it appeared that Lincoln would do neither, pursuing what Greeley described with probable accuracy as 'a Fabian policy, which concedes nothing, yet employs no force in support of resisted Federal authority, hoping to wear out the insurgent spirit, and in due time reestablish the authority of the Union throughout the revolted or seceded states, by virtue of the returning sanity and loyalty of their own people'.[96]

To Bennett this policy was 'unconciliatory. . . ignorant. . . imbecile. . .vicious. . . fanatical. . .mean. . .cowardly. . .fatal'.[97] He sneered that the Lincoln Administration lacked only the nerve and the power to execute its unholy designs on the South.

While the North hesitated the South was organising itself. In contrast to the 'morbid demoralization of the Northern mind upon this thing of Southern slavery', Bennett praised the open avowal by Confederate Vice-President Alexander H. Stephens that human slavery was the 'cornerstone' of the new Southern nation.[98] He also found the Confederate Constitution a 'vast improvement' on that of 1787. Among the features he admired in it was the provision for a one term Presidency of six years, a reform calculated to lessen some of the evils of rotation in office coincidental to American democratic practice. Furthermore he praised the Confederacy for calling slavery by its proper name, as the United States Constitution did not, and for its low tariff policy.[99]

This last matter received a great deal of attention from the *Herald* in the last weeks of peace. The Republicans passed the Morrill Tariff

---

of our great Republic, but the fact is, no one minds what the man writes of anyone, his game is to abuse every respectable man in the country in order to take his revenge on them for his social exclusion, and at the same time to please the ignorant masses who delight in vituperation and scandal.' It is reasonable to infer that Bennett was the subject of this conversation. Incidentally, the early chapters of Russell's diary give a vivid impression of New York during the latter part of the secession crisis.

[95]*NYH* 9 Mar 1861.

[96]NY *Daily Tribune* 27 Mar 1861.

[97]*NYH* 11, 13, 14, 15, 31 Mar 1861.

[98]*NYH* 16, 27 Mar 1861.

[99]*NYH* 17, 19 Mar 1861.

Act which raised protective duties on certain imported manufactured goods. The new rates were due to come into effect on April Fool's day, which Bennett thought appropriate. For once his attitude was representative of the entire press of New York City, with the exception of the devotedly protectionist *Tribune*. There was general and deep alarm at the damage the new measure would inflict on the trade of the Empire City. Bennett complained that the new tariff was cumbersome, unworkable, sponsored by a few 'corrupt' Republican interests, damaging to the city's commerce and injurious to the poor. Duties on cloth and salt contrasted oddly, he pointed out, with Republican professions of concern for free labour (to which Greeley replied by calling Bennett a 'wretched demagogue'). Chiefly though, the *Herald* claimed that the Morrill tariff prevented any chance of reconstruction with the South, and made it a commercial necessity for Europe to trade directly with the Confederacy. To make it cheaper to trade through Charleston than New York was a free gift to Southern independence, it warned. To Bennett it was in any case a foregone conclusion that 'King Cotton' would dictate British and French recognition and protection of the Confederacy, which in turn would make any Northern naval blockade 'out of the question' even had there been enough ships to make it effective. He portrayed the Morrill tariff as a national disaster, a further justification of the Southern Confederacy, and one likely in his view to make the Northwestern states want to join it.[100]

Bennett's final scheme of compromise was for the lower Northern states and the upper South to apply for admission to the Confederacy. If three-quarters of the states of the old Union adopted the Confederate Constitution it would become the official instrument of government of a new United States and the Republicans could then do what they liked.[101] On 19 March he seriously suggested as a 'reasonable compromise' that Lincoln should treat the Confederate Constitution as an ultimatum and discuss it with Confederate commissioners as a basis for reconstruction.

As the weeks passed by, Bennett became more uneasy that the 'conservative' statesmen of the Confederacy were in danger of spoiling the justice of their cause by unconcealed warlike preparations. The cautious nature of official utterances North and South could not disguise the fact that the Confederacy was arming itself for trouble.

[100]*NYH* 25, 28 Jan; 5, 8, 17 Feb; 4, 5, 12-31 Mar; 1, 3, Apr 1861; NY *Daily Tribune* 2 Apr 1861. Buchanan's role is mentioned in chapter 3 above. On press reaction to the tariff see Foner, *Business and Slavery,* pp. 261-4, 277-82.

[101]*NYH* 17 Mar 1861.

Still Lincoln did nothing decisive either to soothe or to provoke. Even his own party became impatient. Republican Senator Zachariah Chandler of Michigan expressed his view that: 'Without a little blood letting this Union will not. . .be worth a rush!' which drew a barrage of invective from the *Herald* on the 'execrable. . .diabolically infamous' nature of the Republicans.[102] On 13 March the *Herald* prematurely announced with relief that the Cabinet had decided to evacuate Fort Sumter, stressing that it was about to do the right thing for the basest of reasons. This report may have been a genuine mistake, or was perhaps gleaned from Secretary Seward, who favoured the surrender of Sumter. At worst it may have been a deliberate attempt to compromise the government. The Republican press castigated Bennett for spreading the false rumour, and charged that his paper was losing circulation as a result of his unpopular views.[103]

In despair of producing any significant reaction against 'abolition treason' the *Herald* at this time took the openly obstructive course of appealing to the financiers of the city and the nation to refuse all loans to either 'revolutionary' government; 'Neither the government at Washington. . . nor the government at Montgomery ought to receive a dollar from any source unless they renounce their nefarious schemes of civil war, and agree to a peaceful solution of the questions at issue'.[104] The business community of the city had contemplated such a course earlier in the year, but by now Wall Street was behind any governmental initiative to restore the Union by the shortest possible means, and the *Herald* was out of tune with their sentiments.[105]

The descent was now irretrievable. On 6 April there was news that the government was outfitting an expedition to sail to either Fort Sumter or Fort Pickens, which the *Herald* interpreted as 'The Administration Dragging the Country into Civil War'.[106] The last days before the arrival of the federal fleet off Charleston and the Confederate attack on Fort Sumter found Bennett cursing and pleading against war. He thought the situation 'never. . .so dark, menacing and desolate',[107] and accused the Republicans of having all but destroyed Unionism in the Upper South and the border states.

[102]*NYH* 11 Mär 1861.

[103]Bennett's rejoinder *NYH* 9 Apr 1861.

[104]*NYH* 1 Apr; see also 26, 29, 30, 31 Mar; 3 Apr 1861.

[105]Such is the interpretation of the motives of the business community expounded in Foner, chs 11-17.

[106]Bennett guessed that Fort Pickens, rather than Sumter, was the object of the expedition, which was the desire of Secretary of State Seward.

[107]*NYH* 11 Apr 1861.

What would the war be for, he asked? To enforce the law? Or, as one Republican paper put it, 'to show that we have a government?' Bennett was contemptuous of such justifications.[108] Were thousands of lives to be lost to collect the revenues and maintain the postal system? All such technical considerations could have been settled peaceably had there been any will to. do it, and Bennett lashed Lincoln's 'affectation' of not recognising the fact of Southern independence. Would it be a war for democracy? The *Herald* answered its own question in the negative. How could a case be made for denying millions of white people the right of self-determination, especially when they had adopted the old Constitution and bill of rights almost intact? On the contrary, coercion would put back the cause of liberalism in Europe. Would it be a war for the Union, when the first effect of coercion was bound to be the secession of the Upper South and the inflamation of sectional hatreds that might be generations dying? No. Bennett was adamant that the war would be one against slavery and for the subjugation of the South – 'that is the naked aspect of the war when stripped of all its disguise'. As such he condemned it as 'the wildest chimera that ever entered the brain of man',[109] and predicted that the war, more easily started than stopped, might last twenty years: 'oceans of blood, and millions of treasure will be wasted, with no other imaginable end than to leave the country exhausted, impoverished and wretched, and, worse than all, despoiled of the freedom purchased at such cost by our forefathers.'[110] In this event, he held, 'the Lincoln administration will be compelled to succumb in disgrace amidst the execrations of the people and the curses of mankind'.[111]

In the *Herald*'s view, Lincoln's policy amounted to no more than that 'if the Southern States make no resistance, when the administration shall be ready to attack them, there shall be peace'[112] and it was sure that nine-tenths of the people of the North would be aroused by this against Lincoln. Bennett accused the President of aiming to throw 'upon the Southern Confederacy the responsibility of commencing hostilities. But the country and posterity will hold him just as responsible as if he struck the first blow. The provocation to assault is often more culpable than the assault itself.'[113]

[108]*NYH* 10 Apr 1861.
[109]*NYH* 8 Apr 1861.
[110]*NYH* 12 Apr 1861.
[111]*NYH* 8 Apr 1861.
[112]*NYH* 9 Apr 1861.
[113]*NYH* 5 Apr 1861.

Having warned New Yorkers that sending troops away to the South might expose their city to the rule of the 'dangerous classes',[114] Bennett added a final observation on the task which the Northern states were about to undertake: 'The magnitude of pauperism and crime [in New York City] should be looked squarely in the face, as a thing we do not find to any great extent in the slave labor States . . . Would it not be better to reflect seriously on this condition of social life before we make war on an institution under which the physical comforts of the laboring class are well provided for?'[115]

It was a time of 'gnawing suspense and feverish excitement'[116] rather than of serious reflection as Americans went to bed on the night of 11 April 1861. As compositors toiled in the *Herald* offices in the early hours to get out the next morning's edition there was activity in Charleston harbour. At 4.30 a.m. Confederate batteries opened on Fort Sumter, having received no satisfactory assurance that the federal garrison had any intention of evacuating.

The first news that civil war had at last broken out reached New York during the afternoon in a telegram to the *Herald* from its Charleston correspondent.[117] The news spread about the city as extra copies of the *Herald* were run off containing the latest details.[118] Citizen George Templeton Strong wrote in his diary that day '*War* has begun, unless my extra *Herald* lies, and its Charleston despatch is bogus. . . The streets were vocal with news boys – "Extry – a *Herald*! Got the bombardment of Fort Sumter!!!" We concluded it was probably a sell and that we would not be sold, and declined all invitations to purchase for about four blocks. But we could not stand it longer. I sacrificed sixpence and read the news.' Next day: 'on coming home, I find Ellie in possession of a still later *Herald* extra. The ships were engaged with the batteries. . . Two are sunk. The rest are shelling the city, which is on fire. I take this to be invented for the sake of stimulating wrath and fury in the Border States. . . The New York *Herald* is non-committal this morning. It may well be upholding the

[114]*NYH* 17 Jan 1861.

[115]*NYH* 3 Apr 1861.

[116]*NYH* 12 Apr 1861.

[117]Felix Gregory De Fontaine: see article on him in *Dictionary of American Biography,* also Louis M. Starr, *Bohemian Brigade* (NY 1954), pp. 25, 29. De Fontaine was a friend of General Beauregard and the author of a pro-Southern history of anti-slavery which had appeared in the *Herald* in February. He stayed in the South and remained loyal to the Confederacy, though he rejoined the *Herald* after the war.

[118]On Friday 12 Apr 1861 the *Herald* sold 94,000 copies; on Saturday the 13th 107,520, and on Sunday the 14th 135,600; figures *NYH* 15 Apr 1861. The latter was a circulation record for any daily newspaper up to that time.

Administration and denouncing the Democratic party within a week. It takes naturally to eating dirt and its own words (the same thing).'[119]

Strong's intuition was correct in that the federal ships had not engaged the shore batteries or shelled the city. As we shall see too, he was right about the *Herald*'s conversion. This was not immediate, however. On 14 and 15 April Bennett's tone was disgruntled and caustic. He announced

'The War Begun – Dissolution of the Union Consummated'

He mourned the final supercession of the Union of 1789 by military governments North and South and the demise of christianity and civilisation. Not for him the joyful renascence of nationalism which pervaded the North generally. He would make no prediction as to how the war might end, but called for a public meeting to protest against it and to urge peace on the Administration. Lincoln was rebuked for having made insincere professions of peace. On the bright side Bennett could see only that the war would prove 'beneficial, pecuniarily, to the Empire City'. Otherwise he thought the situation would please only two groups of people. First, the rowdies and vagrants of the city, who would now be able to find regular employment in their favourite amusement of destroying life and property. Secondly, the abolition fanatics 'who have toiled and prayed for years for the destruction of the Union'.

What general comment should be made about the *Herald*'s course in the secession crisis? It was consistent in demanding what it regarded as 'justice' for Southern demands on slavery, which is to say full concession of everything they asked for. Say this for Bennett – in his main assumptions he was proved right by events; namely that failure to concede the South its full demands must lead to secession, and that failure to recognise the Confederacy and persistence in holding Fort Sumter must lead ineluctably to war. He could not be accused of underestimating the extent of the crisis or the earnestness of Southern intentions, nor of placing a facile faith in the highly conditional Unionism of the Upper South. All these accusations may to some extent be laid against Lincoln, Seward, Greeley, Raymond and their party. After the firing on Sumter and Lincoln's call for 75,000 volunteers to supress the rebellion, Arkansas, Tennessee, Virginia and North Carolina joined the Confederacy. Bennett was wrong only in that Missouri, Kentucky, Maryland and Delaware held (or were

[119]Nevins and Thomas eds., *The Diary of George Templeton Strong* (NY 1952), vol. III, pp. 117-19, entries for 12, 13 Apr 1861.

held) back. As a prophet he could justly claim a measure of vindication, and he did not disguise from his readers the fearful possibilities of civil war. Bennett deserves some credit for having consistently opposed a fratricidal war – a courageous course which rejected all intellectual dishonesty about the cost of maintaining the Union. His was supposedly the paper of vulgar and irresponsible sensationalism, yet it did not succumb to super-patriotic jingoism and flag waving until after the outbreak of war. Bennett may have lacked high moral principles, but he was not a deliberate war-monger.

On the debit side it must of course be said that after the election of 1860 Bennett stands open to the accusation of having deliberately inflamed excitements and encouraged Southern intransigence in the hope of gaining political advantage over a legal and popularly elected Republican administration. He condoned and perpetuated a relentless attempt at moral and political blackmail against the new regime, regardless of the consequences. If he was an above average prophet it must be said that there was an element of self-fulfilment in his prophecies – the financial panic of December 1860 being the clearest instance. Claiming to be 'patriotic' and 'conservative' he was in reality viciously partisan, and his schemes for 'compromise' were in fact nothing of the kind because they simply took no account of the claims and policies of the party he opposed. He pleaded for 'tolerance' towards the South but displayed a feeling of rancorous intolerance towards the majority party of the North; if he tried to soothe animosities towards the South he was very free with the word 'treason' in regard to anti-slavery men. He helped create an atmosphere of intemperate abuse and political suspicion and hatred which was anything but conducive to peace. In one sense his analysis of the causes of the Civil War was no more profound than many since, in that it consisted merely of saying that there would have been no war if one side had not behaved as it did – where to place the blame being solely a matter of personal predilection. His detestation of the anti-slavery basis of the Republican party is in itself just one more evidence of the bitterness and depth of the political divisions which produced war.

Bennett claimed to be for the Union first and foremost. In fact he was wedded to the Southern Democratic conviction that the Union was inseparable from slavery, and that the preservation of slavery was ultimately more important than that of the Union.

7

THE CONVERSION: THE *HERALD* AND THE OUTBREAK OF WAR, 1861

> The *Herald* may be said to represent, in one particular, the genius of the 'universal Yankee nation' – that is, in its supreme regard for what is vulgarly called the main chance. — New Orleans *Picayune*

> Times changes, and men change jist ez fast ez times. I shood like to see the times wich kin change faster than I kin. — Petroleum V. Nasby

Bennett soon discovered that the temper of the North was far different from what he had imagined it to be. In fact, although the recently published census of 1860 went far to refute the *Herald*'s generous estimate of the economic superiority of the Southern States, it came as something of a real shock to Bennett to discover that a self-conscious North did exist, and one remarkably single-minded on the subject of maintaining the Union.[1] Mayor Fernando Wood joined the *Herald* in predicting popular anger against Lincoln's call for volunteers to suppress the Southern rebellion. In reality the response in New York proved overwhelmingly enthusiastic. The only appearance of anything like a riot in the city was when a crowd gathered outside the *Herald* offices to make Bennett hang out an American flag.

On 15 April Lincoln's proclamation calling for 75,000 militia was made public. That same morning the *Times* attacked the *Herald* in a stinging editorial entitled 'A Question a Good Many People Are Asking'.

> Is there to be no limit [demanded Raymond] to the *Herald's* open advocacy of treason and rebellion? That print has done everything in its power to encourage and stimulate the secession movement. It has vilified the Government, belied the people of the Northern States, scattered broadcast throughout the South the most infamous falsehoods concerning the public sentiment in this City, and done everything in its power to incite the South to the open war into which they have at last plunged the country. . .
> The *Herald* announces a meeting in the Park to declare against coercion. It is rather late in the day to stigmatize the effort of the Government to protect itself from destruction as coercion. And

[1] On 17 Apr 1861, Bennett called the unanimity of the North 'startling'.

> when the *Herald* succeeds in getting together a public meeting in
> this City to protest against taking any steps to redress the outrage
> of Fort Sumpter [sic]. . . we trust Mr. Bennett will consent to make
> the opening speech in person. He will receive such a greeting as
> will probably discourage his oratory, if it does not cure his
> treason.

Raymond's indignation was shared by the excited crowd which
gathered outside the *Herald* offices that grey, rainy Monday morning.
The throng soon filled the sidewalk and, according to the restrained
language of the *Times* reporter, 'hooted and indulged in various
expressions of dislike to that establishment', threatening loudly that
they would mob it unless the Stars and Stripes were displayed
promptly. This was a curious situation for a self-styled leader of
majority opinion to be in.

Bennett had apparently expected an attack on Sunday night and a
reserve police force was discreetly kept in readiness at the downtown
stations to protect the *Herald* premises if necessary. However, the
Herald's readiness apparently did not extend to having an American
flag handy. The *Tribune* later hinted that Bennett, anticipating a
different popular sentiment, had provided his establishment with a set
of secessionist colours only and had to send out to purchase those of
the Union. At any rate there was a long delay during which the mood
of the crowd waxed very ugly. Finally, at about 4.30 in the afternoon,
an American ensign was dropped slowly from an upper window where
for several minutes it hung against the building. Commingled groans
and cheers greeted this tardy compliance with the popular wish.
Shortly afterwards a lad was seen running towards the office with
another flag attached to a staff, and this was soon displayed from a
window on the second storey. After this the crowd gradually
dispersed, 'no doubt to the great relief of the establishment', said the
Times man.[2]

Bennett was soon to deny that any of this had happened except in
the malignant imaginations of Republican journalists, though it was
said that from that day forward stands of muskets were kept handy in
the *Herald* offices.[3]

[2]This account follows reports in the *Times* and *Tribune* of 16 and 17 Apr 1861. Other
Democratic journals received visitations from the crowd. The *Sun* of 16 Apr thought
that the issue of the *Herald* for another day would have been 'more than doubtful' if
Bennett had failed to show the flag.

[3]The *Herald* of 17 Apr asserted that the crowd outside its offices had been there to get
news, that the raising of the flag had been a purely patriotic gesture, and that Bennett
had been treated with ordinary courtesy in public. The malignity of the *Times* and
Tribune reports was, said Bennett, a symptom of their jealousy of the *Herald's*
unparalleled success and popularity with the public. The story of the muskets is in
Seitz, *The James Gordon Bennetts* (NY 1928), p. 178.

The effect of the demonstration of 15 April was made plain in the *Herald* for Tuesday morning, 16 April 1861. Bennett now announced that 'the actual presence of war cuts short all debate. . . there will now be but one party, one question, one issue, one purpose in the Northern States — that of sustaining the government'. Approving Lincoln's 'vigorous' war measures, Bennett conceded that although the damage which war must inflict on the South was to be regretted 'it will be none the less well, if it secures final peace to the country'. Yesterday he had called for a peace meeting to oppose this 'causeless and senseless appeal to arms'; now he dismissed such an idea as outdated. Finally he was pleased to come to the defence of Major Anderson and the Sumter garrison against charges by the bellicose Webb in the *Courier and Enquirer* that they had hauled down their flag too soon.[4]

Of course the Republican press had a field day at what Greeley exulted over as 'the most sudden and total change of opinion on record, surpassing in its quickness anything ever effected by the most successful missionary'. Reporting the occurrences outside the *Herald* office and the display of 'the flag of that Union which the *Herald* has done so much to destroy', the *Tribune* nevertheless disapproved of mob action: 'The cause of the Union is the cause of Law and Order. . . The true way to deal with these disloyal sheets is to let them alone. If all good citizens would cease to buy them they would be suppressed much more effectually than by mob violence, which only tends to give them notoriety and to excite sympathy for them by natural reaction in favor of the freedom of the press.'[5] Raymond in the *Times* was more bitter and implacable. Calling Bennett a 'reckless scoundrel', he asserted that 'the fact is the old Harlequin is about "played out". People are beginning to take too serious views of public affairs to render his damnable contortions amusing.'[6]

George T. Strong reflected in his diary on Bennett's volte face and its importance to the North:

> The conversion of the New York *Herald* is complete. It rejoices that rebellion is to be put down and is delighted with Civil War, because it will so stimulate the business of New York, and all this is what 'we' (the *Herald,* to wit) have been vainly preaching for months. This impudence of old J.G. Bennett's is too vast to be appreciated at once. You must look at it and meditate over it for some time (as at Niagara and St. Peter's) before you can take in its immensity. His capitulation is a set-off against the loss of

[4]See NY *Courier & Enquirer* 13-15 Apr 1861.
[5]NY *Daily Tribune* 16, 17 Apr 1861.
[6]NY *Times* 17 Apr 1861.

Sumter. He's a discreditable ally for the North, but when you see a rat leaving the enemy's ship for your own, you overlook the offensiveness of the vermin for the sake of what its movement indicates. This brazen old scoundrel was hooted up Fulton Street yesterday afternoon by a mob, and the police interfered to prevent it from sacking his printing office. Though converted, one can hardly call him penitent. St. Paul did not call himself the Chief of the Apostles and brag of having been a Christian from the first.[7]

On succeeding days the *Herald* manifested all the zeal of the newly converted. Declaring that 'they who are not with the government are against it', the *Herald* was loudest in threatening Maryland with the iron fist if she attempted secession, and warned her that the demoniac roughs of the Northern cities were quite up to suppressing the secessionist 'plug uglies' of Baltimore. Washington must be saved at any price from the 'secession rabble', thundered Bennett, and he pronounced that the Southern Confederacy, by the 'cowardly' attack on Fort Sumter, had 'wantonly and wickedly inaugurated hostilities in order to dissever and destroy the republic'.[8] Making an open breast of things to his readers, he confessed that events had enlightened him: 'We now understand that we have been deceived by a deliberate and comprehensive rebellion. . . . We now perceive that President Lincoln is right in treating this grand conspiracy and its developments as a gigantic insurrection, and in exercising his constitutional powers to suppress it. . . .'[9] He was at pains to show that the *Herald* had always, and in fact before anybody else, favoured the maintenance of Federal authority, and daily defamation of Buchanan became a ritual.[10] Denying accusations of disunionism, he rationalised the *Herald's* change of front: 'the policy of this journal has been to save the Union, to avoid war and to restore harmony through sectional concessions and compromises. To this end we have vindicated the constitutional rights and the cause of the South to the very last day of peace. We had hoped that, in avoiding war, the seceded States might be reclaimed. . .' He professed horror that Southerners should have been guilty of 'deceiving their friends in the North with false professions of attachment to the Union', and concluded that 'thus relieved of the thankless office of a peacemaker, this journal is free to undertake the

---

[7]Nevins and Thomas eds., *The Diary of George Templeton Strong* (NY 1952), vol. III, p. 122, entry for 16 Apr 1861.

[8]*NYH* 20, 22, 25, 27, 28 Apr; 1 May 1861.

[9]*NYH* 20 Apr 1861.

[10]See above p. 104.

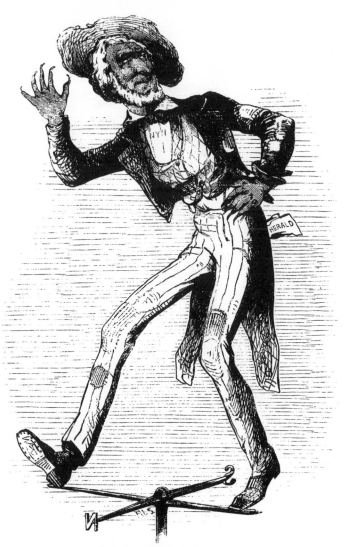

THE EDITORIAL JIM CROW.

Wheel about, an' turn about,
  An' do jis' so,
An' ebery time I turn my coat
  I says I told you so.

The wind veers to northerly.
(From *Vanity Fair*, 17 April 1861).

unqualified duty of sustaining the cause of the government and of the Union. . .'[11]

Bennett had now embraced the belief that the restoration of the Union by warfare was a feasible proposition. So unstinting was the spontaneous offering of money and men in the North that the *Herald* predicted that the conflict would be short. A great mass meeting for the Union was held in the city on 20 April, at which even Fernando Wood advocated re-establishment of the Union by force.[12] Bennett himself subscribed $3,000 to a fund to equip the volunteer regiments, and the *Herald* started a popular subscription to support the families of the departing soldiers.[13] The rally was described in the *Herald* as 'more than a meeting — it was a national ovation'.[14] The Seventh Regiment marched out of the city amid deafening acclaim and the *Herald* celebrated the occasion with a large woodcut representation of the scene at the New Jersey Railroad depot.[15] In the enthusiasm of the moment Bennett saw spiritual values in the war which might outweigh its bloodshed and vindictiveness.

Civil War, he wrote, 'is now the scourge for our national vices and the instrument of restoring health and purity. As the thunderstorm purifies the atmosphere, so does the tempest of war. It will sweep away the miserable wire pullers and politicians and it will bring forth a new set of men, with lofty ideas, high purposes and brilliant talents. . . .'[16] Changing the metaphor he meditated further that without purification in the fires of war 'society would become stagnant and corrupt' and without suffering patriotism and heroism would be lost to a degenerate mankind.[17] Before the war, the *Herald* confessed, the great standard by which Americans judged excellence had been shrewdness in the purchase and sale of stocks and proficiency and cunning in the art of money making; 'Mammon seemed to be our God'. Now, it predicted, nobler sentiments would arise. The whole country was feverishly involved in some way in organising a war effort.

Yet it would be a mistake to exaggerate the extent to which party differences were submerged by the outbreak of war, notwithstanding

[11]*NYH* 18, 20, 24 Apr 1861.
[12]See S. Pleasants, *Fernando Wood* (NY 1948), pp. 120-1.
[13]*NYH* 28 Apr 1861.
[14]*NYH* 20, 21, 22 Apr 1861.
[15]*NYH* 20 Apr 1861.
[16]*NYH* 19 Apr 1861.
[17]*NYH* 29 Apr 1861.

the volume of 'save the Union' oratory from Republicans and Democrats alike. This was after all a civil war. The impression of unanimity was doubtless helped by the fact that Congress was not in session at the time, but April was not out before the political issues of the war years had appeared in embryo.

Bennett's conversion to thorough-going Unionism by no means inclined him to trail in the political wake of the Republican press. The New York papers were soon indulging in mutual recriminations, Republicans and Democrats each claiming to have a premium on patriotism. Bennett claimed that not only was the *Herald* in front of the Republicans in this respect but that the intentions of the majority party were positively inimical to the restoration of the Union. A headline such as 'War Democratic Patriotism Versus Republican Folly and Ferocity' (2 May) was hardly calculated to abate the spirit of party.

The *Herald* claimed that four-fifths (or on some days nine-tenths) of New York's volunteers were Democrats, and conversely complained of the Republican controlled State Military Board. The *Herald*'s dire threats of the economic disaster which secession would entail for New York had gone awry. Instead the need to equip departing regiments meant profitable contracts to manufacturers able to supply shoes, uniforms, tents and other essentials. The war was only a few weeks old when Bennett was charging Republican corruption in awarding contracts, and negligence and swindling against contractors themselves.[18] He was also wrathful that the State Military Board should allegedly be guided by nepotism and favouritism in handing out commissions in the army to Republican politicians. He was tolerably consistent in demanding that Brigadier- and Major Generalships should be filled by Congress mostly from the ranks of West Point graduates.[19] Of course he may have borne in mind that a high proportion of regular army officers were Democrats, but he was on firm ground in arguing that high military rank was too important to be conferred as a political reward and that the regular army should provide the nucleus of a volunteer organisation. The idea that popular opinion demanded 'political' generals finds scant support from the *Herald* files. Non-professional appointments were apparently desired more by the politicians concerned than by the Democracy at large,

[18]*NYH* 7, 13 June 1861.

[19]*NYH* 12, 13, 15 June 1861. But the *Herald* did support the appointments of John C. Fremont and Nathaniel Banks to high rank.

which as the rank and file of the army would suffer the murderous consequences of inexpert leadership.[20]

While it was natural that Democrats should wish to publicise their own role in the great patriotic conflict, they were not just vying with the Republicans for the honours of sacrifice and combat. The question of the aims for which the North was fighting very soon came in for newspaper debate. Bennett represented Democratic opinion in calling for a narrow construction of war aims; that is, for a brief war to reassert the integrity of the Union. He frankly confessed his desire 'to save in the Southern States their peculiar institutions from a violent overthrow'.[21] Not only did he hope that the war would not harm slavery but he called on the government to ensure it 'generous protection. . . regardless of abolition clamors'. He wanted it perfectly understood that even 'with all this ardor at the North, there does not exist the least wish to subjugate the South'.[22]

Yet paradoxically Bennett was outspoken in defending Lincoln's assumption of executive power in the early days of the war because 'self preservation is the first law of governments as it is of nature'.[23] Chief Justice Taney was branded a secessionist by the *Herald* when he filed a protest against a violation of habeas corpus, and the paper praised Lincoln's determination to save the Union regardless of legal niceties.[24] Like other 'War Democrats'[25] Bennett nevertheless

---

[20]*NYH* 2 June 1861.

[21]*NYH* 11 May 1861. On 18 Apr Bennett appealed to Virginia and the other border states to remain in the Union 'in behalf of their institution of slavery, their political and social safety'.

[22]*NYH* 30 Apr; 21 May 1861.

[23]*NYH* 5 June 1861.

[24]*NYH* 9 June 1861. This was the celebrated case *Ex Parte Merryman*. On this and other legal aspects of the war see J.G. Randall, *Constitutional Problems under Lincoln* (1951) and A.H. Kelly and W.A. Harbison, *The American Constitution* (NY 1970), ch 16, esp. pp. 437-41.

[25]Christopher Dell, *Lincoln and the War Democrats* (Rutherford 1975) is a gallant attempt to pioneer an important subject, and contains some useful political data on the wartime activities of Democrats. However, some of its classifications of 'War Democrats' are curious; it actually says little about Lincoln; and in scant references to Bennett mispells his name. There is room for another work in the field. Joel H. Silbey, *A Respectable Minority* (NY 1977), unfortunately dismisses the 'War Democrats' rather briefly (pp. 56-9), confining his study to the rump of the party on the premise that when 'War Democrats' announced themselves as such they became in effect nothing else but Republican converts. This approach seems to minimise the allegiance which many of them retained for their political home, the Democratic Party proper, and the interest which they felt in having it fully support a war policy. The *Herald* had hardly been a Democratic organ as such, but neither did it come close to embracing Republicanism, or the 'Union' party.

remained hypersensitive to any suggestion of infringing the 'rights' of slaveholders, and was horrified at the prospect of the confiscation of rebel property by Congress. He did not feel the incongruity of an interpretation of the Constitution which allowed the killing and imprisonment of Southerners who opposed US authority, but not the alienation of their property. With astounding glibness the *Herald* predicted that after a few months of 'mutual extermination' North and South would learn respect for each other and become better friends.[26] Grasping the truth that the hatred between North and South transcended any of the political issues at stake, Bennett raced on to the conclusion that physical confrontation would satisfy the anger of both sides, and that the issues which had produced division in the first place would be heard of no more after trial by battle had successfully restored the Union. The outbreak of war did not destroy his faith in the Crittenden Compromise as a framework for settlement which might be imposed by Congress after a Union victory.[27]

From the outset Bennett was adamant that the war must not 'degenerate' into an anti-slavery crusade as the 'incendiary' Republican press desired. He warned against the 'vandals of the New York *Tribune*. . . [who]. . . are preaching a ferocious crusade which, if adopted, will carry us into the endless horrors of Mexican anarchy'.[28] His lectures against 'Republican Journalism — Its Brutal and Bloodthirsty Character', delivered in early May, predictably angered the accused who retorted that Bennett, 'the trembling traitor' of the 'Daily Tumbler' had changed his mind but not his heart about the rebellion.[29] When Bennett 'exposed' the perfidy of Jefferson Davis one day in his main editorial, the *Times* rejoined that the Southern President was not half so responsible for the rebellion as was the editor of the *Herald*.[30] So the feud went on, portending more bitter struggles over war aims if the contest were prolonged. Bennett loved Republicans no better because he happened to be on their side in a civil war. They in turn were fearful that the support of the erratic and cynical *Herald* might embarrass and damage the course of the Lincoln administration.[31] Inside the White House John Hay, Lincoln's secretary, while sorting through the obscene and threatening letters

[26]*NYH* 29 Apr 1861.

[27]*NYH* 9, 10 May 1861.

[28]*NYH* 2 May 1861.

[29]*NYH* 5 May; NY *Daily Tribune* 23 May 1861.

[30]*NYH* 30 Apr; 6 May 1861 for the 'Conspiracy of Jefferson Davis and His Associates to Destroy the Union', and NY *Times* 10 May for rejoinder.

[31]NY *Times* 10 May 1861.

sent to the President by secession sympathisers, thought that 'blasphemy rolls as awkward and malformed from a seceding pen, as patriotism or purity from the lips of James Gordon Bennett'.[32]

That thinly smothered party antagonisms were potent and clearly defined in the weeks following Sumter was curtly illustrated by Bennett's threat, made on 1 May, that 'Abolition will hang on the same tree with rebellion'.

Two interesting anecdotes survive concerning Bennett's conversion in 1861. The first and more authentic is related by Henry Villard.[33] Villard, a German American, had been employed by the *Herald* since November 1860 to accompany Lincoln and forward reports from Springfield.[34] In February he was appointed Washington correspondent for the *Herald*. Villard's acquaintance with Lincoln was of great value to Bennett, but the staunchly Republican reporter was rather unhappy about representing a paper which so abused his party editorially. He therefore made it a condition that his news despatches should not be edited in a political sense, and Bennett faithfully stuck to this agreement. On 16 April Villard received a cable from Bennett asking him to come to New York, and the reporter, drawn by the opportunity to learn more about 'this notorious character', took the night train.

Next afternoon he was privileged to accompany Bennett on his regular carriage ride from the *Herald* offices up Broadway and Fifth Avenue and through Central Park to Washington Heights. He found all his prejudices against the editor confirmed. Admitting that his host still had a 'fine tall slender figure, large intellectual head covered with an abundance of light curly hair, and strong regular features', Villard thought his exterior spoiled by his crossed eyes, 'which gave him a sinister, forbidding look'. Conversation with Bennett, Villard wrote, 'quickly revealed his hard, cold, utterly selfish nature and incapacity to appreciate high and noble aims'.

During dinner Bennett interrogated Villard about Lincoln's intentions and characteristics, and afterwards requested him to assure

[32]Tyler Dennett ed., *Lincoln and the Civil War in the Diaries and Letters of John Hay* (NY 1939), entry for 24 Apr 1861; see also Tyler Dennett, *John Hay* (NY 1933), p. 40.

[33]Henry Villard, *Memoirs, 1835-1900* (Boston & NY 1904), vol. I, pp. 153, 161-3. Villard was the father of the same Oswald Garrison Villard who was later to write about Bennett in *Some Newspapers and Newspapermen.*

[34]Tom Reilly, 'Early Coverage of a President-Elect: Lincoln at Springfield, 1860', *Journalism Quarterly,* 49 (1972) reprints many extracts from Villard's Springfield correspondence and shows that Lincoln may have deliberately used the *Herald* , via Villard, as a sounding board for proposed Cabinet appointments.

Lincoln personally that the *Herald* would support the government's war measures. Villard was pleased to carry such a message, though he had to suppress his amusement at the editor's air of magnanimity, for he knew all about the mob scene two days previously. Also present at dinner was Bennett's son and namesake, and the sire asked Villard to convey the offer of his son's sailing yacht to Secretary of the Treasury Chase as a gift to the government for use in the revenue service. In return, he intended to ask for the youth's appointment as lieutenant in the same service. Villard, again seeing the humour of the situation, agreed to see Chase, to whom he had ready access (having worked on the Cincinnati *Commercial,* a Chase organ in Ohio). To his pleasure the reporter learned next day that Bennett had raised his weekly allowance to $35. He covered the first battle of Bull Run for the *Herald.*

Following Villard's mission Bennett's son made his own way to Washington and saw Secretary of State Seward on 6 May. Seward took him to Lincoln, who in turn wrote out a favourable note of introduction to Chase.[35] A week later, on 15 May 1861, James Gordon Bennett Jr. was commissioned third lieutenant in the revenue service, in command of his 160 ton yacht *Henrietta.*[36] He served only a year and apparently had some difficulty with the concept of taking orders. He resigned when his yacht was withdrawn from the service after an uneventful and routine term of service.[37] Bennett senior may well have felt the comparison when the son of his old rival Webb went on to be a major general and a hero of Gettysburg, but at least a Bennett had put on the uniform of his country.[38]

Another dinner table anecdote about Bennett's change of course was written down by no less a personage than Thurlow Weed. Weed recalled the incident when he was in his dotage, and perhaps it should not be given very much weight:[39] for instance he could only date his reminiscence to within 'several weeks' after the outbreak of

[35]Text in R.P. Basler ed., *The Collected Works of Abraham Lincoln,* vol. IV, p. 357.

[36]*Ibid.*

[37]Bennett Jr. resigned on 11 May 1862 — see D.C. Seitz, *The James Gordon Bennetts* (NY 1928), p. 182. Richard O'Connor, *The Scandalous Mr. Bennett* (NY 1962), p. 40, gives an amusing account of his services. Letters from Bennett Jr. to his father dated 31 Jan and 18 Feb 1862 are found in the Bennett Papers, Library of Congress.

[38]For Bennett's sensitivity to his son's reputation see *NYH* 22, 25 Mar 1862. See also Bennett to Salmon P. Chase 9 Sept 1861, Chase Papers, Library of Congress.

[39]Weed, *Autobiography* (2 vols, Boston 1883), vol. I, pp. 615-19.

war, and was insistent that the appearance of the mob on 15 April had not altered the *Herald*'s course — which was incorrect.[40]

Even so Weed's narrative contains an interesting glimpse of Bennett. Weed introduced his little scenario by saying that *Herald* editorials had been giving encouragement to the rebel cause and that US representatives abroad were fearful that the *Herald,* with its large European circulation, was creating a dangerous public sentiment in Europe against the Union. It was true that although before Sumter the *Herald* had fervently decreed Britain's interest to lie in alliance with the South, afterwards it threatened war daily on 'perfidious Albion' for so much as daring to recognize the Confederacy as a belligerent. Only a short while before the battle of Bull Run the *Herald* announced that the people were bored with the 'ridiculous' confrontation of the two armies in Virginia, and it clung to the notion that reunion might be achieved easily by war against a European power. Its free and aggressive language towards neutral powers was calculated to annoy.[41]

Weed recounted how a worried President Lincoln had raised the matter of the *Herald*'s attitude at a cabinet meeting and had resolved to make an 'earnest appeal' to Bennett. Weed was telegraphed and personally requested by Lincoln to bell the cat.[42] Weed recalled that he had been reluctant to comply, for although he and Bennett insulted each other with a will in the columns of their respective newspapers, they had not otherwise been on speaking terms for thirty years. However, Weed secured an invitation to dine with Bennett through an intermediary.

So again to the dining room at Fort Washington. After a servant had cleared away the meal Weed made bold to state his mission, and stressed the importance which Lincoln attached to the *Herald*'s support. Bennett had received Weed cordially, but now burst into a long and bitter denunciation of Greeley, Garrison, Seward, Senator Sumner, Joshua Giddings, Wendell Phillips and Weed himself for having irritated and exasperated the South until the country was plunged into war. Weed, diagnosing that Bennett's mind 'had been so absorbed in his idea of the pernicious nature of abolition that he had entirely lost sight of the real causes of the rebellion', had no choice but

[40]See also Howard K. Beale ed., *The Diary of Gideon Welles* (NY 1960), vol. I, pp. 78-9, entry for 10 Aug 1862. A letter dated 'Sunday July 28' in the Bennett Papers, Library of Congress, indicates that Weed was expected to dinner that day, but was unable to attend. July 28 fell on a Sunday in 1861.

[41]*NYH* 11, 18, 19, 23, 27-30 June; 1-7 July 1861.

[42]This would accord with Lincoln's use of Weed as a semi-official emissary to Europe during the war.

to submit to this diatribe for ten minutes. He then replied, arguing that a deliberate secessionist conspiracy had existed to break up the Union. He claimed to have 'startled' Bennett by this revelation, and to have converted the editor to the Union. Indeed, Weed intimated that he had made Bennett permanently loyal to the Lincoln administration, and that the gratified Lincoln and Seward determined to offer Bennett a diplomatic post as a reward as soon as convenient.

The sketch of Bennett's after dinner monologue seems in character, but it is hard to reconcile Weed's recollection with Villard's, or with the *Herald*'s known course from 16 April onwards. Also, as subsequent chapters will reveal, the *Herald*'s enthusiasm for the Lincoln administration fluctuated markedly during the President's first term, and the eventual offer of a diplomatic post to Bennett had far more to do with the politics of the election of 1864 than with the occurences of 1861.[43] It was also odd that Weed should imagine that his interview with Bennett had restored friendly relations between them, because for the rest of the war the *Herald* hounded Weed with accusations of jobbery and corruption (some of them well founded).[44] Bennett was evidently not so impressed with this love feast as his guest, for even in his more genial editorials thereafter he was apt to refer to Weed in such terms as 'superannuated imbecile'. No doubt Weed flattered himself that he had achieved more than was actually the case, perhaps not grasping the full significance of his own observation that at their parting Bennett was affable but non-committal. It is very unlikely that Weed's visit had more influence on Bennett than the state of Northern opinion as manifested outside his office on 15 April.

[43] See below, chapter 13, where it will be shown that in 1865 Weed was actually astounded to learn that Bennett had been offered a foreign post — a circumstance which hardly squares with the claim in his *Autobiography* to have been instrumental in procuring it.

[44] On Weed's war-time activities see G. Van Deusen, *Thurlow Weed* (Boston 1947).

8

INTERLUDE: THE *HERALD* IN THE CIVIL WAR

> Mr. Bennett desires the best arrangements made for efficiency
> and completeness. — Frederic Hudson to *Herald* correspondent
> W.H. Stiner, 9 July 1862[1]

Getting the News

Whatever else it may have been, the Civil War was the greatest news
story of the age, and it created an enormous public appetite for news
which the *Herald* did its best to satisfy.[2]

Not that the war was an unqualified blessing for the newspaper
industry. It created new opportunities, but the beginning of the war
coincided with rising costs in materials and labour.[3] Its first fruits
therefore included the demise of a number of the smaller New York
papers. Among the journals which gave up the struggle to survive was
the *Courier and Enquirer.* Webb had secured himself the embassy to
Brazil as a reward for loyal support of Seward. Thus the redoubtable
duellist resigned his editorship of a long unprofitable journal and set
sail. Bennett, flinging jibes after him, had lost his sparring partner of a
generation.[4]

The New York *World,* which merged with the *Courier,* soon got
into parlous condition ('The wicked *World* is about to come to an end'

---

[1]Stiner MSS., New York Historical Society.

[2]In this section I have again chiefly relied on the *Herald* itself and the Bennett Papers
in the Library of Congress. Frederic Hudson treats war journalism in his *History of
Journalism,* pp. 482-3, 715-19. Two modern histories of journalism have systematic
chapters on the war — F.L. Mott, *American Journalism* (NY 1962), and E. Emery,
The Press and America (Englewood Cliffs 1972). There is a good chapter on the Civil
War in Joseph J. Mathews, *Reporting the Wars* (Minneapolis 1957), ch 6. Best of a
number of specialised studies is Louis M. Starr, *Bohemian Brigade* (NY 1954). Two
works which deal colourfully and at length with war correspondents are Emmet
Crozier, *Yankee Reporters 1861-5* (NY 1956) and J. Cutler Andrews, *The North
Reports the Civil War* (Pittsburg 1955), which is well illustrated and reproduces some
of the corrrespondence in the Bennett Papers. Bernard A. Weisberger, *Reporters for
the Union* (Boston 1953), considers newspapermen in a political light as party
pamphleteers and it contains a chapter 'Mr. Bennett's War on the *Herald*'s coverage of
events. All these studies have used the Bennett Papers. See also Edward L. Carter,
'The Revolution in Journalism During the Civil War', *Lincoln Herald,* 73 (1971),
229-40.

[3]*NYH* 9 Apr; 2 July 1861; Mott, p. 329.

[4]*NYH* 20 Apr; 4 May; 25 June; 2 July 1861; J.L. Crouthamel,*James Watson Webb*
(Middletown 1969), p. 148 ff.

crowed the *Herald*)[5] and it eventually survived only after changing politics. Under the editorship of Manton Marble it became the leading organ of the Democratic Party in the City.[6] Among the smaller Democratic journals the *Daily News, Journal of Commerce, Day Book, Freeman's Journal* and *Brooklyn Eagle,*[7] which had not followed Bennett's example in swallowing their Southern sympathies, were soon in trouble with public opinion and the authorities.[8]

To meet the challenge of the war, great demands were made on the capital resources of newspaper establishments. The *Herald* was better able than any to meet that requirement, and so not merely survived but developed in the struggle for news and circulation. So much was this so that by the middle of the war Bennett was in favour of heavier taxes on newspapers, knowing that the *Herald* could stand them while some of its competitors could not.[9] The *Herald* had sold for two cents since 1836, but in December 1862 it went up to three cents and in August 1864 to four cents.

During the war Bennett worked on the same principles that had brought success in the previous quarter century and particularly in the Mexican War: he invested lavishly (something over half a million dollars) in obtaining news coverage on the well calculated gamble that increased circulation would justify the outlay.

Getting the news was still an extremely competitive business, despite the institution of the Associated Press and a certain camaraderie among war correspondents. As a contemporary put it: 'Napoleon assures us that the whole art of war consists in having the greatest force at the point of contact. This rule applies to the art of journalism; the editor of the *Herald* knows it, and has the means to put it into practice.'[10] Superior organisation and full staffing were the keys to the *Herald*'s success. Bennett boasted that the *Herald* maintained at least forty correspondents in the field at any one time, and sometimes as

[5]*NYH* 15 Aug 1862.

[6]On Marble and the *World* see George T. McJimsey, *Genteel Partisan* (Iowa 1971) and on the sale of the *World* to Democratic Party interests Irving Katz, *August Belmont* (NY 1968), pp. 116-18. *The Manton Marble Collection* in the University of London Library contains many items of interest on Marble, the *World* and the contemporary press.

[7]See R.A. Schroth, *The Eagle and Brooklyn* (Westport 1974).

[8]*NYH* 29 Aug 1861; see also Robert S. Harper, *Lincoln and the Press* (NY 1951), ch 15.

[9]*NYH* 6 Mar 1861. In 1863 Bennett claimed that the tax due on the *Herald's* carriages, yachts, billiard tables, silver and gold plate was $4,000.

[10]James Parton, 'The New York Herald', *North American Review,* 102 (1866), 373-419.

many as sixty-three.[11] This was a much larger force than any other journal could deploy. A *Herald* waggon, providing reporters with a base and facilities independent of the whims of army commanders, was a common sight at the front.[12]

The 'Special Correspondents' were the aristocracy of journalism and led a glamorous but demanding life. Bennett expected his reporters to give their personal best. A circular to them from the *Herald* office enjoined

> In no instance, and under no circumstances, must you be beaten. You will have energetic and watchful men to compete with. Eternal industry is the price of success. You must be active — very active. To be beaten is to be open to great censure. . .
>
> Remember that your correspondence is seen by half a million persons daily and that the readers of the *Herald must* have the earliest news. . . Again bear in mind that *the Herald must never be beaten.*[13]

To obey this ukase *Herald* men were supposed to work any hours and under all conditions to get a story. Everything had to be subordinated to getting that story to the *Herald* office by foot, horse, train, boat or telegraph before any other paper had the news. Reporters who did this might expect a handsome increase in salary, for Bennett never quibbled about paying the bill if the news was worth it; those who failed got short shrift. This system led to some spectacular 'beats', comparable to the great duels of the 1840s. Sometimes, as with the news of Shiloh, the *Herald* man won the race, sometimes, as with the news of Antietam and the Wilderness, one of his rivals. In 1862 the managing editor of the *Tribune* wrote to one of his correspondents complaining that 'the *Herald* is constantly ahead of us' with news. By ill luck a *Herald* man got hold of this letter, Bennett reprinted it in a gleeful editorial,[14] and the *Tribune* people were not allowed to forget it for months. When the boot was on the other foot there was jubilation in the Greeley camp. Recounting how an irate Bennett had telegraphed his Washington bureau five times in one day to inquire why news from the Wilderness battlefield was late, a *Tribune* reporter confessed that

[11]*NYH* 11 July 1865.

[12]See *Gardner's Photographic Sketch Book of the Civil War,* plate 56.

[13]A.D. Richardson to S. Gay, 11 Apr 1863, enclosure, Sidney H. Gay Papers, quoted in Starr, p. 233. See also Hudson to W.H. Stiner 9 July 1862; 30 Mar 1864, Stiner MSS., New York Historical Society.

[14]*NYH* 16 May 1862.

202

'it does compensate some for one's army discomforts to beat the unconscionable old braggart'.[15]

Herald reporters generally shared the reputation of their establishment for being high in enterprise and low in ethics. They were encouraged to pay for news when necessary,[16] and the system Bennett fostered certainly got results. One of the best reporters, George Alfred Townsend, not only covered the Peninsula battles for the paper but left us this memorable portrait of the *Herald* agent with the Army of the Potomac at that time:

> He was a shrewd, sanguine, middle-aged man, of large experience and good standing in our establishment. . . Such a thorough individual abnegation I never knew. He was part of the establishment, body and soul. He agreed with its politics, adhered to all its policies, defended it, upheld it, revered it. The Federal Government was, to his eye, merely an adjunct of the paper. Battles and seiges were simply occurrences for its columns. Good men, brave men, bad men, died to give it obituaries. The whole world was to him a reporter's district, and all human mutations plain matters of news. I hardly think that any city, other than New York, contains such characters. The journals there are full of fever, and the profession of journalism is a disease.[17]

The story of the 'Special Correspondents' of the period has been well told.[18] The Bennett Papers in the Library of Congress containing reports from Malcolm Ives, S. P. Hanscom, L. A. Whitely, S. M. Carpenter, Finley M. Anderson, D. B. R. Keim,[19] W. H. Stiner, W. G. Shanks, Thomas W. Knox, T. M. Cook and other *Herald* men in the field have long been recognised as an invaluable source for study of how the war was covered by the press. A number of the 'Specials' later wrote narratives of their war-time exploits which revealed how they themselves had given the commanding general or admiral the idea that produced victory, or had carried the vital messages which turned the tide of battle, or saved the general's life by their presence of mind etc.; all of which may or may not be true. General Meade

[15]Homer Byington to Sidney H. Gay, Gay Papers, quoted in Starr, p. 308. On the rivalry of *Herald* and *Tribune* men in the field generally see *ibid.*, pp. 232-9, and the works of Andrews, Crozier and Weisberger cited above, *passim.*

[16]See L.A. Whiteley to F. Hudson, 29 Nov 1863, Bennett Papers, LC.

[17]George A. Townsend, *Rustics in Rebellion* (Chapel Hill, 1950), p. 71. (Originally published as *Campaigns of a Non-Combatant* (NY 1866).

[18]For reference see note 2 above.

[19]Keim's Civil War *Scrapbook,* containing clippings of his war correspondence for the *Herald,* is preserved in the manuscript division of the Library of Congress.

however observed that 'the race of newspaper correspondents is universally despised by the soldiers'.

In fact correspondents could enjoy a rather privileged existence. It was not unknown for newspapermen to serve as military aides — an arrangement which enabled reporters to be conveniently near to the sources of information while providing certain reputation conscious officers with what might now be called a press agent. *Herald* men with the Union armies were the fore-runners 'of the line of war correspondents who became so conspicuous. . . and are now so abundant, enterprising and dangerous, on the outskirts of all wars: men whose personal courage is often equal to their conceit, but who do not hesitate to make or mar the reputation of generals and admirals according to their fancy'.[20] An exchange of 'news for puffs' enabled generals of modest military abilities — Daniel Sickles for instance[21] — to achieve a disproportionate fame at the expense of those (such as General Meade) whose temperaments made them less forward in cultivating the organs of democracy. This was one of the basic conditions of Civil War journalism, which was in general remarkably free of systematic government and military control.

Northern newspapers showed a lack of restraint in publishing troop numbers and dispositions or proposed movements where they could learn of them,[22] and although its record was perhaps not so bad as the *Times*'s and the *Tribune*'s the *Herald* was not exempt from guilt when lives were lost as a result of editorial obtuseness about

[20]Henry K. Douglas, *I Rode with Stonewall* (Chapel Hill 1940), p. 83.

[21] See e.g. Sickles to Bennett 24 May 1863, forwarding army correspondence, Bennett Papers, LC. Little wonder that the *Herald* boosted Sickles as the hero of Chancellorsville and Gettysburg. Under the signature 'Historicus', Sickles penned a series of articles for the *Herald* highly critical of General Meade, his commander at Gettysburg. There is material on Sickles' wartime relationship with the *Herald* in W.A. Swanberg, *Sickles the Incredible* (NY 1956), *passim*. Assistant Secretary of the Navy Gustavus V. Fox was another who took care to bestow favours on *Herald* men — see Malcolm Ives to Bennett, 8 Feb 1862; T.M. Cook to Hudson, 3 Nov 1864, Bennett Papers, L.C.

[22]The whole question of Civil War censorship is well summarised in Emery, pp. 239-45. Long the standard authority on the subject was James G. Randall, 'The Newspaper Problem in its Bearing Upon Military Secrecy During the Civil War', *American Historical Review,* 23 (1918), 302-23. This may be supplemented by Adolph O. Goldsmith, 'Reporting the Civil War: Union Army Press Relations', *Journalism Quarterly,* 33 (1956), 478-87, and Quintus Wilson, 'Voluntary Press Censorship During the Civil War', *Journalism Quarterly,* 19, 251-61. Congress reported on the subject during the war and its findings are in *House Report 64 of the 37th Congress (2nd session).* The committee concluded that censorship by the Secretary of State (Seward) had exceeded reasonable necessity, and that in suppressing press despatches the Censor had 'manifested want of both care and judgement'. For the history of newspaper censorship generally consult Lucy M. Salmon, *The Newspaper and Authority* (NY 1923).

security.[23] In the early days of the war the Confederate State Department was paying $30 per month for freshly smuggled copies of the *Herald*. On the other hand, the *Herald* once managed to compile a complete and up date roster of the Confederate army, for which it was accused by its rivals of being in league with the rebels.[24]

Not that the War Department and many a general did not try after their own fashion to improve security by curbing press reports and providing penalties for disobedience, but these efforts were piecemeal and of varying effectiveness. Although in 1864 the War Department did begin issuing regular bulletins, nothing came of Bennett's suggestion in 1861 that a government Press Bureau should be established.[25] Some exasperated commanders had reporters arrested and court martialled and expelled from their lines, others tried instituting a system of passes or limiting use of the telegraph. *Herald* correspondents frequently complained of erratic censorship. Sometimes censorship was so arbitrary that Bennett cried out 'if there are to be censors, let us have censors who know the business, and have at least a little common sense',[26] which only underlined the problem of finding an enforceable uniform code of practice covering the relations of the military and the press. As a result Northern readers received a vast amount of eye-witness information about the war; more, in all probability, than civilian populations were able to obtain during the wars of the twentieth century, when governments exercised more control over the media. A lot of this information turned out to be speculative or downright fabrication. It is arguable whether the advent of the cheap press eliminated gossip and rumour or merely propagated it more widely. For instance in September 1861 the *Herald* confidently announced the death of Jefferson Davis. In 1863 the capitulation of Vicksburg was proclaimed six weeks before it actually happened. It was not uncommon for a news story to be headed 'Important if True'.

[23]For instances see James E. Pollard, *The Presidents and the Press* (NY 1947), p. 392 and Crozier, p. 227. Conversely, it can be argued that Northern press reports were often so inaccurate that the enemy was as often misled as enlightened.

[24]Hudson, pp. 483-4; *NYH* 13 Oct 1861; 28 Feb 1862. In Richmond the *Herald* report started a hunt for the traitor in the War Department. J.B. Jones recalled the 'tremendous excitement' in the rebel capital and that the Confederate Secretary of War 'told me that if he had required such a list a more correct one could not have been furnished him'. — *A Rebel War Clerk's Diary* (NY 1935), vol. 1, pp. 70-1, entry for 7 Aug 1861. For a hint on how the *Herald* came by such information see J.A. Green to Bennett, 21 July 1862, Bennett Papers, LC. Green revealed that his information was derived 'from one who has a relation in a high station in the rebel War Office, and who has lately run the blockade'.

[25]*NYH* 11 Nov 1861.

[26]*NYH* 26 June 1863. For complaints by correspondents see e.g. S.P. Hanscom to Bennett 26 Feb 1862; L.A. Whitely to Bennett 15 June; 10 Sept 1862, Bennett Papers, LC; W.H. Stiner to his wife 19 Mar 1862, Stiner, MSS., New York Historical Society.

Yet, whatever the value of Civil War reportage to the historian, the Northern public was never denied the daily dish of 'news' which it craved. The telegraph made it a far cry from the days of eighteenth-century or Napoleonic Europe when the result of battles as large as those fought in the Civil War might not be known for weeks rather than days. The battle of Gettysburg was fought near at hand in Pennsylvania over three days in July 1863. Before the fighting was over and Pickett had made his hopeless charge on 3 July New Yorkers knew not only that a battle was in progress but many of the details of the fighting of 1 July. They also had a map of the area before them.

Modern journalism has the technology to approach the ideal (or fetish) of providing instant news. During the Civil War the means but not the will was lacking to achieve this. When some newsmen were reported killed, General Sherman is said to have cried out 'That's good! We'll have dispatches now from hell before breakfast.'[27]

Press and People

The Civil war was doubtless a profoundly individual experience for those who participated in it, but the obvious thing in retrospect is that it heightened the consciousness of nationality among Northerners because it was a communal enterprise — something which involved Americans collectively. To open one of the large daily papers of the time such as the *Herald,* with its high proportion of war news, its maps, its announcements of activities and meetings to do with the war, its lists of advertisements dealing with military enlistments and equipment, its casualty lists, is to be made aware of that collective enterprise in a tangible way. It is a truism worth repeating that what is now history was once news. The American public, and indeed government officials, knew the war chiefly through the daily press and shaped their attitude to it accordingly. The war as it happened — the 'People's war' — would have been inconceivable without the newspaper. Oliver Wendell Holmes insisted that 'we must have something to eat, and the papers to read. Everything else we can give up. . . Only bread and the newspaper we must have.'[28]

Herald circulation rose from a daily average of 75,806 in December 1860 to 104, 480 in December 1861.[29] The issue of extra editions at intervals during the day became regular. Raymond in the

[27]Junius Browne, *Four Years in Secessia* (Hartford 1865), p. 238.

[28]Holmes, 'Bread and the Newspaper' (September 1861).

[29]*NYH* 22 Jan 1862.

Times was once rash enough to bet $12,500 that Bennett's boasts were unfounded in fact, only to find his scheme to embarrass his rival rebound on him.[30]

It did not take the *Herald* long to establish a circulation in the army, where the newsboys were eagerly greeted and the relative merits of Greeley and Bennett debated in camp.[31] In 1863 Bennett estimated that the *Herald* sold 8,000 copies daily in the Army of the Potomac.[32] By 1865 the figure was 11,000 daily, meaning that roughly one man in ten bought it, and copies were no doubt passed around.[33]

At home the spell of military strategy and tactics was perennial, and the *Herald* helped to foster the cult of the soldier, with some strange political consequences to be noted later. The column on its editorial page which before the war had provided a synopsis of 'The News' was now retitled 'The Situation', that readers might have a blow by blow account of the war.

So far as is known Bennett never ventured to the battlefront himself. He knew his place was in New York and he ridiculed the excursions of Greeley and Raymond into the field of war correspondence, but he could not resist the temptation to play armchair strategist any more than the other editors could. In discussions of strategy Bennett's familiarity with the campaigns of Napoleon stood him in good stead, and his commentaries were replete with historical parallels and classical examples. At least it can be said that his strategic appreciations were often less far fetched than those of his rivals.

Bennett was quick to realise the importance of war maps, and the *Herald* surpassed all other journals in its productions. Considering that these maps were often executed very hurriedly they served their purpose well enough. What had been a special feature in pre-war days thus became a commonplace. Bull Run had hardly been fought before the *Herald* produced its own atlas as a supplement.[34] Although in the

---

[30]NY *Times* 11 Dec 1861, which features a front page cartoon of Bennett; *NYH* 5, 10 Dec 1861; Carlson, *The Man Who Made News,* pp. 240-2.

[31]Oliver W. Norton, *Army Letters 1861-5* (Chicago 1903), p. 146.

[32]*NYH* 22 May; 22 Aug 1863. Note though that circulation could drop drastically when the army was on the move.

[33]*NYH* 7 Apr 1865. Newspapers at the front were considerably more expensive than in New York, sometimes selling for ten cents — see Bell I. Wiley, *The Life of Billy Yank* (NY 1952), pp. 153-4.

[34]A *Herald* Civil War Atlas is preserved in the New York Public Library.

1830s and '40s the *Herald* made some notable excursions into the field of pictorial journalism,[35] illustrations were still beyond the range of daily newspapers as a regular feature and had to be left to the more expensive magazines, but vivid journalism had an invaluable aid in clear cartography.[36]

The very brashness and lack of sophistication of the Civil War press made it arguably more responsive to the public mood than the press of the twentieth-century wars. Nevertheless, the *Herald*'s efforts at morale raising were at times rather heavy handed. Virtually every battle was at first reported as a great victory, even those which had in fact been federal disasters, though it is fair to say that this was sometimes as much to do with fitful War Department censorship as with wishful thinking and bad reporting.[37] (A conscientious *Herald* man observed wryly that 'commanders are always anxious to grant correspondents passes after a victory; but they wish to defer the unwelcome publication of a defeat'.)[38] From the beginning of the war to its end the *Herald* proclaimed editorially that the rebellion was about to collapse and that the South was starving, quivering and demoralised. Seizing on one of Bennett's favourite phrases, George T. Strong complained to his diary that 'newspaper gabble about the "backbone of the Rebellion" being "broken at last" is abundant and nauseating'.[39]

At the front soldiers' comments on newspaper patriotism were legion. One of Meade's staff officers wrote to his wife that 'the newspapers would be comic in their comments, were not the whole thing so tragic', and cautioned that reported routs of Lee's army 'exist only in the N.Y. *Herald*'.[40] An illustration of the *Herald*'s reputation for Munchausenism occurred in Virginia in 1862. The Confederates had been victorious in a battle, leaving a field covered with fly-blown Unionist corpses. A truce was called, and a Southern general bet his Federal counterpart a new hat that the Northern papers would claim the encounter as a victory. The Federal took him up, replying that not

[35]Hudson, p. 450 lists some examples of *Herald* pioneering in this field.

[36]The *Herald*'s pride in its own achievement in this respect is expressed in the edition of 9 Nov 1864.

[37]See however Edward Dicey, *Six Months in the Federal States* (London 1863), vol. 2, p. 273 for a comment on the frankness of reports of federal defeats around Richmond in June 1862.

[38]Townsend, *Rustics in Rebellion*, p. 179.

[39]Nevins and Thomas eds., *The Diary of George Templeton Strong*, vol. III, p. 354, entry for 2 Sept 1863.

[40]Theodore H. Lyman, *Meade's Headquarters 1863-5* (Boston 1922), p. 100.

even the New York *Herald* would have the audacity to claim it. He lost his bet. A fine new hat and a copy of the *Herald* announcing victory were mirthfully received in the Southern camp a few days later.[41]

For the Northern public there was more, of course, to reading about thé war than vicarious participation in a spectacle. Relatives at home could discover the whereabouts of kinsmen in the army and to some extent share their experiences through the medium of newspapers. As always, the *Herald*'s advertising and personal columns were an important vehicle of communication between groups and individuals in Northern society. (The paper's role in stimulating volunteering will be considered in another context.) Most important, too, the *Herald* was at pains to gather the names of the killed, mortally wounded and missing after each battle, giving where possible a brief description of the wound. General Sherman, who was no lover of democracy or the press (he once had Thomas W. Knox, a *Herald* correspondent, court martialled)[42] once made a quip to the effect that fame in war consisted of the privilege of having one's name mis-spelled in the newspapers. Even so, the *Herald* reporters were able to do an important and difficult job well in the circumstances and it should hardly be wondered at that mistakes and omissions occured. The *Herald* was able to excel other papers in this respect because it could often afford to detail men to go over the field and into the hospitals enquiring after casualties while others reported the battle. What needs stressing too is that the *Herald* was supplying a service which the government, in the form of the War Department and army administration, did not always perform adequately.

Whatever the faults of Civil War journalism, Bennett grasped the fact that a literate democracy would demand the fullest information about the course and conduct of the war and would be critical of civilian and military leaders, who would have to come to terms with such criticism. The press had become part of the democratic process in asserting the right of the public to know how its affairs were managed. Although the relations of the government with the press

---

[41]C.M. Blackford, *Letters from Lee's Army* (NY 1947), p. 110; W.W. Blackford, *War Years with Jeb Stuart* (NY 1945), p. 98n.

[42]The Knox episode is discussed in Thomas H. Guback, 'General Sherman's War with the Press', *Journalism Quarterly*, 36 (1959), 171-6. Sherman complained that Knox escaped punishment because Lincoln 'fears to incur the enmity of the *Herald*'. The general's attitude to the press is the subject of John F. Marszalek, *Sherman's Other War* (Memphis 1981). Knox's own story is set forth in his *Camp-Fire and Cotton Field* (NY 1865), ch XXV. Knox discusses the general difficulties of being an army reporter in ch XLV.

were permeated by the desire on one side to receive favourable attention and on the other to gain access to information,[43] it remains true that a paper as well established and rich as the *Herald* had to be treated with some respect, because it was big enough to find out important information for itself. It was Bennett's boast that if the US government were run half as efficiently as his newspaper the war would be won very quickly:

> A well organised newspaper establishment is a little nation in itself. It has its President, its cabinet, its administrative, judicial and executive departments, its major and minor officials, its foreign agents and correspondents, its representatives with the army and navy in every section of the country, and its employees of every grade and degree, while the crowds which throng its office present all the phenomena of a busy metropolis. . . Chase, Stanton, Welles, Halleck & Company might learn a thing or two worth knowing by a visit to the HERALD office.[44]

In the following chapters Bennett's editorial attitude towards the Lincoln government will be followed. Although it was open to charges of cynicism and 'irresponsibility' by its opponents, the New York *Herald* was a significant mouthpiece of the many Democrats who supported the war. It was easy for Republicans to denounce the *Herald* and its editor, less easy for them to admit that so far as there existed a 'loyal opposition' to the Republican party in the North, the *Herald* often spoke its sentiments. Lincoln himself made the laconic recognition that 'it is important to humor the *Herald*'.[45]

---

[43]This theme will be illustrated in the next chapter. It is amply documented by some of the correspondence in the Bennett Papers reprinted under the title 'Federal Generals and a good Press', *American Historical Review,* 39, pp. 284-97.

[44]*NYH* 7 May 1863.

[45]See R.P. Basler, *The Collected Works of Abraham Lincoln* (New Brunswick 1953-5), vol. VI, p. 120.

9

THE *HERALD* FOR THE UNION AND LINCOLN, 1861-2

If we are desirous of a short and decisive war for the Union, one great reason is that we do not wish to see the South and its peculiar institutions destroyed; and if the slaveholders of the cotton States are wise they will move without delay for their submission to the Union. The Union will save them; but otherwise who can answer for the consequences? — *Herald*, 3 September 1861

'My dear Mr. Lincoln'

The cordial support which the *Herald* gave to Lincoln from mid-April 1861 endured through the first two years of the conflict. This support, the paper made clear, was given to Lincoln as President, not as head of the Republican party.

The Union rout at Bull Run in July 1861 provided Bennett with an opportunity to affirm his loyalty to Lincoln editorially. At first the *Herald* refrained from publishing the worst details of the disaster, from fear of a repetition of the April mob scene,[1] but on the whole it was unshaken, counselling that 'the wise and the strong make adversity the stepping stone of success, and turn present defeats into future victories'.[2] Besides leading the American press in its excoriation of W.H. Russell of the London *Times* for the embarrassing description of Yankee panic which he gave to Europe, the *Herald* sustained Lincoln against strong criticism from the Democratic *News* and *Journal of Commerce* and helped to heap the whole blame for Bull Run onto the *Tribune*.[3]

The *Tribune* had led the 'On to Richmond!' furore which was believed to have precipitated the army's advance. To Bennett's delight Greeley, with a gnashing of teeth and beating of breast, wrote an editorial confessing his paper's responsibility.[4] Privately Greeley

---

[1] *NYH* 22 July 1861; H. Villard, *Memoirs,* vol 1, p. 200.

[2] *NYH* 23 July 1861.

[3] E. Dicey, *Six Months in the Federal States* (London 1863), vol. 1, pp. 35-7, alleges that Bennett attacked Russell partly because the *Times* man had refused a social invitation from him.

[4] NY *Daily Tribune* 25 July 1861. The editorial was entitled 'Just Once'.

wrote a despairing and defeatist letter to Lincoln for which one of the President's secretaries thought Bennett would willingly have given $10,000.[5] During the autumn of 1861 *Tribune* sales fell off considerably while those of the *Herald* and *Times* grew rapidly.[6]

A Rip Van Winkle waking up in the latter part of 1861 and being told that a civil war was in progress might have been forgiven for assuming that the chief combatants were the rival editors of the New York press. In the absence of military action, mutual recrimination between the *Herald, Times* and *Tribune* ran to new lengths. Bennett called for the 'satanic' and 'criminal' papers to be suppressed and for Greeley to be imprisoned in Fort Lafayette for his abolition 'treason'. Two representative *Herald* headlines at this period were 'The Abolition Incendiaries Conspiring to Overthrow the Union' and 'President Lincoln Nobly Meeting the Crisis'.[7] Both illustrated Bennett's effort to claim ownership of the President and to dissociate him in the public mind from what he increasingly described as the 'Jacobin' or 'Radical' wing of the Republican party which favoured abolition as a war aim. Emancipation, said the *Herald,* would be a declaration that the South's secession had been justified.[8]

Though Bennett was nothing daunted by the task of claiming Lincoln as a War Democrat in all but name, he had to work hard to convince the voters of New York. The *Herald* minimised the political significance of the elections to the state legislature in November, in which the Republicans drew many normally Democratic votes and were overwhelmingly victorious.[9] (Among those elected, despite Bennett's calumnies, was Henry J. Raymond.)[10] In the

---

[5]The letter appears in H.H. Horner, *Lincoln and Greeley* (Univ. Illinois 1953), pp. 233-5. Lincoln's secretary John Hay thought it 'the most insane specimen of pusillanimity I have ever read'. When John G. Nicolay, the President's other secretary, remarked 'that would be nuts to the *Herald'* and suggested the price Bennett would pay, Lincoln replied 'I need $10,000 very much but he could not have it for many times that' — *Lincoln and the Civil War in the Diaries and Letters of John Hay,* ed. Tyler Dennett, (NY 1939), p. 178, entry for 30 Apr 1864.

[6]L.M. Starr, *Bohemian Brigade* (NY 1954), p. 54, gives details of the *Tribune's* eclipse.

[7]*NYH* 16, 18 Sept 1861 respectively.

[8]*NYH* 31 Oct 1861.

[9]The ticket, though described as 'Union' was predominantly Republican and gained a huge majority of 107,000. Bennett himself had attacked the platform of the Albany Regency Democratic regime as treasonable. For background see Sidney D. Brummer, *Political History of New York State during the the period of the Civil War* (NY 1911), ch V; D.S. Alexander, *A Political History of the State of New York* (NY 1906-9), vol 3, ch 2.

[10]*NYH* 6 Nov 1861.

mayoral contest which followed the paper was again out for Fernando Wood, arguing for his re-election on the grounds that he was a 'national' man who supported the 'conservative' policies of Lincoln. To vote for the Republican nominee, merchant George Opdyke, would on the other hand be a blow to the Administration – or such was the reasoning of the *Herald*.[11]

The burden of the *Herald*'s campaign against Opdyke was the charge that he was an abolitionist whose election would presage the overthrow of the Constitution and a war of extermination on the South. Moreover, he supposedly favoured putting Negroes in the army, and Bennett asked his readers 'what white man, possessed of esprit de corps, would move forward cheerfully against an army with a filthy nigger at his right hand, and another at his left?' 'Yet', he warned, 'this is the condition of things to which the *Tribune* and *Post* [both campaigning for Opdyke] would bring us'. It was fortunate, Bennett thought, that the Union army was composed of 'gentlemen' who would never fall prey to such fanaticism.[12]

The *Herald*'s forceful appeals to the Irish and German communities not to let Opdyke elevate the Negro at their expense recalled those of the 1859 mayoral fight, as did its identification of the Republican candidate as the representative of 'shoddy' capitalism. There was a slight religious undertone to the contest too, for Roman Catholic Archbishop Hughes had recently voiced disapproval of abolitionism while some Protestant clergy had declared (blasphemously, said Bennett) that God would not permit reunion until slavery were abolished.[13]

International issues were also brought into the canvass. The *Trent* crisis was brewing and in colourful language the *Herald* was threatening Britain with war unless she ceased her 'insolent' and 'insulting' demands for the release of two rebel ambassadors taken off a British vesel by a US boarding party. The *Times* and the *Tribune* accused Bennett of deliberately trying to provoke a war between Britain and the USA in order to aid the Confederacy. Bennett retorted that they were unpatriotic.[14] The Republican press was able to take advantage of an anti-Administration speech by Wood made on 27 November to a largely German audience at the Volks Garten to paint

[11]*NYH* 27-9 Nov 1861. On Opdyke's wartime career see Steven L. Carson, 'Lincoln and the Mayor of New York', *Lincoln Herald,* 67 (Winter 1965), 84-91.

[12]*NYH* 27, 29 Nov; 1, 2 Dec 1861.

[13]*NYH* 8 Oct; 30 Nov 1861.

[14]*Herald, Times, Tribune* 17 Nov 1861-7 Jan 1862.

him as the treason candidate. The *Herald* itself disapproved the speech and could only ignore these charges rather than try to answer them.[15]

As remarkable as Bennett's claim that Wood could be identified with Lincoln was Opdyke's indignant letter to the *Herald* just before the election denying that he was an abolitionist.[16] This letter at least enabled Bennett to accept Opdyke's victory with a show of grace. Wood lost votes heavily compared with 1859 and was also beaten by C. G. Gunther, the regular Tammany candidate. Once again Democratic division had handed victory to a Republican with little more than a third of the city's vote.[17]

But if Republican ascendancy locally was unbreakable for the moment, the *Herald* could still take satisfaction in President Lincoln's continued sensitivity to the feelings of Democrats who supported the war. Lincoln retained Democratic general George B. McClellan in command of the Union armies despite mounting Republican dissatisfaction at his military inactivity.[18] Democrats were appointed to positions of trust throughout the armed services. Nor did Lincoln show himself in any hurry to push matters to extremes on the slavery question. In July Congress had resolved, with the *Herald*'s hearty approval, that the restoration of the Union was the sole purpose of the war,[19] and Lincoln seemed quite content to stand on that ground. When the President revoked an emancipation order by General John C. Fremont in September 1861 the *Herald* was properly gratified, claiming that although the President had offended 'a few hundred fanatics' he had made 'millions of friends'.[20] Although Bennett had always discountenanced the colonisation of freed Negroes in Africa or Central America, he managed a respectful enthusiasm for the idea

---

[15]For the speech see S. Pleasants, *Fernando Wood* (NY 1948), pp. 127-30.

[16]*NYH* 3 Dec 1861.

[17]The *Herald* of 4 Dec compared voting figures with those of 1859:

	1859		1861
Wood	30,339	Wood	23,350
Havemeyer	26,813	Gunther	24,644
Opdyke	22,716	Opdyke	25,451

[18]On Lincoln's conciliatory appointments system see specifically *NYH* 18 Mar 1862.

[19]The Crittenden-Johnson Resolutions were passed on 22 July in a virtually unanimous vote. For text see H.S. Commager, *Documents of American History* (NY 1968), vol. 1, pp. 395-6. There is a good discussion of them in Herman Belz, *Reconstructing the Union* (Ithaca 1969), pp. 24-8, 39.

[20]*NYH* 20 Sept 1861.

as mooted in Lincoln's annual message.[21] If Lincoln's aim was to carry loyal Democrats with him by his 'conservative' approach to the slavery problem, then the files of the *Herald* for 1861-2 may be cited as evidence that his efforts were appreciated.

Considering the *Herald*'s past record in opposing Lincoln's election and its course before Sumter it would not have been surprising if the Republican administration had shown more favour to its rivals in the matter of news. Lincoln, however, soon indicated that he appreciated the *Herald*'s more recent support. Whether or not it was true, as the ferocious Count Gurowski had it, that Lincoln 'reads no paper, that dirty traitor, the New York *Herald* excepted',[22] when a question of passes issued to reporters came to his attention the President took the opportunity to write to Bennett. The letter, dated 28 September 1861, must have relieved the editor, although it combined flattery with an obvious threat: 'I . . . assure you that the administration will not discriminate against the *Herald*, especially while it sustains us so generously, and the cause of the country so ably as it has been doing.'[23] Bennett replied warmly, 'every aid that I can give will be most cheerfully given'.[24]

That the *Herald* would not be discriminated against was pleasing, but Bennett wanted the news first, and something had to be done to offset the influence of a *Tribune* correspondent with the Secretary of War, Simon Cameron.[25] Before long the *Times* and *Tribune* realised that 'Old Satanic' was up to something when they reported that Mrs. Lincoln had been observed on the arm of the *Herald*'s ubiquitous emissary, the rakish 'Chevalier' Henry Wikoff.[26]

The cultivation of Mrs. Lincoln had apparently not been difficult. Bennett occasionally sent her a bouquet of flowers. In October, unbidden, he defended her editorially against criticism, and the *Herald* social columns began reporting her appearance and movements with heavy sycophancy.[27] This brought a gushing letter from Mrs.

[21]*NYH* 4 Dec 1861.

[22]Adam Gurowski, *Diary* (2 vols. Boston 1862), vol. 1, p. 81.

[23]Lincoln to Bennett 28 Sept 1861 in R.P. Basler, *The Collected Works of Abraham Lincoln* (New Brunswick 1953-5), vol. IV, p. 539.

[24]Bennett to Lincoln 22 Oct 1861, Lincoln Papers, Library of Congress, item 12602. Bennett sent the note by Judge Russell whom, he informed the President, was a worthy man ready to serve his country in any capacity.

[25]Starr, pp. 67-74.

[26]NY *Daily Tribune* 7 Dec 1861; Henry Villard, *Memoirs,* vol. 1, p. 157.

[27]*NYH* 21 Oct 1861 etc.

Lincoln. In expressing 'more than ordinary gratitude', she confessed to Bennett what he had doubtless counted on, that 'my own nature is very sensitive', and went on, 'I trust it may be my good fortune . . . to welcome both Mrs. Bennett & yourself to Washington; the President would be equally as much pleased to meet you. . . .'[28] Indeed, the Bennetts received an invitation to the Grand Union Ball in the White House at the New Year.

Wikoff's friendship with Mrs. Lincoln had by that time paid a handsome dividend in news when he was able to telegraph to the *Herald* the text of Lincoln's first annual message in advance of its delivery on 3 December. This scoop however had consequences which went beyond the outcry of beaten rivals. There was consternation in Congress, which delegated a committee chaired by Pennsylvania congressman John Hickman to investigate the matter. Wikoff was imprisoned, but would admit no more than the unlikely story that a White House gardener had committed the message to memory and repeated it to him. The general assumption was that Mrs. Lincoln had given Wikoff access to the message, but the matter was not pursued after Lincoln visited the committee and in effect asked to be spared further embarrassment.[29]

In the *Herald* Bennett blandly denied any direct connection with Wikoff, whose usefulness as a correspondent was ended for the moment. Rather than being abashed Bennett was able to use the occasion to advantage, for the *Herald* posed as the defender of the President and his family against the intrusions of the 'Jacobins' in Congress. The editor desisted from lampooning the commitee only when he received a warning from a Washington informant imploring him 'Bennett, for christian charity, have done with Hickman . . . his friends, and they are many . . . threaten to visit your sins upon your son – and will insist . . . that Lieutenant Bennett shall be ousted or displaced.'[30] Still the *Herald* continued to pay assiduous court to Mrs. Lincoln, and the first lady retained her trust in Bennett.

[28]Mrs Lincoln's extant correspondence is printed in J.G. & L.L. Turner, *Mary Todd Lincoln* (NY 1972) — see p. 110, letter dated 25 Oct 1861.

[29]*Herald, Tribune, Times* Jan-Mar 1862; *Congressional Globe,* 37th Congress, 2nd session, pp. 775, 784, 785, 831; Ben Perley Poore, *Reminiscences* (Philadelphia 1886), vol. 2, p. 143. See further Margaret Leech, *Reveille in Washington* (NY 1941), pp. 290-1, 298-300; Oliver Carlson, *The Man Who Made News* (NY 1942), pp. 336-8; Starr, pp. 75-6; Turner & Turner, pp. 97-100; Ruth P. Randall, *Mary Todd Lincoln* (Boston 1953), pp. 303-5; W.A. Swanberg, *Sickles the Incredible* (NY 1956), p. 136-8; F. Marbut, *News From the Capital* (Carbondale 1971), pp. 117-19. Wikoff himself did not write about the episode in his autobiographical works.

[30]E.W. Dennison to Bennett, 18 Feb 1862, Bennett Papers, LC.

The *Herald*'s honeymoon with Lincoln endured through the turbulent summer of 1862. Although disappointed that the President signed the bill for ending slavery in the District of Columbia,[31] Bennett was delighted when he made public his objections to a confiscation bill proposed by Congress[32] and was ecstatic when Lincoln declared in reply to Greeley's celebrated plea for emancipation entitled 'The Prayer of Twenty Millions' that 'my paramount object in this struggle *is* to save the Union. . . . If I could save the Union without freeing *any* slave, I would do it. . . .'[33] Bennett's joy would have palled had he known that Lincoln already had the draft of an emancipation proclamation in his desk, but the secret was well kept. Ironically, Bennett wrote to Lincoln that summer 'on occasions I have found myself groping in the dark in endeavouring to sustain your admini- stration, but generally try to come out right'.[34] Every public and private announcement of Lincoln's seemed to indicate that he would not venture to free the slaves. Bennett bragged that the abolitionists were defeated: 'Do they not see that twenty-three millions of white men will never get down on their knees and beg three millions of Southern darkeys to aid them? Do they not see that the President cannot be deluded into justifying the rebellion, at home and abroad, by making this a war against Southern slavery?'[35] The *Herald* lauded Lincoln as 'the only man of moral and political stamina in the country. . . . He is the only popular man in the United States.'[36] Privately too Bennett wrote to the President to assure him of his popularity:

> My dear Mr. Lincoln I do verily believe that you yourself are the only man in the government that possesses the confidence of the people. You can exercise more control over public opinion than half a dozen cabinets or a whole bevy of generals – They believe that of all the men in the government, you alone have a single

[31]*NYH* 1, 3 Apr 1862.

[32]*NYH* 27 May; 18, 19 July 1862. The *Herald* thought the Confiscation Act 'absurd', 'folly' and 'treason'. Lincoln angered members of his own party by publishing his misgivings about the constitutionality of parts of the bill. He signed a revised version.

[33]Greeley's plea in NY *Daily Tribune* 19 Aug 1862. The letter and Lincoln's reply are conveniently printed in Commager, *Documents,* pp. 415-18.

[34]Bennett to Lincoln 6 June 1862, Lincoln Papers, LC, item 16331. Bennett ventured to advise, 'from what I know of human nature and human action, I fear you will have more trouble with the politicians in the coming restoration of the several states, than you have had with the generals and the armies in the recent conflict'. In order to 'aid and assist', Bennett promised to try to visit the White House. The editor added his sympathies at the loss of 'your fine boy — I lost just such a boy myself a couple of years ago'. Willie Lincoln had died in February 1862; Cosmo, Bennett's son, had died in 1859.

[35]*NYH* 26 July 1862.

[36]*NYH* 18 July 1862.

mind for the good of the Republic – This I speak from what I see and hear. . . .[37]

Having claimed proprietorship of the President and regarding him as above criticism for the moment, the *Herald* also made itself the champion of the Army of the Potomac and its commander.

The *Herald* eagerly stirred the political cauldron in which the ideological struggle over slavery beame inextricable from controversies over the military conduct of the war. In Congress the vehement 'Jacobins' insinuated that the North's embarrassing want of military success was due to General McClellan's timidity. They believed that the war could be won but for McClellan's tender regard for secessionist property and his pro-slavery sympathies. McClellan and his staff officers, on the other hand, were obsessed with the idea that the radical anti-slavery men were witholding reinforcements and supplies in a deliberate attempt to prolong the war, even at the cost of sacrificing the Army of the Potomac.[38]

From the very beginning of this bitterly partisan debate the *Herald* was a leading champion of McClellan against the 'abolition bloodhounds'. Readers of the *Herald* were expected to be thoroughly indoctrinated with the idea that the abolitionists had conspired to cause the war, and now Bennett explained to them daily that these same men were actively seeking Union defeat. He did not hesitate to suggest that McClellan would be justified in playing Cromwell and turning Congress out at bayonet point. The word 'treason' was freely bandied about on both sides: as always Bennett knew the value of having some imposing domestic enemy to attack. In the *Tribune* one could read that the army favoured emancipation and chaffed at poor leadership while in the *Herald* news and editorial columns it was claimed that the soldiers worshipped McClellan and were pro-slavery to a man.[39]

[37]Bennett to Lincoln 11 Aug 1862, Lincoln Papers, LC, item 17554. Bennett regretted that he had not been able to visit Washington as planned and asked Lincoln to 'speak a good word. . . with Chase' for the bearer of the letter, a Mr Dickinson.

[38]On the well-canvassed 'McClellan Question' see particularly T. Harry Williams, *Lincoln and His Generals* (NY 1952) and *Lincoln and the Radicals* (Madison 1941) and Don E. Fehrenbacher ed., *The Leadership of Abraham Lincoln* (NY 1970). I have used the term radical only as Bennett used it for partisan purposes, referring to those members of the Republican party who wished to destroy slavery: just as 'conservative' in the *Herald* meant one who wished to conserve slavery. Needless to say Bennett's 'radicals' included many republicans who regarded themselves as moderates.

[39]The political colouring of much Civil War reporting is looked at in Bernard A. Weisberger, *Reporters for the Union* (Boston 1953). Mr Weisberger comments dryly but justly, 'according to journalistic accounts Civil War fighting men had the

Both sides were aware that the next presidential election was a mere two years away. Even before he left Washington on campaign the *Herald* was grooming McClellan as a likely Democratic candidate for 1864. In January 1862 a correspondent forwarded to Bennett some detailed military information which McClellan had divulged to him. The *Herald* man reported enthusiastially that McClellan had said to him

> Mr. Bennett has stood by me in the hour of the bitterest anxiety of my whole life. . . . He has done so disinterestedly, nobly and with the whole force of his paper. He and he alone, has upheld me, cheered me and encouraged me, when every other newspaper heaped on me calumny and abuse, at the very time that I was saving them from the horror of invasion. . . . I shall *never, never, never* forget his kindness and I want him to know that I cherish him in my heart and that I shall strive . . . to prove . . . that his confidence has not been misplaced.[40]

In return the *Herald* continued to 'puff' the general to the skies. When McClellan's feeble grasp of military reality caused the army to be repulsed from in front of Richmond in June, the *Herald* informed the country that the abolitionists in Congress and the cabinet were entirely to blame. In the name of a 'furious' and 'indignant' public, the *Herald* demanded that Lincoln purge his cabinet of all 'radicals' in order that the war might be won.[41]

Attacks on cabinet members and demands for their replacement by War Democrats had become an almost daily staple of the *Herald* by the summer of 1862 and were to remain so for the rest of the war. Bennett found no incongruity in supporting President Lincoln while aiming fearsome tirades against his closest advisers. Indeed, such attacks were one means of expressing dissatisfaction with the management of the war while remaining loyal. Just as the barons of medieval England ascribed misgovernment to the 'evil councellors' around the king, so Bennett cushioned the head of state himself from criticism by blaming all mistakes on government officers.

Secretary of the Navy Gideon Welles came in for heavy onslaughts from the *Herald* throughout the war. To readers of the paper 'the

temperamental instability of operatic leads. They burst into either tears or "oaths" at any unusual development in the news. . . . One could find an army to suit one's taste merely by selecting the right journal of fearless and impartial opinion.' — *ibid.,* pp. 196, 202.

[40]Malcolm Ives to Bennett, 15 Jan 1862, Bennett Papers, LC. Ives wrote to Hudson next day that McClellan 'is as guileless and innocent as a child, and we must be careful not to injure him, even to promote *Herald* interests'.

[41]*NYH* 4, 6, 7 July etc 1862.

Connecticut fossil' was presented as a somnolent old incompetent who urgently needed replacing with 'a living man'. It was not unusual for the *Herald* to carry a leading article on the insolence and malignancy of Britain for questioning the efficiency of the Union blockade, while the next column would be devoted to taking Welles to task precisely for the weakness and mistakes of the federal fleet. This criticism may have arisen from the natural fears of New Yorkers that not enough was being done for the protection of their commerce or the safety of their harbour. Welles himself, though, had another explanation for the assaults.

The dour New Englander thought Bennett 'a vagabond editor without principle or reputation . . . whose aims are often wickedly and atrociously levelled against the best men and the best causes, regardless of honor or right'. Welles recalled that he had been visited by W. O. Bartlett,[42] 'the jackall of Bennett', a 'mercenary rascal' who sought to have himself made an agent to purchase vessels for the navy in New York.

> Because I would not prostitute my office and favour his brokerage [Welles continued] he threatened me with increasing hostility and assaults, not only from the *Herald* but from nearly every press in New York which he said he could control. I was incredulous as to his influence over other journals, and at all events I shook him off. . . . In a short time I found the papers slashing and attacking me, editorially and through correspondents . . . this Bartlett . . . boasted of his work and taunted me through others. . . .[43]

Secretary of War Edwin M. Stanton also came in for a drubbing from Bennett, and after the defeat of the 'Seven Days' it was Stanton's resignation which the *Herald* demanded most loudly. Stanton had ingratiated himself with the 'radicals' and was considered a personal enemy by McClellan.

In January 1862 the *Herald* had welcomed Stanton's appointment, for the departure of Simon Cameron had broken the *Tribune*'s cosy monopoly of official confidence in that quarter.[44] Unfortunately the paper's relationship with the new Secretary was soon marred by the

---

[42] On Bartlett see further chapter 13 below.

[43] H.K. Beale ed., *The Diary of Gideon Welles* (NY 1960), vol. 2, pp. 258-60, entry for 16 Mar 1865. See also entry for 10 Aug 1864 where Welles argues that the *Herald,* 'with a deservedly bad name, gives tone and direction to the New York press'. Welles also endured heavy attacks from Congress, see John Niven, *Gideon Welles* (NY 1973), chs 18-20.

[44] *NYH* 15 Jan 1862.

activities of one of its Washington staff. 'Dr' Malcolm Ives, the same who had written to Buchanan about Bennett's attitude during the election of 1856, had joined the *Herald* in 1858, having previously been connected with the *Times* and the *Journal of Commerce*. A defrocked Roman Catholic priest of extreme political opinions, the unstable Ives had apparently written some of the *Herald*'s more rabid anti-abolitionist and pro-Southern diatribes.[45] Ives won, or believed he had won, Stanton's favour, but presumed upon it when he threatened the Secretary with attacks in the *Herald* unless he divulged some secret information. It seems that he was drunk at the time and had no authorisation from Bennett, who publicly disowned him and let him cool his head in the jail where Stanton threw him.[46]

Stanton seemingly bore no animus, for on 2 May he 'took the liberty' of sending Bennett his political views with an obvious eye to their publication.[47] On the 18th of that month however the *Herald* carried an editorial entitled 'President Lincoln and his Happy Cabinet' which ridiculed Stanton and hinted that he was an unprincipled time-server. This elicited a prompt letter from Lincoln to Bennett, defending Stanton.[48] Bennett replied that he had availed himself 'at the earliest moment of the hints you gave me relating to the Secretary of War – a gentleman and a patriot of whom I have a high opinion. . . .'[49] (That 'high opinion', which Bennett expressed privately elsewhere, was that Stanton's 'whole characteristics were exhibited in this, that when a youngster going to school he kissed the – of the big boys and kicked those of the little ones'.)[50] The President's hint notwithstanding, the *Herald* soon became a remorseless critic of Stanton, taking it for granted that if anything went wrong with the war it was his fault, while if anything went right the credit went to the officers and men of the

[45] On Ives see L.R. Shepherd to James Buchanan 3 Sept 1856; John A. Dix to Buchanan 6 Mar 1858, Buchanan Papers, Historical Society of Pennsylvania; NY *Daily Tribune* 11, 12, 13 Feb 1862. See also chapter 3 above. On his career in Washington at this time see Crozier, *Yankee Reporters,* p. 181 ff.; also Starr, pp. 77-81; Marbut, *News from the Capital,* pp. 115-16.

[46] *NYH* 11, 14 Feb; 21 May; 10 June 1862. Greeley claimed that Ives was not merely a correspondent for the *Herald,* as Bennett said, but a trusted editorial assistant. He thought 'the prospect is fair that the N.Y. *Herald* will soon be issued from Fort McHenry' — *Tribune* 12 Feb 1862.

[47] Text of the letter in Hudson, *History of Journalism,* pp. 484-5.

[48] Lincoln to Bennett 21 May 1862 in Basler, vol. V, p. 225. Lincoln wrote 'thanking you again for the able support given by you, through the *Herald,* to what I think the true cause of the country, and also for your kind expressions towards me personally', but protested the President, Stanton 'mixes no politics whatever with his duties'.

[49] Bennett to Lincoln 6 June 1862, Lincoln Papers, LC, item 16331.

[50] Schuckers Papers, LC, quoted in H.M. Hyman and B.P. Thomas, *Stanton* (NY 1962), p. 7.

services, who found in the *Herald* their self-appointed watchdog and defender against civilian mismanagement.[51] A *Herald* man would shortly write that Stanton 'absolutely stinks in the nostrils of the people and the army . . . to the *Herald* he is inexorable in his hate'.[52]

Would President Lincoln be swayed by Bennett's 'conservative' pressure? The signs were ambiguous. He did not remove Welles or Stanton. On the other hand, although McClellan was put on the shelf in August 1862, he was restored to command following the second débâcle at Bull Run, which was the cost of the generalship of John Pope, a favourite of the 'radicals'. The *Herald* seemed to have been proved right in its view that anti-slavery sentiments were no guarantee of military competence. But could McClellan win the war? Bennett believed he could. On 20 September the *Herald* announced that McClellan had won a great victory and 'broken the backbone' of the rebellion. Let the radical traitors now hang themselves, it exulted.

The ironical truth, lost on McClellan, Bennett and all who thought like them, was that on 15 and 16 September the general's caution had lost a real chance to destroy Lee's army and end the war. So passed the last chance of the 'conservative' settlement Democrats craved so much. The 'great victory' of Antietam was only another horribly bloody stalemate. The *Herald* continued in the belief that reunion should be effected with slavery intact but Lincoln, impatiently watched by his party, pondered now whether reunion could be effected at all unless more drastic measures were adopted. On 22 September he did what Horace Greeley had urged him to do and gave notice of his intention to free the slaves, and incidentally of the fact that, after all, he did not see eye to eye with the editor of the New York *Herald*.

Emancipation – 'The Pope's Bull Against the Comet'

Lincoln's proclamation that all the slaves in the rebel states would be freed on 1 January 1863 unless those states returned to the Union in the meantime,[53] was a defeat for everything the *Herald* had argued for in the previous decade. The President must have been heartened

---

[51] The Bennett Papers, LC, contain a number of letters from soldiers complaining of injustices, such as failure to be paid, and asking for the *Herald*'s support, e.g. letter to J.G.B. from a soldier of the 12th Regiment, NY Volunteers, 22 Oct 1862.

[52] L.A. Whiteley to F. Hudson 30 Mar 1863, Bennett Papers, LC.

[53] On the genesis and provisions of the proclamation, and reaction to it, see John Hope Franklin, *The Emancipation Proclamation* (NY 1963).

when the *Tribune* thundered 'God Bless Abraham Lincoln',[54] but what would be the reaction of the snubbed 'conservatives'? Bennett might have been expected to produce one of his famous paroxysms of editorial rage, but in fact his first reaction was resigned and even temperate.

Of course the *Herald* was disapproving. Emancipation was 'social revolution', it correctly observed, and it feared that Lincoln's advice to the slaves not to revolt was disingenuous. On the other hand it conceded that Lincoln had been anything but precipitate. After all, the *Herald* had advised the representatives of the loyal border states to accept Lincoln's plan of compensated emancipation, made some months before.[55] They had not done so, yet the proclamation exempted their slaves, which Bennett interpreted as a 'peace offering' to them.[56]

Bennett hesitated to abandon the President. He announced his faith in Lincoln's sincerity in wishing to end the war rapidly. Obviously the President must hope that his conditional proclamation would cause the South to surrender before the New Year. Therefore, the *Herald* reasoned, Lincoln's purposes were still 'conservative' – for if the war ended the federal government would have no power whatever to interfere with slavery. Bennett began quoting fondly and gleefully Lincoln's own remark that emancipation might prove only as effective as 'the Pope's bull against the comet', and professed to see in it a clever device to silence the abolitionists.[57] In all, he informed his readers: 'We accept this proclamation . . . not as that of an armed crusade against African slavery, but as . . . a liberal warning to our revolted States, in order to save their local institutions by their timely restoration of the Union . . . Men look through the wretched but transparent negro in it, and see clearly the end of the war.'[58] and again later: 'We must conquer the white population before we can get hold of the blacks, and when the whites are subdued nobody but a handful of impotent fanatics will desire the sudden freedom of the black race.'[59] Bennett appealed to the Southerners to use their three months grace to return – let them save themselves by joining in a war on England and France. Now, the *Herald* warned, the 'radicals' in and out

[54]NY *Daily Tribune* 23 Sept 1862.

[55]*NYH* 7, 8, 9 Mar 1862.

[56]*NYH* 23, 24 Sept 1862.

[57]*NYH* 27-30 Sept 1862.

[58]*NYH* 24 Sept 1862.

[59]*NYH* 4 Dec 1862.

of the cabinet had a traitorous vested interest in prolonging the war, and they must be thwarted.[60]

The irony of the situation was, once again, that if any one man had the power to forestall the operation of the proclamation it was General McClellan who, however, kept his army inactive as the precious weeks advanced towards 1 January. The *Herald*, predictably, failed to comment on this fact, just as it passed over the failure of the army to stage the mutiny which it had long predicted would be the inevitable consequence of 'abolitionizing' the war.

The fall elections were approaching; in New York a new governor was to be elected to replace the retiring Republican, Edwin D. Morgan. It might have been expected that emancipation would be the main issue to be contested, but a reading of the *Herald* suggests that the party division between supporters and opponents of the Administration was a little blurred on the Democratic side.[61]

The question of abolition was debated hotly. Republicans charged treason on all who opposed it. They nominated a radical, upstate landowner General James S. Wadsworth,[62] as their candidate. Like other Democrats, Bennett was angered by the treason accusation. Wadsworth, the *Herald* charged, was a 'firebrand', a 'malignant abolition disorganiser, and the inveterate enemy of Gen. McClellan and every other officer of the army who has had the presumption to consider the abolition of slavery a secondary question, and the Union the paramount object of the war'.[63]

Wadsworth's record of making military arrests in Washington and his comparative lack of combat experience laid him open to charges of being a 'political general'. If he won, said Bennett, all who opposed him would be subjected to a reign of terror – their property would be confiscated and they would be imprisoned and flogged: bloodshed and

[60]*NYH* 23 Sept; 1 Oct 1862. In the South such appeals only encouraged resistance. In Richmond war department official J.B. Jones wrote in his diary on 13 Oct 1862, 'The *New York Herald,* and even the *Tribune,* are *tempting* us to return to the Union by promises of *protecting slavery* and an offer of a convention, giving us such guarantees of safety as we may demand. *This is significant.* We understand the sign.' *A Rebel War Clerk's Diary,* vol. 1, p. 168.

[61]On the campaign see Brummer, VII, VIII; D.A.S. Alexander, vol. 3, ch 2; Allan Nevins, *The War for the Union,* vol 2, ch 12, esp. pp. 302-5, 310-20; *American Annual Cyclopedia 1862,* pp. 654-6. Very worthwhile also is an unpublished thesis by Mary P. Hodnett, 'Civil War Issues in New York State Politics' (St. John's 1971).

[62]See H.G. Pearson, *James S. Wadsworth of Geneseo* (London 1913).

[63]*NYH* 26 Sept 1862. See also H. Leackin to F. Hudson 12 Mar 1862, Bennett Papers, LC.

endless civil war would ensue. He insisted that Wadsworth was going to seize power by fomenting riots on election day.[64]

There was also an element of old fashioned Jacksonianism in the *Herald*'s assaults. Wadsworth, it reminded voters, was as much an aristocrat as any southern slaveholder, and his claim to be a champion of the popular will was 'all fudge and fustian'.[65] Wadsworth's paternalism was reflected in the affectionate Republican nickname of 'Pap' Wadsworth, which Bennett immediately amended to 'Treasury Pap' Wadsworth.

The significant point is that the *Herald* led New Yorkers to believe that Lincoln opposed Wadsworth's election, just as Seward certainly did.[66] In fact, Bennett told the electorate, Lincoln must be trusted, and the best way to support him against the 'radicals' in an energetic prosecution of the war was to vote for a 'conservative' Democrat: 'A conservative triumph will kill Jeff. Davis and end the rebellion. An abolition triumph will kill the nation to end negro slavery.'[67]

As usual the *Herald* – that incomparable instrument for finding and bludgeoning an enemy's weak spots – was only luke warm in positive support for the Democratic candidate. Horatio Seymour, Governor in 1853-4, was noted for his strict attention to 'legality'.[68] The *Herald* distrusted his identification with the Albany Regency state organisation, and while Seymour was outspoken on the Administration's infringements of civil liberty and on the constitutional rights of the South, he was not positive enough for Bennett's liking about pressing the war to victory. Bennett feared that Seymour would spoil the Democratic campaign with too much defeatism. Professing alarm at the growing excitement of the canvass, the *Herald* proposed that both Seymour and Wadsworth should withdraw in favour of a true Union man, General John A. Dix.[69]

Dix would undoubtedly have made a good candidate. His unionism and probity were beyond cavil and he possessed the full confidence of the mercantile community. Nor was Bennett alone in

[64]*NYH* 26 Sept – 4 Nov 1862.

[65]*NYH* 1 Oct 1862.

[66]See particularly *NYH* 3 Nov 1862.

[67]*NYH* 28 Oct 1862.

[68]A highly sympathetic biography is Stewart Mitchell, *Horatio Seymour of New York* (Cambridge, Mass. 1938).

[69]The *Herald* first suggested that Seymour should withdraw on 11 Oct, because it thought he could not win. It first advocated Dix's candidacy on 14 Oct. The regular Democratic *World* was quick to pooh-pooh the idea.

advocating his adoption. John Van Buren, son of the former President and a formidable orator and personality in his own right, favoured the idea. On the other side Thurlow Weed, who disliked Wadsworth's radicalism, paired with his old enemy Bennett in pressing Dix's candidacy. But the scheme was fruitless, for Dix preferred to remain in his command at Fortress Monroe and declined to run for the governorship.[70]

Bennett need not have worried. On 4 November Seymour was elected governor by a 10,700 majority. Like other states throughout the North, New York returned more Democratic representatives to Congress than Republicans – among them Fernando Wood. For the first time in ten years Bennett could declare that the election results were 'wonderful'.[71] Although the Republicans would still control Congress, the reaction against them seemed at last to be in motion.

The 'radicals', the *Herald* pontificated, had been repudiated because they had failed to support Lincoln and were corrupt. The new Congress would not meet until December 1863, but Bennett wanted the victorious Democrats to lose no time in making their views known to Lincoln, whom he called upon to 'harmonise' with the wishes of the people by changing his cabinet.[72] (So determined was Bennett on this point that he privately even tried to enlist Mary Lincoln to influence her husband.)[73] Instead of heeding the *Herald* the President waited until the elections were over to dismiss McClellan, whose inability to press his military advantage had grown too chronic to tolerate longer. Lincoln showed no inclination to 'balance' this act by inviting a Democrat into his cabinet.

---

[70]*NYH* 11-25 Oct 1862. Weed had hoped to have Dix nominated as the Republican candidate — see Albany *Evening Journal* 30 Sept; 1, 4 Oct 1862; Brummer, p. 429; Pearson, Wadsworth, p. 152. On Dix see *Dictionary of American Biography* and Morgan Dix, *Memoirs of John A. Dix* (2 vols, NY 1883) and Martin Lichterman, 'John Adams Dix, 1798-1879' (unpublished thesis, Columbia University 1952).

[71]*NYH* 4, 5 Nov 1862. Seventeen Democrats were returned from New York, as against fourteen Republicans.

[72]*NYH* 5-8 Nov 1862.

[73]Bennett's letter to Mrs Lincoln is not extant, but its substance may be inferred from her reply to him, dated 4 Oct 1862, which read in part, 'I have a great terror of *strong* minded ladies, yet if a word fitly spoken and in due season, can be urged in a time like this, we should not withold it. As you suggest the C [abinet] was formed, in a more peaceful time, yet some two or three men who compose it would have distracted it — our country requires no ambitious fanatics to guide the helm, and were it not, that their Counsels, have very little control over the P [resident] when his mind, is made up, as to what is right, there might be cause to fear...' — see Turner and Turner, p. 138 and Ruth P. Randall, *Mary Lincoln,* p. 250.

Bennett persisted in seeing McClellan – 'the hero of Antietam' – as the victim of 'radical' intrigue.[74] Giving McClellan unstinting praise, the *Herald* promised with unmistakable meaning that the country would do him justice after his 'temporary retirement'. Throughout 1863 the *Herald* frequently extolled McClellan's virtues, and would often call for his restoration to command of the Army of the Potomac or even for his appointment as Secretary of War. It would cross swords with the *Times* and *Tribune* again and again over the facts of McClellan's campaigns and the responsibility for their failure.

Meanwhile events seemed to justify Bennett's pessimism with regard to the change. Under its new leadership the Army of the Potomac went to an appalling and futile carnage. In one day 12,000 federals fell on a frozen Virginia plain at Fredericksburg. The intensity of party feeling was revealed in Bennett's description of 'The Bloodthirsty Atrocity of the Radicals'.[75] The defeat, screamed the *Herald,* was entirely the fault of the 'imbecile' Stanton and the General-in-Chief Halleck – 'a thick headed and conceited martinet'. Expressing the frustration and bereavement felt in thousands of Northern homes, and building into it the assumption that military disaster was the inevitable consequence of anti-slavery ideas, Bennett warned that

> The people are willing to expend their treasure and their blood to any amount for the restoration of the Union, but not a cent or a drop of blood to carry out the visionary, impracticable ideas of fanatics; nor will they patiently look on while their sons and brothers and neighbours are slaughtered by wholesale through the criminal carelessness or ignorance of pretenders, who have never seen a battle, and who undertake, at Washington, to lead in the field armies of 150,000 men, at sixty or one hundred miles distance, by click of the telegraph.[76]

Simultaneously his own party was trying to make Lincoln give his cabinet a more pronounced anti-slavery tone, but although the war was going so badly the President refused to make any change. This satisfied neither 'radicals' nor 'conservatives'.[77] The end of 1862 brought gloom to the latter. Nothing had been done to avert the issue of the final emancipation proclamation. When it was promulgated on New Year's day, 1863, Bennett could see in it only 'the opening of a

[74]For imediate reaction to the removal see *NYH* 10-14 Nov 1862.

[75]*NYH* 18 Dec 1862.

[76]*NYH* 20 Dec 1862.

[77]*NYH* 10-23 Dec 1862. On the 'Cabinet Crisis' see Nevins, *The War for the Union,* vol. 2, ch 14.

Pandora's box of evils upon the country', a portent of ruthless and interminable war, and perhaps the death warrant of the Union. The expiry of the hundred day period of grace had hardened his attitude and he pronounced the edict 'unnecessary, unwise and ill-timed, impractical, outside of the constitution and full of mischief'.[78]

[78]*NYH* 31 Dec 1862; 1, 3 Jan 1863. Bennett had continued to hope against hope that Lincoln would not sign the proclamation.

10

NIGGERHEADS AND COPPERHEADS: THE CONSERVATIVES' DILEMMA, 1863

I hev prayd that Linkin will spare the South this bitter cup. Hez the wretch no sole? . . . Ef the nigger fites alongside uv the white man, he is acknowledged ez his ekal, and away goes the corner-stun uv Dimokrasy. It hez allus bin a consolashen to the Northern Dimekrat to feel that ther wuz a race meaner than they are. Shel this pleasin deloosion be roodly dissipatid? Forbid it, Hevin! — Petroleum V. Nasby

The Peace Agitation

Politically, the year 1863 was one of frustration for Bennett. Dissent began to take organised political form, but not the form that the *Herald* advocated. The policies it favoured were increasingly ground between the upper and nether millstones of Republican anti-slavery and Democratic pro-Southern defeatism. Abroad, Bennett watched with impatience the progress of the French invasion of Mexico and resented what he considered covert British aid to the rebel cause.

The Union seemed to go from defeat to defeat. The news from Chancellorsville in May caused Bennett to reflect on the civil strife in a gloomy vein: 'cui bono! . . . It is only the Anglo-Saxon race destroying itself . . . from the battles of the civil war no glory can be reaped. The laurels of the conqueror, on whichever side victory turns the scale, are dripping with kindred blood. . . .'[1] The *Herald*'s criticism of the generalship of the boastful 'Fighting Joe' Hooker was so sarcastic and withering that the irate general – a favourite of the *Times* and *Tribune* – ordered copies of the paper in his camp to be burned.[2] Chancellorsville seemed a microcosm of the Union war effort – superior numbers and resources deployed partially and without intelligence. In New York stock jobbing operations and prize fighting seemed to attract more attention than the war, and Bennett doubtless expressed a widespread sentiment of exasperation and weariness with the abysmal management of the war when he said:

> The public has been so often misled, duped, deceived, disappointed and trifled with by the authorities at Washington that, in spite of

[1]*NYH* 6 May 1863.
[2]*NYH* 15, 20, 22 May; 14 June 1863.

the splendid fighting on the Rappahannock it has at length relapsed into comparative indifference and settled into the conviction that this administration is totally incompetent to conduct the war, and that there is no longer any prospect of the very speedy suppression of the rebellion.

Would the war go on in some form or other for generations; as, in a sense, it had already been waged for thirty years by the abolitionists?[3] Within the Democratic party a vociferous faction favouring peace began to make itself heard. The peace orators claimed that the emancipation proclamation stood in the way of reunion, and although their logic was questionable it wàs emotionally seductive, since casualties were running into hundreds of thousands and no end was yet in sight.

For Clement L. Vallandigham of Ohio, leading spokesman of the 'copperheads', as the Peace Democrats were generally known, Bennett had utter contempt.[4] The *Herald* at first viewed Vallandigham's military arrest in May for making a 'disloyal' speech as a consequence of his own folly.[5] Shortly thereafter a Democratic meeting in New York's Union Square was treated to violent peace harangues by speakers who advocated forceful resistance by the state authorities to the federal government while gangs of 'Bowery Boys' and 'Dead Rabbits' applauded and called for the hanging of the cabinet. Bennett characterised these proceedings as 'reckless' and 'absurd revolutionary excesses' though he was all the time lambasting Stanton and Halleck unmercifully. It was a curious thing, Bennett

---

[3]*NYH* 5 May 1863.

[4]On Vallandigham see Frank L. Klement, *The Limits of Dissent: Clement L. Vallandigham and the Civil War* (Lexington 1970). Still the best overall work on the Copperheads is Wood Gray, *The Hidden Civil War* (NY 1942) although it deals mainly with the Northwest and only incidentally with the peace faction in New York. Richard O. Curry, 'The Union as it was; Recent Interpretations of the Copperheads', *Civil War History,* 13 (1967), 25-39, argues that the Peace Democrats should be seen as old fashioned constitutionalists rather than traitors, as Republicans branded all Democrats as a matter of course. So far as New York is concerned, I think the rabidly pro-confederate tone of the copperhead press makes such a view unrealistic. After all, the Confederates in arms regarded themselves as 'old fashioned constitutionalists'. The indispensable background to dissatisfaction with the war in New York is Basil Leo Lee, 'Discontent in New York City, 1861-5' (unpublished thesis, Catholic University of America, Washington, D.C. 1943). Good studies of wartime issues and the peace movement in a major eastern urban centre are N.B. Wainwright, 'Loyal Opposition in Civil War Philadelphia', *Pennsylvania Magazine of History and Biography,* 88 (1964), 294-315, and William Dusinberre, *Civil War Issues in Philadelphia, 1856-65* (Philadelphia 1965), an analysis which suggests to the reader that the *Herald*'s political attitudes were by no means confined to the Empire City.

[5]*NYH* 8 May 1863. Vallandigham had said that the 'wicked and cruel war' was an attempt to erect a Republican despotism on the ruins of slavery — see Klement, chs 10-13.

himself dryly observed, that 'by a strange paradox, the war democrats are exceedingly peaceable fellows, while the peace democrats are inclined to muscular developments'.[6]

The rising fever of peace agitation caused Bennett, fearful that 'deeply excited popular elements' might 'be inflamed to the most fearful extremities of resistance',[7] to warn Lincoln that:

> Ill judged repressive measures always create a determined opposition . . . this Vallandigham affair furnishes the very capital to these democratic radicals which they have most desired, and puts them in a constitutional position from which they cannot be displaced. The public sentiment of New York and of all the loyal States on this point is with them, and the administration must squash these military proceedings against Vallandigham, and recognise the vitality of the civil law in the loyal states, or there will be civil war in the North . . . the great majority of those who have made their remonstrances heard against such arbitrary assumptions care nothing for Vallandigham, but they do care for the great constitutional principles involved in this case.[8]

Although Lincoln banished the 'wily agitator' to the Confederacy, thus evading the issue of military arrest, the Supreme Court was to declare after the war in *Ex Parte Milligan* that the military had no jurisdiction in areas where the civil courts were open, so vindicating the *Herald*'s arguments.

Bennett took the same ground in relation to the military suppression of the Chicago *Times,* against which he protested strongly even though he regarded his copperhead contemporary as a bad 'party hack' paper run by the 'vilest and meanest politicians'.[9] Lincoln disavowed the suppression, but still Bennett could not resist asking 'Why should the Chicago *Times* be suppressed and the New York *Tribune* which is a thousand times more dangerously treasonable, be permitted to rave on unrebuked?'[10] Had Lincoln arrested Wendell Phillips, Henry Ward Beecher and Greeley rather than Vallandigham, the *Herald* indicated in plain terms that it would manage to overcome its constitutional scruples.[11]

[6]*NYH* 20-22 May; 10 June 1863.

[7]*NYH* 20 May; see also 5 June 1863.

[8]*NYH* 22 May; see also 28 May;1, 2, 13 June 1863.

[9]*NYH* 9 June 1863. On the suppression see Robert S. Harper, *Lincoln and the Press* (NY 1951), ch 29.

[10]*NYH* 4 June 1863.

[11]*NYH* 15 May; 4 June 1863, etc.

Arbitrary use of federal authority only exacerbated the growing peace movement. On 3 June Fernando Wood and his Mozart Hall Democracy organised a peace rally in New York which an estimated 30,000 people attended. Quite suddenly, the *Herald* capitulated completely to the popular excitement. It declared that the people had lost all faith in the war, that the peace men were in a majority in the Democratic party and that the 'peace revolution' was bound to be successful. Predicting the extermination of the abolitionists, it praised Wood as 'the Stonewall Jackson of the Democratic party' (slightly strange, since Jackson had recently been killed by his own men). If the war went on for another year, said Bennett, a peace President would be elected to proclaim an armistice and call a Convention of Northern and Southern states which would 'restore constitutional rights' North and South and 'the cause of the strife and alienation – the slavery question – will be finally settled by a return to the principles on which the government was founded: the old fabric will be reconstructed as a white man's government. Negro slavery will be established more firmly than it ever was before, and North as well as South the whole race will be enslaved or exterminated. All the trouble the country has seen has arisen from emancipation.'[12] Yet, unlike the copperheads, Bennett did not call for an immediate armistice, and when the euphoria of the moment had passed he dissociated the *Herald* completely from Wood's peace movement.[13] His opportunistic dalliance with it proved to have been a mere temporary aberration – the only week in the whole war when he advocated anything less than restoration of the whole Union following the defeat of the Southern armies.

It was the advance of the Confederate Army into Pennsylvania which caused a resurgence of 'win the war' patriotism in New York. Lee provided the cure for creeping demoralisation. As the *Herald* itself later observed:

> Every time a Southern army comes to the Potomac it strengthens
> the administration, because it simplifies all questions and issues
> that are before the people. It boils all politics down to the two

[12]*NYH* 5, 6 June 1863. Yet on 26 March Bennett had tartly remarked that Wood seemed desirous of being locked in Fort Lafayette, to judge by his recent speeches, and only a fortnight before the June meeting the *Herald* had scoffed that the Copperheads favoured peace 'on any terms acceptable to Jeff Davis' (23 May). The suddenness of the *Herald*'s conversion may be seen by the fact that it warned its readers to stay away from the Wood meeting for fear of violence and pronounced on 1 June that 'we are no partisans of conventions which are called together for the purpose of making a show of violent opposition to the administration, or with the intent of agitating questions which produce schisms, party quarrels and ill feeling'.

[13]*NYH* 23 June 1863.

facts of the public enemy on one hand and the government on the other, and everyone stands by the government, of course.[14]

The *Herald* reported that a grim joke was current in the ranks of the invading Southern infantry, to the effect that they were coming North to hold peace meetings. On 18 June Bennett announced bluntly that 'the peace party is squelched for the present'.

The Reconstruction and Race Issues in 1863

Lee's repulse at Gettysburg did more than submerge the peace agitation. It raised the question of reconstruction as a current issue. A Northerner reading his paper in the week after Gettysburg might well believe that the war would be won before the summer of 1863 was out. The fall of Vicksburg made headlines on 8 July and the capture of Charleston was momentarily expected. Every day between 9 and 13 July the *Herald* carried headlines warning of the impending battle in which Lee's army would be annihilated. Bennett could 'hardly resist the conclusion that the tide of victory has turned so decidedly against the rebel army of General Lee that the end of this campaign will be the end of the rebellion'.[15] This was the time, he believed, for President Lincoln to take the initiative by issuing a liberal amnesty to the Southern masses:

> the helpless rank and file of the rebel armies should be invited to their old allegiance, with the assurance of forgetfulness of the past and the protection of the constitution for the future, including the important item of slave property, and the remaining armed forces of Jeff. Davis will be broken up and disbanded without further bloodshed. A general Southern popular reaction in favor of submission and peace will speedily put an end to the war, and send into exile Jeff. Davis, his Cabinet, his Congress and all his most guilty fellow conspirators in this disastrous experiment of their Southern Confederacy.[16]

Although he realised, as the copperheads seemingly did not, that only defeat would halt the bid of Southern leaders for independence,[17] Bennett shared the notion that seems to affect both sides in most wars, namely that the enemy soldiers have been dragooned into fighting by despotic leaders. Early in 1861 faith in latent Southern Unionism had

[14]*NYH* 9 July 1864.
[15]*NYH* 4 July 1863.
[16]*NYH* 9 July 1863.
[17]*NYH* 2 June 1863.

influenced Republican policies. Bennett had ridiculed it then but believed it now, giving prominence to every sign of disaffection and weakness in the South and tenaciously expounding the view that Davis represented only a few criminals holding out against punishment. This kind of thinking even led him occasionally to advocate an implausible scheme for peace based on federal aid to the Confederate government. The proposal was that the Southern States should be restored to the Union in return for a subsidy to Jefferson Davis and his followers to establish their government in Mexico. This, thought Bennett, would not only end the Civil War but drive the French out of Mexico and bring the native 'mongrel' population the benefits of Anglo-Saxon rule.[18]

Perhaps only a New Yorker, perhaps only Bennett, could have contemplated buying off the enemy on such a grand scale. Suffice it to say that, like the proposed amnesty and guarantee of slavery intended to precipitate the collapse of the Confederacy in July 1863, the idea was never tried.

In a broader sense though, the amnesty scheme showed that Bennett grasped the fact that every day the war continued made a restoration of the 'Union as it was' more difficult, and he deplored the fact. Like Lincoln, Bennett always remembered that white Southerners would have to be lived with in harmony after the war. Unlike Lincoln, he saw the reconstruction problem only in terms of white people. The *Herald* still regarded the Emancipation Proclamation as negotiable and agitated for its revocation. For Bennett the moral problem of what to do about slavery simply did not exist. He wanted a return of fugitive slaves to their owners at the end of the war, or if that proved impossible, the payment of compensation to the owners. He yearned to restore the old Democratic hegemony by an early readmission of Southern Senators and representatives to Congress with all their 'rights' guaranteed and no questions asked. His utter contempt for Negroes, of course, allowed him to be scrupulously legalistic in expounding those 'rights'. In Louisiana, for instance, the *Herald* challenged Lincoln's right to make abolition a requisite for the reorganised state government.[19] It also rejected the radical Republican 'state suicide' theory which would have regarded the beaten South as just so much conquered territory. Even though he would sometimes descant on the war as part of a general civilising and amalgamating

[18]*NYH* 4, 9, 28 Oct 1863.

[19]*NYH* 20 Aug 1863. On Lincoln's attempts to form a loyal government in Louisiana see H. Belz, *Reconstructing the Union* (Ithaca 1969), ch VI, esp. p. 147 ff.

process in world history,[20] Bennett was adamant in asserting that 'It is not an international or foreign war, but an insurrectionary or domestic one. The whole theory of the war assumes that the Southern States are still legally a part of the Union, and consequently under the jurisdiction of the constitution and laws of the Union, notwithstanding their secession and rebellion.'[21]

From there he proceeded to describe the issues between the 'conservative masses' (He used this term in much the same way that politicians of a later age invoked the 'silent majority') and the 'radicals' in dramatic terms. The 'radicals' were out not only to 'overthrow slavery at any cost to the nation and humanity' but 'to destroy the white race of the South root and branch; to make the country a waste, howling wilderness; to give the land to the negroes in reward for the massacre of the old men, the women and the children who now inhabit it.'[22] He predicted that they would try to build a Republican party ascendancy based on Negro votes and portrayed them all as cast in the mould of Senator Jim Lane of Kansas, 'red handed, rapacious, utterly unscrupulous as to veracity, making a joke of homicide and ready to base political power on the devastation of a region half as large as Europe'.[23]

When Bennett doubted that the majority in the North 'desire the prosecution of this war to the extinguishment of Southern slavery, when peace and the Old Union are within our reach' he was making a rather large assumption, but one which it was very convenient to attack the Republicans with. Because they frankly did not desire 'the Union as it was' he branded them as unpatriotic and worse. Bennett differed from the Peace Democrats in holding that the war was just and that the Confederacy could and should be defeated, but he shared their view of the goals of reconstruction and their fixation that abolition stood in the way of victory.

It was August 1863 before the *Herald* came grudgingly to the major admission that slavery might have to take its chances among the casualties of the war.[24] Even then Bennett was anxious that the states should be allowed to preserve at least a remnant of it. This political retreat did not involve any revision of the paper's attitude towards

[20]*NYH* 25 Aug; 8, 13 Oct 1863.

[21]*NYH* 20 May 1863.

[22]*NYH* 28 Aug 1863. Stanton was accused of encouraging depredations by black troops in South Carolina for this purpose — *NYH* 28 June.

[23]*NYH* 14 Oct 1863.

[24]*NYH* 20 Aug 1863.

Negroes. On the contrary, the prospect of the war being prolonged on their behalf made Bennett if possible more bitter against blacks in the summer of 1863. He anticipated wistfully the time when 'the abolition leaders will be all banished from the country or hanged, and it will be a penal offence of the highest magnitude against the dignity of the white race and the white man's government to agitate the question of slavery hereafter, or blaspheme the handiwork of God by asserting that a black man is equal to a Celt, a Saxon, or a Teuton or any other division of the great Caucasian race'.[25]

He did come to approve letting Negroes fight in the federal armies. Although in 1862 he had predicted that arming blacks would be suicidal, in 1863 he reconsidered that military training could only improve the lazy, worthless fellows: and although white soldiers detested them and might exterminate them, once at the front 'they are just as good for killing as anyone else'.[26] He hoped that as many as possible would be captured by Southerners and not exchanged, so allowing the North to use more 'sturdy and intelligent' Irish and German labour.[27] Bennett surprised Republican editors when he admitted that black regiments could be effective in battle, but he considered nevertheless that Negroes' innate barbarism put them beyond the pale of civilised warfare.[28] He steadfastly defended the system of slavery just as he had before the war, portraying the well provided 'happy nigger' as the envy of the white workers of Europe. He now definitely opposed colonisation on the straightforward grounds that slavery ensured the prosperity of the United States. What was the use in banishing the Southern labour force? Could slavery, he asked, be called barbarous in comparison with the consequences of trying to destroy it?[29]

He blamed hostility to blacks in New York on the 'niggerhead' (he could not resist the counterpoint) abolition newspapers of the city, whose constant agitation of the 'mischievous doctrine' of Negro equality 'very naturally inflames the inborn prejudice of the white race against the unfortunate black race upon the slightest provacation'.[30]

The black race in the city was, in fact, about to suffer most unpleasantly from the inflamed 'inborn prejudice' of the whites. Ten

[25]*NYH* 6 June 1863.
[26]*NYH* 22 May; 5, 20 June 1863.
[27]*NYH* 28 May 1863.
[28]*NYH* 28 June 1863.
[29]*NYH* 1 Aug 1863.
[30]*NYH* 24 June 1863.

days after Gettysburg, New York City erupted in four days of rioting which were the worst in its history. When order had been restored a controversy scarcely less violent broke out (though only ink, not blood was spilled). The *Herald* was in the thick of this row, and Bennett found himself assailed more bitterly than at any time, perhaps, since the 'moral war' of 1840.

The Draft Riots and their Aftermath

The draft riots were unexpected in their size and ferocity.[31] They were directly attributable to the draft, which began in the city peaceably enough on Saturday 11 July. The following day gave the malcontents time to feel their grievances and to organise, and on the Monday morning, when drawing for the conscription was resumed, pandemonium broke loose. On the third day, before the violence had run its full course, the newspapers began to attack each other for having provoked them. What was the *Herald* saying?

During the preceding week the paper had been too busy printing details of Gettysburg and Vicksburg to spare much space for political comment. On 6 July the *Herald* had printed the text of a speech made by Governor Seymour to an overflowing audience at the Academy of Music on Independence Day in which he had said, with reference to arbitrary arrests and the draft, 'Remember this, that the bloody and treasonable, and revolutionary doctrine of public necessity can be proclaimed by a mob as well as a government'.

Now Bennett, it has been seen, was no supporter of arbitrary arrests. Moreover, he had lately been pleased with Seymour for the promptness with which he had forwarded state militia to serve in Pennsylvania to save that State, as Bennett made a point of telling the Philadelphia editors, from the cowardice and panic of its own inhabitants.[32] Gettysburg put him in no mood, however, for this latest effusion from the Peace Democracy. He had called upon Fourth of July orators to rise above the stereotyped eloquence usual to the occasion and declare themselves unequivocally for the suppression of

---

[31] Discounting exaggerated estimates of the casualties in the riots which appeared for a century afterwards, a superior recent analysis places the dead with some confidence at not more than 119 and not less than 105 — see Adrian Cook, *The Armies of the Streets* (University of Kentucky 1974). A spirited narrative of events is James McCague, *The Second Rebellion* (NY 1968). See also the older works of Joel T. Headley, *The Great Riots of New York* (NY 1873, 1971), chs X-XX inclusive, and Herbert Asbury, *The Gangs of New York* (NY 1928), chs VII, VIII.

[32] *NYH* 21, 23, 26, 29 June; 1 Aug 1863. The absence of these troops in Pennsylvania was of course the reason why New York was so vulnerable to disorder.

the rebellion.[33] What Seymour actually delivered disgusted Bennett, and the editor let off his spleen on 7 July. His fulmination was titled 'The Great Historical Crisis and the Small Politicians':

> On the Fourth of July Governor Seymour, of this State, ex-Governor Seymour, of Connecticut, and the Hon. Mr. Pendleton of Ohio, delivered speeches at the Academy of Music before a new democratic club, composed of politicians as small and unappreciative as the speakers themselves. We took the trouble to publish these addresses in yesterday's HERALD, and are almost sorry that we wasted so much valuable space on such trashy productions. In the midst of the greatest crisis the world ever saw – with the news of the greatest victory of the war just electrifying the country – these political trimmers spent the precious hours of our national anniversary in talking about the arrest of Vallandigham and the suppression of a few tupenny papers, and the awful despotism which these actions of the administration had imposed upon the country. We are sick to nausea of such silly, brainless prattle. It is designed merely for political effect. The more these small fry politicians chatter, the firmer becomes our conviction that if a couple of hundred niggerhead and copperhead organs had been suppressed, and about five thousand niggerhead and copperhead leaders thrown into a common prison long ago, the country would have been in a far better position today and in the future.

Bennett was convinced that these 'Lilliputian politicians' would soon be 'swept away with the other dirt and rubbish of the past'.

He also continued to be squarely in favour of the draft. Mass conscription had become law in March, and in some states it was resisted to the point of murdering enrolling officers. Bennett, though, was critical of the government for not implementing the draft rapidly enough.[34] The previous year he had assured Lincoln by private letter that he would be happy to give 'a most active support' to enlisting and enlarging the army, and this he had done according to his lights.[35] He

---

[33]*NYH* 1 July 1863.

[34]Eugene C. Murdock deals with the draft in New York in *Patriotism Limited, 1862-65* (Kent, Ohio 1967), and in the North generally in *One Million Men* (Madison 1971).

[35]Bennett to Lincoln 11 Aug 1862, Lincoln Papers, LC, item 17554. Bennett had been invited to serve as a Vice-President at a Union Mass Meeting for recruitment at the Cooper Institute on 1 July 1862. Shortly afterwards a *Herald* employee suggested to Bennett that a 100-man company should be recruited from the paper's offices and enlisted as the 'Bennett Guard' in a crack regiment. A 'Herald Guard' militia company had existed in 1851. See Peter Y. Everett to J.G. B., 28 July 1862, Bennett Papers, LC; A.E. Coleman, 'A New and Authentic History of the *Herald*', *Editor and Publisher*, 56-58 (1924-5).

thought that Governor Seymour could have taken more energetic steps in co-operation with Washington to fill out the state quota with volunteers (and of course he never tired of declaring that 100,000 volunteers would immediately step forward if only McClellan were reappointed to command).[36] Bennett urged the government to press on with the draft in order to raise an army to fight the French in Mexico rather than the Confederates.[37]

So encouraging seemed the quiet and even good humoured reception given the first drawings on 11 July that the edition of the *Herald* going onto the streets on Monday morning, the 13th, just as the violence was getting under way, contained editorial assurances to the government that no opposition need be feared from a population anxious to assist in winning the war. Ironically, Bennett drew the lesson that the tranquillity with which the draft was being carried out showed that it had not been want of patriotism but despair at the capacity of the Administration which ever caused the draft to meet opposition. Only briefly had he paid attention to some 'unprincipled and designing' Democratic politicians who were making speeches calculated to stir up a moblike spirit which could 'raise a storm that will terminate in insurrection and bloody scenes in this city'. Yet the *Herald* on 13 July carried news reports which did not quite square with the optimistic editorial page. A reporter on the streets found the feeling in the city in relation to the draft 'very excited' among those fortunate enough, as he put it, to have procured Sunday's *Herald* with its long list of draftees. In some wards the reporter found labourers organising resistance with every means in their power.

The riots themselves kept the *Herald* busy in the ensuing days giving fully detailed coverage of this doorstep sensation, with its grisly atrocities against Negroes and murderous confrontations between the police and the crowd. Pressure on space kept editorials perfunctory. The *Herald* hoped for a return of reason and an end to scenes 'which everyone must deplore', though its news columns suggested that 'excuse must be made for the conduct of the crowd by the glaring fact that a number of their kindred had been shot down in cold blood by their sides'.[38]

[36]*NYH* 20 May; 16-19, 27, 29 June; 1 July 1863. On Seymour's inglorious role see Eugene Murdock, 'Horatio Seymour and the 1863 Draft', *Civil War History*, 11 (1965), 117-41.

[37]*NYH* 2 June; 9, 10 July 1863. Another reason which Bennett alleged for supporting conscription was that it would avoid the financial panic and collapse which it was supposed would follow a rapid demobilization. Presumably he imagined that the prospect of fighting the French would fill the draftees with enthusiasm.

[38]*NYH* 14 July 1863,

Such was the *Herald*'s record immediately before and during the riots. Republican editors found its tone of detachment insincere. Greeley said 'The . . . *Herald* of yesterday had not one editorial word concerning the mob which its counsels had originated and inflamed. Nothing which it could have said was so significant as this silence'.[39] The *Times* thought that every true patriot should have referred to the rioters as 'the mob', and that the *Herald*'s description of them as 'the people' was a libel that ought to have paralysed the fingers that penned it.[40]

On the 16th Bennett loftily noted the verbal war between the 'copperhead' *World, News* and *Express*[41] on one hand and the 'niggerhead' *Tribune, Times* and *Post* on the other. He found the assaults of both parties on the *Herald* 'laughable' and roundly condemned 'these mischievous papers all scandalously attempt[ing] to make political capital out of the riots before the rioters are fairly suppressed'. Then he descended to the plain and retaliated in kind. The *Tribune* accused him of being a 'Mob Jackal', stirring up the feelings of the 'Jeff. Davis ruffians' against the unfortunate Negro. Bennett answered by blaming the *Tribune* itself for holding the Negro constantly before the people and exciting feelings by 'endeavouring to degrade the white race to a level with him': the murdered Negroes were but a few of the thousands of blacks sacrificed to abolitionism during the war. Greeley was inflamed because the mob had surrounded the *Tribune* building and threatened his life. Here at last, Bennett crowed, was a taste of his own medicine, for he had been glad enough to see the *Herald* offices suffer in April 1861. Paraphrase cannot do justice to Bennett's rejoinder to Raymond, who was 'exceedingly aggrieved because one of our reporters called the rioters "people". Well, they are people are they not? They have heads, bodies, legs and arms . . . they are possessed of minds and souls, and, if their intelligence is not very great, it is at least equal to that of the niggerheads and the editors of the niggerhead organs.'[42]

Bennett never denied Mozart Hall or the extreme Democratic press its share of blame for the riots. He accused the copperheads of having deliberately misrepresented the conscription act in order to

[39]NY *Daily Tribune* 15 July 1863, and see also 17 July.

[40]NY *Times* 15 July 1863.

[41]On the reaction of the *Express* to the draft riots see chapter XIII of Russell H. McLain, 'The New York *Express:* Voice of Opposition' (unpublished thesis, Columbia University, 1955).

[42]*NYH* 16 July 1863.

make it odious to the people.[43] The *Herald* found nothing to praise in Seymour's handling of the situation, though it refrained from criticising his address to the rioters as 'my friends' on which Republicans were to ring the changes for years to come. It found him guilty of not working cordially enough with Washington but acquitted him of Republican charges of treason.[44]

The brunt of the *Herald*'s ire during the newspaper inquest on the riots fell on the abolitionists. They had tried to make the draft as onerous as possible, Bennett now discovered, with a view to imposing martial law on the Democratic city. Although the mobs had acted with some show of concert he utterly rejected the Republican contention that the riots were the work of Southern agitators or that New Yorkers were actively disloyal: 'the very classes said to have been engaged in the recent riots have contributed more soldiers to the Union armies than all the niggerheads in the nation.' He turned the charge around and accused Republicans of being in league with Southern leaders in deliberately misrepresenting the popular disturbances. Their motive?

> They know that the rebels are beaten. They know that unless something is done to prolong the war the Union will be restored before their conspiracy to abolitionize every seceded state can be accomplished. They know that to prolong the war it is necessary to inspirit Jeff. Davis and weaken our armies . . . they aim to keep up the war until the last cent is stolen from the national treasury and the last slave is transformed into an abolition voter.[45]

This charge was in a spirit typical of the press in the days following the riots, each paper trying to represent the others as being the most incendiary.

The *Herald* defended the city's Irish population from the attacks of the Republican press. Certainly the Irish had been prominent in the rioting, but Bennett justly pointed out that the police to whom credit was due for the suppression of the disorder had a large proportion of Irish members.[46] His own seemingly accurate analysis of the crowd was that it was basically composed of labouring men enraged against the draft but had been augmented and finally taken over by every species of vagabond and criminal in the city.[47] This was certainly a

---

[43]*NYH* 21, 30 July 1863.

[44]*NYH* 21, 26 July 1863.

[45]*NYH* 21 July 1863.

[46]*NYH* 25 July 1863.

[47]*NYH* 26 July 1863. The *Herald* also commented on the role of youths and viragos in making trouble. An analysis of the occupations of the rioters, based on city criminal

more dispassionate appraisal than that of the eminently respectable Republican and college man George Templeton Strong, who wrote in his diary at this time 'I would like to see war made on the Irish scum as in 1688'.[48] The *Herald* added the charge of trying to start a religious war against Roman Catholics to the crimes of the 'beastly radicals of the Black Republican Press', Raymond and Greeley, who 'appear to hate the white race as intensely as they adore the black'.[49]

What can be said then, in summary of the *Herald*'s role in the riots? In the first place there was no justification for charges that it directly condoned bloodshed and the destruction of property in the period immediately preceding the riots or during them. Also, it plainly supported the draft and favoured co-operation between the state and federal authorities. Its reporting of the riots was sensationalist, after the manner of the time, but generally very full. This in itself may have aroused a certain professional jealousy among the city press.

On the other hand, while the *Herald* was by no means so extreme against the Administration as smaller circulation Democratic papers such as the *World, Express* and *Daily News,* it filled its readers with hatred of Negroes. It had also hammered home the message in the preceding months that the abolitionists were responsible for the war and its prolongation. Bennett had threatened them with vengeance on numerous occasions, repeating that abolitionists and secessionist fire-eaters should be hung on the same gallows.[50] In a particularly venomous editorial on 1 July he had reviewed the crimes of the anti-slavery 'radicals' and had reminded his readers that:

> Their leaders still walk in high places and fill their pockets from the national Treasury, and their journals are still supported by official patronage and government contracts; but the end of things is at hand . . . the duty of the hour is to remember and punish. First let the rebels be defeated and driven back, and then, without hesitation or delay, let those northern abolition traitors who are responsible for the rebellion and for the success it has achieved be held to strict and final account.

Furthermore he had attacked Greeley incessantly. Of course this was nothing new. Assaults on Greeley were good space fillers in the editorial columns and the 'wretched Horace' made a fine target.

records, may be found in Cook, *Armies of the Streets,* pp. 195 ff. and Appendix VI. Some of the *Herald*'s more important judgements seem verified by the facts.

[48]Nevins and Thomas eds., *The Diary of George Templeton Strong,* vol. III, p. 343, entry for 20 July 1863.

[49]*NYH* 21, 28 July 1863.

[50]*NYH* e.g. 12, 27 June 1863.

Bennett enjoyed himself no end in ridiculing his rival's eccentric clothing, wondering whether the old white coat and cowhide boots might one day be venerated like the green breeches of Mahomet; but such attacks seldom remained good natured. The *Tribune* editor was accused of having brought on an abolition war, then having turned secessionist and defeatist, and in a macabre bit of satire Bennett warned that the North would take vegeance on him: 'Time was, and we hope will come again, that when the brains were gone the man would die. There is yet hope for the nation if the rule is once again a fact.'[51] Greeley was not in the slightest squeamish about returning these compliments with interest. Nevertheless when the mob threatened to sack the *Tribune* offices and hang Greeley the *Herald* shared moral guilt as an accessory. The *Herald* offices were not threatened.

In all, the violence of Bennett's language on occasions makes his claims to having been above the mêlée of the party press disingenuous to say the least. He did not start the debate over responsibility for the riots,.but he gave as good as he got. His mind was free from the set of conspiracy theories that Republicans carried in their intellectual baggage concerning Confederate agents and the Irish, but he carried his own set concerning the abolitionists. Both cases built an absurd edifice of overstatement on genuine political differences over the interpretation of facts.

Unrepentant, the *Herald* continued after the riots to denounce anti-slavery leaders as bitterly as ever, and to belabour Greeley as 'the strenuous advocate of . . . every social and political abomination of the day' and delighted in repeating rumours that the dedicated vegetarian had saved his skin from the mob by hiding in a meatbox in Windust's restaurant.[52]

So far as the draft itself was concerned, the *Herald* now discovered that the terms of the conscription act had been 'odious and oppressive', that the city's quota was far too high and that the aportionment between Republican and Democratic districts was unfair. Bennett did not, however, support the view of Governor

---

[51]*NYH* 1 July 1863. In this editorial Bennett said: 'He, above all men, has brought on the present crisis by his persistent folly in assailing, abusing and threatening the South, giving them all the provocation they wanted to excuse their crime. He, by his journalism, has infected the fools of the country with the desire to become philosophers.' Greeley had favoured schemes for foreign mediation during the winter of 1862-3 and had recently said 'If Lee can conquer us, so be it'. For other attacks on him see *Herald* 19 May; 2, 12, 21, 27 June 1863.

[52]*NYH* 8 Aug 1863. Greeley of course hotly denied these imputations of cowardice, and his biographer agrees that the tale about the meatbox is a 'malicious falsehood' — Glyndon Van Deusen, *Horace Greeley* (Philadelphia 1953), p. 299.

Seymour and the copperheads that the conscription act was unconstitutional, and chided them for their error. Seeing its worth as a future
election issue, he held rather that the act was inexpedient and
unnecessary.[53]

Yet although he continued to believe that the volunteering system
assisted by bounties was the best way to raise an army, from this time
until the war's end Bennett supported the Administration in its
successive calls for three year men. In October he assured Lincoln
privately, 'I shall help your government all I can to get the 300,000
new troops. The sooner you get them, the sooner the peace.'[54] The
Herald was in the forefront in encouraging volunteering to fill
enlistment quotas before a draft became necessary. It exhorted the
rich of the city to empty their pockets to create a fund to provide
attractive municipal bounties to volunteers – Bennett himself contributed $1,000.[55] A typical appeal ran: 'Let our merchant princes,
banks and financiers lead the way; and let the gold speculators, the
shoddy contractors, the stockjobbers and all others who have been
coining money out of this war, step forward to assist. . . .' In the
immediate wake of the riots the *Herald* joined in the call for a city
ordinance to provide for bounty payments to relieve the poor of the
'onerousness of the draft' and so allay discontent, but Mayor Opdyke
vetoed this proposal on the grounds that it appeared to be a concession
to violence.[56] However, in the following February the State Legislature
established a bounty fund, to the *Herald*'s hearty approval.

It was all very well for Bennett to complain during 1864 about the
abuses and frauds to which the bounty system gave rise but, as he
admitted, action to reform them might hinder the state's recruiting
effort. The social price to be paid for putting a premium on patriotism
became evident as the unscrupulous breed of 'bounty brokers'
proliferated and preyed on unwary recruits. Yet the *Herald* reserved
its most bitter criticisms for Massachusetts or New Jersey brokers
who lured New York recruits away with higher bounties or 'cheated'
by enlisting Negroes to fill up their state quotas.[57] Its only answer to

[53]*NYH* 2, 4, 11, 13 Aug 1863.

[54]Bennett to Lincoln 26 Oct 1863, Lincoln Papers, LC, item 27504. The draft calls
were in summer 1863, spring 1864, autumn 1864 and spring 1865; see e.g. *NYH* 18
May; 10, 15 Aug 1864.

[55]*NYH* 14 Aug; 25 Oct; 16, 17 Nov; 5, 6, 8, 25 Dec 1863; 4, 6, 13 Feb; 4 Mar; 11, 18
Apr; 11, 12, 21, 26 May; 3, 29 June; 4, 13, 19, 22 July; 3 Aug 1864; 15, 21 Feb; 5, 6,
10, 15, 16, 17, 20, 24 Mar 1865.

[56]*NYH* 29 July; 24, 26, 29 Aug 1863.

[57]*NYH* e.g. 14 Sept; 9, 16 Dec 1863; 9, 12, 29 Jan; 8 Feb; 22 July; 6, 12, 17, 25, 31
Aug 1864. Bennett accused Republican 'Loyal Leaguers' of having a hand in the trade

these and other abuses was to call for yet higher competitive bounties. Such was New York's eagerness to buy her way out of the draft that Bennett could cite the city's ability to donate thousands of dollars to military and naval heroes and still pay $4 million for exemption fees as a proof of 'the public spirit of her citizens'.[58] The draft riots made a deep impression on the city, and well into 1864 Bennett could see sinister incendiarism in the anti-conscription diatribes of copperhead journals and would remain touchy about sending militia away when a draft was imminent.[59]

Otherwise the occurrences of 13-16 July 1863 became a fixed feature in the realm of political mythology for both Republicans and Democrats. The draft had gone into effect but no social reform followed the outbreak. The *Herald* had complained some time before the riots at the laxity of the city authorities in disarming gangs of roughs. Bennett saw that the dependence of ward politicians on these gangs for their election stood in the way of effective action, but this condition of affairs seemed ineradicable. All sides preferred to draw morals about national politics and cry 'treason' at their opponents rather than suggest ways of tackling crime and poverty amongst the 'dangerous classes'.[60]

The Autumn Elections: Political War on Two Fronts

The year 1863 was politically an 'off year' in New York, which is to say that only a number of subordinate state posts were to be filled by election. Like the term of the New York City Congressional delegation, the governorship of Horatio Seymour still had another year to run, although his record so far was bound to be an issue. The *Herald* was busy early in campaigning. What did it think were the issues?

Bennett produced his political manifesto at the end of July. Modestly crediting the *Herald* with the leadership of the 'conservative masses' of the country since the collapse of the Democratic Party in 1860, he called for the union on a war platform of all Republicans who

of driving recruits to other states. In his view bounty swindles of all kinds ran unchecked because the local politicians were financially interested in bounty brokerage — *NYH* 23 Oct 1864.

[58]*NYH* 2 Jan 1865. He did express the pious hope that, although the government could not actually fight rebels with greenbacks, it would be able to use them as bounty money to induce the reinlistment of veterans.

[59]*NYH* 23 Apr; 6, 26 May; 13, 23 July; 30 Aug 1864.

[60]*NYH* 27 May 1863. On the persistence of the social conditions underlying the 1863 outbreak ten years later see Charles L. Brace, *The Dangerous Classes of New York* (NY 1872).

rejected the abolitionists and all Democrats who repudiated the copperheads. He used the results of recent elections in New England to point the moral that for 'conservative' War Democrats to make political bargains for office with peace men would be to ensure defeat: 'Let the conservatives refuse to coalesce with the copperheads. Let such conservative organisations as Tammany Hall set the example in this policy. If it be perservered in the copperheads will soon be crushed with the abolitionists.'[61]

As Bennett predicted the Albany Regency ignored this advice. At the Democratic Party state convention in September both city organisations (Tammany and Mozart) were admitted on an equal basis. For making up a ticket and distributing political spoils this policy made sense, and the mistake of 1860 was avoided, but the price of harmony was the submersion of clear principle. The party appeared to express no preference between the War Democrat Tammany Hall and the Wood brothers' Peace Democrat Mozart Hall. Worse, in October Tammany and Mozart Halls combined their forces in the city, although the *Herald* had felt confident that on a strong war platform Tammany could have won the contest and crushed its rival decisively.

After these developments the *Herald* lost enthusiasm for the campaign. In the summer it had been possible for Bennett to imagine a successful tide of Democratic condemnation of emancipation, confiscation, conscription and arbitrary arrests sweeping all before it and putting the war back on a 'sound' Union basis – with the prospect of Horace Greeley and Jeff. Davis being caged together in Barnum's Museum of freaks for the 'conservative masses' to gape at. As the weeks passed, however, it became clear that the Republicans were succeeding in portraying all Democrats as copperheads and using the history of the draft riots to good effect. In fact the Republicans had some time previously adopted the name 'Union Party', and although Bennett might protest that this was merely donning the livery of heaven to serve the devil in, they had undoubtedly gained a clear psychological advantage over the Democrats, thereby attracting the very conservative voters whom Bennett had hoped would defeat them.

It was incomprehensible to Bennett that Seymour and the Woods could have interpreted victory in the elections of 1862 as a vote for peace; could they not see, he demanded, that the conduct of the war had been the issue, and that 'there can be no political hereafter for those who array themselves against their country'?[62]

[61]*NYH* 30 July 1863.
[62]*NYH* 28 Sept 1863.

The answer was given in the continuing peace diatribes of Ben Wood's *Daily News* which were so much grist to the Republican mill. In disgust and frustration Bennett exclaimed that 'the silly copperheads, with their professions of devotion to the constitution, excite only the disgust and contempt of every man who is not a knave or a fool'.[63] Nor did the *Herald* attempt to defend Seymour's record, which was a serious handicap to the Democrats. Indeed, said Bennett, the Governor had slipped off the safe, conservative war platform 'like an obstinate donkey off a greased plank . . . he has been equally distinguished by imbecility and verbosity. He can talk more without saying anything and write more without meaning anything than any other man we know . . . We consider Seymour not much of a man, and no Governor at all.'[64]

The dilemma of self-defined 'War Democrats' such as Bennett who wanted a viable alternative to Republican rule was certainly acute. The *Herald* was found rejoicing at copperhead defeat in Ohio yet bemoaning Republican victory in Pennsylvania, attacking administration measures as inexpedient and obnoxious yet defending their constitutionality, threatening the South with defeat yet giving assurances that it would not be 'subjugated'.

It is easy to say of course that secession had doomed the Democratic party to eclipse for the duration of the war, but there is something in Bennett's thesis that the Republican administration was fortunate in its opponents. As the *Herald* was continually pointing out, despite the growing industrial and financial power of the Union the party in power had 'wasted oceans of blood and mountains of

[63] *NYH* 18 Sept 1863. Still Bennett thought Greeley worse than Ben Wood 'for he is Satan, while Ben Wood is merely Moloch'.

[64] *NYH* 11, 23 Sept 1863. Seymour's sympathetic biographer (Stewart Mitchell, *Horatio Seymour,* Cambridge, Mass. 1938), p. 305, claims that Bennett's animus against the Governor stemmed from pique that Seymour did not appoint Bennett's friend to the Board of Police Commissioners. Bennett wrote to Seymour on 2 Jan 1863, 'your note of a few days ago was received and is satisfactory. The bearer of this letter is Judge Russell, an old friend of mine and of yours. . . . In the proposed removal of the Police Commissioners, I would be much gratified if you could give him one of the vacant seats.' — Seymour Papers, New York Historical Society. It is certainly true that the *Herald* agitated for the removal of the Republican commissioners early in the year, see *NYH* 3 Jan; 5 June 1863. On the other hand Bennett may have needed no such venal motive for feeling that Seymour was a liability to the Democrats. After the draft riots, from which the Police Commissioners alone emerged with enhanced reputations, the *Herald* became much more sympathetic to the police. When Seymour made a further ineffectual attempt to have them removed Bennett attacked his action as foolish and unjust, and hoped to see control of the police removed from the Governor and restored to the mayor of the city — *NYH* 4, 5 Jan 1864. On 12 Sept 1863 George T. Strong noted in his diary 'Bennett comes out against Governor Seymour. A good sign. The sagacious old rat knows when his ship is unseaworthy.' In fact we have seen that the *Herald* was disenchanted with Seymour as early as 7 July.

money and . . . not yet accomplished the object of the war'. There was another Union disaster in September at Chickamauga. Here was an opportunity for a vigorous and well led opposition, but by dallying with the peace alternative and making the war itself rather than its management an issue, the Democrats squandered their chance. Had the *Herald* spoken for the party leadership things might have been different, but instead of building on the initiative of 1862 the Democrats lost it.

In the elections the Democratic gains of 1862 were wiped out, a result which Bennett ascribed to Seymour's 'double faced, do-nothing policy'.[65] The editor had seen what was happening with his usual acuity, and he clearly grasped the urgent need for a new rallying point for the party in 1864 if the 1863 débâcle were not to be merely a dress rehearsal for the fate which awaited the Democracy in the Presidential election.

[65]*NYH* 4 Nov 1863. On the election see also S.D. Brummer, *Political History of New York State during the Period of the Civil War* (Columbia 1911), pp. 321-54. In a vote slightly less than the previous year the party lost roughly 21,000 votes against a gain for the Republican Unionists of 18,000. The swing was very marked in the city itself.

11

THE CAMPAIGN AGAINST THE POLITICIANS, 1863-4

The Herald drops Lincoln and Slavery

The notion that Lincoln could be dissuaded from an anti-slavery policy died very hard in the *Herald*. Five months after emancipation, in May 1863, it actually came out for Lincoln's re-election to the presidency in 1864 as the candidate of a 'conservative' coalition because 'his well known conservative views and inclinations, and his unquestioned honesty, patriotism and singleness of purpose in the prosecution of this war, will render him to a great extent acceptable to thoughtful men of all parties'.[1]

Bennett snatched at every straw in the news which might suggest that the President was about to declare political war on the 'radical' members of his party, declaring with a mixture of wishful thinking, political pleading and threat that 'we cannot believe. . . that President Lincoln has abandoned the safe landmarks of his own patriotic and eminently popular Union policy for the violent, revolutionary abolition programme of Senator Summer and Secretary Chase and his radical faction'.[2] The public were continually alerted by the *Herald* to the supposed 'War in the Cabinet' between Seward and Chase and their adherents. Bennett was fond of quoting Wendell Phillips ('the direct agent between Satan and the Satanic party at Washington')[3] to the effect that Lincoln's Cabinet had resolved itself into two committees for managing the next presidential election.[4] The *Herald* gave all the publicity it could to latent differences in the Republican camp. On the supposition that Secretary of the Treasury Salmon P. Chase (fondly known to *Herald* readers as 'the Mephistopheles of the Cabinet') would seek the Republican nomination in 1864, Bennett worked hard to torpedo his ambition by unflagging abuse.

While the *Herald* obviously hoped for a split in the Republican party the President had an equally obvious interest in preventing one. If he was not completely at one with 'radicals' it was becoming

[1]*NYH* 23 May 1863.
[2]*NYH* 2 Aug 1863.
[3]*NYH* 11 Aug 1863.
[4]*NYH* 24 Sept 1863.

increasingly difficult to portray him as almost a Democrat on the reconstruction and slavery issues. Troubled with regard to Lincoln's intended reconstruction in Louisiana without slavery, Bennett wrote in August that 'latterly . . . we have observed indications of his weakness and backsliding in bringing the eternal nigger into the question of the war for the Union, and this has rather cooled our ardor and enfeebled our support of him'.[5] By September Bennett was complaining that 'the President's great failing does not consist in want of intellect, integrity or love of truth, but in deficiency of moral courage in giving way to the clamors of a faction and the seductive advice of the knot of fanatical and treacherous politicians who aspire to lead it. Let him, even at the eleventh hour, sever his connection with the juggling knaves and visionary fools who have hitherto swayed his counsels.'[6]

As late as October Bennett was giving Lincoln private assurances that 'if your labors can accomplish. . . [peace]. . . in the next six months you may rely upon it, the people will remember you whatever Conventions may do',[7] and publicly coaxed him to disown his party and 'throw himself on the people' who would then gratefully re-elect him. Very possibly it was Lincoln's failure to respond to these overtures and growing disenchantment at the President's 'niggerism' which accounted for the *Herald*'s lack of editorial comment on his speech at Gettysburg in November.[8] The final break came in December, on the occasion of the President's amnesty proclamation. Although the *Herald* perceived some small offering to conservative opinion in the President's non-acceptance of Sumner's 'state suicide' theory and in his reminder that the Supreme Court had yet to rule on the legality of the Emancipation Proclamation, the gist of the message was plainly that the President had no intention of repudiating emancipation even if that displeased the War Democrats. High ranking Confederate officers were excluded from amnesty. In Lincoln's plan for reconstruction of reclaimed states on the basis of ten per cent of those who went to the polls in 1860 (if that many loyal men could be found), Bennett saw only a half-cooked plan intended more to conciliate 'radical' opinion than anything else.[9] It was apparent, too,

[5] *NYH* 20 Aug 1863.

[6] *NYH* 23 Sept 1863.

[7] Bennett to Lincoln 26 Oct 1863, Lincoln Papers, LC, item 27504.

[8] A version of the Gettysburg Address appeared in the *Herald*'s news columns on 20 Nov 1863.

[9] *NYH* 10, 11 Dec 1863. For an analysis of the proclamation see H. Belz, *Reconstructing the Union* (Ithaca 1969), p. 155 ff.

that the *Herald*'s campaign for the dismissal of the Cabinet had made no impression in Washington. Lincoln could not be captured by the War Democrats, and the end of the war scarcely seemed in sight.

So on 16 December 1863, Bennett told his readers that although the *Herald* had laboured to support Lincoln despite his mistakes the President had failed to crush the rebellion even with the resources available to him, and should be judged accordingly. It could no longer be pretended that Lincoln was not personally responsible for all the 'gross errors' of his administration and therefore, 'We abandon "Honest Old Abe" as a hopeless case'.[10]

The oddest thing about Bennett's abandonment of Lincoln as a tool of the 'radicals' was that it coincided with his recognition of the fact that slavery was dead beyond recovery. Indeed the *Herald* now began advocating the abolition of slavery by constitutional amendment.

Bennett had first championed this idea in late November, a little reluctantly, certainly, because he still felt that if the war could be ended by leaving a remnant of slavery then it should be done. But if emancipation was inevitable then the only legal way to accomplish it (since the Constitution recognised slavery) was for the Constitution to be amended.[11] Paradoxically the New Year found the *Herald* attacking Lincoln because his proclamations against slavery were timid, ineffectual and not in earnest, and boasting that it had stolen a march on the abolitionist Senator Sumner.

Public opinion had advanced so far for Bennett to admit that although slavery had been a great civilising influence it had now outlived its usefulness and was no longer an acceptable system of labour. He gave the frank opinion that 'not one man out of a thousand is now a pro-slavery man'.[12] When other editors raised their eyebrows at this apparent change of heart he simply reminded them that the *Herald* was independent and progressive, and rejoiced that in support of the amendment 'such hitherto antagonistic bodies as Charles Sumner and Reverdy Johnson are found revolving in harmony around that great central light, the NEW YORK HERALD'.[13] Needless to say, when the measure was introduced in Congress the *Herald* proudly claimed paternity.

[10]*NYH* 16, 18, 21 Dec 1863.

[11]*NYH* 22, 23 Nov 1863.

[12]*NYH* 13 Feb 1864.

[13]*NYH* 9, 18 Feb 1864. Reverdy Johnson was a distinguished jurist and hitherto pro-slavery Democratic Senator for Maryland who had denounced the emancipation proclamation as illegal — see Bernard C. Steiner, *Life of Reverdy Johnson* (Baltimore 1914).

Bennett now proposed that the acceptance of an abolition amendment should be the condition for re-admission of any rebellious state. This seemed advanced ground, but was 'conservative' in that it recognised the continued existence of the Southern States as entities. Not only did Bennett's plan discountenance the enforcement of the Confiscation Acts passed by the 'insane radicals' in Congress, it also advocated the payment of compensation at the rate of $300 per slave to 'loyal' owners in the seceded states.[14] What device could be logically simpler to quieten the slavery question than to undercut it by yielding to the 'radicals' ' most basic demand? 'There being no slavery, of course, there can be no anti-slavery. . . this knocks the foundations from under this association of pestilent agitators and crazy fanatics.'[15]

But why drop Lincoln and slavery together, when for so long the *Herald* had professed its support of the President despite his anti-slavery leaning? The answer is that both these editorial departures were looking towards the presidential contest of 1864.

To remove 'this harassing incubus of African slavery from the country absolutely and forever' by constitutional amendment would do more than baffle the Anti-Slavery Society. It would remove the Republican party's prime reason for existence, and so separate its conservative members, who would be content with such an achievement, from the radical fringe. If the amendment could be passed, as Bennett hoped, before the November election, the way would be clear for a new party fusion. It would be the liberation of the Democrats as well as the slaves. Nothing better illustrated Bennett's changing strategy than the caption to one of his leaders at the end of 1863: 'The Slavery Question All Fudge.'[16] He contended that the 'inevitable negro' was in any case being exterminated by the efforts of the abolitionists. As Confederate territory diminished under Northern attacks, so the remaining slaves were being herded southwards or becoming refugees and dying in droves, the victims of the abolition crusade and Jefferson Davis's attempt 'to anticipate Providence with violent measures'.[17] The blacks were dying out through the intervention of the white man just as surely as the 'nobler' Red Indian; miserable Negro survivors of the failed colonisation experiment on Ile à Vache proved as much at the cost of $30,000 of public money, argued Bennett.[18] Nor did he

[14]*NYH* 6, 7, 11 Feb; 20 Mar; 30 Apr; 3 May 1864.
[15]*NYH* 17 Apr 1864.
[16]*NYH* 29 Dec 1863.
[17]*NYH* 22 Nov 1863.
[18]*NYH* 24 Dec 1863; 22 Mar 1864.

regret this, for 'our Yankee soldiers now carry in their brains and their knapsacks the plans of machines which will develop the South without the comparatively feeble aid of the African machine'.[19] Under free labour, disease and 'African idleness' would ensure the demise of the race.

Plainly Bennett reasoned that the Democrats would be helped if slavery were replaced by race as an issue in the 1864 election. A constitutional amendment would not involve 'such fallacies as negro equality, political or social, with the white race'.[20] If the 'radicals' wanted more than simple abolition or quibbled as to terms the *Herald* could, and did, brand them as hypocrites intent on making political capital out of the agitation. Claiming that anti-slavery leaders were working to frustrate the amendment Bennett demanded, with truly breathtaking nerve, 'What will be the next dodge proposed by these political traitors to keep in check the great emancipation movement in the North?'[21] More than that, the *Herald* could stigmatise them as 'racial amalgamationists'; strong ground, perhaps, for forcing the anti-slavery movement away from the centre of power and back onto the fringe.

Simultaneously with its advocacy of final abolition the *Herald* accordingly began an effort to expose 'The Beastly Doctrine of Miscegenation and its High Priests', 'proving' that this 'vile pollution' of white blood etc., etc., was what Greeley, Beecher, Wilson, Sumner, Garrison and anybody else actively concerned with the advancement of the Negro was aiming at all the time.[22] Bennett, describing a supposed fashion among Republicans for marrying blacks, starting off a libel against white women school teachers in occupied South Carolina, crossed swords with Greeley over it, and having cast his slurs and had his fun, retreated.[23] When Congress

[19]*NYH* 13 Feb 1864.

[20]*NYH* 3 May 1864.

[21]*NYH* 31 Mar 1864.

[22]*NYH* 23 Mar 1864. The term 'miscegenation' had only recently been coined to supersede 'racial amalgamation'. On its orgination in the offices of the NY *World* as part of an elaborate hoax to embarrass the Republicans see Sidney Kaplan, 'The Miscegenation Issue in the Election of 1864', *Journal of Negro History,* 34 (1949), 274-343, and Forrest G. Wood, *Black Scare* (Berkeley 1970), ch 4.

[23]*NYH* 23, 26, 28, 31 Mar 1864. Bennett alleged that sixty-four New England women school teachers arriving at Port Royal all produced mulatto children nine months later. When Greeley defended their honour, Bennett retorted that of course he had never meant to imply that the women weren't properly married to Negro husbands and how dare Greeley suggest that they were infected with his own free love doctrines — see also 1,30 Dec 1863; 18, 19 Feb 1864. The *Herald* had been a consistent enemy of the 'hypocrites' and 'bloodthirsty fanatics' who were trying to construct a free black labour

refrained from stipulating that citizens of the new Territory of Montana should be white, Bennett suggested that the area should be renamed 'Miscegenia'.[24] Obviously the Negro wasn't being killed off by abolitionists so fast that the *Herald* couldn't make some election capital out of him. This was one prong of its campaign against the party of anti-slavery, and the dropping of Lincoln was another.

It is possible that Bennett had been intending to cease his support of Lincoln anyway as soon as the 1864 election came near enough, and was merely waiting for an opportunity to make a break. In support of this argument it can be said that *Herald* readers had the virtues of General McClellan kept before their eyes regularly during 1863, as if the paper were grooming him but was not yet ready to bring him into the open as a candidate. It seems likely though that Bennett's support of the President was genuine enough so long as he looked like a winner, but by December 1863 Lincoln's record seemed so tarnished that he could not, after all, beat Chase for the Republican nomination in 1864.[25] If this was so and voters had only a choice between abolition or a copperhead peace at the election then they would go for the former.[26] A stronger candidate was needed to beat the 'radicals', and one who could attract the important soldier vote.[27]

When Bennett turned his editorial guns on Lincoln he was announcing that he thought he had found the answer to his political equation. He had not lost his political shrewdness so far as to cast off into the political wilderness, for he had found a candidate more

community at Port Royal, S.C., claiming that the 'dangerous' blacks ought to be forced to work under stricter supervision and that the war was 'not to take care of the Negro or introduce among them ideas of equality and amalgamation of races' — *NYH* 2, 8 Apr 1862. The history of the community has been sympathetically told by Willie Lee Rose, *Rehearsal for Reconstruction* (NY 1964).

[24]*NYH* 2 Apr 1864.

[25]*NYH* 15 Dec 1863.

[26]*NYH* 20 Dec 1863.

[27]On 8 Sept 1863 Bennett had said 'we are not in a prophetic mood today, and so we shall utter no predictions. . . . But, above all, let us impress upon the politicians that the army will vote at the next Presidential election, and that no candidate can succeed whose supporters do not take this interesting fact and these five or six hundred thousand voters into account.' To enable the soldiers to vote was an issue in itself in New York, since it required a change in the state constitution. At least, Governor Seymour insisted that it did when Republicans in the state legislature tried to effect soldier voting by enactment. Seymour's wishes were observed, and the constitution was changed by popular vote, but the delay involved made it appear that the Democrats were reluctant to give the soldiers the vote, and this may have damaged them. Bennett had urged that if soldiers had a right to fight they had a right to vote, but his rather contorted argument that the Republicans bore the responsibility for delaying the grant of the franchise probably convinced few. See *NYH* 3, 7, 26, 31 Mar 1874; Charles Z. Lincoln, *The Constitutional History of New York* (Rochester 1906), vol. 2, pp. 235-40.

popular than either Lincoln, Chase or McClellan. Good newspaperman that he was, he had also found a means of satisfying the public thirst for sensations which he had recently noted.[28] On 15 December 1863 the *Herald* announced that General Ulysses S. Grant was the 'People's Candidate' for President.

'Grant is the Man for the Crisis'

The *Herald* had actually been intimating for some weeks that a soldier might be the man to win the 1864 election, and had played with the names of McClellan, Banks, Grant, Meade, Rosecrans, Gillmore and Dix as possible successors to Lincoln if he didn't get on and win the war.[29] Bennett had been generous in his praise of Grant when that general took Vicksburg, and his victory at Chattanooga late in November made him clearly the most successful soldier in the North.[30] Having mused on 14 December that both Republicans and Democrats might wish to nominate Grant 'because they shrewdly guess that the party which secures him as its candidate will walk over the Presidential course', Bennett suggested next day that here was the candidate who could run well ahead of both party tickets and emerge as the leader of a middle ground war party bearing neither the Republican nor the Democratic label. Grant's achievements could not be detracted from by critics as easily as McClellan's and he had no political record to defend. To an editor who had supported Jackson, Harrison and Taylor this was exceptionally pleasing. If the drum beating tactics of 1828 and 1840 could be made to work in 1864, then the *Herald* had picked a winner. Although it seems certain that Bennett had no kind of prior arrangement with Grant he might hope, if his man were elected, to be liberally recognised for having been his first public champion.

So the *Herald* went all out for General Grant — 'The man who knows how to tan leather, politicians and the hides of rebels'.[31]

In this 'hard sell' campaign to advertise his candidate, Bennett kept Grant as the subject of his lead editorials every day for weeks, with lesser items repeating or reinforcing the same themes with apt

[28]*NYH* 13 Dec 1863.

[29]*NYH* 5, 15, 19, 24 Nov; 8, 9 Dec 1863.

[30]In part Bennett attributed Grant's success to his remoteness from the War Department interference which the editor claimed had thwarted McClellan — see *NYH* 3 Sept 1863.

[31]*NYH* 16 Dec 1863.

anecdotes and captions. Such headings as 'General Grant a Great Man'[32] were thoroughly in keeping with the none too subtle ways in which quack medicines were recommended to readers in the paper's advertising columns. The modest Ulysses was presented as a panacea for all the nation's ills.

The main theme of Bennett's arguments for Grant was that the General would be an 'independent' President, nominated and elected by popular acclaim and so above politics. He would thus owe no debts to the 'hack politicians' and their corrupt party machines and the election of 1864 would be fought between the people and the politicians. The history of the Lincoln administration, said Bennett, proved that civilians were totally unfitted to win the war, but at last the people had a champion whose services spoke for themselves. Grant's election would show rebels and foreigners that the Union meant business. For, having put down the rebellion, Grant would undoubtedly break from the supposedly cowardly and truckling foreign policy of Lincoln to force the French to withdraw from Mexico. Leading the nation against Canada, he would exact a tribute of $20 million for damage done by British built rebel 'privateers'. He would drive down the price of gold and restore confidence in an inflated currency. He would force corruption and political scheming from high places, and make the United States respected abroad; in fact by his victories he had already done more towards achieving this than Lincoln. Grant's victory would allay partisan passions; Lincoln's world excite them.[33]

The *Herald* exulted that its campaign was putting 'Greek fire' among the newspapers and politicians. Rumours appeared in suspicious rival papers that Bennett had been bribed $30,000 to kill the Grant cause by a surfeit of enthusiasm.[34] Raymond's *Times* of 21 December feared that the *Herald* might stir Grant's ambition and so spoil him as a good general. George T. Strong commented in his diary: 'The New York *Herald* has discovered that within a day or two General Grant is to be next President and expatiates on his claims and merits in slashing, slangy editorials. Its former pet, McClellan, seems forgotten. Grant is certainly our most successful general and might probably make a good President, but that the *Herald* takes him up so earnestly is against him.'[35] Still, Grant's popularity was such that rivals could not

[32]*NYH* 17 Dec 1863.

[33]*NYH* 15-27 Dec 1863; 4, 6, 8, 12, 22, 23, 30 Jan 1864.

[34]The Chicago *Tribune* 25 Dec 1863; 1 Jan 1864, objected that the *Herald* 'cannot be allowed to paw and slobber over our Illinois General'. Even some Democrats were baffled; see P.J. Benson to Bennett 3 Feb 1864, Bennett Papers, LC.

[35]*Diary of George Templeton Strong,* entry for 19 Dec 1863. For similar reaction see NY *Daily Tribune* 18 Dec.

attack him with impunity. Bennett rejoiced in embarrassing Greeley because the *Tribune* could not defend Lincoln wholeheartedly while its editor was known to be hoping for Chase's nomination.[36] The politicians were aghast, crowed Bennett, because the *Herald* had gone over their heads in appealing to the people: party caucuses and nominating conventions were only interested in nominating weak men of contemptible intellect like Pierce, Buchanan and Lincoln, whom they could control. In fact, conventions were mere humbugs on the people because 'the fact that a man is a member of a nominating convention is prima facie evidence that he is either a place holder or hunter, or a contractor, or that expects to be bought by a place holder or hunter, or a contractor'.[37] Let them not stand in the way of the will of the people!

The counterpart of these endeavours to prove the virtues of military leadership was the *Herald's* continuing identification of the Lincoln administration with 'shoddy' and corruption. Bennett may not have invented the term 'shoddy' but he gave it wide currency from 1861 onwards. To him it meant not only sub-standard goods but the whole new aristocracy of manufacturers which had grown up during the war by supplying the immense demands of the government for war material. As a class the *Herald* characterised these men as corrupt through and through: 'Six days a week they are shoddy businessmen. On the seventh day they are shoddy Christians.'[38] It flayed them as boors who were taking over the fashionable watering places of New York State during the summer season and whose ill manners when driving carriages and hacks caused enormous traffic jams around Central Park.[39] It was the shoddy merchants who conspired to create the monopolies which made food, coal and many other necessary items exorbitantly expensive in the city, and yet had the nerve to introduce a bill in the legislature to prohibit strikes by working-men to raise their wages; a plot, said Bennett, 'to wring out of the workingmen what the shoddyites fail to steal from the government'.[40] These were

[36]Greeley's preference for Chase is followed in Horner, *Lincoln and Greeley,* ch 10.

[37]*NYH* 2 May 1864.

[38]*NYH* 6 Oct 1863, also 26 Apr 1864. The first use I could find of the term 'shoddy' in the *Herald* was 24 Aug 1861.

[39]*NYH* 13, 17 Oct 1863. Bennett threatened a continuous and personalised onslaught on the culprits until they mended their ways.

[40]*NYH* 9, 10 Apr 1864. A comprehensive social history of the wartime North is one of the great gaps in American historiography. However, there is a good source anthology in George W. Smith and Charles Judah eds., *Life in the North During the Civil War* (Albuquerque 1966). On conditions in New York the best introductions are an essay by James A. Frost, 'The Home Front in New York during the Civil War', *New York*

the men who swindled small investors at the Stock Exchange.[41] 'Shoddy' were the whisky lobby in Congress, trying to have the new excise law tailored to their own desires: the *Herald* found paper so expensive because the rag required in the manufacturing process was in heavy demand by contractors making 'shoddy' army uniforms.[42] Everywhere these men had their hands in the government's pocket, said Bennett, recklessly robbing it of what they could while the war lasted. They had a vested interest in prolonging the war: the Republican party was their machine and Lincoln their tool for this purpose.[43]

Bennett's efforts to characterise the Administration as rotten with jobbery asked New Yorkers to believe that the federal regime was but a grand version of their own profligate city government. But apart from a few instances of 'exposing' fraudulent timber contracts made by the Navy Department and the cotton operations of Treasury agents in the South, the *Herald* did very little by way of providing names and facts in this barrage of insinuation. It confined itself to strident demands for congressional investigations into these matters.[44] In an editorial entitled 'The Unparalleled Corruptions of the Administration' Bennett admitted that Lincoln, though politically insincere and vacillating, was personally honest 'because he is too imbecile to be otherwise'.[45]

The President's record of military management was a steady handle of abuse to the *Herald,* and its readers were persuaded that when Congress revived the grade of Lieutenant General for Grant in February 1864, the measure was intended as a rebuke to Lincoln's incompetency.[46] Meanwhile the paper which had once professed amusement at Lincoln's pithy wit now found that his coarse jokes were an offence to all respectable people, and in any case were mostly stolen from the English comedian Joe Miller. In fact 'President Lincoln is a joke incarnated. His election was a very sorry joke. The

History, 42 (1961), 273-97, and a full length study by Basil Leo Lee, *Discontent in New York City, 1861-5* (NY 1943).

[41]*NYH* 29 Nov 1863.

[42]This was the relationship, Bennett explained to his readers, of a call for 300,000 volunteers to a rise in the price of newsprint from 12 to 16 cents per pound — *NYH* 28 Oct 1863.

[43]*NYH* 28 Dec 1863; 15 Jan; 10 Feb; 25 May 1864.

[44]*NYH* 6, 31 Dec 1863; 9, 16 Jan; 1 Feb; 27 Mar; 17 Apr 1864.

[45]*NYH* 14 Jan 1864. Bennett soon changed his mind: on 10 Feb the *Herald* accused Lincoln, Stanton and Chase of being in collusion to make enormous profits out of confiscated Southern lands.

[46]*NYH* 15 Jan; 2, 6 Feb; 11 Apr 1864.

idea that such a man as he should be the President of such a country as this is a very ridiculous joke. . . His title of "Honest" is a satirical joke."[47] Bennett now revealed that the *Herald*'s own renomination of Lincoln in 1863 had been only a joke (a charge he had vehemently denied at the time).

The Republican party thus became, in the columns of the *Herald,* the faction of shoddy politicians and smutty jokers. The Republican Party Convention scheduled for June 1864, was christened the 'Shoddy Convention' and the cabinet became the 'Washington Directory'. Continuing the historical parallel Bennett suggested that if Grant cared to imitate Napoleon by staging a military coup the people would support him, a call which invited cries of 'Treason!' from the Republican press and jibed ill with the paper's newly affected suspicion of Lincoln's imperial ambition. At any rate, said Bennett, Grant must be the master of the 'radical' politicians in Washington if the country were to avoid anarchy and ruin. He must not allow himself to be victimised as McClellan was.[48] If Grant's spring campaign failed, readers should know in advance that it would be entirely because of treachery at Washington.[49]

As spring approached, and with it the time when both military and political battling would begin in earnest, the *Herald*'s attitude to Lincoln became even more bitter. From Florida came news in late February of a military fiasco at Olustee. A Northern force met defeat in an attempt to reclaim the state for the Union, and the fact that John Hay, Lincoln's private secretary, had been on a confidential mission there gave the *Herald* plausible grounds for informing the country that Lincoln had bid one thousand lives in an attempt to secure three electoral votes towards his own re-election. In publicising these events the *Herald* suggested that an investigation might render the President liable to impeachment. Bennett roundly announced that 'Lincoln, Stanton and Welles are alike incompetent drivellers' who 'must never again be permitted to govern this great country'.[50]

[47]*NYH* 19 Feb 1864; see also 31 Dec 1863.

[48]*NYH* 11-18 Mar; 12 Apr 1864.

[49]*NYH* 21, 23, 25 Mar 1864.

[50]*NYH* 1, 13 Mar; 13, 27 Apr 1864. Hay wrote to Charles G. Halpine on 13 Apr 'I thank you for offering to set me right with the pensive public. But the game is not worth so bright a candle. The original lie in the *Herald* was dirty enough & the subsequent commentaries were more than unusually nasty. But the Tycoon [Lincoln] never minded it in the least and as for me, at my age, the more abuse I get in the newspapers the better for me. I shall run for constable some day on the strength of my gory exploits in Florida' — Tyler Dennett ed., *Lincoln and the Civil War in the Diaries and Letters of John Hay* (NY 1939), p. 171.

An even more vitriolic onslaught, perhaps the most furious that the *Herald* ever delivered against Lincoln, came when the Republican Convention at Baltimore was less than one month away.

The third week in May was a difficult one for the New York press in its relations with Washington because the *World* and the *Journal of Commerce* were suppressed temporarily for publishing a bogus Presidential proclamation.[51] Yet it was not this incident but a pro-Lincoln Republican political meeting which provoked Bennett's ire. He penned an editorial so horribly replete with the imagery of the charnel house that it might almost have been written in dried blood. This was, after all, the time when the murderous holocaust in Virginia was at its most terrible. Readers of the *Herald* of 20 May might turn from the casualty lists of Spotsylvania to what won notoriety as the 'ghoul editorial'. It began as follows:

> The Recent Lincoln Meeting — A Gathering of the Ghouls
> The Lincoln Meeting at the Cooper Institute last Friday evening was one of the most disgraceful exhibitions of human depravity ever witnessed in this wicked world. It was a gathering of ghouls, vultures, hyenas and other feeders upon carrion, for the purpose of surfeiting themselves upon the slaughter of the recent battles. We remember nothing like it in the history of politics. The great ghoul at Washington, who authorised the meeting, and the little ghouls and vultures who conducted it have succeeded in completely disgusting the people of this country, and have damaged themselves irretrievably. . .

More in this vein suggested that while the truly patriotic were sacrificing themselves for the national cause the Lincolnites were thinking of re-election and so

> proceeded to dig up the graves of our soldiers, to tear open the wounds of the wounded, to riot amid the carnage and make themselves fat with gore. . . the trick of claiming credit for carnage and trying to make capital out of wholesale slaughter is too transparent and too boldly played. . . Lincoln has shown himself as incompetent, during the present administration, as he has shown himself destitute of any sentiment, any feeling, any judgement, by indulging in vulgar jokes at the most solemn crisis of our history.

[51] The story of the suppression has been told a number of times — the *Herald* joined the other papers in offering a reward for the perpetrator of the hoax and in petitioning for the victims on the grounds that their crime was credulity and negligence rather than disloyal malice. See *NYH* 19-24 May; 13, 14 July 1864; and accounts in Robert S. Harper, *Lincoln and the Press* (NY 1951), ch 34; Louis M. Starr, *Bohemian Brigade* (NY 1954), pp. 315-20. Hudson has some documentary material on the *Herald*'s role in his *History of Journalism,* pp. 670 ff.

The point of all this was that Lincoln could be and should be annihilated at the polls in November by a 'conservative' coalition; and its vehemence was perhaps to be accounted for by the fact that, despite the *Herald*'s denials, Lincoln looked politically much stronger in the spring of 1864 than he had done when Bennett started the boom for Grant in December 1863. Chase's presidential prospects had been badly hurt by an early and tactless exposure by his friends, and in his embarrassment he had stayed in the cabinet but denied all intention of running. The *Herald*, scoffing at his insincerity, conjectured that Chase's mouthings about patriotic harmony meant an admission that he could not even carry his own state against Lincoln.[52]

Splendid as it had seemed as a tactical device to rally the War Democrats, the *Herald*'s nomination of Grant had run very early into difficulty. The general, unfortunately for Bennett, was not interested. Disregarding the editor's public advice to remain silent and write no letters, Grant discreetly but very definitely let it be known through the western press that he was not a candidate.[53]

Bennett at first denied then affected to be unabashed by this news. It simply showed, he asserted, how modest and patriotic Grant was in comparison with the politicians, and anyway it would not be the first time in the republic's history that a candidate had affected coyness prior to accepting a nomination. If Grant were nominated then Bennett was confident that he would consent to run and be elected.[54] The *Herald* consequently never deserted the general's cause and continued to advocate his candidacy right up to the election, praising and sustaining his military endeavours until the end of the war. Even in the mid-summer of 1864, when the high hopes of spring had faded and Grant was deadlocked in front of Richmond after heavy losses, the *Herald* defended him against criticism and the dissatisfaction of other papers.[55] (It is related that on receiving the *Herald* in the field Grant would remark with wry sarcasm 'Now, let me see what my organ has to say, and then I can tell better what I'm going to do'.)[56] There was always

[52]*NYH* 23, 24 Feb; 1, 12 Mar 1864. On Chase's discomfiture, and for a thorough analysis of the political campaign of 1864 generally, see William E. Zornow, *Lincoln and the Party Divided* (Norman, Oklahoma 1954).

[53]For Grant's reaction to these moves on his behalf see Bruce Catton, *Grant Takes Command* (London 1970), pp. 103-12.

[54]*NYH* 21, 26 Feb 1864.

[55]*NYH* e.g. 9 June 1864, responding to a criticism of Grant in the *Times*. On Bennett's personal admiration for Grant see John Russell Young, *Men and Memories* (NY 1901), p. 209.

[56]Horace Porter, *Campaigning with Grant* (NY 1961), p. 168.

the possibility that if Grant took Richmond before November nothing could keep him out of the White House.[57] But the bold political initiative which the *Herald* had seized in December 1863 suffered a fatal blow when Grant declined to run. Even in this year when intra party divisions were so important to electoral fortunes, it was becoming apparent that the regular Republican and Democratic organisations had more strength than the *Herald* gave them credit for.

Accepting this situation with as much enthusiasm as he could in the face of his own predictions, Bennett came in early March to 'presume that the candidate of the opposition will be General McClellan; and he is undoubtedly the most popular and available man upon whom they can combine. . . he will, we venture to say, prove more than a match for Mr. Lincoln. . . '[58]

What would have happened if the War Democrats nationally had taken the *Herald*'s cue in starting a really vigorous initiative on a war platform remains impossible to say. Bennett could only reprove their pusillanimity: 'we find them much more amenable to kicks than to good advice'.[59]

[57]*NYH* 27 Apr 1864.
[58]*NYH* 5 Mar 1864.
[59]*NYH* 15 Feb 1864.

12

'SHODDY', 'SHENT-PER-SHENT' AND
STALEMATE: SUMMER 1864

Late in March John Hay, Lincoln's secretary, noted in his diary that 'Seward says Wykoff is in town to sell out the *Herald* to the highest bidder. S. is bored by him but will not see him.'[1] The shady Wikoff was not above using Bennett's name to further his own interests.[2] As for Hay, the lampooning he had received in the *Herald* over the Florida fiasco may have jaundiced his observation. Nevertheless, documentary evidence has survived that Bennett was using his editorial columns to play a devious political game during the election campaign of 1864. To understand that evidence[3] the course charted by the *Herald* through a close and exciting contest must be kept firmly in view, for readers of the paper knew nothing of the secrets of the editorial room. To all appearances the *Herald* had reverted to its old stance of 'armed neutrality' between the warring parties once its boom for Grant had lost steam. In this summer of drought and slaughter and stalemate at the front and war weariness at home, no political party seemed entirely safe from the *Herald*'s maulings, or from its advice and prophecies either. The only seemingly predictable feature of the *Herald*'s political course in midsummer was its dogged opposition to the re-election of President Lincoln.

For instance, the *Herald* flirted with the movement which nominated John C. Fremont for the presidency at Cleveland in May. What he might have dismissed contemptuously as a motley band of radicals Bennett dignified by describing as 'an extensive organisation of intelligent and earnest men, who conscientiously believe that Abraham Lincoln is a deplorable failure'.[4] Certainly Fremont's denunciation of 'executive usurpation' was music to some Democratic ears. Even when the movement proved to be only what the *Herald* described ruefully as an 'abolition fiasco' and Fremont stood down in September, Bennett was to praise his refusal to be reconciled with Lincoln.[5]

---

[1] T. Dennett ed., *Lincoln and the Civil War in the Diaries and Letters of John Hay* (NY 1939), p. 168.

[2] See L.A. Whiteley to JGB, 29 June 1862, Bennett Papers, LC.

[3] To be discussed in the second section of ch 13 below.

[4] *NYH* 7 June 1864. See also 8, 10, 16, 17, 20 May; 2 June.

[5] *NYH* 23, 26 Sept 1864.

The President easily achieved renomination by his party at its Baltimore convention in June (dubbed the 'Shoddy Convention' by the *Herald*), despite Bennett's prediction that there would be riots if the people were denied Grant and had Lincoln with his 'heavy budget of cruel jokes and costly blunders, and with the enormous schedule of corruptions and spoliations that have marked his administration' foisted on them again by the politicians.[6]

The *Herald* asserted that Lincoln's only chance of re-election would be extensive use of Treasury funds and made great play of the 'raids' by Thurlow Weed and Henry J. Raymond on the New York Custom House for party funds. There were divisions within the Republican Party to be exploited too. The *Herald*, reflecting increasing disquiet at inflation in the North, had long agitated for Chase's removal from the cabinet. When Lincoln accepted the Secretary's resignation on 30 June the paper claimed a War Democrat victory, though Lincoln replaced Chase with Fessenden of Maine who was scarcely less 'radical'.[7] The *Herald* was gleeful at the prospect of an imminent Republican split when Lincoln's reconstruction policy was attacked by the extreme spirits in his own party in the Wade-Davis Manifesto. Bennett observed with some justice that a copperhead could scarcely have penned a more vicious attack, and he suggested that the honourable thing for Lincoln to do would be to resign and join the army as a private.[8]

War-weariness in the North reached a peak in midsummer. Another draft for 500,000 men was pending and no decisive Union victory had yet been achieved. In this atmosphere Bennett argued that a vote for Lincoln would be a vote for continued arbitrary arrests, martial law and military mismanagement, and the retention of a cabinet comprising a clique of squabbling imbeciles who were prolonging the war by their criminal blunders. Lincoln might regard lack of co-operation and rivalry within the cabinet as jokes, wrote Bennett tartly, but the public were unable to see 'the fun of defeats, the amusement in heavy taxes, the pleasures of conscription and the ridiculousness of death'.[9]

In the month of July Horace Greeley, motivated by a humanitarian desire to end the 'wholesale slaughter' of the war, gained authorisation

[6]*NYH* 27-9 May; 4-7 June 1864.

[7]*NYH* 28-30 June 1864. The *Herald*'s ideal Cabinet would have included McClellan, John A. Dix, Admiral S.F. DuPont and conservative Republican Charles Francis Adams.

[8]*NYH* 10 July; 6 Aug 1864.

[9]*NYH* 29 June 1864.

from the President to negotiate with three self-styled Confederate commissioners on the Canadian shore of Niagara Falls.

In the event the negotiations turned out to be a fiasco: the *Herald* dismissed the whole affair as a 'ludicrous and undignified joke'[10] and Bennett could congratulate himself on having declined to be personally involved. He had been invited to Niagara to try his hand at peacemaking by one William Cornell Jewett. 'Colorado' Jewett was a speculator in minerals and self-appointed diplomat well known for his pretensions in New York journalistic circles. He was the intermediary by whose agency Greeley had become involved with the Southerners at Niagara, and seems to have been responsible for giving Greeley the false impression that the men were regular Confederate commissioners. Bennett had a low opinion of the amateur negotiators spawned by the civil war, and was much more astute than Greeley in refusing to have anything to do with such an adventurer.[11] At Niagara one of the rebel commissioners, James P. Holcombe, remarked to Greeley, 'I wanted old Bennett to come up, but he was afraid to come'.[12]

That the Confederates' original intention was to deal with the federal government via the two most prominent New York editors of the day tells not only a good deal about the power and reputation of Bennett and Greeley and their respective journals: it also lends credence to the argument that these 'commissioners' wanted publicity for their cause as much as they wanted a sincere effort at peace. Doubtless they reasoned that both objectives could be happily combined and that the editors could somehow be persuaded to rouse Northern sentiment for a negotiated peace, which would be by implication a disunion peace. In the event Greeley's good intentions and lack of judgement provided the Southerners with a first-rate opportunity to make propaganda, Jewett being the instrument by which their letter blaming Lincoln for the continuation of the war was made public. Thereafter these same Confederates devoted themselves to organising the fifth column raids of which New York was to know more by and by. By his refusal to go to Niagara Bennett did himself and his country a considerable favour.

Nevertheless the *Herald* found Lincoln more to blame than Greeley. In the peace terms which he presented to the 'commissioners'

[10]*NYH* 22-5 July 1864.

[11]On Jewett *NYH* 14 Sept 1863; 18 Apr; 5 May 1864, and some clippings in Bennett Papers, LC. On the Niagara negotiations and other attempts to parley see E.C. Kirkland, *The Peacemakers of 1864* (NY 1927).

[12]Wm. R. Thayer, *The Life and Letters of John Hay* (2 vols, Boston & NY 1915), vol. 1, pp. 180-1.

(he addressed his note 'To Whom it May Concern' to avoid recognition of the Confederate government)[13] the President had assumed the responsibility for making abolition a precondition for reunion. By what right did he do so, asked a disgusted Bennett? Asserting that the Northern people 'care nothing about slavery', he again accused Lincoln of prolonging the war for party ends. With its usual disregard for consistency the *Herald* would argue one day that Lincoln's inflexibility on abolition gave the Southerners no alternative but to fight to their much vaunted last ditch, and the next that re-election of the blundering Lincoln would encourage the rebels and was desired in Richmond, whereas the triumph of a Democratic soldier candidate would convince the Confederates that they had no chance of success.[14]

The *Herald*, clinging to the notion that Union and emancipation were still separable, questioned whether the price being paid for liberating the slaves was justifiable. Lecturing his readers unctuously on 'What Nigger Freedom Costs', Bennett estimated that it took one white man killed or maimed and $5,000 to free each Negro. For him the great and pessimistic moral lesson of the war was that 'we have learned to our sorrow that there is not much morality in murdering and maiming thousands of white men in order to free negroes, nor much benevolence in freeing negroes in order to bury them. Theoretically the freedom of the negro is a very nice thing; but practically it is only exchanging his easy fetters for bullets or starvation.'[15]

If he was critical of Lincoln's handling of the Niagara episode, Bennett did come forward with his own armistice proposition on 12 August. Northern opinion demanded that any new negotiations should be open and official, he stressed, and he claimed that an armistice in the present position of the armies would be to Northern advantage and allow Southern Unionism to come into play against the Davis government. If Davis refused to treat he would bear the odium with his own people.[16] In trying to rouse public support for his plan Bennett was careful to differentiate it from the chorus of pro-rebel peace demands from the Northern copperhead press, warning that 'no copperheads need apply'. More practical than Bennett's original

---

[13]The relevant documents to this episode are in R.P. Basler, *The Collected Works of Abraham Lincoln* (New Brunswick 1953-5), vol. VII, pp. 435, 440, 441, 451, though they are conveniently reprinted with additional material and commentary in Harlan H. Horner, *Lincoln and Greeley* (Illinois UP 1953), pp. 289-330.

[14]*NYH* 26-9 July; 1 Aug 1864.

[15]*NYH* 1, 6 Aug 1864.

[16]*NYH* 12-25 Aug 1864. See also Abram Wakeman to Lincoln, 12 Aug 1864, Lincoln Papers, LC, item 35261.

scheme perhaps was his pressure in late August for negotiations with individual Southern States as a means of fragmenting the Confederacy.[17] Then a season of spectacular federal victories caused the armistice question to drop out of discussion with everybody except the copperheads. The *Herald* was soon to the fore in discountenancing any peace but a military conquest.[18] The period of serious doubt about the outcome of the war was already past by the onset of autumn in the North, but this was a situation which the Democratic party had rendered itself incapable of exploiting politically.

Despite its continued hostility to the Administration, the *Herald* had blown hot and cold about the Democrats all summer long. As Bennett once said of them, 'They have a peace leg and a war leg, but, like a stork by a frogpond, they are as yet undecided which to rest upon'.[19] When they rested on the war leg they had the *Herald*'s support, when they rested on the peace leg they drew its bitter denunciation. It loyally beat the drum for McClellan during July, comparing his oratory with the classics in the most extravagant way and defending his record at length against the *Tribune*'s indictments.[20] When veteran politician Francis P. Blair visited Bennett in his office on 20 July he got the impression that the old Scot was all enthusiasm for the general's cause.[21] Yet the *Herald* publicised grave divisions in the Democratic ranks, and its habitual diatribes against the party managers equalled anything in the Republican press. Taking a dig at August Belmont, wealthy Jewish-born chairman of the national party and by profession a banker who acted as American agent for the Rothschilds, Bennett christened the planned Democratic assembly the 'Shent-per-Shent' Convention.[22] From the start he believed that if the Democratic campaign succeeded it would be in spite of such management rather than because of it. The secession of the South had left the initiative for Democratic leadership with New York, and Bennett was too familiar with the methods of his inveterate antagonists of the Albany Regency to expect any good of it.

Indeed, after the 'Shoddy' Republicans nominated Lincoln, Bennett argued that the Democratic leadership was failing to mobilise

[17]*NYH* 27, 29 Aug 1864.

[18]A spirited defence of the armistice plan appeared as late as 3 Sept, but this would have been sent to print before news of the fall of Atlanta had percolated fully to the North. For copperhead comment see *NY Daily News* 13, 15, 18 Aug 1864.

[19]*NYH* 31 Oct 1863.

[20]*NYH* e.g. 25 June 1864.

[21]W.E. Smith, *The Francis Preston Blair Family in Politics* (NY 1933), vol. 2, p. 280.

[22]*NYH* 14 Apr 1864; I. Katz, *August Belmont* (NY 1968), ch 8.

the strength of its rank and file support. The party convention at Chicago, previously scheduled for July, was now postponed until the end of August, supposedly to be able to take advantage of developments; but this postponement, wrote a disgusted Bennett, might just as well have been a cancellation: with it the cause of the War Democrats was compromised and time was given to the copperhead wing of the party to organise and make mischief.[23] For the national organisation to give countenance to the Peace Democrats, or even to admit them to the Chicago convention would in Bennett's view be to commit political suicide. Visions of a 'foolish and senseless squabble in Chicago over the platform' resulting in a fatal party split appalled him: 'As they are going on, the danger is that the opposition party will dwindle down to a copperhead faction, and thus the opportunity that is and has been offered to rescue the country from the rule of fanaticism and blundering mismanagement will be thrown away, and the reign of the smutty joker continued for four years more.'[24]

The Albany Regency might be prepared to let this happen, but Bennett was not. How could true Democrats want a peace by submission to the South, which was what the demands of these 'infatuated fools' amounted to?[25]

The battle between Peace and War Democrats was something more than a simple sectional contest between eastern business and western agricultural interests. In New York City itself a great deal of political heat was generated over the congressional elections. Since February 1864 the *Herald* had been fighting against reindorsement of the copperhead delegation which represented (or misrepresented, Bennett insisted) the city in the 38th Congress. Most prominent in this delegation was Fernando Wood, with whom Bennett had now broken politically.[26]

In mid 1863 Bennett had enthusiastically described a call which Wood paid Lincoln as a meeting of 'two of the greatest men in the country' and had pushed Wood's claims for the speakership, pleading that he was just the man to expose 'the corruption and malfeasance in office' of the Radical Republicans 'in all their awful details'.[27] Since

[23]*NYH* 17, 18, 28 June 1864. On the Democratic campaign generally see Joel Silbey, *A Respectable Minority* (NY 1977), ch 5.

[24]*NYH* 10, 11 July 1864.

[25]*NYH* 30 June; 28 July 1864.

[26]*NYH* 28 Jan; 19, 28 Feb 1864. Also in the delegation was James Brooks, proprietor of the *NY Express*.

[27]*NYH* 9 June; 13-18 Aug 1863.

then, as we have seen, Bennett had opposed Ben Wood as the emerging 'evil genius' of the Democratic party during the political campaign in New York in the autumn of 1863. During and after that contest Bennett held the Woods jointly responsible with Governor Seymour for the wreck of Democratic strength, and fought against their influence unremittingly. Maledictions against the *News* and Mozart Hall became part of the regular litany of the *Herald*'s editorial page and Fernando Wood was written down as a small time ward politician, a 'blockhead' and 'political rake' whose popularity vanished when he began advocating 'silly and impractible' peace theories in Congress. 'All that Wood intends now', said Bennett of the ex-mayor, 'is to work the peace party in this State into that prominence which will enable him to strike a bargain profitable to himself, and which will secure his own and Brother Ben's re-election to Congress.'[28]

The *Herald* accused the Woods (and the *World* and *Express*) of trying to incite riots in the city and of discouraging volunteering – a crime under the enrolment act for which he wanted them duly punished. More serious still, the *Herald* charged that the copperheads were actually in the employ of the Confederate government, and in contact with Jacob Thompson and George N. Sanders, two of the rebel 'commissioners' at Niagara Falls. When a Confederate army corps was repulsed from Washington in July the *Herald* announced the fact editorially under the caption 'Ben Wood Dished'.[29] Bennett accused Ben Wood of having received $20,000 from Thompson for subversive purposes.[30] With less justification but a nice eye for symmetry Bennett added that Wood was in collusion with Lincoln to undermine the Democracy. Another *Herald* headline ran 'British Agents Stirring Up a Northern Insurrection' – the gist of the 'exposure' being that a correspondent of the London *Times* had contributed an article to the *Daily News*. Given the rabidly pro-Confederate views of the *Times* this charge was calculated to arouse indignant Northern opinion.[31]

[28]*NYH* 8, 26 Nov; 17 Dec 1863; 11 Feb; 22 June 1864. On Wood at this time see also Basil Leo Lee, *Discontent in New York City 1861-5* (NY 1943), chs 7 & 8.

[29]*NYH* 15 July 1864.

[30]*NYH* 13, 16, 18 July 1864. The Confederates certainly paid for propaganda; see *Official Records of the War of the Rebellion* (Washington 1880-1901, series 1, vol. 43, pt 2 for reports of C.C. Clay 12 Sept 1864 and Jacob Thompson 3 Dec 1864, pp. 930-6. The *Daily News* was knowingly the medium of communication between the Confederate Secretary of War and his agents in Canada. Union authorities were aware of the treasonable connections of the *Daily News*, see *OR* series 3, vol. 4, pp. 1064-8. See also Joe Skidmore, 'The Copperhead Press and the Civil War', *Journal Quarterly*, 16 (1939), pp. 345-55. For Ben Wood's vigorous reply to JGB's charges see NY *Daily News* 18, 19 Aug 1864.

[31]*NYH* 21 May; 22, 24 June; 10, 18, 30 July; 17, 19, 24 Aug; 3, 11 Sept 1864.

Although the *Herald* sneered that the copperheads were merely a 'small, insignificant, contemptible clique' up for auction to the highest bidder, it feared that if the more extreme members of the 'let Jeff. Davis alone' party had their way only Confederate agents would be admitted at the party convention. As August passed Bennett saw the opportunity of attracting conservative Republicans to the Democracy being consistently ignored. The Vallandigham-Wood wing of the Democracy, insistent on offering voters what they considered the real alternative of peace, stood in the way of any such coalition. Continuing to hope for the best at Chicago, the *Herald* feared the possibility that a deal between the copperheads and the Albany Regency would result in the nomination of some 'poor drivelling politician' (Bennett was thinking of the covert ambitions of Horatio Seymour) instead of a military candidate on a war platform. The course certainly doomed to demoralising failure, he warned on 24 August, would be the nomination of McClellan on a peace platform. Finding fault with the *World* over the feeble way the Democratic campaign was being managed, the *Herald* frankly admitted during August that if the Republicans were yet to adopt Grant or Sherman on their ticket they would win easily.[32]

It is interesting that at a time when Lincoln himself was privately expressing serious doubts about his re-election Bennett predicted that the President actually had 'the game in his hands'. The trend of recent elections, the soldier vote, the power of government patronage – all seemed favourable to the Republicans.[33] Nor did Bennett any longer hold out hope that radical malcontents within the Republican party would inflict serious damage on Lincoln. What, he asked, did all the noise which the 'Republican Soreheads' were making against Lincoln mean? He predicted that it was merely a ploy to get better terms from the party leadership as the price of their support: 'When your professional politician blusters the loudest that he is going to break the party crockery he is simply playing the auctioneer for a bargain and sale.'[34] They wanted Lincoln to give them 'more shoddy' and 'more nigger' although the people already had too much of both. They were not serious in seeking another candidate, said Bennett, because Lincoln's renomination meant that they needed the President even more than he needed them:

> The Republican leaders may have their personal quarrels, or their shoddy quarrels, or their nigger quarrels with Old Abe; but

[32]*NYH* 2, 11 Aug 1864. For comment on the *Herald*'s growing coolness towards McClellan see *Philadelphia Press* 11 Aug 1864.

[33]*NYH* 21, 24, 26 Aug 1864.

[34]*NYH* 25 Sept 1864.

he has the whiphand of them and they will soon be bobbing back into the Republican fold, like sheep who have gone astray. . . Whatever they say now, we venture to predict that Wade and his tail; Bryant and his tail; and Wendell Phillips and his tail; and Weed, Barney, Chase and their tails; and Winter Davis, Opdyke and Forney who have no tails; will all make tracks for Old Abe's plantation, and soon will be found crowing and blowing, and vowing and writing, and swearing and stumping the state on his side, declaring that he and he alone, is the hope of the nation, the bugaboo of Jeff Davis, the first of Conservatives, the best of Abolitionists, the purest of patriots, the most gullible of mankind, the easiest President to manage, and the person especially predestined and foreordained by Providence to carry on the war, free the niggers, and give all the faithful a fair share of the spoils. The spectacle will be ridiculous, but it is inevitable.[35]

Before long he would have cause to congratulate himself on his powers of prophecy with regard to both Republicans and Democrats.

[35]*NYH* 23 Aug 1864; and see also 31 Aug; 29 Sept. 'Bryant' refers to William Cullen Bryant, editor of the NY *Evening Post.* Hiram Barney, a protégé of Chase, was collector of New York Port until 31 Aug 1864.

13

THE *HERALD* FOR THE UNION AND BENNETT, 1864-5

> We presume that Mr. Lincoln has been making Bennett the victim of one of his cruel jokes, and has touched his weak point with a suggestion that in the event of his re-election the long cherished vision of the mission to France may be realized. Poor Bennett! that dream of diplomatic honours has governed his political action throughout four Presidential elections. . . . – NY *Daily News,* 5 September 1864

Two months before the election, the Presidential contest entered a new phase. On the first day of September the *Herald* reported that General McClellan had been nominated at Chicago as the candidate of the Democratic National Convention. Two days later the headlines announced that General Sherman had delivered a crippling blow to the Confederacy by capturing Atlanta after a four months' campaign. It was now apparent that after a summer of stalemate the war was being won by the Union, and military success redounded to the credit of the Lincoln administration. This chapter describes the *Herald*'s view of the final weeks of the contest between Lincoln and McClellan. It then reviews the evidence surrounding the enigma of Bennett's motivation.

The Campaign of Failures

The first news of McClellan's nomination revived Bennett's political enthusiasm, for it seemed to confirm that the copperheads were a powerless minority after all. The *Herald* indicated its strong support for the General but at the same time modified its tirades against Lincoln. Adopting, for the occasion, an attitude of exemplary moral purity, the paper hoped that the coming campaign would be free from violence of language. The nation was still experiencing the consequences of a disagreement over an election, and Bennett pleaded: 'Let us discuss the whole question like Americans and like gentlemen.' With a serenity quite different from his tone during the previous winter, he solemnly pronounced 'Let it be understood at the very outset that Mr. Lincoln is not a "scoundrel" and that General McClellan is not a "traitor".'[1]

[1]*NYH* 1, 2 Sept 1864.

By 3 September the editor had digested the news that while nominating McClellan the Democratic convention had adopted a platform which instead of confining itself to the defence of civil liberties declared:

> that after four years of failure to restore the Union by experiment of war . . . justice, humanity, liberty and the public welfare demand that immediate efforts be made for a cessation of hostilities, with a view to an ultimate convention of the States or other peaceable means, to the end that, at the earliest possible moment, peace may be restored on the basis of the Federal Union of the States.[2]

This produced rage in the *Herald* office. Bennett acused Vallandigham, Seymour and the Woods of having an 'understanding' with the rebels to re-elect Lincoln and so cause insurrection in the North. They seemed intent on undermining McClellan's candidacy, and the *Herald* reproachfully cautioned its former idol:

> For three years past the HERALD has sustained and defended the hero of Antietam. We have done full justice to his generalship, his statemanship, his honesty and his patriotism. But when McClellan takes his stand upon a cowardly peace platform we are at a loss how to follow him and defend him. . . The Chicago platform invites defeat, and it must be broken up, either by McClellan himself or by the voice of the people at the polls.[3]

When McClellan seemed slow and indecisive in disavowing the peace plank Bennett showed the degree of his disillusion by saying of the man he had defended so stoutly for so long that 'McClellan has proved a failure in that supreme necessity of war – success. His military record – no matter what may be the excuse for it – has been one of results in no degree adequate to the means at his command.'[4] At this moment he thought that if the Republicans were to withdraw Lincoln and put Grant and Sherman on one ticket they would sweep the electoral board, and hinted that the *Herald* would be happy to support them. All was soon forgiven, however, when McClellan 'came right' in a

---

[2] For party conventions and platforms (state as well as national) in the 1864 election see *American Annual Cyclopedia for 1864,* pp. 579 ff., 786 ff. On the circumstances of the Chicago Convention which led to the framing of the peace plank see also I. Katz, *August Belmont* (NY 1868), ch 8; Wood Gray, *The Hidden Civil War* (NY 1942), chs 8,9; S. Pleasants, *Fernando Wood* (NY 1948), ch 10; F. Klement, *The Limits of Dissent* ch 18; A.C. Flick, *Samuel Jones Tilden* (NY 1939), pp. 147-50; W. Zornow, *Lincoln and the Party Divided* (Norman, Oklahoma 1954), chs 12, 13.

[3] *NYH* 3 Sept 1864.

[4] *NYH* 9 Sept 1864.

letter accepting the Democratic nomination but in effect repudiating the Chicago platform:

> The Union is the one condition of peace. We ask no more . . . I could not look in the face my gallant comrades . . . who have survived so many bloody battles, and tell them that their labors and the sacrifice of so many of our slain and wounded brothers had been in vain – that we had abandoned the Union for which we have so often periled our lives.[5]

This was civilly done, but the *Herald*, applauding McClellan with relief, would have preferred stronger language against the copperheads and a clearer definition of the differences between himself and Lincoln.[6] If the *Herald* approved the mass rally held by McClellan supporters in the city, its enthusiasm was not so unqualified as that of the *Express, World* and *Journal of Commerce.* Cheer boisterously for the general by all means, the *Herald* urged the crowd, but be sure to hiss Seymour and Fernando Wood loudly. Bennett counselled the Democrats to save face by reconvening their convention at once. The copperheads were suggesting that since McClellan had not accepted the party platform he should stand down,[7] whereas in fact, said the *Herald*, the only safety for the party was in dropping the Chicago platform and keeping McClellan on his own ground.[8]

Bennett was little inclined to help politicians who would not help themselves. He attributed August Belmont's apparent lack of vigour as party chairman to sinister motives, amusing his readership with the charge that since Belmont was related to Confederate diplomat Slidell and was American agent for the Rothschilds, who supplied Napoleon III with the funds to maintain the French expedition in Mexico, and since Napoleon III wished for the success of the Confederacy and the break up of the United States, *ergo*, the Albany Regency was in league with Napoleon and with Confederate agents in Canada to break up the Democratic party. The Chicago platform was the tool designed to produce this result.[9] Hardly less incredible was the adherence of the Democracy to a defeatist platform at a time when the papers were full of exciting news of Union victories.[10]

[5]*American Annual Cyclopedia for 1864,* pp. 793-4.

[6]*NYH* 17 Sept 1864.

[7]e.g. NY *Daily News* 10-15 Sept 1864.

[8]*NYH* 11, 13, 14, 18, 20, 21, 22 Sept; 5, 6 Oct 1864.

[9]*NYH* 7, 17, 30 Sept; 2, 5, 6 Oct 1864. Belmont was dogged throughout his career by similar attacks from the press, see Katz, *passim.*

[10]As Joel Silbey expresses it; 'The Democrats' institutional imperatives got in the way of their electoral needs' — *A Respectable Minority* (NY 1977), p. 171. Silbey

By now the Presidential race was a straight one between Lincoln and McClellan. Fremont withdrew his candidacy at the end of September, although he remained unreconciled to Lincoln and said so plainly. For this the *Herald* applauded him, and damned as hypocrites those 'radicals' who had ceased their fractiousness and were now on the stump for Lincoln. The convention which Greeley and other radical Republicans had talked of assembling at Buffalo, New York, to supersede Lincoln with another candidate, came to nothing.[11]

In the face of a united Republican party Bennett became increasingly critical of the 'unparalleled stupidity' of the Democracy.[12] His appeals for the abatement of partisan spirit had produced little effect in New York. The *Herald* took the *Tribune* and *World* to task for their intemperance of language, commending to their notice the success of the *Herald* as a 'patriotic and fair' journal. Bennett certainly seemed impartial when he took to declaring that both Lincoln and McClellan were failures. The tone in which he wrote against Lincoln was certainly much milder than in the days of the 'ghoul editorial' four months previously, but still he found the President 'a failure in manners and administration, in manliness and management' and believed him to be 'honest but weak'. On the other hand he pointedly enquired what the failed General McClellan would do with the successful Grant and Sherman if he were elected.

Hence Bennett argued that since both candidates stood on a war platform the only choice before the voters was concerning the personal capacity of the contestants, and in this respect, said he, McClellan was obviously superior even if he was not the best man in the country.[13]

Carefully contrived also was the *Herald*'s avoidance of making an issue of slavery. Lincoln's platform did have 'more of the nigger' in it, admitted Bennett, but slavery was dead and the fate of the Negro was 'a matter of indifference'.[14] Any voter who relied exclusively on the *Herald* for his political knowledge would hardly suspect that there was any real element of choice concerning slavery in the Presidential election. Bennett virtually suspended discussion of the slavery and reconstruction issues until after polling day. Maryland was in the

gives a generally convincing picture of why the Democrats pursued the course they did, and of how they viewed themselves at this juncture.

[11]*NYH* 23, 26 Sept 1864.

[12]*NYH* 22 Oct 1864.

[13]*NYH* 9, 14, 15, 18, 21-4, 27 Sept;8, 9, 11 Oct 1864.

[14]*NYH* 14, 26 Sept; 1 Oct 1864.

process of freeing her slaves and, said the *Herald*, this was a strictly local matter. Until the constitution was amended slavery was the business only of individual state legislatures, and Bennett was more than willing to leave it there for the moment.[15]

The *Herald* continued to 'sit tight' through the modest Republican electoral victory in Pennsylvania in mid-October. Bennett was hazarding none of his famous prophecies: McClellan was the more popular man but, even allowing for a marginal swing against Lincoln in local elections since 1860, Bennett reckoned that the President still had enough strength to be re-elected, despite his 'imbecility'.[16] But for the pro-rebel copperheads, he snarled, the victory of McClellan would be certain over the 'fanaticism, profligacy and recklessness' of the administration.

At least McClellan could be certain of carrying the Democratic citadel of New York City by a good majority; Bennett expected that he might win by 40,000 votes in a poll that would be swollen by large numbers of naturalised foreigners and by a sizeable displaced population from the border and Southern states which had found refuge in the metropolis.[17] But the fight over the congressional delegation would be the real test of local strength between the peace and war wings of the party. Matters augured well for War Democrat success because at the party's state convention that year Tammany delegates on a war plank were admitted to the exclusion of Mozart Hall and other city groups. Most of the current congressional delegation were repudiated for renomination. What would Ben Wood do for a livelihood now, sneered Bennett, for Lincoln would surely see that he was without influence and stop financing him to break up the opposition party?[18] Tammany nominated Judge Russell, Bennett's kinsman, for city judge, possibly as a compliment to the *Herald*.[19]

Outside the city things did not go so well for the War Democrats. The Democratic State Convention renominated Horatio Seymour for the governorship. Bennett was astonished: 'Seymour did not deserve to be nominated and does not deserve to be elected', he wrote.[20]

[15]*NYH* 16, 31 Oct 1864.

[16]*NYH* 30 Sept; 5, 14, 15, 16, 19, 26 Oct 1864. Bennett's straddle was by now becoming so obvious as to excite the mirth of some journals, e.g. Philadelphia *Press* 1 Oct 1864; NY *Daily News* 1, 12 Oct 1864.

[17]*NYH* 29 Oct 1864.

[18]Wood replied that he would willingly run for Congress if Bennett would consent to oppose him — *Daily News* 22 Sept; 3, 5, 8, 24 Oct 1864.

[19]*NYH* 13 Sept 1864.

[20]*NYH* 13 Sept 1864.

Otherwise Bennett was loftily unconcerned with State politics – all he wanted from aspirants to the legislature was a declaration that they would stand up against the pressure that the railroad and gas companies were bringing to the lobby in order to have their charters revised to allow them to charge higher prices. Against this kind of monopolistic connivance to mulct the city Bennett wanted a firm legislative stand. Otherwise his view of local politics was encapsulated a few days before the election by the laconic headline 'Election Frauds – The Usual Dreadful Disclosures on Both Sides'.[21]

In the last two weeks of the Presidential race the tone of the *Herald*'s editorials became if anything even less enthusiastic about both Presidential candidates. But it may be argued with pardonable paradox that the *Herald*'s 'impartiality' began to weigh rather less heavily against Lincoln. Bennett was certainly not campaigning all out for either party, neither praising one nor disparaging the other excessively.

Posing as arbiter, the *Herald* on 23 October came out with its own Presidential platform comprising: first and foremost, reunion through military victory; secondly, when this had been achieved, the direct readmission of Southern representatives (even ex-Confederates) to Congress; thirdly, an ultimatum to Napoleon III to leave Mexico and to Britain to pay reparations to the United States; and lastly a review of the unconstitutional acts of the abolitionists by the Supreme Court. With the exception of the first point this platform was entirely Democratic in tone and principle. It was poles apart from Republican aims as expressed at Baltimore. This became even more evident a few days later when Bennett reiterated his list, omitting the last provision about the legality of abolition but substituting one that slavery should be left to die a natural death. This platform has been described as 'the kind of straddle that appealed to every corner grocery loafer with bellicose prejudices'.[22] For the moment the *Herald* had forgotten its championship of abolition by amendment which was now identified as a Republican party measure. Now Bennett invited both candidates to declare their standing on the war platform which the *Herald* presented to them in its capacity as the 'organ of the independent, thinking masses of the American people'.[23]

On 27 October (neither candidate having responded) the *Herald* announced itself still desirous of a more positive assertion of war

[21]*NYH* 24, 26, 29 Oct 1864.

[22]Allan Nevins, *The War for the Union,* vol. IV, p. 126.

[23]*NYH* 25 Oct 1864.

principles from McClellan. Of the President's attitude to winning the war Bennett said 'we accept Mr. Lincoln as he stands'. Lest the prospect of continued war alarm potential conscripts the *Herald* had already given soothing assurances that New York had filled its draft quota, so that 'married men with their large families and small incomes may possess their souls in peace, and no longer tremble at the possible chances of the wheel. Bachelors may also burn their memoranda of railroad fares to Canada, and relinquish their stooped shoulders, hard coughs and rheumatic pains.' Now it cautioned that rumours of an impending new draft were merely being put about to damage Lincoln. (They were true as it happened.)

Had the *Herald* done a quick change to the side of the seeming winner at the last minute? Not to judge by the leading editorial of 29 October, which pronounced that 'Lincoln and McClellan are failures, and Grant is our Presidential Candidate'. Armed neutrality indeed. But how was the election of Grant to come about, since he was not even a candidate? Bennett's solution was strikingly simple. The Electoral College, he argued, was not bound by anything in the Constitution to elect the Presidential candidate with the greatest number of popular votes. Lincoln and McClellan were the choices of the politicians, not of the people, and weren't even faithful to their party platforms. Therefore, said Bennett, the opportunity had arisen for members of the Electoral College to make themselves illustrious by disregarding the election of 8 November and exercising their moral right to choose the most popular man in the country, General Grant, for the Presidency. Thus the *Herald* reverted to its first choice of the year.

On 4 November Bennett was in a philosophic frame of mind about the election – 'Our manifest destiny is to remain one nation and rule the world, and we have yet to see the politicians who can prevent this consummation.' Party excitement was high, but Bennett had every confidence that troops brought to the city under Ben Butler's command would ensure a quiet and orderly election. The *Herald* advised voters to go to the polls early, if only to do homage to republican institutions, but didn't proffer any last minute persuasion to cast ballots this way or that. In Lincoln and McClellan the country was offered a choice of evils, said Bennett, yet the election of neither one would be the ruin of the country, any more than it would be paradise regained.[24] The war would be won and the Union restored whoever won. Reconstruction would be a difficult problem for any executive to face, but a foreign war would help matters along nicely.

[24]*NYH* 6, 7 Nov 1864.

Once the election returns were in Bennett wasted little time on post mortems. Overall Lincoln had won by 2,213,645 popular votes to 1,802,237 for McClellan, and would have an overpowering majority in the electoral college of 212 votes to 21. Within New York State the Republican victory was by a much smaller margin – Lincoln had lost ground there to the Democrats since 1860 and had a majority in the state of only 6,749 out of a total poll of over 730,000.[25] 'Killed by copperheads' was Bennett's short epitaph on McClellan,[26] and he would have been less than human (and much less than a journalist) had he failed to claim that if the Democrats had only followed the *Herald*'s advice General Grant would now be their President-elect. He laid the blame for failure squarely on the 'cowardice and mismanagement' of the Albany Regency and maintained that had the opposition been directed intelligently Lincoln's 'budget of blunders' should have been enough to ruin him.[27]

For Horatio Seymour, defeated for the governorship by Republican Reuben E. Fenton (who in fact ran ahead of Lincoln on the ticket), Bennett had short shrift. Reviewing Seymour's career, he reflected on how the governor had botched the chance of entering the White House which had seemed so bright in 1862. He bade political *au revoir* to Seymour with a terse epithet – 'He is a small, weak, slippery man. . .'[28] As 1864 ended, the *Herald* made a small gesture of condolence to the defeated 'hero of Antietam'. The paper collected a fund of $692.10 to buy a sword for McClellan. At the general's request the money was donated to an orphans' home.

Amid the general Democratic wreck Tammany candidates had triumphed within the city, leading Bennett to call for the final disbandment of rival factions. To his immense satisfaction, Fernando Wood was defeated in the ninth congressional district, and Bennett tweaked brother Ben for his sparse analysis of the election: 'Hereafter let us hear no more of Wood, Mozart Hall and the copperheads.'[29] Yet ironically, just at the moment when Confederate sympathisers in the North had seemingly received a decisive drubbing, New York City found itself the target of a new kind of Southern offensive. One night in

[25]The vote in New State stood at:

	Lincoln	McClellan
	368,735	361,986

[26]*NYH* 9 Nov 1864.

[27]*NYH* 10, 12, 16 Nov 1864.

[28]*NYH* 13 Nov 1864.

[29]*NYH* 10 Nov 1864.

late November Confederate agents unsuccessfully attempted to start a general conflagration in the city by firing several major hotels. The *Herald*, voicing the shock and anger of New Yorkers at suddenly finding themselves in the front line, whipped up feelings against the 'rebel press' and its editorial feud with Ben Wood and his *Daily News* became intensely bitter. The tendency of copperhead papers to play up Southern victories with as much enthusiasm and less regard for truth than even the Richmond press could no longer be laughed at, and Bennett called for the military suppression of 'journalistic abettors of murder and treason'.[30]

Once this excitement was over New York City returned to a normality which seemed almost like obliviousness to the war. If regiments had marched off amid cheering crowds in 1861, by the autumn of 1864 nobody seemed to notice soldiers returning on leave or to treat even the wounded among them with much courtesy. Like the growing army of women wearing black, they were an uncomfortable reminder of a reality which the city semed intent on keeping at bay.

Whether because of callous indifference or because of a frantic desire to forget the sufferings of the front and of Southern prison camps, the city's theatres, hotels and amusement places were packed to overflowing. Fashions in the fourth winter of the war were more brilliant than ever, and the *Herald* occasionally reproached the rich for their tasteless flaunting of diamonds and expensive silks. The traffic of carriages in the city's streets was now so busy that the *Herald* suggested that vehicles going in opposite directions ought to stick to different sides of the road.[31]

Bennett had been called a cynic because in April 1861 he had said that the war would make New York City rich. Time had proved him right, but the prosperity of 1864 was by no means evenly spread. The *Herald*'s continuing strictures against railroad, gas and coal monopolists and profiteering grocers and its calls for firewood for the poor told their own story of deepening social rift: 'The cost of rents, food and raiment is becoming intolerable. . . . Such, however, is the tendency in our own, as in other wars – the poor poorer, the rich richer; heavy taxation and an increasing national debt, with large rates of interest – a vortex for drawing the nation's property into the hands of the few,

[30]*NYH* 27-30; 1, 16, 19 Dec 1864. For Ben Wood's equally bitter retorts see NY *Daily News* 29 Nov; 1, 2, 5, 6, 7, 11-14 Dec 1864. On the abortive Southern arson attempt see N. Brandt, 'New York is Worth Twenty Richmonds', *American Heritage*, 22 (Oct 1971), 74-80. When Richmond did finally fall the *Herald* carried the caption: 'ALAS! POOR BEN WOOD — What next?'

[31]*NYH* 3, 12 Sept 1864; see also 13, 17 Oct 1863.

permanently diminishing the means and prospects of the masses.'[32] Inflation and strikes had increased during the year. Defending groups of low paid workers whose employers were prospering out of the war and spending money with vulgar ostentation, the *Herald* suggested that the Albany legislature should curb monopolists instead of trying to prohibit strikes by 'unfair, impolitic and dangerous' laws: 'Reduce the cost of living by judicious legislation, and workmen will not be forced to combine to defend their interests.'[33] Skilled workers protested against the influx of cheap foreign labour which the new Contract Labor Law enabled employers to bring into the city, although in this case the *Herald*'s eagerness to see the state draft quota filled by the new arrivals caused it to take the employers' side. Bennett called Mayor Gunther a 'rank copperhead' for his efforts to protect native labour.[34]

Union victories in late 1864 did something to ease inflation by stabilising the price of gold and hence of other commodities. Certainly when its better off citizens could contribute an estimated $50 million to election expenses and still find money to buy themselves out of the latest draft, New York was in flush times.

In the distant days of 1860, the *Herald* had poked fun at the 'Cotton, Hardware and Codfish' aristocracy which had dominated the city. Commerce and finance retained their traditional prestige, but the war had seen the social arrival of the railroad operators, monopolists and manufacturers who had done well out of supplying the government's war needs. We have seen how the *Herald* used the 'shoddy' theme against the Republicans in the early days of the election campaign. By late 1864, however, a new set of grandees had arrived in town, portending the post-war social scene. These were people who had made their money out of western gold and silver and Pennsylvania oil. So lavishly did the new arrivals spend their wealth (little regarding the fires caused by poor storage of the new oil in populated areas) that Bennett sardonically suggested that the metropolis be renamed 'Petrolia'.[35]

New prosperity brought an accentuation of New York's old problem of lawlessness. Sneak thieves had become such a plague that Bennett demanded that a few be shot as an example. Drink had

[32]*NYH* 18 Mar 1864.

[33]*NYH* 9 Apr 1864. See also 10 Apr; 26 Sept. The strikes Bennett most approved of, needless to say, were those amongst the typographical staff of rival papers.

[34]*NYH* 25 Sept 1864.

[35]*NYH* 19 Sept; 7, 20 Oct 1864; 11 Feb 1865.

become such a bane that he called for a new temperance movement by public men. Violence, always a prodigious problem in the urban area, had reached the scale of an epidemic according to the editor, who claimed that, 'at present in and around this city the ruling mania appears to be bloodshed by the reckless use of the revolver'.[36] By early 1865 there was serious talk of forming citizens' vigilance committees to combat the evil.

Another of New York's old problems could not be blamed on the war. Francis I. A. Boole had been the *Herald*'s favourite for mayor in 1863. Failing to be elected, this Tammany politician had stayed on in his post as City Inspector, and in that capacity was a disaster for the city although the *Herald* continued to puff him loyally. The nauseating stench from heaps of uncollected rubbish in the streets seemed to threaten another epidemic, and the city's air was not made any sweeter by odours from broken sewers, unregulated hogpens, bone boiling establishments and gasworks. These abuses, and the continuing squalor of the city's overcrowded housing, were the prelude to a public health reform programme introduced by the Republican State government in 1865.[37] For once the *Herald* regarded the problem as too serious for partisan politics, and there was no repetition of the city's opposition to police reform in 1857. One contributory reason for Republican victory in the 1864 state election may have been that the Democrats were as negative in their attitude towards the government of the country's largest city as towards the restoration of the Union.

In Which Mr. Bennett is Offered a Reward

The *Herald*'s reception of the re-elected President Lincoln was somewhat grudging, and hardly suggested that Bennett had felt any interest in Republican success. The paper pledged its continued support of the government in putting down the rebellion, but was unrepentant of its past criticisms. The people, said Bennett, had conceded much to Lincoln by re-electing him, and now he had the opportunity to concede something to them by replacing the present cabinet with an 'able and harmonious Cabinet, selected with a generous recognition of the rights of war democrats'. Bennett still considered it beyond debate that such a measure would unite the

[36]*NYH* 8 Oct; 19 Dec 1864.

[37]*NYH* 27 Mar; 6, 21, 22 Apr; 1, 5, 6, 8, 9, 14, 19 May; 1, 3 June; 1, 2, 7, 29 July; 18 Aug; 23, 24 Sept; 13, 15, 21 Oct; 24, 28 Dec 1864; 13, 14, 17, 20 Jan; 6, 13, 18 Feb 1865. On post-war reform see James C. Mohr, *The Radical Republicans and Reform in New York during Reconstruction* (Ithaca 1973).

North, but if Lincoln had found it unnecessary to conciliate War Democrats in this way before the election, yet had won, the editor did not explain why he should do so afterwards.[38] Nor was Lincoln perturbed by the *Herald*'s strong objections to his appointing Chase to the vacant Chief Justiceship, though it seems that Bennett joined with two leading conservative Republicans, ex-Postmaster Montgomery Blair and Thurlow Weed, to make a personal protest against this move.[39]

As for the reconstruction issue, the *Herald* enjoined the President to make 'no compromise with Jeff. Davis' on the integrity of the Union, though it did urge that on the strength of his victory Lincoln could now afford to offer a liberal amnesty to the South. For once it was in agreement with General Benjamin F. Butler, who had made a speech in the city on this very subject.[40] Bennett was still fearful that the Southerners might be pushed into their last ditch unnecessarily but, as the *Evening Express* remarked, such advice was now no more likely to be heeded 'than the screechings of the owl'.[41]

Only in the matter of the new draft did the *Herald*'s objections help to modify administration policy. Early in 1865 the paper joined in a chorus of protest that Stanton and Provost Marshall James B. Fry were being deliberately unfair to Democratic New York City in deciding its draft quota. Bennett argued that the city had already sent 140,000 men to the war and 'a willing horse should not be driven to death'.[42] To make its point the *Herald* impishly raised a collection to buy a book of primary arithmetic for General Fry. On this occasion Lincoln took some notice of the clamour and intervened to modify the quota.

By the time Lincoln began his second term, on 4 March 1865, Bennett had had time to reflect that this man, intended only as a one term compromise by the Republican managers in 1860, had actually matched the achievement of the revered Jackson: he had won re-election. Accordingly he made a generous estimate of Lincoln, for the editor had as much reason as anybody to realise that the President was 'a most remarkable man. . . . He has proved himself, in his quiet way,

[38]*NYH* 9, 11 Nov 1864.

[39]*NYH* 16, 18 Oct; 23 Nov; 4 Dec 1864; W.E. Smith, *The Francis Preston Blair Family in Politics* (NY 1933), vol. 2, p. 298.

[40]*NYH* 9, 17-20 Nov 1864; L.T. Merrill, 'General Benjamin F. Butler in the Presidential Campaign of 1864', *Mississippi Valley Historical Review,* 33 (1946-7), 537-70.

[41]NY *Evening Express* 9 Nov 1864.

[42]*NYH* 10, 28, 30 Jan; 1, 3, 6, 9 Feb 1865.

the keenest of politicians, and more than a match for his wiliest antagonists.' But Bennett was not moonstruck with the Inaugural Address; he found it an orthodox piece of 'glittering generalities'. He guessed that the speech was an effort to avoid discussing the reconstruction question and the Monroe Doctrine and that the President's phrases about the causes of the war were intended to divert his audience from more pressing questions. Bennett was unhappy about Lincoln's fatalism. If Lincoln accepted as the will of God that the war should continue 'until all the wealth piled by the bondsman's two hundred and fifty years of unrequited toil shall be sunk, and until every drop of blood drawn with the lash shall be paid by another drawn with the sword', was he threatening war to the extermination of Southern life and property? Was such a declaration calculated to do any good, queried Bennett, and how much 'charity for all' was implied in it?[43]

As he wrote this Bennett was contemplating another of Lincoln's literary efforts, in which there was nothing mystical. It was a personal letter to Bennett, dated from Washington on 20 February, and read:

Dear Sir,

I propose, at some convenient and not distent[44] day, to nominate you to the United States Senate, as Minister to France.

Your Obt. Servt.
A. Lincoln[45]

What had Bennett done to deserve such generous recognition? The French mission was hardly one of those minor diplomatic sinecures with which faithful Republican politicians could be rewarded for services rendered. In 1861 James Watson Webb had had to rest content with the ministry to Brazil, even though the redoubtable editor of the *Courier and Enquirer* had supported Seward through thick and thin. Horace Greeley, for all his differences with Lincoln, was a thorough Republican and the *Herald* rumoured that Lincoln had promised him the cabinet post of Postmaster General in return for his support in the election.[46] There is no record that this offer ever materialised, while the offer to Bennett is a matter of record. The *Herald* was tight lipped about the affair. On 6 January it had reported

[43]*NYH* 4, 5 Mar 1865.

[44]*sic.*

[45]Text in R.P. Basler, *The Collected Works of Abraham Lincoln* (New Brunswick 1953-5), vol. VIII, p. 307.

[46]The standard work on Lincoln's appointment policies is Harry J. Carman and Reinhard H. Luthin, *Lincoln and the Patronage* (NY 1943).

in the most matter of fact way that forty or fifty Republican 'political donkeys' and time servers, hardly any of whom could even speak French, were pestering Lincoln for the Paris mission, but advised the President to keep consul John Bigelow in the post as acting minister until a new ambassador could be named. That was all. Later, the *Herald* contented itself with reprinting an article from the *Tribune,* dated 15 March 1865, reporting the offer.[47]

Only at the end of April, when the matter had become academic, did the *Herald* report that the tender of the French embassy was the sensation of the moment in the city and the press rooms and salons of New York, London and Paris. It commented that 'Mr. Bennett' was much amused by this, and would confirm that the rumour was true, adding that although news had not yet been received from India, China or Japan, the people of those countries were undoubtedly engrossed in speculation about the matter.[48]

When prominent Republicans got wind of the offer they were incredulous. Thurlow Weed sent a hurried note to Consul Bigelow in Paris

New York, April 26, 1865

> I dare not tell all about the Bennett matter on paper. It was a curious complication for which two well-meaning friends were responsible. Seward knew nothing about it until the Election was over, when he sent for me. I was amazed at what had transpired.[49]

Within the cabinet, Gideon Welles was still in the dark three weeks after the President had made the offer. He noted in his diary on Wednesday 15 March that

> A rumor is prevalent and very generally believed that the French mission has been offered Bennett of the *New York Herald.* I discredit it. On one or two occasions this mission had been alluded to in Cabinet, but the name of B. was never mentioned or alluded to. There are sometimes strange and unaccountable appointments made but this would be . . . disreputable.

The next day Welles picked up some more gossip from the ex-Postmaster General, but was still unbelieving:

> Blair believes the President has offered the French mission to Bennett. Says it is the President and not Seward. . . . He says he

[47]Portions of this article are quoted and its origin explained in the text below.

[48]*NYH* 29 Apr 1865.

[49]Quoted in John Bigelow, *Retrospections of an Active Life* (NY 1909), vol. 2, p. 250.

met Bartlett, the jackall of Bennett, here last August or September; that Bartlett . . . [told Blair] . . . that he was here watching movements and that they [i.e. the *Herald*] did not mean this time to be cheated. . . .[50]

It was, Blair says, the darkest hour of the Administration, and when the President himself considered his prospect of a re-election hopeless. Soon after [this] the *Herald* [came out] for the re-election [of Mr. Lincoln] and he had little doubt that the President made some promise or [gave some] assurance at that time. At a later day, Bartlett alluded again to the matter, and he [Blair] told him if he had got the President's word he might rely upon it implicitly.

This has some plausibility and there may have been something to encourage the *Herald* folks, but I cannot believe promised [*sic*] or [that] will give him the French mission. . . [51]

Despite Welles' doubts, Blair was very near to the truth. Parts of the affair are still tantalisingly mysterious. Contemporaries avoided committing much to paper. The business was so secret that even the President's private secretary was not privy to Lincoln's motives and actions, but when the Lincoln papers became available some eighty years after the Civil War certain facts could be verified.

To return to the election campaign of the summer of 1864. The two 'well-meaning friends' Weed alluded to were W. O. Bartlett and Abram Wakeman. At about the time of the Niagara peace negotiations in July Lincoln had written a confidential letter to Wakeman, who was Republican Postmaster in New York City. Gideon Welles described Wakeman as 'affable, insinuating and pleasant, though not profound nor reliable. . . Wakeman believes that all is fair and proper in party operations which can secure by any means certain success, and supposes that every one else is the same.'[52] Wakeman was apparently on good terms with Bennett because the *Herald* pumped his claims to be appointed Collector of Customs at New York Port.[53] In return, Postmaster Wakeman let the *Herald* charge the government its usual advertising rates for publishing the weekly lists of mail for collection.[54]

---

[50]It has been suggested in chapter 9 above that this refers to Bartlett's desire for naval contracts: we shall see later that Bennett had also expected Blair to secure the appointment of G.G. Fleurot as consul at Bordeaux.

[51]H.K. Beale ed., *The Diary of Gideon Welles* (NY 1960), vol. 2, pp. 258-60.

[52]*Ibid.*, vol. 2, p. 122, entry for 27 Aug 1864. It should be said, though, that Wakeman had suffered in the Republican cause — his house was burned by the draft rioters in 1863.

[53]*NYH* 5 Sept 1864.

[54]*NYH* 17, 22 Oct 1864.

Lincoln wrote to Wakeman as one who had some influence in the *Herald* office:

Executive Mansion
Washington
July 25, 1864

My dear Sir,

I feel that the subject which you pressed upon my attention in our recent conversation is an important one. The men of the South, recently (and perhaps still) at Niagara Falls, tell us distinctly that they *are* in confidential employment of the rebellion; and they tell us as distinctly that they are *not* empowered to offer terms of peace. Does anyone doubt that what they *are* empowered to do, is to assist in selecting and arranging a candidate and a platform for the Chicago convention? Who would have given them this confidential employment but . . [Jefferson Davis] . . . who only a week since declared . . . that he had no terms of peace but the independence of the South – the dissolution of the Union? Thus the present presidential contest will almost certainly be no other than a contest between a Union and a Disunion candidate, disunion certainly following the success of the latter. The issue is a mighty one for all people and all time; and whoever aids the right, will be appreciated and remembered.

Yours truly
A. Lincoln[55]

What had he and Wakeman talked about? Lincoln was outlining Republican campaign strategy, and offering a reward to 'whoever' would help pursue it. That this letter was intended for Bennett's eyes is confirmed by Wakeman's reply to Lincoln, dated 12 August 1864:

Your excellent letter was duly received. I have read it with proper explanation to Mr. B. He said, after some moments of silence, that so far as it related to him 'It did not amount to much'. I supposed, if anything was written, something more specific would be expected. However, I hope to avoid the writing of anything further. . . . I will indicate my views as to its form, personally. . . . I have ventured to show this letter to several of our friends (of course without indicating a word as to what drew it out) and it has met with universal approval.[56]

Bennett, in other words, was too shrewd to be won with fair words alone. Exactly what happened between August and the week of the

[55]Basler, Vol. VII, p. 461.

[56]Abram Wakeman to Lincoln, 12 Aug 1864, Lincoln Papers, LC, item 35261. The latter part of the letter states explicitly that 'Mr B' is Bennett.

election is rather mysterious, but Lincoln obviously gave more thought to Bennett's support than he revealed to his associates. For instance Leonard Swett, an Illinois friend of Lincoln's, naively believed that the President would not lift a finger to improve his own electoral prospects, and later wrote:

> Mr. Bennett of the *Herald* with his paper, you know, is a power. The old gentleman wanted to be noticed by Lincoln, and he wanted to support him. A friend of his, who was certainly in his secrets, came to Washington and intimated if Lincoln would invite Bennett to come over and chat with him, his paper would be all right. Mr. Bennett wanted nothing, he simply wanted to be noticed. Lincoln in talking about it said, 'I understand it; Bennett has made a great deal of money, some say not very properly, now he wants me to make him respectable. I have never invited Mr. Bryant or Mr. Greeley here; I shall not, therefore, especially invite Mr. Bennett.' All Lincoln would say was that he was receiving everybody, and he should receive Mr. Bennett if he came.[57]

Swett was misled. Lincoln received advice on the Bennett matter from his personal friend Republican Senator James Harlan of Iowa, who was in charge of the committee responsible for levying election campaign funds from Republican officeholders. John Hay made an interesting entry in his diary for 23 September 1864 about this which shows that he doubted whether the President were actually in the market for Bennett's support. The secretary wrote:

> Senator Harlan thinks that Bennett's support is so important, especially considered as to its bearing on the soldier vote, that it would pay to offer him a foreign mission for it, & so told me. Forney has also had a man talking to the cannie Scot who asked plumply, 'Will I be a welcome visitor at the White House if I support Mr. Lincoln?' What a horrible question for a man to be able to ask. I think he is too pitchy to touch. So thinks the Presdt. apparently: it is probable that Bennett will stay about as he is, thoroughly neutral, balancing carefully until the October elections, & will then declare for the side which he thinks will win. It is better in many respects to let him alone.[58]

On the same day however Mary Lincoln wrote privately to her friend Wakeman that 'a little notice of. . . [Bennett]. . . would strengthen us

[57]Swett to W.H. Herndon 17 Jan 1866, quoted in W.H. Herndon and Jesse W. Weik, *Herndon's Life of Lincoln* (NY 1949 ed.), p. 428.

[58]T. Dennett ed., *Lincoln and the Civil War in the Diaries and Letters of John Hay* (NY 1939), p. 215.

very much I think. The P[resident] . . . appreciates a kind expression of Mr. B's very much . . . '.[59]

By this time Wakeman was not the only envoy between Lincoln and Bennett. On 3 September the Republican party worker mentioned by Welles, W.O. Bartlett, wrote to Lincoln in the hope of assuring him that McClellan would not accept the Chicago nomination, and adding cryptically that 'I am just starting for Fort Washington'.[60]

William O. Bartlett was 'a prominent member of the New York bar',[61] but though a lawyer first and a writer incidentally, he was described by a newspaper man who knew him as 'not only the peer of any of the contemporary group of writing journalists in New York, but the master of most of them and the teacher of them all'.[62] He had influence in the offices of the *Tribune* and the *Evening Post* as well as the *Herald* and is known to have contributed editorial articles to all three papers. Secretary of the Navy Welles had discovered to his cost that Bartlett's claims to speak for the course which this or that paper would take were more than idle threats.[63] (After the war Bartlett became legal counsel for the *Sun* and exercised a powerful influence over its editor, Charles A. Dana. His moment of fame was to come during the Presidential campaign of 1880, when he described the Democratic candidate, General Hancock, as 'a good man, weighing two hundred and fifty pounds'. From this dart of ridicule the general's electoral prospects never really recovered.)

What occurred at Bartlett's September meeting with Bennett is not recorded, but he visited the editor again late in October, and reported to Lincoln: 'Mr. B. expressed the opinion to me, this morning, that you would be elected, but by a very close vote. He said

[59]Mary Lincoln to Abram Wakeman 23 Sept 1864 in J.G. & L.L. Turner, *Mary Todd Lincoln: Her Life and Letters* (NY 1972), p. 180. On Mrs Lincoln's acquaintance with Wakeman see *ibid.,* p. 165.

[60]Bartlett to Lincoln 3 Sept 1864, Lincoln Papers, LC, item 35858.

[61]A.K. McClure, *Abraham Lincoln and Men of War Times* (Philadelphia 1892), pp. 90-2.

[62]C.J. Rosebault, *When Dana was 'The Sun': A Story of Personal Journalism* (NY 1931), pp. 177-9, 219 includes this quotation and other information about Bartlett. For this reference I am indebted to an important article by David Quentin Voigt, 'Too Pitchy to Touch — President Lincoln and Editor Bennett', *Abraham Lincoln Quarterly,* 6 (1950), pp. 139-61. That my conclusions do not entirely coincide with Mr Voigt's does not lessen my debt to his exploration of the topic.

[63]See chapter 9 above. Bartlett's acquaintance with Bennett went back to at least 1851 — see his letter of 19 Nov of that year in the Bennett Papers, New York Public Library, and Bartlett to Buchanan 21 May; 19 June 1860, James Buchanan Papers, Historical Society of Pennsylvania.

that puffs did no good and he could accomplish most for you by not mentioning your name.'[64]

According to Bartlett, then, Bennett had been wooed secretly to the Republican cause. Already the copperhead *Daily News* had jeered that Bennett had been bought with the offer of the coveted French mission, and had warned true Democrats against the 'chorus of anarchy' which the *Herald* had been 'chosen to lead'.[65] Yet it seems that Lincoln had not definitely committed himself to any reward, for a week later Bartlett found it necessary to nudge him:

> Permit me to call your attention to the *Herald* of this date as a model paper for our side.
>
> Mr. Bennett told me yesterday that he had accomplished more for you than he could have done any other way, because he had carried his readers along with him.
>
> Please read his leader of today calling on Gen. McClellan for a more definite avowal of his policy, and at the same time distinctly accepting you as satisfactory.
>
> The enclosed article was written at my suggestion.
>
> Mr. Bennett said that it would benefit you more than anything else that could be said.[66]

It would appear that Bennett was now asking for his pound of flesh, and four days before the election, on 4 November 1864, Bartlett wrote to assure him he would have it:

> My dear Sir: I am from Washington, fresh from the bosom of Father Abraham. I had a full conversation with him, alone, on Tuesday evening, at the White House, in regard to yourself, among other subjects.
>
> I said to him: There are but few days now before the election. If Mr. Bennett is not *certainly* to have the offer of the French Mission, I want to know it now. It is important to me.
>
> We discussed the course which the *Herald* had pursued, at length, and I will tell you, verbally, at your convenience, what he said; but he concluded with me the remark that in regard to the understanding between him and me, about Mr. Bennett, he had been a 'shut pan, to everybody': and that he *expected to do that thing* (appoint you to France) *as much as he expected to live.* He repeated '*I expect* to do it as certainly as I do to be reelected myself'.[67]

[64]Bartlett to Lincoln 20 Oct 1864, Lincoln Papers, LC, item 37390. During September and October Bartlett had been doing campaign work for the Republicans in Pennsylvania — see his correspondence with Lincoln *ibid.,* items 37247, 37265, 37386, 37938.

[65]NY *Daily News* 27 Aug; 5 Sept; 8, 11, 12 Oct 1864.

[66]Bartlett to Lincoln 27 Oct 1864, Lincoln Papers, LC, item 37641.

[67]Bartlett to Bennett 4 Nov 1864 in Basler, Vol. VIII, pp. 239-40.

A. K. McClure, a Pennsylvania Republican politician writing in 1892, knew of Bartlett's role and the offer of the French mission, but he had evidently not seen the correspondence and he wrote as though on hearing of the offer of the foreign mission a proud and grateful editor immediately switched horses and came squarely to advocate Lincoln's re-election. But it has already been suggested in the first part of this chapter that on reading the files of the *Herald* for the first week of November 1864, one finds that Bennett did no such thing.[68] If the President thought he was to gain instant and enthusiastic support then he was duped. What did Lincoln think he was buying at such a price? Perhaps he remembered the advice Joseph Medill had given him about Bennett during the campaign of of 1860: 'We deem it highly important to spike that gun; his affirmative help is of no great consequence, but he is powerful for mischief. He can do much harm if hostile. If neutralized a *point* is gained. . . .'[69]

Apart from its influence nationally and abroad, the *Herald*'s voice might prove crucial to the voting in New York State. Remember that, by all accounts, Lincoln was by no means confident of the result of the election right up until the last moment. Four weeks before election day, on 13 October, Lincoln jotted down a memorandum on a blank telegraph form. It was his conservative estimate of the number of electoral votes he might obtain.[70] He reckoned that he might pick up 117 electoral votes. Against this he set 114 votes to the credit of the Democrats. At the top of the list of opposition states he put New York, the largest single state in the Union with 33 electoral votes of its own. With the power of hindsight it is easy to take for granted the fact that Lincoln could have been re-elected even if he had lost New York. But with the election still in the future and a close-run race in prospect it is quite understandable that Lincoln may have felt that to secure New York was to make sure of the Presidency for a second term by a decisive margin. The fate of New York State might (as the case proved) depend on a few thousand floating voters beyond the reaches of the regular party machines but who might just be influenced by Bennett. And if Lincoln thought that the price of the *Herald*'s support, or neutrality, was just a little social recognition or an invitation to tea

---

[68]Most historians who have noticed the matter have been content to swallow McClure's simple tale of a 'deal' between Lincoln and Bennett, without taking the trouble to actually read the *Herald* files for 1864. A notable exception, by two scholars who seriously question what Lincoln practically gained, is an article by John J. Turner Jr. and Michael D'Innocenzo, 'The President and the Press: Lincoln, James Gordon Bennett and the Election of 1864', *Lincoln Herald,* 76 (1974), 63-9.

[69]David C. Mearns ed., *The Lincoln Papers* (NY 1948), vol. 1, pp. 261-2; see chapter 5 above.

[70]Basler, vol. VIII, p. 46.

at the White House, as Medill in 1860, Hay in 1864 and Swett later imagined, he was soon disillusioned. Bennett's terms to Lincoln were what they had been to Pierce and to Buchanan – a foreign mission.

Lincoln carried New York State by 6,749 votes. It has been said that in the last week of the campaign Bennett called the President a failure and declared that it did not matter whether Lincoln or McClellan won. The point is that if the *Herald* had gone all out for McClellan in the last fortnight before the election, and had assailed the President with the same intensity as it had during the spring and early summer, those 6,749 votes might have gone the other way. To say that it did not matter if the opposition lost was to give tacit support to the Administration – the gun was spiked, and the caustic tongue was silent, when the balance might have been tipped against the Republicans. Lincoln was apparently satisfied with the journalistic service rendered and the divisions wrought in the Democratic camp; hence the offer of the French mission was duly forthcoming, while politicians of the President's own party went disappointed.

In bidding for Bennett's support, Lincoln had been well aware that the opposition was also in the market. Bartlett seems to have been playing Bennett's game in drawing the President's attention in October to the fact that 'Gen. McClellan has been up to Fort Washington and spent a day with Mr. Bennett'.[71] It was not until three days before the election and the day *after* Lincoln confirmed the promise of the French mission that Bartlett wrote to the President as if to confirm the deal: 'Mrs. James Gordon Bennett has become *a very ardent Lincolnite*. Little Mac's visit to Fort Washington was like most of his advance movements, altogether unsuccessful.'[72] John Hay saw this letter and wrote in his diary: 'Poor Mcs visiting those people and compromising himself to them has been of no avail and must be terribly humiliating to a man so well bred as Mc is.'[73] (Bennett, by the way, also spoke highly of John Hay – he once called him 'that infinitely little parasite'.)[74]

Presumably McClellan called on Bennett to ask for his support. Why else do Presidential candidates call on newspaper editors? Is it implausible that Bennett tried to exact a promise from McClellan of

[71] Bartlett to Lincoln 20 Oct 1864, Lincoln Papers, item 37390. The *Daily Tribune* of 22 Oct reported that McClellan's lengthened visit to Bennett's Fort Washington home took place 'last Tuesday', i.e. 18 Oct. See also report in NY *Daily News* 21 Oct.

[72] Bartlett to Lincoln 5 Nov 1864, Lincoln Papers, item 37938.

[73] Dennett, p. 232, entry for 7 Nov 1864.

[74] *NYH* 10 Aug 1864.

some political reward under a new Democratic regime in return for editorial support – the mission to France, for instance?[75] If this was so then the scale of Bennett's 'armed neutrality' takes on the proportions of black farce. If one considers the possibility of McClellan's victory, the delphic ambiguity of the *Herald*'s editorials for a fortnight before the election, and especially during the final three days, comes more sharply into focus. As late as 2 November the *Tribune* described the *Herald* as a 'McClellan Journal'. If McClellan had won, would Bennett have claimed a reward? Had he not been loyal to McClellan all through the war and supported his nomination? Had he not said that he was a better man than Lincoln, despite the hindrance of the Chicago platform? Had he not fought his battles against the copperheads, while opposing the abolitionists and the administration? Had the *Herald* advised anyone to vote against McClellan? On election day, had the paper not said that if McClellan won the Union would be restored?

Seen in this light Bennett's 'neutrality' becomes more than a shift in Lincoln's favour, as it has sometimes been described. It was a shift in favour of Lincoln *or* McClellan, whichever won. As with Buchanan and Fremont in 1856, Bennett was covering both eventualities in the hope of playing jackal to the victor.

If this was Bennett's blackmail scheme it had a certain justice in it for if the politicians were bargaining with Bennett's ambition he was also playing with theirs. He would be safe from exposure by the losing party because they stood to damage their own reputation more than his.

Bennett's own sympathies may fairly be said to have been with the Democratic party originally, but if the Democrats had helped themselves earlier by disowning the copperheads, as Bennett advised, the *Herald* might have more enthusiastically helped them to win the floating vote. If the Peace Democrats received undue publicity in the *Herald*, the War Democrats could only blame their own supineness. Had they been more active and less timid about taking a stand against the peace wing, Bennett might never have found it tempting to seek 'insurance' from Lincoln. It should be considered that a powerful newspaper editor could only make such terms in a very closely contested election which each party considered crucial to win, like the one in New York State.

It must have given Bennett great pleasure to be courted by the mighty and still tell the nation on election day that it had a choice of

[75]Carl Sandburg guessed at this possibility in *Abraham Lincoln: The War Years* (NY 1939), vol. 3, p. 248.

evils. But the final trump came when Bennett replied to Lincoln's offer of the French mission. Sixteen full days elapsed between Lincoln making the offer on 20 February 1865 and Bennett's answer on 6 March. Perhaps the editor was savouring his honour.

Bartlett wrote to Lincoln on 28 February saying 'Mr. J. G. B. informed me this morning that he would give his answer Monday next . . . [i.e. 6 March] . . . I propose to leave for Washington with it the same evening, and to call on you Tuesday morning.'[76] In fact Bartlett was three days late, detained in Pennsylvania by ice.

The Senate was due to adjourn on 11 March. If Bennett were to be confirmed as United States Minister to France time was short. Lincoln cabled Bartlett at Philadelphia on the 9th – 'It will soon be too late, if you are not here'.[77] There was no hurry: Bennett's letter was a refusal.

It was probably as remarkable a letter as the President ever received in his experience of editors and hungry office seekers. Having sought the post, Bennett now declined it in the following terms:

Fort Washington,
6th March 1865.

To His Exelency

The President of the United States

My Dear Sir,
   I have received your kind note in which you propose to appoint me Minister Plenipotentiary to full [*sic*] up the present vacancy in the important Mission to France. I trust that I estimate, at its full value, the high consideration which the President of the United States entertains and expresses for me by proposing so distinguished an honor. Accept my sincere thanks for that honor. I am sorry however to say that at my age I am afraid of assuming the labors and responsibilities of such an important position. Besides, in the present relations of France and the United States, I am of the decided opinion that I can be of more service to the country in the present position I occupy.

---

[76]Lincoln Papers, item 40961. Lincoln had telegraphed Wakeman on 26 Jan 1865 asking to see Bartlett — the first direct evidence of co-operation between Bartlett and Wakeman in the negotiations with Bennett. See Basler, vol. VIII, pp. 239-40; Bartlett to Lincoln 26 Jan 1865; Wakeman to Lincoln 26 Jan 1865; Bartlett to Lincoln 14 Feb 1865, Lincoln Papers items 40267, 40285 and 40686 respectively.

[77]Basler, vol. VIII, p. 346.

While, therefore, entertaining the highest consideration for the offer you have made, permit me most respectfully to decline for the same reasons assigned.

I am, my Dear Sir
With sentiments of the highest respect, your most
Obt. Sert.
James G. Bennett[78]

A. K. McClure thought that nothing in Bennett's career gratified him so much as the offer of the French mission.[79] That may be so, but it is just possible that refusing the honour gratified him even more. Almost any other editor in the country would have jumped at such a reward for political service. On one level the letter may be seen as Bennett's personal revenge on all his critics and detractors. Martin Van Buren had pushed him away thirty years earlier when the editor had solicited a reward which he felt he had earned for political loyalty. Now Bennett had the satisfaction of delivering a polite snub to the President of the United States who had sought his support. It is not inconceivable that he had solicited political preferment merely for the opportunity to refuse it.

But on another level, although he modestly declined to make his letter public, Bennett was teaching a lesson about the independent press. His proud boast that 'the notion which some people appear to entertain that the HERALD can be purchased except for four cents a copy at news stands – is beneath contempt'[80] has a rather hollow ring considering the cynical manner in which the French embassy was solicited. Nevertheless, Bennett had been offered a higher political post than Raymond, Webb or Greeley had ever attained, and had refused it. Like them, Bennett was engrossed in politics and relished his own influence. But he was content to exercise that influence as editor of the *Herald* and not as a professional politician. The *New York Herald* was his life and work, and he valued it too highly to share the notion that politics was somehow a finer and more important vocation than editing a paper. When he told the Chief Magistrate of the nation that 'I can be of more service to the country' in the *Herald* office than in one of the highest political positions which could be offered, there is no reason to doubt that he meant it.

Still, Bennett did ask one favour in patronage. He tried to have his old friend G. G. Fleurot re-appointed as Consul at Bordeaux, but

[78]Lincoln Papers, item 41070.

[79]*Abraham Lincoln and Men of War Times,* pp. 90-2.

[80]*NYH* 30 June 1865.

apparently Lincoln had taken no action on this at the time of his death.[81]

As for Lincoln, one can only wonder whether any motives other than the desire to pay a political debt for electoral support influenced his choice of Bennett for the French mission. If Bennett's name had been put up for confirmation in the Senate Lincoln must have anticipated protests from Republican ranks. To risk them he must have had positive reasons for choosing Bennett.[82] A point worth stressing is that the previous US minister to France, William L. Dayton, was still in office at the time of the Presidential election. As it happened Dayton died before the year was out, on 1 December, but if Lincoln did indeed promise Bartlett in November that Bennett should have the French mission then he must have contemplated the recall of the incumbent Dayton, who in truth enjoyed no very brilliant reputation.

Perhaps one should not underrate Mrs. Lincoln's influence on her husband, for she was known to take an interest in rewarding Bennett. On 12 March 1865 she wrote to Wakeman, 'I am sure you will always say a kind word to Mr. & Mrs. B[ennett] whose favour it would be most *impolitic* to ignore'. A week later: 'The papers appear to think it is one of Mr. L's "last jokes", the offer made to Mr. B. Lest he [Bennett] might consider, that it was intended as a jest, please do not fail to express my regrets to him – you will understand . . . that . . . [he] did not accept.'[83] On 13 April 1865 Mary Lincoln wrote to Bennett personally, as if to reassure him: 'We are rejoicing beyond expression, over our great and glorious victories and appreciate most gratefully your devotion to our cause and great influence exerted in crushing, this terrible rebellion.'[84] Whatever the feminine role, Lincoln must also have considered Bennett's personal recommendations. Prominent among these were his knowledge of French and his domestic connection with Paris – very few American representatives in those days had any such local familiarity or linguistic skill.

Bartlett himself wrote the tribute to Bennett which appeared in the *Tribune* of 15 March, in terms which he thought would gratify Lincoln:

[81]Bartlett to Lincoln 22 Mar 1865, Lincoln Papers, item 41290. Bartlett wrote cryptically, 'it was in reference to this matter that Mr. Blair's assurance proved delusive four years ago'. See chapter 3 on Fleurot's appointment by Buchanan.

[82]James Parton in 'The New York Herald', *North American Review,* 102 (April 1866), 373-419, frankly opined that Lincoln had blundered in overrating Bennett's influence — but again this was with post-election hindsight.

[83]Mary Lincoln to Abram Wakeman 12, 20 Mar 1865 in J.G. & L.L. Turner, p. 180. See also Ruth P. Randall, *Mary Lincoln* (Boston 1953), p. 349.

[84]Turner and Turner, p. 219.

> Since Benjamin Franklin – in every sense our first ambassador to France – we do not remember that an Editor has till now been designated for that post, which demands in its incumbent a full and intimate knowledge of our own and of European politics, a ripe general experience, and a special familiarity with the character and career respectively of the leading statesmen of Europe. These qualifications, we presume, dictated the selection of the veteran Editor of the *Herald*.[85]

Did Lincoln have anything else in mind? In domestic policy did he want to be sure of the *Herald*'s strong support for a conservative reconstruction programme to offset radical opposition? Was he at last making that bid for War Democrat support which Bennett had always urged on him? Or was he intent on getting Bennett out of the country to clear the path for a more radical course? Nor can Lincoln have been oblivious to the effect that Bennett's appointment would have had on Europe. The *Herald*'s editor was celebrated as the staunchest and most vociferous champion of the Monroe Doctrine. To send Bennett to Paris would have been interpreted as due notice to Napoleon III that the United States intended to take a firm line on Mexico and that America was not to be trifled with by foreign monarchs. With the end of the war in sight Lincoln may have planned to use Bennett's aggressive republicanism to diplomatic advantage. One can only speculate.[86]

Anyway, Bennett was now reconciled with Lincoln. On 4 April, as the war was drawing to its cathartic close and excited crowds thronged in and around the *Herald* office waiting expectantly for war news, Bennett commented that Lincoln's bulletins from the front (the President was visiting the army in Virginia when Richmond fell) were so good that he would give him a job as a reporter on the *Herald* when his term expired. On 13 April the editor was full of praise for Lincoln's tentative approach to reconstruction and his generous spirit. In this Lincoln was the spokesman of the American people and the philosopher of common sense, said the *Herald*.

The *Herald* appeared in mourning after the President's assassination, with column rules reversed from 16 to 27 April, and Bennett paid a fulsome and manly obituary tribute to the generous hearted Lincoln, the 'morally magnificent' leader of American democracy.[87]

---

[85]NY *Daily Tribune* 15 Mar 1865; Bartlett to Lincoln 14 Mar 1865, Lincoln Papers, item 41244.

[86]Consul John Bigelow was eventually confirmed as ambassador to France.

[87]*NYH* 16, 17 Apr 1865.

14

THE *HERALD*, CHAMPION OF PRESIDENTIAL RECONSTRUCTION, 1865-6

> I think it is my duty to the country that your administration should be supported to the utmost – Bennett to President Johnson, 1 February 1866[1]

The sacrifice made by the North to maintain the Union had been terrible indeed. Of the 400,000 New Yorkers who served in the war (comprising one sixth of the total Union forces), 53,000 lost their lives – the greatest numerical loss of any state.[2] In early 1865 however the *Herald* reflected the elation of complete victory in calling for a speedy settlement without vengeance. 'Mercy to a fallen foe is one of the highest characteristics of manhood',[3] proclaimed Bennett: if Jefferson Davis should imitate Judas and hang himself it would be fitting and convenient, but the *Herald* actively opposed according the honour of martyrdom to the Southern leaders (save perhaps Jacob Thompson and his incendiaries in Canada). Let the others flee to Mexico. With Southern independence, states' rights and slavery dead, the *Herald* argued that the North could well afford generosity over such matters as confiscation and amnesty. The second half of 1865 might thus see a thoroughly reunited country able to confront the monarchies of Europe while getting on with the job of exploiting its own material resources.[4]

Lincoln's murder temporarily converted the *Herald* to a vindictive line against 'traitors'. It bowed to none in its enthusiasm to demonstrate Jefferson Davis's complicity in the assassination plot and it clamoured for a hasty military trial of the conspirators. Bennett now believed that at least 'a few exemplary cases of the halter' among Southern leaders would be necessary, and suggested that Davis, that 'son of a horsethief', should be hanged in the petticoats in which the *Herald* alleged he had been captured.[5]

[1] Andrew Johnson Papers, Library of Congress.

[2] For statistics on the state's military participation in the war see Frederick Phisterer, *New York in the War of the Rebellion, 1861 to 1865* (Albany 1890), esp. pp. 48, 84, 529. See also *NYH* 10 Jan 1865.

[3] *NYH* 15 Apr 1865. This editorial would have been set in print before the first news of Lincoln's shooting.

[4] See *NYH* e.g. 29 Jan 1865.

[5] *NYH* 19 Apr 1865 ff.; on Davis see esp. 28 Apr; 3, 15, 16, 17, 20, 28 May; 1 June. (Though see Don C. Seitz, *The James Gordon Bennetts*, NY 1928, pp. 205-6, for the

The man on whom the execution of justice ultimately depended now was President Andrew Johnson. Until Congress met in December reconstruction would be in his hands. In common with nearly every other political group and newspaper in the country the *Herald* hastened to express its confidence in Johnson and sought both to discover his policy and to identify itself with it.[6] The chief interest of the *Herald*'s history in the early years of reconstruction is the remarkable extent to which it made itself the leading Johnson paper in the country. Yet, more than being a mere mouthpiece, the *Herald* also attested the extent to which Johnson disappointed his supporters and threw away opportunities for achieving reunion on terms satisfying to Northern opinion.

For instance, in the critical weeks of April and May 1865, when the *Herald* was groping to align itself with the new President, it assumed that stern measures would be necessary to maintain order and to protect loyal white men in the South. Furthermore, astounding though it may seem, the *Herald* assured Johnson that it would sustain him if he took the expected step of requiring Negro suffrage from the South.[7] Bennett had actually determined in February to bring the *Herald* out for black suffrage.[8] Mere sensationalism? Such a verdict rather begs the question. He judged the *Herald* to be in tune with popular wishes. True, he assured his readers that:

> There need be no fear that this concession will lead to negro social equality. Negroes vote in New York, and yet in New York there is no approach to negro social equality . . . negro suffrage in the reconstruction of the insurgent States will effectually spike the last gun of the Northern abolitionists and will expel or neutralize the fire eating political elements of the South for all time to come . . . best of all, the political agitation of the negro question, in every shape and form, will be ended, North and South.[9]

story that sometime in the late 1860s Davis was Bennett's house guest at Fort Washington). The *Herald*'s enthusiasm of the moment for the punishment of Southern leaders never undermined its regard for the Southern people generally as 'a portion of our own people, relieved of a savage, usurping despotism' — 3 May.

[6]*NYH* 16 Apr 1865, onwards.

[7]*NYH* 3, 6, 18, 20, 22 May 1865. The *Herald* also favoured heavy Northern immigration to the South at this time.

[8]W.O. Bartlett to A. Lincoln 28 Feb 1865, Lincoln Papers, LC, item 40961: 'The *Herald* is going to advocate extending the right of suffrage to negroes.' As late as 14 Apr 1865 however (the very day of the assassination), the *Herald* had surmised that Lincoln 'does not recognise the expediency of rushing the black slave, before breakfast, with all the disabilities of slavery upon him, to his own guidance as a freeman, including the right to vote'.

[9]*NYH* 3 May 1865. This theme had been foreshadowed in Bennett's headline of 1 Mar, 'The Almighty Nigger Gone at Last, North and South'. On 22 May the *Herald* again warned that Negro suffrage ought not to be an issue in 1868.

Nevertheless, when the *Herald*, even the conservative *Herald,* could speak of the utter impossibility of a free and enlightened people abandoning Negroes who had fought for the Union to 'political degradation',[10] the iron was hot indeed if President Johnson cared to strike by imposing a comprehensive plan of reconstruction.[11]

Johnson did not strike. His harsh threats against the South on taking office were soon moderated, and his customary scrupulous regard for states' rights began to reassert itself. Emboldened by the lack of provisions on the subject in the President's proclamations of 29 May,[12] the *Herald* qualified then abandoned its advocacy of Negro suffrage through executive intervention, although Bennett had temporary misgivings that the President was yielding an electioneering plank to the Republicans.[13]

By degrees the *Herald* came to appreciate that Johnson's political position was so anomalous as to make him what the paper had always yearned for – a President above (or at least aside from) party politics. For all its efforts the *Herald* had never succeeded in seducing Lincoln from his strong party allegiance. Now the White House was occupied by a man whose antecedents were strongly Democratic, although the war had made him a Republican almost by default. Johnson's experience as the loyal war governor of Tennessee had confirmed his independent instincts, and his attachment to the party which had chosen him as Lincoln's Vice-President from motives of political convenience had yet to be seriously tested.

The war had been a Republican triumph, but once the first shock of Lincoln's death had passed the *Herald* realised that the new President might be willing and able to make a peace acceptable to conservative opinion. In January the paper had exhorted Democrats to heartily endorse the thirteenth Amendment, abolishing slavery, so burying the issues and mistakes of the war years.[14] Johnson's apparent disposition to secure a speedy readmission of the Southern States suddenly made Democratic prospects much brighter than they had seemed after the 1864 débâacle. A chance to break Republican dominance was emerging almost providentially.

[10]*NYH* 19 June 1865.

[11]The times were indeed propitious for change when the *Herald* could discuss woman suffrage seriously, as it did on 27 May.

[12]Johnson issued an amnesty proclamation for restoring a loyal state government in North Carolina which became a model for other states.

[13]*NYH* 31 May 1865.

[14]*NYH* 28 Jan; 1, 2 Feb 1865. Bennett had harsh words for those Democratic 'Bourbons', including Fernando Wood, who had voted against the amendment in Congress.

True to its traditions, before May was out the *Herald* had begun to define and dramatise the differences between Johnson and the Radical Republicans over reconstruction, encouraging the President to defy the wrath of the 'negro worshippers' and pursue his 'popular, practical, conservative and constitutional policy' of rapid restoration of the South to full participation in the Union.[15] By June the *Herald* was campaigning for the formation of a 'Soldiers' and Sailors' Party', to be composed of veterans, War Democrats and conservative Republicans.[16] This party would sustain Johnson against the still dangerous 'Jacobins' whose latest ploy, the *Herald* revealed, was to incite Southern Negroes to a race war against their former masters, which would lead to racial 'amalgamation' and a ruinous national debt to maintain their political power in the South.[17] To combat such 'treacherous schemes' the *Herald* sought to promote its new party by organising a pro-Johnson demonstration in New York in August.

Bennett sent Henry Wikoff to the White House to explain his views on reconstruction, and in an introductory letter informed the President that 'We are preparing to get up a demonstration in opposition to the Boston agitators which I think will be successful at all hazards. . . .'[18] Small wonder that the *Tribune,* commenting on its political correspondence from North Carolina, complained that

> When scarcely any other newspaper circulates in all the State [North Carolina] the lying and insidious New York *Herald* worms its slimy way everywhere. On all railroad trains, on all steamboats, in all hotels, one meets its disgusting presence, and its iterated and reiterated tale of a division of the Northern friends of the Union on the [negro] suffrage question – that the President, with a portion of the Union party, is to disentomb the old democratic party, and then, uniting with a pro-slavery, negro-hating party of the South, be in good condition for dividing the national patronage.[19]

From this time onward the *Herald* was apparently encouraging and abetting Johnson in the provocative course which led to a disastrous collision with the Republican dominated Congress. Yet retrospect may be deceptive. Bennett did not intend to take on the bulk of the

[15]*NYH* 31 May; 1, 2 June 1865.

[16]*NYH* 4, 8, 9, 10, 11, 13-19, 21, 25 June 1865.

[17]*NYH* 23, 24, 27 June 1865.

[18]Bennett to Johnson 26 Aug 1865, Johnson Papers, Library of Congress. See also *NYH* same date.

[19]NY *Daily Tribune* 15 Aug 1865.

Republican party by championing a reactionary and unpopular course, although that is what Johnson eventually did.

The *Herald* assumed that if Johnson could persuade the restored Southern state governments to recognise a minimum programme of obligation to the victors – an acceptance of the Thirteenth Amendment and the disqualification of high ranking ex-Confederates from office-holding, plus *local* initiative on civil rights for Negroes – then he could secure a broad conservative support in the North adequate to ensure readmission before 1865 was out. Those Radical Republicans contemplating more extensive and severe federal reconstruction measures would be left out on a limb. The *Herald* loved nothing better than to have an unpopular minority to attack.

Thus in the summer of 1865 the *Herald* advised the South that its best interest lay in co-operation with the President. As late as 1 July it carried this advice for the defeated:

> The Question for the South –
> Whether the Southern States shall make their four millions of emancipated blacks a political balance of power for the South, or permit the Northern abolition radicals to use this element of political strength against the South? . . . If the loyal whites authorized by the President to re-organize the late rebel States will only face the new order of things like wise men, and practically admit the principle that the emancipated negro is a citizen, and, under certain restrictions, is entitled to the right of suffrage, they cannot be kept out of Congress, and they will soon have the game for the next Presidency in their own hands.[20]

When even the *Herald* advised it to give ground to Northern opinion the South might have done well to comply. Instead the notorious 'black codes' denying Negroes civil rights, provoked Bennett to call Southern legislators 'stupid'. The *Herald* pleaded with them to strengthen Johnson's arm against the radicals by meeting him half way, but they did not.[21] Johnson was left in the position of having dealt generously with the South without exacting the political guarantees thought necessary by most Republicans.

Nevertheless, with Congress meeting in December, the *Herald* chose to fall in behind Johnson, trusting his popularity and ability to forestall the radicals and achieve reunion. In October Johnson wrote to Bennett 'simply to render you my thanks, for the able and disinterested manner in which you have defended the policy of the

[20]See also *NYH* 30 June 1865.

[21]*NYH* 21 Sept; 7, 8, 31 Oct 1865.

Administration, since its accession to power. It is the more highly appreciated, because it has not been solicited, but voluntarily tendered. I feel grateful for your timely help. . . .' The President went on to say that he believed his liberal reconstruction terms to be the most popular, although perhaps significantly he failed to express with any clarity what his terms were. He concluded: 'There is no man in America who can exercise more power in fixing the government upon a firm and enduring foundation than you can – with such aid the task will be made easy. . . .'[22]

Bennett, thanking Johnson for his 'noble letter', replied: 'I take a deep interest in the success of your administration because I think that your policy is . . . right . . . and will lead to reunion and prosperity.'[23]

When Congress met it refused to seat Southern members, so in effect condemning Presidential reconstruction. Accordingly during the winter of 1865-6 we find the *Herald* extolling 'Andy' as its own, attacking 'Mephistopheles' Thaddeus Stevens and the radical leadership in Congress with all its habitual venom, and declaring that 'the secession rebellion is over, the radical rebellion has begun'.[24] Just as the *Herald* blamed the Civil War on abolition 'agitators', so it held the Republicans solely responsible for the perpetuation of disunion during this phase of reconstruction. In both cases the arguments and analyses supplied by Bennett against the Republican party were to reappear in 'milk and water' versions (to employ one of the editor's own phrases) in certain 'revisionist' histories in later decades. Indeed, Bennett's ingenuity in impugning the motives and actions of the Republicans left little for elaboration by later historians.

The *Herald* was particularly thorough in its indictment of the Freedmen's Bureau, the government agency charged with the welfare of Southern Negroes. It poured forth tirades charging the Bureau with being a mere scheme to keep blacks in idleness at the expense of Northern taxpayers, or else to channel the funds into corrupt Republican pockets.[25] Johnson, the *Herald* trumpeted, 'unlike the members of Congress, does not forget that there are white men in the country'.[26] In February 1866, after sending in his veto (on states' rights grounds) of the Congressional Bill for the extension of the

---

[22]Johnson to Bennett 6 Oct 1865, Johnson Papers, LC.

[23]Bennett to Johnson 15 Oct 1865, *ibid.*

[24]*NYH* 22 Feb 1866.

[25]*NYH* 13, 14 Sept 1865; 28 Jan; 17, 20, 21 Feb 1866.

[26]*NYH* 9 Feb 1866.

Freedmen's Bureau, Johnson had his private secretary write that the *Herald*'s latest article supporting the President's action was 'highly approved'.[27] Johnson had evidently ignored the warning given him earlier by Joseph Medill of the Chicago *Tribune* not to judge 'the political opinions of the twenty millions of Northern people from the columns of the New York *World* or *Herald*'.[28]

Meanwhile, seeing the inability of Congress to agree on its own terms for a settlement with the South, Bennett had counselled Johnson privately.

> Stevens and the radicals have now declared war against your administration – It is clear now that something should be done of a practical character – I believe that with proper skill the conservative interests of Congress could now be invited under the programme of your administration so as to give you a majority for all public purposes – I am perfectly satisfied that the extreme radicals are in a minority in the Congress but they intend to do everything they can to prevent any division in their ranks so as to be able to carry the next elections for Congress. Now or pretty soon is the time for your friends to act.[29]

In other words, Bennett still expected Johnson to undercut the exremists on reconstruction by rallying conservative Republicans and Democrats around him. To do this the *Herald,* notwithstanding its opposition to the Freedmen's Bureau Bill, naturally assumed that Johnson would sign the Civil Rights Bill in March 1866. It called the bill, making Negroes citizens, both 'practical' and 'constitutional' and believed Johnson would sign it to ensure rapid readmission of the South.[30] To its surprise, the President vetoed the bill. He had, as the *Herald* had always desired, made clear his utter hostility to the 'Jacobins', but Johnson had exceeded even Bennett's counsel by in effect throwing down the gauntlet to the whole array of Republican opinion.

The *Herald* loyally reversed itself and now discovered that the Civil Rights Bill had contained 'the most flagrant devices for overriding the reserved rights of the States in their legislatures and tribunals ever attempted by Congress . . . [it is] . . . nothing less than a

[27]W. Rives to James G. Bennett Jr. 19 Feb 1866, Johnson Papers, LC.

[28]Quoted in James E. Pollard, *The Presidents and the Press* (NY 1947), p. 401.

[29]Bennett to Johnson 1 Feb 1866, Johnson Papers, LC; see also *Herald* for Jan-Feb 1866.

[30]*NYH* 17 Mar 1866. Text of the bill and Johnson's veto in H.S. Commager, *Documents of American History* (NY 1968), vol. 1, pp. 464-8.

bill of unconstitutional abominations from beginning to end'.[31] The *Herald* challenged its readers,

IS THIS A WHITE MAN'S GOVERNMENT

for white men?

The Civil Rights bill says that it is not.[32]

Nevertheless Congress repassed both the Civil Rights and Freedmen's Bills over Johnson's veto and the President was in dire danger of appearing to Northern voters as a mere defender of unrepentant rebels. The *Herald*'s editorial course in the following weeks made it clear that Bennett believed that Johnson must devise some new means of rallying support to his own reconstruction policies other than mere obstructionism: 'Something better than this is wanted, Mr. President, to bring your administration in front of the Republican party and not behind it.'[33]

The editor believed that bold and sensational strokes were the recipe for success in politics as well as in journalism, and the *Herald* was fertile in expedients. It pressed Johnson to pursue a vigorous foreign policy, especially towards England. It also advised him to purge federal officeholders from the cabinet downwards and replace them with his own appointees, and to bring forward financial and banking questions as 'live issues'.[34] It may be doubted with hindsight whether such initiatives would have strengthened Johnson,[35] but both publicly and privately Bennett urged the President to try them.

Fortunately we have some intimate glimpses of the way in which *Herald* editorial opinion was formed during this period. A series of letters survives to the President from one W. B. Phillips, an editorial writer for the *Herald*. Phillips was a southern sympathiser, 'some might be disposed to call me a secessionist', though he denied having taken part in the rebellion and had come North from New Orleans in

[31]*NYH* 28 Mar 1866.

[32]*NYH* 28, 30 Mar 1866.

[33]*NYH* 15 June 1866.

[34]For Bennett's suggestions for a vindictive patronage policy see *NYH* 12, 13, 25 Apr; 19 May: on foreign expansion 5, 9, 12, 15 June; 1 July 1866. In his letter to Johnson of 26 Aug 1865, Bennett had suggested to the President that foreign policy was equally as important as domestic and had hinted 'if I had any idea what your government thought on that subject I could in my own way aid and assist your administration with more efficiency'. See also chapter 2 above.

[35]The feasibility of Bennett's suggestions is examined and adversely criticised in Eric L. McKitrick, *Andrew Johnson and Reconstruction* (Chicago 1960), pp. 364 ff.

December 1862.[36] Besides having aspirations as a novelist[37] Phillips was politically a devoted Johnson man. He was importuning the President for a position as his personal secretary, or else as an unofficial government agent to Europe,[38] and he sent Johnson cuttings of the editorials he had written for approval. If Johnson should desire to express his views or wishes on any subject, Phillips volunteered himself 'happy to attend to them'.[39] In February 1866, he was assuring Johnson that he had Bennett's word that 'the paper will heartily support you in the great and good work', but cautioning that 'although I have some influence with Mr. Bennett and my advice is often taken, he takes a stand sometimes entirely independent of the opinions of anyone'.[40]

By late May 1866, Phillips had to report apologetically that Bennett was privately less than happy about Johnson's political management of the reconstruction issue:

> Mr. Bennett has manifested lately a good deal of impatience with regard to your course with the cabinet and radical office-holders. He came down to the office on yesterday and discussed the matter pretty fully with me. The leading editorial in yesterday's paper will give you an idea of the views he entertains. But he was more emphatic in conversation than that. He is firmly convinced that you cannot sustain yourself in any other way than by a bold,. striking and prompt action with the opponents of your administration. His arguments are that the radicals are able to carry the timid and wavering conservatives with them because you are not decisive and bold enough in using patronage in your hands against them and in favour of those who do support you. You 'are gone' he says unless you take the boldest and most decisive course and thus rally all the conservatives to you. The country he argues is impatient and tired of the present unsatisfactory state of things . . . The paper may take a turn unfavourable to you unless you take the course mentioned. The *Herald*, as you are aware, goes with the strongest, or with the party it believes to be the strongest, and Hercules like it will help those who do and can help themselves. Mr. Bennett believes your policy as to reconstruction and in general a good one, and he is satisfied the

[36]See W.B. Phillips to Johnson 5 Mar 1866, Johnson Papers, LC.

[37]See Phillips to Johnson 3 June 1866, Johnson Papers, in which Phillips hopes the President will have time to read his novel.

[38]Phillips to Johnson 25 June; 7 Aug 1866, Johnson Papers. In the latter note Phillips complained that the Secretary of State 'seemed to think I was disposed to be unnecessary troublesome'.

[39]Phillips to Johnson 5 Dec 1865; see also same to same 24 Nov, Johnson Papers.

[40]Phillips to Johnson 23 Feb 1866, *ibid.*

sentiment of the country is with you, but he thinks you may lose all the advantage of this by the persistency, tact and ability of the radicals if you do not disarm them and separate the wavering conservatives from them.[41]

One week later Phillips felt that the President should be alarmed at the 'manifest disposition in our editorial conference yesterday to find fault with the Government' and that the *Herald* was 'strongly inclined to make a new start'.[42]

Johnson was at last trying to mobilise political support for himself, although half a year had passed since Bennett had advised him: 'Now or pretty soon is the time for your friends to act'. According to Phillips, the feeling in the *Herald* office was that Johnson had left it rather late to expect success from the Union Convention planned for Philadelphia in August.[43] Consequently he wrote to the President on 1 July: 'The *Herald* is a little on the fence relative to the proposed Convention. If the movement takes a vigorous start and it looks looks like being successful the paper will support it.'[44]

The Philadelphia Convention did indeed start generating some enthusiasm. The presence of Southern delegates there would symbolise reconciliation. Raymond of the *Times* lent his active support to the movement. Since his election to Congress Raymond had been increasingly at odds with the more radical members of his party and had become a champion of moderation towards the South. For once the *Herald*'s sense of expediency and the *Times*' principles led in the same direction. On 17 July Phillips assured the President that 'I think we are fairly committed to sustain the Philadelphia Convention movement'.[45]

From that time onwards the public was certainly given no reason to suspect that the *Herald* was not as wholeheartedly in favour of Johnson as ever. 'Our strategy, like General Grant's, consists in getting as close to the enemy as possible', said Bennett,[46] and he waded into the congressional campaign with all the bitter animosity characteristic of the 1850s, denouncing the Republican party, from 'the cadaverous, pale faced and canting New England parson to the

[41]Phillips to Johnson 20 May 1866, *ibid.,* Phillips added that he would do his best to influence Bennett in Johnson's favour.

[42]Phillips to Johnson 3 June 1866, *ibid.*

[43]Phillips to Johnson 25 June 1866, *ibid.*

[44]*Ibid.*

[45]*Ibid.*

[46]*NYH* 19 Sept 1866.

blackest and strongest smelling African',[47] as traitors seeking to perpetuate disunion. The love feast at Philadelphia, where former rebels, copperheads, War Democrats and Republicans mingled in the Convention chaired by John A. Dix, was reported as a great success.[48] When Johnson effectively upheld local white authorities responsible for bloody race riots in New Orleans, Bennett met Republican protests with charges that they were merely playing the 'bleeding Kansas' game again. The *Herald* accused the Republicans of instigating the riots and making the unfortunate Negroes 'human sacrifices for political capital'.[49] Plus ça change. . . .

By the first week in September the *Herald* was brimful of campaign fight. The issues were now before the people to its utter satisfaction. The President, it explained, stood for the final settlement of the Civil War by the readmission of the South with no conditions save the Thirteenth Amendment. All questions of civil rights, labour relations and enfranchisement would be left with the individual Southern states, and the nation would be rid of the sectional problem. On the other hand the Republicans wanted to exclude the South from Congress until some guarantee of Negro rights had been secured, and they realised that it would be impossible to impose any conditions on the South once ex-Confederates were seated with their rights unimpaired. When President Johnson arrived in New York to begin his speaking tour of the Northern States, the *Herald* claimed that his vindication at the polls was certain.[50]

Phillips' previous correspondence prepares us for what followed. Within a fortnight, by the third week of September 1866, the *Herald* had reversed itself and abandoned Johnson to his fate. What had happened was simply that Johnson had made a fool of himself by his stump speeches in his notorious 'Swing around the Circle'. The reception he got in the North persuaded Bennett of the President's unpopularity. Phillips could only apologise to Johnson for his own failing influence:

> You have noticed, probably, that the *Herald* has commenced a new course, and one less cordial to your administration and the conservative party than heretofore. I need hardly say that I regret this very much and that I was unable to prevent it. . . . The *Herald* cares nothing for party and likes to 'pitch in' (to use its

[47]*NYH* 4 Sept 1866.
[48]*NYH* 12-18 Aug 1866.
[49]*NYH* 4, 6, 14 Aug 1866.
[50]*NYH* 30, 31 Aug; 2 Sept 1866.

own peculiar expression) to all parties in turn. Nor does it care about individual public men, though for some there exists always a personal regard and for others a persistent dislike. It aims to be independent, and like the *London Times* in this respect, but its course is decided more by capricious moods or personal feeling than by large and liberal views or fixed principles. Yet at the bottom Mr. Bennett is not without patriotism or generous sentiments; nor are these apparent fitful words without a motive. While he is naturally disposed to change with the changing tide, or when he believes the tide is going to change, he makes this subservient to his business interests. His business is in the midst of an . . . excitable people and he attracts attention to his paper by doing startling or exciting things . . . the election in Maine had impressed Mr. Bennett with the belief that the whole of the States will go the same way this fall, that, in fact, the voice of the majority of the Northern people is in favor of the republicans . . . [but he] . . . will continue to assail the radicals as fiercely as ever. He thinks your trip to Chicago was unfortunate, and has done you no good. Another motive for the course he is now taking is his opposition, on personal grounds in part, to Mr. Hoffman, the nominee of the state conservative [Democratic] convention for governor.[51]

The *Herald* itself chronicled Bennett's conversion to the view that the President had exhausted his own and the 'conservatives' political capital, and was heading for a clash with Congress which could do nothing for the South.[52] Not only did Bennett concede with some grace, for the first time in a dozen years, that the Northern majority were in favour of Republican measures, but he counselled both the President and the South to accept the Fourteenth Amendment, which aimed at conferring citizenship on Negroes,[53] as the best bargain available. Bennett was at least being consistent in advocating the quickest practical means for readmission of the South. As Phillips expressed it, the South would do well 'to take what she can get – to swallow even the constitutional amendment, as a man would a nauseous dose of medicine to relieve himself from a painful disease'. Otherwise, 'the political disabilities of the South may become

[51]Phillips to Johnson 16 Sept 1866, Johnson Papers. Bennett's own preference for Governor would have been John A. Dix. Aside from Dix's personal merits, there was about this time some talk of Bennett's son becoming engaged to Dix's daughter — see James Buchanan to 'Mr King', 2 May 1867, in J.B. Moore ed., *The Works of James Buchanan* (NY 1960), vol. XI, p. 445.

[52]*NYH* 15 Sept 1866 onwards. For the campaign in New York generally see Homer A. Stebbins, *A Political History of the State of New York, 1865-1869* (Columbia 1913), ch V; and for the Democratic reaction to Bennett's desertion *ibid.,* p. 113.

[53]The Fourteenth Amendment had passed through Congress on 16 June 1866, and up to this time the *Herald* had attacked it.

chronic'.[54] After all, Bennett reasoned, no confiscation or direct enfranchisement was involved in the amendment; the South would never get better terms, and once back in the Union would have enough strength to defeat the 'radicals' and nullify their acts.[55]

The sequel is quickly told. Victory at the polls in November 1866, gave the Republicans a two thirds majority in Congress. Johnson was rebuked by the voters and the *Herald* conceded that by the 'law of necessity' both the President and the South must go under the yoke of the Fourteenth Amendment as the Republican ultimatum. When neither would do so willingly the *Herald* disowned them. Continuing intemperance and obstruction south of the Mason-Dixon line caused the paper to declare that the former rebels had insured Republican rule for twenty years and had voluntarily chosen exclusion.[56]

As for Johnson, by early 1867 the *Herald*'s latest sensation was to lead the clamour for his impeachment and to denounce his 'wilful and wicked' obstructionism.[57] But this departure too proved only temporary. When in the summer of 1867 Johnson attempted to oust Stanton from office, Bennett's cordial dislike for the Secretary of War caused him to rally again to the President's support.[58] In 1868 the *Herald* finally opposed Johnson's impeachment, seeing no sense in punishing him more severely than Jefferson Davis. But although Johnson wrote to Bennett that 'I am glad that you have come so vigorously to the rescue',[59] the editor apparently did not bother to reply. He had little time for failures, and had long since understood that 'General Grant, whether he desires it or not, is destined to be the next President'.[60] The course of the *Herald* was shaped accordingly, and it was left for Phillips to write another of his consoling letters to Johnson, regretting his employer's lack of enthusiasm for the idea of a second term.[61]

Even before the political struggle of 1866, Bennett had been looking for viable financial and foreign issues to replace the flagging

[54]Phillips to Johnson 7 Oct; 8 Nov 1866, Johnson Papers.

[55]*NYH* esp. 15, 18, 19, 20, 21, 24, 29 Sept; 5, 6, 10, 13, 17, 19, 22 Oct 1866; Phillips to Johnson 16 Sept 1866, Johnson Papers.

[56]*NYH* 8, 10, 14, 17 Nov; 4, 7, 9, 16, 25, 27 Dec 1866

[57]The *Herald* had predicted for many months that impeachment would be attempted, but had of course opposed it. For comment on its volte face see NY *Daily Tribune* 21 Jan 1867; and Phillips to Johnson 25 Jan 1867, Johnson Papers.

[58]See *NYH* Aug 1867; Phillips to Johnson 7 Aug 1867, Johnson Papers.

[59]Johnson to Bennett 21 Mar 1868, Johnson Papers.

[60]*NYH* 23 Feb 1866; see also Phillips to Johnson same date, Johnson Papers.

[61]Phillips to Johnson 8 July 1868, *ibid.*

sectional quarrel as a source of headlines. He had the newspaperman's sense that Americans now wanted to read about other things than North and South, and to maintain its circulation the *Herald* must anticipate and obey their wishes.

15

'SHOULD HISTORY CONDESCEND TO PEN IT, WHAT WOULD ITS VERDICT BE ON BENNETT?'

— Anon. poem, *c.*1865, Ford Collection, NYPL

From 1867 onwards the story of the *Herald* is properly that of Bennett's son. In fact, during 1866 James G. Bennett Jr. had been taking the prominent role in the management of the *Herald* for which his father had carefully groomed him. Gradually Bennett senior came less frequently to the office, save when a particular political theme struck his imagination. Hudson left early in 1866, so breaking a working partnership of thirty years. He retired to write his history of journalism, supposedly sponsored by Bennett to the extent of $6,000.

The founder of the *Herald* gave his son his 'entire confidence'[1] to carry on the paper, but some *Herald* staff had misgivings. Warning Johnson in June 1866, that the political opinions of Junior were now of some consequence in the *Herald* office, W.B. Phillips had mentioned that 'young Mr. Bennett, who has a great deal to do with the paper since Mr. Hudson left. . . is self-willed and not very steady or comprehensive in his views'.[2]

In April 1867, the *Herald* moved to impressive new premises on the former site of Barnum's Museum.[3] On 21 April under the familiar centre page heading

JAMES GORDON BENNETT — EDITOR AND PROPRIETOR

the paper reviewed its own history and prophesied a glorious time when there would be *Herald* bureaux in all the major cities of the world and when the paper might be delivered within minutes of

---

[1]Bennett to Johnson 15 Oct 1865, Johnson Papers, Library of Congress: 'what is said to him will be the same as if said to me. . . . No other person has my exclusive confidence but my son.' Phillips described the old man's confidence as 'overweening'.

[2]Phillips to Johnson 3 June 1866, *ibid.* The writer added that the younger Bennett presided at editorial conferences in his father's absence and was even more inclined to desert the President at that stage. On another occasion (16 Sept) Phillips wrote that Bennett Jr. 'is more changeable than his father, while his judgement is more defective and his information limited'.

[3]For opposing versions of how the *Herald* acquired these premises see *NYH* 2, 3, 9 Oct etc; 23 Nov 1865; P.T. Barnum, *Struggles and Triumphs* (London 1869), ch XLI, and Don C. Seitz, *The James Gordon Bennetts* (NY 1928), ch 6.

publication by 'pneumatic express'. Next day there was a change. The centre page heading read

JAMES GORDON BENNETT, PROPRIETOR
JAMES GORDON BENNETT JR., MANAGER

April 22 1867, may be designated the beginning of a new era for the *Herald*.[4] Although the founder still influenced the paper's politics and contributed the occasional article, *Herald* editorials never quite regained their old flair and bite. By 1870 it was a rather conservative, well-printed journal costing five cents and bearing little resemblance to the cheerful little scandal sheet of 1835.[5] Although in the years after the Civil War intelligent observers could indulge in the rather smug belief that sensationalism was a thing of the past,[6] ironically in the following decades Pulitzer and Hearst were to 'out-Bennett Bennett' by rediscovering a class which the advance of 'serious' journalism had left behind. They applied to the newspaper market in the last quarter of the nineteenth century the formulas Bennett had developed in the second. During the 1880s Pulitzer's *World* succeeded the *Herald* as the cheapest, most sensational, most popular paper of the day.[7] Later the *Herald* was slow to adopt the banner headline and photographic illustration, which made Hearst's 'Yellow Press' such a dramatic financial success;[8] though in response to changing times it is said that during the 1890s the younger Bennett considered abandoning the editorial column altogether as a superfluous feature.[9]

Despite the colourful eccentricity of the younger Bennett, whose capriciousness and fabulous despotism parodied and surpassed the autocratic tendencies of his father, the *Herald* remained in the front

[4]See also A.E. Coleman, 'A New and Authentic History of the *Herald* of the Bennetts', *Editor and Publisher*, 56-8 (1924-5).

[5]In the late 1860s the *Herald* reverted to placing its advertisements on the front page.

[6]See for instance James Parton, 'The New York *Herald*', *North American Review*, 102 (1866), 373-419. 1865 saw the foundation of E.L. Godkin's *The Nation* in New York as an organ of liberal middle class opinion.

[7]A recent study is George Juergens, *Joseph Pulitzer and the New York World* (Princeton 1966). Commenting on the *Herald*'s tendency to grow conservative in the 1870s, Juergens recounts that the younger Bennett kept a list in the *Herald* office of his personal friends whom his editorial writers were not allowed to attack or criticise — p. 10.

[8]There is some material on the later history of the *Herald* during the rise of the 'Yellow Press' in the general histories of journalism by Mott, Emery and Kobre cited in chapter 1.

[9]'New York Editors and Daily Papers' — magazine clipping in box 84 of the Manton Marble Collection, University of London.

rank of American newspapers until the twentieth century.[10] Its news gathering service remained peerless, and the fulness of its reporting continued to command respect. In 1866, with the completion of the Atlantic telegraph cable, the *Herald* was spending more money than anyone else ($7,000 for one message)[11] for European news, and this tradition was maintained. In 1867 the younger Bennett purchased the NY *Evening Telegram,* and one of his early successes for the *Herald* was his despatch of Henry M. Stanley in search of Dr. Livingstone in darkest Africa.[12] Although by the time of his death in 1918 Bennett Jr. had drained the *Herald* of many of its resources and had lost ground to competitors, the paper was still a highly desirable inheritance.

The elder Bennett had intended to found a dynasty, and he meant the *Herald* to be a perpetual institution — a force in world politics as it had been in America. It was not to be. The younger Bennett left no heir. In 1920 the paper was sold for $4 million to Frank A. Munsey, whose brief tenure only emphasised the fact that the *Herald* without a Bennett in the chair was an impossibility. To any who remembered the great duels of Bennett and Greeley in the 1850s it must have seemed a supreme irony that in 1924 their two papers were merged. The elder Bennett's will had insisted that the name 'Herald' be retained always,[13] and so the *International Herald-Tribune* continues to be published to this day, chiefly for Americans in Europe.

In the years of his retirement Bennett Senior remained mentally active. Occasionally the septuagenarian would sweep in, carrying his familiar umbrella, to inspect the journalistic machine he had created and the examine the news exchanges. Even when pottering in his carpet slippers in his Fort Washington home, talking to the caged birds which he had individually named after the leading politicians and celebrities of the day, he kept complete files of the *Herald* to hand and was in touch with the office by his private telegraph line. He continued to be very much a man alone — 'He reigned apart, looking down upon. . . [the world]. . . with scorn.'[14] Although highly cultured personally, his

[10]As a starting point for reading on the younger Bennett there is Seitz; James Creelman, 'James Gordon Bennett', *Cosmopolitan,* 33 (1902); O.G. Villard, *Some Newspapers and Newspaper-Men* (NY 1923); and the fullest account by Richard O'Connor, *The Scandalous Mr Bennett* (NY 1962) which includes a bibliography. There is also a sketch in the *Dictionary of American Biography* and a recent article 'The Commodore' by Julia Lamb in *The Smithsonian,* Nov 1978, 132-40.

[11]*NYH* 11 Aug 1866. It printed a speech by the King of Prussia.

[12]For details see Oliver Carlson, *The Man Who Made News* (NY 1942), pp. 384-6.

[13]The Provisions of Bennett's will are summarised in Coleman, 'New and Authentic History', *Editor and Publisher,* 15 Nov 1824.

[14]John Russell Young, *Men and Memories* (NY 1901), pp. 210-12.

few acquaintances tended to be men of lower mental calibre than himself. Feeling towards him was generally softer than it had been in previous years, but still the faint odour of blackmail clung to him.[15]

The summer of 1872 was to have been spent in another visit to Europe. Bennett's wife and children had already departed across the Atlantic when, on 25 May, he suffered a slight convulsive fit. Twelve hours later he had another, more severe fit after which it was apparent that death was inevitable. At his request Archbishop McCloskey administered last rites at the bedside. As Bennett lay dying amid the gilded splendour of his town residence,[16] an accident to the *Herald*'s machinery caused it to miss a day's production — an incident significant to the superstitious. Only Frederic Hudson, Thomas B. Connery (then editor of the *Herald*), a cousin and a doctor were with Bennett when he died peacefully at 5.25 p.m. on Saturday 1 June 1872.[17]

Next day the *Herald* appeared in mourning, with column rules turned, just as it had after the assassination of Lincoln. Over the next fortnight it reprinted scores of obituaries from both the national and local press, without correction of factual inaccuracies but with adverse comments carefully edited out. That Bennett had been known more by reputation than in person was attested by the failure of a dozen or so biographical sketches to agree on even such basic facts as his age.

The *Herald* itself, as might be expected, praised Bennett's 'wonderful success' and the 'benefits conferred upon mankind by the genius, energy and liberality of the deceased'. Although the nation at this time was enjoying an orgy of corruption in business and politics, the paper did not doubt that the independent press had exercised a 'healthful influence over the politics and public men of the country', nor that to Bennett 'more than to any other individual the American newspaper owes its present high and honorable position'. It had praise for his private charity and for the 'loyalty and affection' in which his staff held him. (Who can avoid the suspicion that 'the Emperor' had prepared the article himself in advance?) A memorial service was held

---

[15]For sketches of Bennett in his last years by contemporaries see John Russell Young, pp. 207-14; Junius H. Browne, *The Great Metropolis* (NY 1869), pp. 491-8; and James H. Wilson, *The Life of Charles A. Dana* (NY 1907), pp. 485-9. See also Seitz, pp. 202 ff. and Carlson, ch 17.

[16]Number 425 Fifth Avenue, purchased in 1865.

[17]*NYH* 30 May - 2 June 1872. The *Tribune* used the accidental circumstances of the absence of Bennett's family to improve the moral picture of the sinner dying alone. Bennett's wife survived him by less than a year, dying on 28 Mar 1873.

in a Roman Catholic church at Washington Heights which he had endowed generously.[18]

At the other extreme the literary magazine, *American Bibliophilist,* testified that Bennett was still cordially hated in some quarters. It congratulated New Yorkers on Bennett's death, though it rather regretted that Providence had permitted him to die in his bed:

> His career is a conspicuous example of prosperous infamy... He deliberately and for purely selfish purpose appealed to the worst side of a democratic society, fawning upon the multitude, exalting its prejudices and caprices, and ministering eagerly to its prurient appetites and mean jealousies, and it can hardly be doubted that the result of his labors was to intensify the despotism of majorities and the truculence of the mob. . . . One opinion was just as good in his eyes as another. . . . His open cynicism and contempt for what he deemed the affectations of sincerity and earnestness, perhaps did more harm than his outrages on good taste and public morality. His abominable attacks on private character had not even the justification of honest indignation; they had no other motive than to make sport for the public, and possibly to add to the profits of his paper in another way... the success of what has been called Bennettism is a fact which cannot be got rid of and which can hardly be regarded as a healthy symptom.[19]

Other papers, searching for something good to say about 'Old Satanic', were just in according Bennett his place as the uncrowned king of the newspaper world. The consensus of opinion was with the *Sunday News,* which termed Bennett simply 'the greatest journalist the world ever produced'.[20] His death brought home to a generation of newspapermen which had grown up since 1830 just how far the press had advanced during Bennett's lifetime and under his influence, and indeed how 'the press' had become a self-conscious entity during that time. No one gainsaid his ability as a gatherer of news. Though the *Evening Express* thought the *Herald* capable of being hateful, vindictive and merciless, it admitted that his enemies had been little better, and that Bennett had many friends.[21] The *Times* went so far as

[18]*NYH* 2 June 1872. Carlson errs in saying that the *Herald* printed no obituary for its founder — it produced a full page article on 10 June.

[19]*Sabin & Son's American Bibliophilist,* 4 (1872), 394-6. In his *Diary* George T. Strong commented: 'I suppose that no one man can be named who has done as much to blunt the moral sense of the people on public questions as J.G. Bennett has done during the last thirty years... his paper has been, and is, a national curse' — see entries in vol. IV, pp. 86, 428, 430 (21 May 1866; 1, 13 June 1872).

[20]NY *Sunday News* 2 June 1872.

[21]NY *Evening Express* 3 June 1872.

to praise his 'indomitable energy and resolute will'. As preparations were made to lay him in Greenwood Cemetery, it was generally agreed that his true monument was the *Herald* itself.

The *Brooklyn Eagle* thought that Bennett's funeral on 13 June was the largest tribute that New York City had ever paid to a journalist.[22] Flags were flown at half mast by order of the Aldermen and Common Council, who attended as a group. Present at the service were Generals Nathaniel P. Banks, John C. Fremont and John Cochrane[23] and ex-Governor of the State Washington Hunt. Heavily represented also were the commercial grandees and the Democratic leadership of the city — Moses Grinnell, A.T. Stewart, August Belmont, Judges Barnard, Daly and Cardozo, Charles Delevan, Charles O'Conor, A. Oakey Hall, along with Roosevelts and Jeromes and lesser social and political lights. The pall bearers signified the unity and prestige of the journalistic world. Besides the ever faithful Hudson they included the most prominent editors and proprietors in the city — Charles A. Dana of the *Sun* (who considered Bennett 'the most brilliant, original and independent journalist I have ever known')[24], Erastus Brooks of the *Evening Express*, George W. Jones of the *Times*, and for the *Tribune* none other than Horace Greeley himself. Greeley was at this time a candidate for the Presidency as head of the Liberal-Republican movement.[25] In helping to bury his old rival he doubtless felt that his own generation was passing.

Greeley himself had penned the obituary on Bennett which had appeared in the *Tribune*.[26] In it he admitted that Bennett's career was an example of what unremitting industry could achieve, but he questioned whether this 'toilsome and sombre' life of pecuniary success was not also a warning. He recalled Bennett's coldness, his inconsistency and recklessness, his unjust and relentless personal prejudices, the suspicious nature which since 1840 had made him isolated, embittered and cynical. Trying to encapsulate a generation of

[22]The account which follows is based chiefly on the reports in the *Herald, Tribune* and *Times* for 14 June 1872.

[23]On 1 Feb 1866 Bennett had privately urged President Johnson to appoint Cochrane to the Collectorship of New York Port — Johnson Papers.

[24]Quoted in James H. Wilson, *Life of Charles A. Dana,* p. 485.

[25]The *Herald* was for Grant, but it had greeted Greeley's candidacy with a not ungenerous editorial on 5 May 1872. Greeley was not destined to survive the year: defeated in the election, he died broken in spirit in November. Henry J. Raymond had died in 1869, after over-exertion with his mistress in an episode the *Times* never found 'fit to print'. The *Herald's* obituary on Raymond is partially reprinted in Augustus Maverick, *Henry J. Raymond* (Hartford 1870), p. 212.

[26]Coleman, 'New and Authentic History'.

opposition to the *Herald*, the *Tribune* found Bennett's greatest failing in his neglect of 'public conscience'. Because his concept of journalism did not include 'a respect for the dignity of human nature', Greeley pronounced, 'he made the newspaper powerful, but he made it odious'.[27]

Now that we have followed Bennett to the end of his career, can we usefully add anything to Greeley's solemn judgement?

Even in the perspective of a century the editor of the *Herald* presents the historian with teasing paradoxes. It must be admitted that he, more than any other man, made 'the news' the democratic institution which it remains: yet his career raises many questions about the possible abuse of the press in a free society. Bennett had argued that the party press could not be relied upon to give the news impartially: yet the *Herald* had amply demonstrated that the 'independent' press is never in reality independent of the need to market its news to the largest possible number of buyers. Moreover, we have seen that Bennett's surviving correspondence with Pierce, Buchanan and Lincoln, revealing his desire for reward and recognition, makes nonsense of his claims to immunity from party considerations. The 'free press' can never be more virtuous or enlightened than the men who control it. If Bennett's wit, individualism and sometimes engaging roguery recall the spirit of John Wilkes, his unscrupulous manipulation of public opinion for financial and personal gain foreshadows the rise of Hearst and the race of cold-blooded press barons of the twentieth century. Indeed, for all the warmth of personality which infused his editorials, Bennett's contempt for 'man, shallow man'[28] was never far concealed.

But if Bennett's moral legacy to democracy is ambiguous, and if he defies ready classification, we can go further than previous biographers in placing him firmly in the context of his times. We can now see that he was more than merely a freak or gadfly on the American scene, as some contemporaries insisted. Indeed, although endlessly abused as a 'foreigner', Bennett followed an honoured American tradition, exemplifying (like Carnegie after him) the 'rags to riches' success story of the poor immigrant making good in the New World and dying fabulously rich. 'Enterprise' was Bennett's watchword and even his enemies had to admire his skill in that most hallowed of national pursuits — business. The *Times* admitted that 'as a successful

---

[27]NY *Daily Tribune* 3 June 1872.

[28]Bennett to William L. Marcy 15 Mar 1833, Marcy Papers, Library of Congress.

journalist and man of business James Gordon Bennett will be remembered among the representative men of the City of New York'.[29]

More than this, the historical continuities exhibited by the *Herald* are quite as significant as its dramatic turn-abouts. We have seen that Bennett, the renegade Democrat, was in many ways the exemplar of Jacksonian attitudes throughout his career. In Jackson's support in 1828 Bennett had denounced privilege and monopoly, upheld the cause of 'the people' and of equality of opportunity. The *Herald* very much embodied these ideas, not only in its editorials but most obviously in its price, content and presentation, and this, as we saw in chapter 1, was a vital element in its success. Typically Jacksonian too was the *Herald*'s brash expansionism and pride in American nationality and power: sentiments which contributed greatly to Northern victory in the Civil War. In 1864 the *Herald* was four years premature in nominating Grant, but Bennett's penchant for military heroes as candidates was also a throw-back to the successful formula of 1828.

Ironically too Bennett had learned in the school of Jacksonian Democracy in the 1820s and '30s the amoral spoilsman's attitude to politics which he carried into the 1850s and '60s. In his Democratic apprenticeship, too, he had learned how to personalise a political fight, a talent which he was to capitalise in the *Herald*. The paper's personalisation of issues, and the fact that it does not fit neatly under a party label, has caused the *Herald* to be historically neglected. Yet Bennett's bile against politicians was something more than the pursuit of a personal vendetta. He exploited the realisation that anti-politicianism and anti-partyism are, paradoxically, considerable influences on electoral behaviour. For a people so engrossed in political procedures, Americans have always shown a hearty scepticism about their elected representatives, and no one ever expressed that scepticism more pungently and wittily than Bennett. If the historian dismisses this attitude as unworthy of his attention he neglects something important about the way in which Americans thought about their affairs, as well as much of the colour and irony of the contemporary scene.

The 1850s and '60s saw the culmination of a debate over slavery, and historians have often drawn a contrast between the heroic era of Lincoln and Lee and the sordid world of Tweed, Fisk and Gould which arose from its ashes. But familiarity with the *Herald* can in

[29]NY *Times* 3 June 1872.

some respects provide a deeper perspective on the realities of the age. Certainly the reader of the *Herald* files, picking over its musty tales of bribery, 'shoddy', prizefighting, train crashes, street thuggery, tenement fires, overcrowded sweatshops and grogshop politics, will not be impressed by the existence of some golden age of innocence which ended in 1861. He will constantly be reminded that the era of Lincoln and Lee was also the era in which the likes of Thurlow Weed, Fernando Wood, and indeed Bennett himself were flourishing. The *Herald* reminds us that local personalities and issues and corruption at all levels of government shaped New York politics to an unsuspected degree, with effects on national affairs which few accounts have sufficiently emphasised.

Does the history of the *Herald* then support those who have denied the importance of slavery and race as moral issues in this period? Bennett himself would have fervently agreed with those historians who have explained the Civil War as an 'artificial' crisis, contrived by selfish and incompetent politicians and abolition 'fanatics'. He would have agreed with that school too in blaming Lincoln and his party for their apparent blindness to the possibility of war in 1860-1. Most of the arguments advanced by those who have laid a 'needless war' at the door of 'irresponsible agitators' were given a vigorous airing by the editor of the *Herald* during the crisis. The irony is of course that Bennett's inflammatory journalism actually added fuel to the sectional confrontation and helps us to understand why a 'conservative' solution was unacceptable to Republicans. Bennett insisted that it was impractical and even wrong to contemplate limiting slavery. The Republicans contended just the contrary. To see Americans in 1860 being dragged uncomprehendingly towards war over 'artificial' issues is therefore merely to beg the question. The *Herald's* scorn of the moral validity of the anti-slavery movement rather reinforces the impression that the Republicans and their opponents understood each other only too well on the crucial issues concerning the future of slavery within the Union. Ironically the 'conservative' Bennett dramatised the real and overriding debate between North and South so effectively that he seems to have done much to create amongst white men in both sections fear that their own rights in relation to Negro slavery were seriously imperilled by the aggressive policies of their opponents.

The *Herald's* virulently racialist attitudes towards Negroes and the values which it associated with the Union add a dimension to our understanding of the abolitionists, the Republican party and Lincoln's policies. To see anti-slavery men such as Greeley or Wendell Phillips through the columns of the *Herald* is to be forcibly reminded of the hostility their opinions met in large sections of Northern society and provides a measure of their achievement. Historically, too, it is more illuminating to see Lincoln through the eyes of his conservative critics of the 1860s than to measure him against the Civil Rights ideals of the 1960s. Although his approach to the slavery problem was too cautious for some of his own party, Lincoln was mindful of the weight of 'conservative' opinion he had to take with him if his policies were to receive general support. Thus while the *Herald* was the natural foil of the anti-slavery movement on its home ground it also became a barometer of its wartime progress. Because it confronts us afresh with the issues of the Civil War era as they were presented to Northern contemporaries, Bennett's paper remains an invaluable source for the politics and social life of its age.

Finally it would be naive to conclude, as Parton did in 1866, that Bennett's acknowledged gift for knowing what his readers wanted to find in the *Herald*'s news columns suddenly failed him when he prepared his editorials. When Parton pronounced Bennett 'the best journalist and the worst editorialist this continent has ever known',[30] he was passing a moral judgement that would hardly satisfy the market researcher or the historian. Furthermore, Bennett possessed one of the keenest iconoclastic minds of his generation, and it is quite wrong to dismiss him as just a colourful character unworthy of serious study. If his view of America was one-sided, it was at times remarkably clear and penetrating. It was left for the *Sun,* the *Herald*'s predecessor in the Penny Press experiment, to question the easy assumption of its rivals that it was news alone which made the *Herald* great, or whether its success and popularity were not due to the wit, genius and 'fascinating kind of eccentricity' of its editor. Its obituary conceded that Bennett was hardly 'fashioned to meet with our conventional approbation', but who could affirm, it asked, 'that if he had been constituted otherwise than he was he would have suited his day and generation so well as he has done. . . ?'[31]

[30] Parton, 'The New York *Herald*'.
[31] NY *Sun* 3 June 1872.

APPENDICES

APPENDIX 1

HERALD CIRCULATION

(a) **Daily circulation**

It is impossible to present a graph of *Herald* circulation during the period with anything like precision. Newspapers did not publish their circulation figures regularly, and even when they did one has to allow for an element of inflation for advertising purposes. For instance, Bennett was apt to make very boastful claims for the *Herald* in comparison with its competitors by taking its best daily circulation figure for a certain period for *all* editions and setting it against the monthly average for one edition of a rival. (Or sometimes, one suspects, he simply invented the figures for effect). Thus in January 1859 he could claim a circulation of 90,000 for the *Herald* against 19,000 for the *Tribune*.

The *Herald* apparently did keep sales records, though they are not now extant. Occasionally it published figures from them which contrasted with the estimates of Bennett's more bombastic moments. From these figures one may at least draw a broad picture of the generally upward growth of sales. Sworn statements of circulation submitted in competition for municipal advertising provide only a partial check because they refer only to sales within the most populous part of New York City. It should also be remembered that newspaper circulation is highly variable from month to month, week to week and day to day, depending on the excitement of the moment. Thus in 1856 the highest daily circulation for the *Herald* was 79,680 while the lowest was 56,090, and the average for the year something like 62,000. In March 1860 *Herald* sales averaged only 63,777 daily, yet news of a prize fight in England at the end of April boosted circulation to 104,160 on one day and 97,080 the next. Without claiming them as definitive, I therefore give the following estimates of average sales per day of the *Herald* in its daily edition only:

Sources for Appendix 1: *NYH* 15 Jan; 10 May; 21 Dec 1854; 10 Jan; 28 July; 6 Aug; 5 Sept 1856; 5 Jan 1857; 13 Jan; 20 June; 11 Sept; 10 Dec 1859; 14 Jan; 21, 30 Apr; 8 Nov 1860; 9 Jan; 4 Feb; 9, 15 Apr; 5 Dec 1861; 22 Jan 1862; 6 Jan; 10 June 1864; 5, 7 Apr; 19 July 1865; NY *Times* 8 May; Dec 1861; NY *Tribune* 6 Nov 1860; W.T. Coggeshall, *The Newspaper Record* (Philadelphia 1856), pp. 128, 142, 144, 147, 149-50; Daniel J. Kenny, *The American Newspaper Directory and Record of the Press* (NY 1861), pp. 47, 109, 121; Alfred M. Lee, *The Daily Newspaper in America* (NY 1937), pp. 728, 731.

		Daily Average Sales of the 'Herald'	Daily Average Sales of all US Newspapers
1840		17,000	2,200
1845		12-15,000	
1849		33,000	2,986 (1850)
1854		53,000	
1855		57,000	
1856		62,000	
1859		70,000	
1860	December	75,806	3,820
1861	January	85,303	
	March	84,813	
	December	104,480	
1864		110,000	

In 1861 the *Herald* sold 135,600 copies with the story of Fort Sumter – a record. In 1865 the news of the fall of Richmond and its sequel sufficed to sell 133,200 copies. In the year ending 1 May 1865 *Herald* receipts from all sources totalled $1,095,000.

(b) National distribution of *Herald* sales, 2 August 1856.
The following table appeared in the *Herald* for 6 Aug 1856, showing sales of the daily edition of the *Herald* on 2 August by state:

Free States		Slave States	
Maine	58	Delaware	235
New Hampshire	139	Maryland	1,153
Vermont	135	D.C.	317
Massachusetts	1,058	Virginia	176
Rhode Island	322	N. Carolina	41
Connecticut	2,146	S. Carolina	139
New York	47,275	Georgia	170
New Jersey	3,330	Kentucky	68
Pennsylvania	2,510	Tennessee	42
Ohio	200	Alabama	80
Indiana	36	Louisiana	88
Illinois	858	Mississippi	11
Wisconsin	38	Missouri	41
Michigan	256	Florida	45
Iowa	49	Texas	5
	58,410		2,611

Total   61,021

(c) **The *Herald* and its rivals, 1856.**

The following figures are derived from sworn statements submitted to the Post Office in New York in December 1856, and are based on averages over a period of weeks. (Advertising of lists of letters for collection was awarded to the paper with the highest circulation.)

Paper	Edition	Circulation
Herald	Daily	57,840 per day
	California	12,000
	European	2,000
	Weekly	21,500
	Total	93,340
Tribune	Daily	29,000
	Weekly	163,000
	Semi-Weekly	15,500
	California	6,000
	European	750
	Total	214,250
Times	Daily	42,000
	Weekly	35,000
	Semi-Weekly	10,000
	California	2,000
	Total	89,000
Sun	Daily	50,000
	Weekly	8,000
	Total	58,000

(d) **Newspaper reading in New York City.**
Athough the cheap press was pioneered in England, the *Herald* had a
greater circulation than the London *Times* in the 1850s. At this period
too, three times as many newspapers were read daily in New York as
in London, although the American metropolis had a smaller population.
Education, kerosene lamps and cheaper newspapers were all factors
in the growth of newspaper reading:

	Number of Daily and Sunday Papers in NYC	Total Average Circulation per day	Population of greater NYC
1833	12	29,200	
1836	16	60,000	
1840	18	60,000	391,114
1842	16	92,700	
1850	14	153,621	696,115
1855	19		
1860	18	300,000	1,174,779
1865	21	425,000	
1870	26	590,000	1,478,103

APPENDIX 2

A NOTE ON ISAAC C. PRAY'S
BIOGRAPHY OF BENNETT

Memoirs of J. G. Bennett and his Times by a Journalist was published in New York in 1855. It was generally highly sympathetic to its subject, seeking to show his nobler qualities and venturing apologies for his misdemeanours. So much was this so that despite formal denials in the *Herald* of any editorial connection with the book,[1] sceptics wondered whether it had been inspired by Bennett to offset the success of the *Life of Horace Greeley* by James Parton, the famous biographer, which appeared that same year.

Yet in his introduction the author, Isaac C. Pray, disclaimed any consultation with Bennett or 'any one connected with him'. Taking him at his word Allan Nevins, in his sketch of Bennett in the *Dictionary of American Biography*, rather unkindly censures Pray for the 'many inaccuracies' caused by his lack of scholarly enterprise. In fact Pray laboured under disabilities with which one may sympathise, or so it would seem from the narrative of veteran journalist William A. Croffut, which was published many years later. As a boy Croffut had been apprenticed to Pray, and he left this highly interesting account of his role as an intermediary between his employer and Bennett:

> 'You will board with me', he [Pray] resumed. 'Breakfast, eight, dinner, six – be punctual! Meanwhile you can take this down to the *Herald* office and deliver it to Mr. Bennett in person. In person. Be sure and leave it!' And he handed me a large sealed envelope from his desk. I took it, bowed myself out, and in a few minutes found my way to the den where the elder Bennett forged his thunderbolts. It was at the top of a building adjoining the American Museum at the junction of Broadway and Park Row, and Underhill had pointed it out to me as a fearsome cavern where ambitious reporters were tortured. I trembled as I handed the great man the parcel.
>
> The Scotch editor who terrorized New York at that time was, as I recall him, rough hewn and bony, six feet high, with a harsh and strident voice, a crescent of white whiskers under his chin and so terribly cross eyed that when he looked at me with one eye, he looked out at the City Hall with the other. 'Who from?' he bluntly asked, without taking the document. 'Mr. Isaac C.

[1]*NYH* 8 Mar 1855.

Pray', I answered. 'Nothing to do with Mr. Isaac C. Pray! Nothing to do with Mr. Isaac C. Pray!' he exclaimed angrily. But he took the parcel and tore off the envelope, disclosing a quantity of printed matter. With a savage gesture he flung it out the door into the hall, fixed me with one good eye and shouted, I don't want it! I won't have it! Carry it back and tell him to keep his stuff!' And he turned his back on me.

I went out at once and collected the matter before it could blow away, but not before I had discovered it to consist of galley proofs. Notwithstanding the order, 'Be sure and leave it', I made my way uptown again with it, bewildered and amazed at the reception, and wondering if my job depended on the singular performances and ungovernable temper of the master of the *Herald*. I was reassured by my reception at Irving Place, where the author pleasantly accepted the package, merely exclaiming, 'Yet that fool once got his living as a proofreader!'

Without more mystery or concealment, Mr. Pray now took me into his confidence.

'You must say nothing at any time to any person of anything you may hear in this house', he said quietly, 'Or of my business'. He added, 'I have undertaken to write a life of Mr. Bennett, rather against his protest. He doesn't like the idea wholly and gets angry about it. He is odd, but will come around all right. These are some of the early proof sheets, and I wanted to give him a chance to revise them and correct errors. Bennett does not want his life written at all, and declares he will not contribute a word.' Hereupon the author handed me the rejected proofs to read, saying I had 'better get the hang of it'.

It was still a riddle to me, as week after week I went on making copy from his dictation, and the riddle was not wholly solved when the handsome finished book issued, the next year, from the press of Stringer and Townsend. In the introduction, as there printed, will be found the following illuminating paragraph: 'The author of these pages has sought no person's counsel upon his theme or its mode of treatment. Neither Mr. Bennett nor any one connected with him has been consulted either directly or indirectly, with respect to the writing or publication of these memoirs. It would have been easy, had circumstances permitted and he been willing, for Mr. Bennett himself to supply some points in his career which he alone can justly elucidate; but the desire of the author has been to be free from influences which might arise from personal inquiry.' It is obvious that Mr. Pray had imposed upon himself a terribly difficult task; to write a friendly biography of an unfriendly man without the active assistance or even the passive sympathy and acquiescence of the subject of it, and even under his prohibition. . . I was repelled once more in a second visit to the *Herald*, but I always suspected, though I never knew, that while the volume was in course of preparation Mr. Bennett's wrath subsided, without being placated. . . Mr. Pray himself later. . . [told] me that in 1850 and '51 he was the musical and dramatic editor of the *Herald*, and that he resigned that position to become manager of the National Theatre. I drew some inferences and kept still.

I was not long in discovering that well defined hostilities still existed between Mr. Bennett and his biographer. In the 'moral war' which had been waged for years against the *Herald* by almost all the newspapers of New York, the object of which was its suppression and annihilation, Mr. Pray had defended Mr. Bennett, but not in that exclusive and wholehearted manner which the editor claimed as a right. Pray, a highly educated and refined man, insisted that the assailants, whom he called 'assassins of character' were indeed a disgrace to journalism and to the city, but he also insisted that in the battle of invective and vituperation Mr. Bennett had placed himself upon their level. This is a sufficient explanation of Bennett's repudiation of the volunteer biographer. . .[2]

[2]Source: William A. Croffut, 'Bennett and his Times', *Atlantic Monthly*, 147 (1931), 196-206.

BIBLIOGRAPHY

The bibliography is divided into the following sections:

A   Manuscripts
B   Newspapers
C   Periodicals
D   Printed Sources:
    Documentary and Statistical Compilations/Press Data/
    Editorials/Diaries/Correspondence etc./Pamphlets
E   Books and Articles Relating to Bennett:
    The Nineteenth century/The Twentieth century
F   Other Secondary Works

A: Manuscripts

The *James Gordon Bennett Papers* are divided between the New York Public Library and the Library of Congress.

The New York Public Library has one box of Bennett Papers dated between 1841 and 1851, with a heavy concentration for the years 1844 and 1850. In those days the *Herald*, in common with other papers, relied largely on voluntary correspondents to fill its columns. A full complement of professional reporters only came into existence gradually. It was common for the *Herald* to advertise for correspondents to cover particular events, especially in other States, offering payment at so much per column. (Occasionally too Bennett had to warn the public against the pretensions of bogus *Herald* reporters who took advantage of the paper's reputation in order to enjoy social privileges.) The Bennett Papers therefore largely comprise a mixed bag of articles submitted for publication in the *Herald*: some successfully, many not. The articles deal with a wide range of subjects, including the doings of the State legislature, the Forrest divorce case, Britain and the Slave Trade, the misbehaviour of a country clergyman, etc., etc. In addition there are miscellaneous invitations, poems, complaints, disclaimers, suggestions for editorials, requests for jobs or money or favourable notice, and so forth.

Also in the New York Public Library is Bennett's manuscript *Diary* for 1831, or rather a fragment of it, for it begins rather abruptly at 12 June and breaks off at 18 August. The *Diary* is chiefly a narrative of Bennett's journey through New York State, describing the political feeling in different towns, relating conversations with local politicians and describing the feelings of each in considerable detail. This narrative may well have been intended to serve as a source for the letters on political matters which Bennett was sending clandestinely to banker Nicholas Biddle, but their more obvious purpose would seem to have been to serve as a source of raw material for newspaper articles. In the entries for 15 and 18 July Bennett interpolates some remarkable passages of self-revelation, apparently born of depression at the disappointment of his ambitions.

The Manuscript Division of the Library of Congress holds one box (225 items) of Bennett Papers, mostly dated 1861-4; a miscellaneous collection which throws little direct light on editorial policy or on the man who ran the *Herald*. The core of the collection is a series of letters from *Herald* correspondents with McClellan's army in 1862, addressed to Bennett or to Frederic Hudson and dealing with military events, staffing, censorship, sources of information etc. (These papers have been drawn upon for chapters eight and nine above). The collection also includes some handwritten drafts by various authors for editorials which appeared in the *Herald* during the war.

The New York Historical Society holds ten Bennett items, dated 1823-63, including letters from Bennett to Nicholas Biddle and Senator Levi Woodbury and a letter from S. Beman to Bennett, dated from Washington 1844, dealing with the *Herald's* relationship to the Tyler administration. In the *Horatio Seymour Papers* in the same library is a letter from Bennett to the Governor dated 2 Jan 1863, asking for a favour for Judge Russell (see chapter ten).

Manuscript collections relating to the *Herald's* coverage of the Civil War include the *William H. Stiner Papers* in the New York Historical Society Library. Stiner became chief *Herald* staff man with McClellan's army in 1862. Besides various letters of instruction from Hudson, his papers include descriptive letters to his wife of a reporter's life at the front. Hudson's own papers are in the Concord, Mass., Free Public Library. The *Scrapbook* of De Bow Randolph Keim in the Library of Congress contains clippings of that reporter's newsletters for the *Herald*, mostly covering the war in the western theatre, 1862-4. The scrapbook is a unique record of one man's contribution to the paper.

A number of letters highly revealing of Bennett's early political ambitions and struggles are contained in the *Levi Woodbury Papers, William L. Marcy Papers, Nicholas Biddle Papers* and *Martin Van Buren Papers,* all in the Library of Congress. For specific references see chapter one of the text.

Very revealing also (and fundamental to the writing of this book) are the items of Bennett correspondence contained in the collections of Presidents Pierce, Buchanan, Lincoln and Johnson.

In the *Franklin Pierce Papers* in the Library of Congress, is the letter in which Bennett disclosed his ambition for the French mission (see chapter three). The *James Buchanan Papers*, Historical Society of Pennsylvania, contain a small mine of information about the *Herald's* course in the election campaign of 1856, as observed by such political correspondents as Henry Wikoff, Malcolm Ives, Albert C. Ramsey, Daniel Sickles, Fernando Wood, besides letters from Bennett and his wife which suggest a great deal about their respective motives and personalities. Although annoyingly cryptic at times, this material makes rewarding reading for any student of Bennett, and I have tried to indicate its scope in chapter three.

The *Abraham Lincoln Papers* in the Library of Congress contain some letters from Bennett to the President during 1861-3 when their relationship was comparatively sunny. Some use is made of these in chapter nine. Correspondence from Abram Wakeman and W.O. Bartlett in 1864-5 allows one to reconstruct at least something of the rather shady negotiations by which Bennett sought and finally obtained the offer of the French mission. This correspondence is the foundation for much of chapter thirteen.

The *Andrew Johnson Papers* in the Library of Congress, besides containing letters between Bennett and Johnson concerning post-war politics, include the series of letters to the President from *Herald* editorialist W.B. Phillips extracted in chapter fourteen.

Other collections in the Library of Congress which contain letters in Bennett's autograph are the Francis Markoe Papers (*Galloway-Maxcy-Markoe Papers*), *John M. Clayton Papers* and *Salmon P. Chase Papers*.

The *Manton Marble Collection*, in the University of London Library, includes a number of miscellaneous clippings relevant to the history of the press at this period.

B: Newspapers

The foundation of this study throughout has been the daily editions of the *New York Herald* itself for which, fortunately, complete files are available. Other newspapers used were:

334

NEW YORK: *Courier and Enquirer; Daily News; Day Book; Enquirer; Evening Express; Evening Post; Globe; Journal of Commerce; National Advocate; Sun; Times; Tribune* (Daily and Semi-Weekly); *World*
ALBANY: *Atlas and Argus; Evening Journal*
BROOKLYN: *Eagle*
CHARLESTON (S.C.): *Courier; Mercury*
CHICAGO: *Tribune*
LONDON: *Times*
PHILADELPHIA: *Daily Pennsylvanian; Pennsylvanian; Press*
RICHMOND: *Enquirer*
WASHINGTON: *Daily Globe; Daily Union*
UTICA: *Morning Herald and Daily Gazette*

C: Periodicals

Abraham Lincoln Quarterly; American Bibliophilist; American Heritage; American Historical Review; Atlantic Monthly; Civil War History; The Cosmopolitan; Democratic Review; Editor and Publisher; Foreign Quarterly Review; Harpers' Weekly; History Today; Illinois State Historical Society Journal; Indiana Historical Bulletin; Journal of American History; Journal of American Studies; Journal of Negro History; Journalism Quarterly; Lincoln Herald; Mississippi Valley Historical Review; New York Historical Society Quarterly; New York History; North American Review; Pennsylvania Magazine of History and Biography; Studies: An Irish Quarterly Review; Vanity Fair; Western Political Quarterly

D: Printed Sources

Documentary and Statistical Compilations
American Annual Cyclopedia (NY 1861 etc).
Henry Steele Commager ed., *Documents of American History* (2 vols, NY 1968).
　　　The Income Record. . .Taxable Income for the Year 1863 of the Residents Of New York (NY 1865).
Frederick Phisterer, *New York in the War of the Rebellion, 1861 to 1865* (Albany 1890).

Press Data
William T. Coggeshall, *The Newspaper Record* (Philadelphia 1856).
Daniel J. Kenny, *The American Newspaper Directory and Record of the Press* (NY 1861).

Editorials
Dwight L. Dumond ed., *Southern Editorials on Secession* (NY 1931).
Howard C. Perkins ed., *Northern Editorials on Secession* (2 vols, NY 1942).

Diaries
GUROWSKI: *Diary of Adam Gurowski* (2 vols, Boston 1862).
HAY: Tyler Dennett ed., *Lincoln and the Civil War in the Diaries and Letters of John Hay* (NY 1939).
HONE: Allan Nevins ed., *The Diary of Phillip Hone, 1828-51* (NY 1936).
JONES: J.B. Jones, *A Rebel War Clerk's Diary* (2 vols, NY 1935).
RUSSELL: William H. Russell, *My Diary North and South* (2 vols, London 1863).
STRONG: Allan Nevins and Milton H. Thomas eds., *The Diary of George Templeton Strong* (4 vols, NY 1952).
WELLES: Howard K. Beale ed., *The Diary of Gideon Welles* (3 vols, NY 1960).

Correspondence etc
ADAMS: W.C. Ford ed., *A Cycle of Adams Letters, 1861-5* (2 vols, London 1921).
BENNETT: 'Federal Generals and a Good Press', *American Historical Review* XXXIX, 284-97 – selections from the Bennett Papers in the Library of Congress illustrating how 'news for puffs' worked.
'The Yellow Press a Century Ago', *History Reference Bulletin* X (Cambridge, Mass. 1937) – a selection of *Herald* editorials and other items illustrating the paper's early history.
BIGELOW: John Bigelow, *Retrospections of an Active Life* (NY 1909).
BUCHANAN: J.B. Moore ed., *The Works of James Buchanan* (12 vols, NY 1960).
DICKINSON: John R. Dickinson ed., *Speeches, Correspondence etc. of. . .Daniel S. Dickinson of New York* (2 vols, NY 1867).
JACKSON: J.S. Bassett ed., *Correspondence of Andrew Jackson* (Washington 1931).
LINCOLN: Roy P. Basler ed., *The Collected Works of Abraham Lincoln* (8 vols, New Brunswick 1953-5).
David C. Mearns ed., *The Lincoln Papers* (2 vols, NY 1948).
J.G. & L.L. Turner, *Mary Todd Lincoln, Her Life and Letters* (NY 1972).
NASBY: David Ross Locke, *The Struggles of Petroleum V. Nasby* (Boston 1963).

Pamphlets

Anonymous, *The Life and Writings of James Gordon Bennett, Editor of the New York Herald* (NY 1844) – expressing the viewpoint of his enemies in the 'Moral War' (and possibly under Webb's auspices), this pamphlet sought to indict JGB as a 'great scoundrel' chiefly by reprinting a number of spicy extracts from the early *Herald* in order to 'expose' their scurrility.

Frank Freidel ed., *Union Pamphlets of the Civil War* (2 vols, Cambridge, Mass. 1967).

John Hughes, *A Letter on The Moral Causes that have produced The Evil Spirit of the Times; Addressed to the Honorable James Harper, Mayor of New York, Including a Vindication of the Author from the Infamous Charges made against him by Jas. Gordon Bennett, William L. Stone and Others* (NY 1844) – In this counterblast against the *Herald*'s onslaught on Hughes's position in the Public Schools controversy, the bishop accused Bennett of malignantly exciting religious and racial feelings. Hughes concluded of Bennett that 'if he were even *more* depraved or *less* despised, he would not be so dangerous; but being without any fixed principle of good, he occupies that ambiguous position which renders him too contemptible for notice, and yet not sufficiently so, to be below the power of mischief'.

John Graham, *New York County: Court of General Sessions: The People ex rel. Daniel E. Sickles vs. James Gordon Bennett, Complaint for Libel. Arguments of John Graham Esq., October Term, 1857* (NY 1857) – John Graham had assaulted JGB in the street in 1850. When Sickles sued Bennett for libels in the *Herald* he deliberately employed Graham to represent him. The pamphlet is only a partial record of the hearing, and consists mostly of Graham defaming Bennett's character. See chapters one and three above.

'Three Lookers-on in Venice', *The War of the Giants Against James Gordon Bennett, and other recent matters* (NY 1840) – condemns Bennett's behaviour in the 'Moral War' but questions the motives and purity of his attackers and concludes that they are little better.

Miscellaneous

Anonymous, *Poem* (n.p., n.d., but possibly c.1865) in Ford Collection, New York Public Library. Three verses of doggerel in execration of Bennett, in which he is called 'a coward, liar, pimp and sneak;/ A heartless robber of the weak;. . ./ With face like Pan's – if Pan had squinted – /And heart more foul than facer e'er hinted' etc.

U.S. Congress, *House Report 64: 37th Congress (2nd Session)* – deals with telegraphic censorship in the first year of the Civil War.

E: Books and Articles Relating to Bennett

The Nineteenth Century
Among contemporary works about Bennett, two by former *Herald* employees must be rated of primary importance. The circumstances in which Isaac C. Pray produced his *Memoirs of J.G. Bennett and his Times by a Journalist* (NY 1855) have been recounted in Appendix 2. Though written in the ornate literary style of the day and interspersed with curious digressions, Pray's book remains the fullest source on Bennett's life before 1855. Much of its value lies in Pray's extraction from the *Herald* files of some of Bennett's choicest editorials about himself – for Bennett was directly and indirectly his own best interpreter. Later biographers have drawn heavily on Pray's selection of materials. Frederic Hudson was Bennett's right hand man on the *Herald* for thirty years, and his history of *Journalism in the United States from 1690 to 1872* (NY 1873), published in the year after his employer's death, contains much information about Bennett unavailable elsewhere. Hudson's book lacks organisation but it was a pioneering work in its field and reprints some interesting documentary material in the text.

Pamphlet attacks on Bennett engendered by the 'Moral War' and the *Herald*'s role in the Public Schools controversy have been listed in the section above. Another virulent attack on Bennett and the *Herald* in its early days may be found in the *Foreign Quarterly Review*, vol 30 (London 1843) 197-222 – an attack which pleased Bennett because it testified to his notoriety across the Atlantic. Far warmer was 'The *Herald* – Onward!', an eulogy of Bennett from the 'Young America' viewpoint which appeared in the *Democratic Review*, vol 31 (NY 1852), 409-19, in appreciation of the editor's services to the party in the recent election. Also published in 1852, in Charleston was *Glimpses of New York City by a South Carolinian (who had nothing else to do)* by William M. Bobo, which contained a glowing tribute to the enterprise of the *Herald* and the character of its editor. As a southerner, Bobo appreciated the *Herald*'s 'strictly national' course and attempted to vindicate Bennett from calumnies with what for him was evidently the ultimate accolade: 'I would rely upon his word. . . as I would upon JOHN C. CALHOUN'S'.

In England anti-slavery journals condemned Bennett for his influence on the press on both sides of the Atlantic: *The Anti-Slavery Advocate* (London) for October 1853 (pp. 102-3) retailed the old blackmail charges, while the *Anti-Slavery Watchman* (London 1854), pp. 70-3, interestingly condemned the London *Times* as being 'indebted for its views of the Anti-Slavery movement' to Bennett.

A vivid pen portrait of Bennett as he appeared in 1854 is in George W. Bungay, *Off-Hand Takings;* or, Crayon Sketches of the Noticeable Men of our Age (NY 1854), pp. 389-90. The illustrated magazine *Harpers' Weekly* carried a feature article on Bennett's career in its edition of 10 July 1858, which spoke well of his contribution to the growth of journalism and included a page length engraved portrait. But, just as the 1857 pamphlet by John A. Graham (see Section D) had shown that the old charges against Bennett's integrity were still very much in circulation, so in 1859 Lambert A. Wilmer's splenetic *Our Press Gang: A Complete Exposure of the Corruptions and Crimes of the American Newspapers* (Philadelphia 1859) revived by innuendo the blackmail accusations against the editor of the *Herald*. The burden of Wilmer's nativist diatribe was the evil of foreign control of the press, and Bennett's chief crime in his eyes seems to have been his foreign birth.

That Bennett had become something of a legendary character even in his own lifetime was suggested by his appearance as a character in the novel *Marion* by 'Manhattan' (3 vols, London 1864). 'Manhattan' was the pseudonym of Joseph Alfred Scoville, to whom Bennett had earlier given aid and employment as a reporter. *Marion* is dedicated to Bennett, and it presents a mostly favourable picture of the editor as a generous, enterprising and even genial employer.

An English journalist, Edward Dicey, recorded some reflections on the *Herald*'s success and some uncomplimentary anecdotes of Bennett's social ostracism in the first volume of his *Six Months in the Federal States* (London 1863). Like Dicey, the famous biographer James Parton was fascinated by the contrast between Bennett's unpopularity and the success of his paper, and set himself the evidently disagreeable task of explaining the latter phenomenon in an article, 'The New York Herald', *North American Review*, 102 (April 1866), 373-419. This essay was reprinted in Parton's *Famous Americans of Recent Times* (Boston 1867), pp. 261-305. As a staunch Republican, Parton was thoroughly hostile to Bennett, but he was a perceptive critic and produced an assessment of lasting value in the literature about the *Herald*.

Amongst notable sketches of Bennett in the post-war years by journalists who knew him, Junius H. Browne emphasised his opportunism and cynicism in *The Great Metropolis* (NY 1869). Picturing Bennett in his retirement, John Russell Young in *Men and Memories* (2 vols, NY 1901) found underneath the misanthrope a man of considerable wit and culture. Even more appreciative was fellow editor Charles A. Dana, whose interesting comments on

Bennett were reprinted in James H. Wilson, *The Life of Charles A. Dana* (NY 1907), pp. 485-9. The famous showman P.T. Barnum quarrelled with Bennett in 1865 over the sale of the site of Barnum's Museum, on which the new *Herald* building was eventually raised. He got his revenge for attacks in the *Herald* by indicting Bennett in his autobiographical *Struggles and Triumphs* (London 1869), ch.XLI.

When Bennett died a number of periodicals carried obituary articles: Paul Peebles admired Bennett's innovations in 'James Gordon Bennett's Scintillations', *Galaxy*, XIV (August 1872), p. 258, while a vicious condemnation of Bennett's career appeared in Sabin & Son's *American Bibliophilist*, vol 4 (1872), 694-6.

In succeeding decades some of the men who had known Bennett gave him a place in their memoirs. His crony Henry Wikoff left an engaging account of his first acquaintance with the editor in 1838 in *Reminiscences of an Idler* (NY 1880), pp. 464-6, 473-4, 486-90. Ben Perley Poore recalled Bennett's days as a Washington correspondent in *Perley's Reminiscences of Sixty Years in the National Metropolis* (2 vols, Philadelphia 1886). Bennett's enforced change of heart in 1861 was variously remembered by Henry Villard, *Memoirs, 1835-1900* (Boston & NY 1904), vol 1, and by Thurlow Weed, *Autobiography of Thurlow Weed* (Boston 1883), vol 1, pp. 615-19. A.K. McClure speculated on Bennett's reaction to the offer of the French mission in *Abraham Lincoln and Men of War Times* (Philadelphia 1892), pp. 90-2, while Hugh McCulloch, Secretary of the Treasury under Lincoln and Johnson, gave a brief but favourable estimate of Bennett in his *Men and Measures of Half a Century* (NY 1900), p. 493.

William A. Croffut recalled his acquaintance with the editor in 'Bennett and His Times', *Atlantic Monthly,* 147 (1931), 196-206, an important memoir which is quoted in Appendix 2 above. The 'high toned' journalist E.L. Godkin contributed a measured (if slightly priggish) assessment of the *Herald* to the NY *Evening Post,* 30 Dec 1899.

The Twentieth Century

A detailed and factual history of the *Herald* by Albert E. Coleman, 'A New and Authentic History of the *Herald* of the Bennetts', was serialised in *Editor and Publisher* LVI-LVIII (29 Mar 1924-13 June 1925). Coleman worked for the younger Bennett for forty years and dealt with his subject favourably. He recorded much information well-known to *Herald* employees, but which would otherwise have been lost.

Two book length studies of Bennett have appeared to date. In *The James Gordon Bennetts* (NY 1928), veteran journalist Don C. Seitz accorded more space to the son than the father. Seitz made no attempt to be comprehensive nor to provide 'scholarly apparatus'; his account is therefore brief and sometimes insubstantial. Nevertheless he incorporated some original documentary material and produced an interesting cameo of his subject's career. Seitz's treatment was superseded by the full length biography by Oliver Carlson, *The Man Who Made News: James Gordon Bennett, 1795-1872* (NY 1942). Mr Carlson included a bibliographical list but did himself and his readers an injustice by not providing references in the text of his well written account. As the title suggests, he was chiefly concerned with Bennett's contribution to journalism, rather than with the *Herald* as a political or social force, and his narrative emphasised the breadth of Bennett's professional enterprise. He made little use of manuscript material, and was in any case writing before the Lincoln Papers became available.

Two review articles are worth mentioning in connection with these biographies: Francis McCullagh had reported for Bennett Jr. and he incorporated a discussion of the *Herald* in his review of Seitz entitled 'The Gordon Bennetts and American Journalism', *Studies: An Irish Quarterly Review*, XVIII (Dublin 1929), 394-442. The *American Historical Review*, XLVIII (1942-3), 606, included a critique of the Carlson biography by Ray Allen Billington.

Allan Nevins contributed the profile of Bennett included in the *Dictionary of American Biography*.

Oswald Garrison Villard included a chapter on the Bennetts in *Some Newspapers and Newspapermen* (NY 1923), ch XVI, though his condemnation of Bennett's sensationalism is criticised by G.H. Payne, *History of Journalism in the United States* (NY 1924). Certainly the historians of journalism have not failed to appreciate Bennett's role in creating the modern newspaper. Outstanding interpretations are Charles H. Levermore, 'The Rise of Metropolitan Journalism', *American Historical Review*, VI (1900-01), 446-65; James Melvin Lee, *History of American Journalism* (NY 1917), pp. 193-205, and Willard G. Bleyer, *Main Currents in the History of American Journalism* (NY 1927). Modern histories of journalism which contain significant treatment of Bennett and the *Herald* are Frank L. Mott, *American Journalism* (NY 1962); Sidney J. Kobre, *Development of American Journalism* (Dubuque 1969), and Edwin Emery, *The Press and America* (Englewood Cliffs 1971). Harold Herd included a chapter on Bennett in *Seven Editors* (London 1953).

A recent discussion of the penny press is in Michael Schudson, *Discovering the News: A Social History of American Newspapers* (NY 1978), where it is argued that the *Herald* was the embodiment of an emerging Jacksonian 'democratic market society'.

Notable articles are Louis M. Starr, 'James Gordon Bennett-Benificent Rascal', *American Heritage*, vol 6, no 2 (Feb 1955), 32-7, and Harvey Saalberg, 'Bennett and Greeley', *Journalism Quarterly*, 49 (1972), 538-46,50. Wallace B. Eberhard considers the questions of censorship raised in Bennett's famous challenge to the court in the White-Crowinshield case of 1830 in 'Mr. Bennett covers a Murder Trial', *Journalism Quarterly*, 47 (1970), 457-63.

Richard O'Connor's informal biography of the younger Bennett, *The Scandalous Mr. Bennett* (NY 1962) deserves mention because of its suggestion of the consequences for his family of the fame and fortune of the founder of the *Herald*, as well as its entertaining narrative of some of the more hilarious episodes in the family history. Bennett was the subject of a college commencement address by Charles Penrose curiously entitled '. . . that this Nation' (Newcomen Society 1941) which is a rank specimen of that literary genre.

Some aspects of the *Herald's* role in politics and society are ably treated in the following articles: Maurice E. Bloch shows how in 1851-2 Bennett exploited the grievances of a discontented artist and was instrumental in destroying by law suit one of America's most prestigious cultural establishments in 'The American Art Union's Downfall', *New York Historical Society Quarterly*, 37 (1953), 331-59. Arnold Whitridge compares the editors of the New York *Herald* and the London *Times* as exacerbators of hostile public opinion during the Civil War in 'Anglo-American Troublemakers – J.G. Bennett and J.T. Delane', *History Today*, VII, no 2 (Feb 1956), 88-95. Possible reasons why Bennett deserted Buchanan in the 1856 election campaign are considered by Phillip G. Auchampaugh, 'Political Techniques 1856 – or Why the *Herald* went for Fremont', *Western Political Quarterly*, I (1948), 243-51. David Quentin Voigt, 'Too Pitchy to Touch – President Lincoln and Editor Bennett', *Abraham Lincoln Quarterly*, 6 (1950), 139-61, reviews the relationship between the two and the circumstances surrounding the offer of the French mission in 1864. The same subject is considered by John R. Turner Jr. and Michael D'Innocenzo, 'The President and the Press: Lincoln, James Gordon Bennett and the Election of 1864', *Lincoln Herald*, 76 (1974), 63-9, who arrive at the same conclusion as Parton in 1866, i.e. that Lincoln drove a bad bargain.

F: Other Secondary Works

Albion, Robert G., *The Rise of New York Port 1815-60* (NY 1939).

Alexander, D.A.S., *A Political History of the State of New York* (3 vols., NY 1906-9).

Andrews, J. Cutler, *The North Reports the Civil War* (Pittsburgh 1955).

Asbury, Herbert, *The Gangs of New York: An Informal History of the Underworld* (NY 1928).

Auchampaugh, Phillip G., 'The Buchanan-Douglas Feud', *Illinois State Historical Society Journal*, 25 (1932), 5-48.

_____ *James Buchanan and his Cabinet on the Eve of Secession* (Boston 1965).

Auchampaugh, P.G., 'Politics and Slavery, 1850-60', see Flick, A.C.

Belz, Herman, *Reconstructing the Union: Theory and Policy during the Civil War* (Ithaca 1969).

Berger, Mark L., *The Revolution in the New York Party System, 1840-60* (Port Washington, NY 1973).

Berger, Meyer, *The Story of the New York Times, 1851-1951* (NY 1951).

Betts, John R., 'The Technological Revolution and the Rise of Sport, 1850-1900', *Mississippi Valley Historical Review*, 40 (1953-4), 231-56.

Billington, Ray Allen, *The Protestant Crusade 1800-1860: A Study of the Origins of American Nativism* (NY 1938).

Bleyer, Willard G., *Main Currents in the History of American Journalism* (NY 1927).

Blue, Frederick J., *The Free Soilers: Third Party Politics 1848-54* (Chicago 1973).

Bobo, William M., *Glimpses of New York City* (Charleston 1852).

Bonham, M.L., 'New York and the Civil War', *see* Flick, A.C.

Bonham, Milledge L., 'New York and the Election of 1860', *New York History*, 15 (1934), 124-43.

Booth, Mary L., *History of the City of New York, from its earliest settlement to the present time* (NY 1859).

Brace, Charles L., *The Dangerous Classes of New York* (NY 1872).

Brown, Francis, *Raymond of the Times* (NY 1951).

Brown, H.C., *Glimpses of Old New York* (NY 1917).

Browne, Junius H., *Four Years in Secessia* (Hartford 1865).

_____ *The Great Metropolis* (NY 1869).

Brummer, Sidney D., *Political History of New York State during the Period of the Civil War* (Columbia, NY 1911).

343

Buchanan, James, *Mr. Buchanan's Administration on the Eve of the Rebellion* (NY 1866).

Carman, Harry J., & Luthin, Reinhard L., *Lincoln and the Patronage* (Columbia, NY 1943).

Carpenter, Francis B., *Six Months at the White House with Abraham Lincoln* (NY 1866).

Carson, Steven L., 'Lincoln and the Mayor of New York', *Lincoln Herald*, 67 (1965), 84-91.

Carter, Edward L., 'The Revolution in Journalism During the Civil War', *Lincoln Herald,* 73 (1971), 229-40.

Catton, Bruce, *Grant Takes Command* (London 1970).

Chalmers, Leonard, 'Fernando Wood and Tammany Hall: The First Phase', *New York Historical Society Quarterly,* 52 (1968), 379-402.

_____ 'Tammany Hall, Fernando Wood and the Struggle to Control New York City, 1857-9', *New York Historical Society Quarterly,* 53 (1969), 7-33.

Coben, Stanley, 'Northeastern Business and Radical Reconstruction: A Re-examination', *Mississippi Valley Historical Review,* XLVI (1959), 67-90.

Collins, Bruce, 'The Ideology of the Ante-Bellum Northern Democrats', *Journal of American Studies*, 2 (1977), 103-21.

Cook, Adrian, *The Armies of the Streets: The New York City Draft Riots of 1863* (University of Kentucky 1974).

Cortissoz, Royal, *The New York Tribune* (NY 1923).

Crenshaw, Ollinger, 'The Speakership Contest of 1859-60', *Mississippi Valley Historical Review*, 29 (1942-3), 323-38.

Crook, D.P., *The North, The South and the Powers, 1861-1865* (NY 1974).

Crouthamel, James L., *James Watson Webb: A Biography* (Middletown, Conn., 1969).

_____ 'Did the Second Bank of the United States Bribe the Press?'*Journalism Quarterly,* 36 (1959), 35-44.

_____ 'The Newspaper Revolution in New York, 1830-60', *New York History,* 45 (1964), 91-113.

Crow, Duncan, *Henry Wikoff, the American Chevalier* (London 1963).

Crozier, Emmet, *Yankee Reporters, 1861-65* (NY 1956).

Cruden, Robert, *The War that Never Ended* (Englewood Cliffs 1973).

Curran, Thomas J., 'Seward and the Know-Nothings', *New York Historical Society Quarterly*, 51 (1967), 141-59.

Curry, Richard O., 'The Union as it Was: Recent Interpretations of the Copperheads', *Civil War History*, 13 (1967), 25-39.

Davis, Elmer, *History of the New York Times, 1851-1921* (NY 1921).

Dell, Christopher, *Lincoln and the War Democrats: The Grand Erosion of the Conservative Tradition* (NJ 1975).

Dennett, Tyler, *John Hay* (NY 1933).

Dix, Morgan, *Memoirs of John A. Dix* (2 vols., NY 1883).

Donovan, H.D.A., *The Barnburners: A Study of the Internal Movements in the Political History of New York State, etc. 1830-52* (NY 1925).

Dudley, Harold M., 'The Election of 1864', *Mississippi Valley Historical Review,* 18, 500-18.

Duffy, John, *A History of Public Health in New York, 1625-1866* (NY 1968).

Dusinberre, William, *Civil War Issues in Philadelphia, 1856-1865* (Philadelphia 1965).

Ellis, David M., et al., *A History of New York State* (Ithaca 1967).

Emery, Edwin, *The Press and America* (Englewood Cliffs 1971).

Ernst, Robert, *Immigrant Life in New York City, 1825-1863* (NY 1949).

Fahrney, Ralph R., *Horace Greeley and the Tribune in the Civil War* (Cedar Rapids 1936).

Fehrenbacher, Don E., *The Leadership of Abraham Lincoln* (NY 1970).

Field, Phyllis F., 'Republicans and Black Suffrage in New York State: The Grass Roots Response', *Civil War History,* 21 (1975), 160-71.

Fite, Emerson D., *The Presidential Campaign of 1860* (NY 1911).

––––––– *Social and Industrial Conditions in the North During the Civil War* (NY 1910).

Flick, Alexander C., ed., *History of the State of New York* (10 vols, NY 1933).

––––––– *Samuel J. Tilden* (NY 1939).

Foner, Eric, *Free Soil, Free Labor, Free Men: The Ideology of the Republican Party before the Civil War* (NY 1970).

Foner, Philip S., *Business and Slavery: The New York Merchants and the Irrepressible Conflict* (Chapel Hill 1941).

Forney, John W., *Anecdotes of Public Men* (2 vols, NY 1873).

Fox, Dixon R., *Yankees and Yorkers* (NY 1940).

Franklin, John Hope, *The Emancipation Proclamation* (NY 1963).

Frost, James A., 'The Home Front in New York During the Civil War', *New York History,* 42 (1961), 273-97.

Gibson, Florence E., *The Attitudes of the New York Irish towards State and National Affairs, 1848-1892* (Columbia, NY 1951).

Giddings, T.H., 'Rushing the Translatlantic News in the 1830s and

1840s', *New York Historical Society Quarterly,* 42 (1958), 47-59.

Ginsberg, Judah B., 'Barnburners, Free Soilers and the New York Republican Party', *New York History,* 57 (1976), 475-500.

Goldberg, Isaac, *Major Noah, American-Jewish Pioneer* (NY 1937).

Goldsmith, Adolph O., 'Reporting the Civil War: Union Army Press Relations', *Journalism Quarterly,* 33 (1956), 478-87.

Gossett, Thomas F., *Race: The History of an Idea in America* (Dallas 1963).

Govan, Thomas P., *Nicholas Biddle, Nationalist and Public Banker 1786-1844* (Chicago 1959).

Gray, Wood, *The Hidden Civil War: The Story of the Copperheads* (NY 1942).

Greeley, Horace, *Recollections of a Busy Life* (NY 1869).

Guback, Thomas H., 'General Sherman's War on the Press', *Journalism Quarterly,* 36 (1959), 171-6.

Hale, William H., *Horace Greeley: Voice of the People* (NY 1950).

Hallock, W.H., *Life of Gerard Hallock* (NY 1869).

Hammond, Bray, *Sovereignty and an Empty Purse: Banks and Politics in the Civil War* (Princeton 1970).

Harper, Robert S., *Lincoln and the Press* (NY 1951).

Hartman, William, 'The New York Custom House: Seat of Spoils Politics', *New York History,* 34 (1953), 149-63.

Headley, Joel T., *The Great Riots of New York* (NY 1873).

Heale, M.J., 'Harbingers of Progressivism: Responses to the Urban Crisis in New York c.1845-60', *Journal of American Studies,* 10 (1976), 17-36.

Herndon, W.H., & Weik, Jesse N., *Herndon's Life of Lincoln* (NY 1949).

Hershkowitz, Leo, *Tweed's New York: Another Look* (NY 1977).

Higham, John, *Strangers in the Land: Patterns of American Nativism 1860-1925* (New Brunswick 1955).

Holt, Michael F., 'The Democratic Party, 1828-1860', in Schlesinger ed., *History of US Political Parties* (NY 1973), 497-536.

_____ *The Political Crisis of the 1850s* (NY 1978).

Hoover, Merle M., *Park Benjamin: Poet and Editor* (NY 1948).

Horner, Harlan H., *Lincoln and Greeley* (Illinois U.P. 1953).

Isely, Jeter A., *Horace Greeley and the Republican Party 1853-61: A Study of the New York Tribune* (Princeton 1947).

Jenkins, Brian, *Britain and the War for the Union* (Montreal 1974).

_____ *Fenians and Anglo-American Relations during Reconstruction* (Ithaca 1969).

Johannsen, Robert, *Stephen A. Douglas* (NY 1973).

Juergens, George, *Joseph Pulitzer and the New York World* (Princeton 1966).

Kaplan, Sidney, 'The Miscegenation Issue in the Election of 1864', *Journal of Negro History,* 34 (1939), 274-343.

Katz, Irving, *August Belmont* (NY 1968).

Kendall, John C., 'The New York City Press and Anti-Canadianism: A New Perspective on the Civil War Years', *Journalism Quarterly,* 52 (1975), 522-30.

Kirkland, Edward C., *The Peacemakers of 1864* (NY 1927).

Klein, Philip S., *President James Buchanan* (Univ. Park, Pa., 1962).

Klement, Frank L., *The Limits of Dissent: Clement L. Vallandigham and the Civil War* (Lexington 1970).

Knox, Thomas W., *Camp-Fire and Cotton Field* (NY 1865).

Kobre, Sidney J., *Development of American Journalism* (Dubuque 1969).

Lamb, Martha J., *History of the City of New York: Its Origin, Rise and Progress* (2 vols., NY 1877-80).

Lannie, Vincent P., *Public Money and Parochial Education: Bishop Hughes, Governor Seward and the New York School Controversy* (Cleveland 1968).

Lee, Alfred M., *The Daily Newspaper in America* (NY 1937).

Lee, James Melvin, *History of American Journalism* (NY 1917).

Leech, Margaret, *Reveille in Washington* (NY 1941).

Lincoln, Charles Z., *The Constitutional History of New York* (5 vols, Rochester, NY 1906).

Litwack, Leon F., *North of Slavery: The Negro in the Free States 1790-1860* (Chicago 1961).

Lyman, Susan E., *The Story of New York* (NY 1964).

McCague, James, *The Second Rebellion: The New York City Draft Riots of 1863* (NY 1968).

McJimsey, George T., *Genteel Partisan: Manton Marble, 1834-1917* (Iowa 1971).

McKitrick, Eric L., *Andrew Johnson and Reconstruction* (Chicago 1960).

McPherson, James, *The Negro's Civil War* (NY 1965).

Mandelbaum, Seymour J., *Boss Tweed's New York* (NY 1965).

Marbut, Frederick B., 'Decline of the Official Press in Washington', *Journalism Quarterly*, 33 (1956), 335-41.

———— 'Early Washington Correspondents: Some Neglected Pioneers', *Journalism Quarterly*, 25 (1948), 369-74.

———— *News From the Capital: The Story of Washington Reporting* (Carbondale, Ill., 1971).

———— 'The United States Senate and the Press, 1838-41', *Journalism Quarterly*, 28 (1951), 342-50.

Mathews, Joseph J., *Reporting the Wars* (Minneapolis 1957).

Maverick, Augustus, *Henry J. Raymond and the New York Press for Thirty Years* (Hartford 1870).

Meerse, David E., 'Buchanan, Corruption and the Election of 1860', *Civil War History,* 12 (1966), 116-31.

_____ 'Origins of the Buchanan-Douglas Feud Reconsidered', *Journal of the Illinois State Historical Society,* 67 (1974), 154-74.

Merrill, L.T., 'General Benjamin F. Butler in the Presidential Campaign of 1864', *Mississippi Valley Historical Review,* 33 (1946-7), 537-70.

Miller, Douglas T., *Jacksonian Aristocracy – Class and Democracy in New York, 1830-1860* (NY 1967).

Mitchell, Stewart, *Horatio Seymour of New York* (Cambridge, Mass., 1938).

Mohr, James C., *The Radical Republicans in New York During Reconstruction* (Ithaca 1973).

Morris, Lloyd, *Incredible New York* (NY 1951).

Mott, Frank L., *American Journalism* (NY 1962).

_____ 'Facetious News Writing 1833-53', *Mississippi Valley Historical Review,* 29 (1942-3), 35-54.

Murdock, Eugene C., 'Horatio Seymour and the 1863 Draft', *Civil War History,* 11 (1965), 117-41.

_____ *One Million Men: The Civil War Draft in the North* (Madison 1971).

_____ *Patriotism Limited, 1862-5: The Civil War Draft and the Bounty System* (Kent, O., 1967).

Mushkat, Jerome, 'Ben Wood's "Fort Lafayette": A Source for Studying the Peace Democrats', *Civil War History,* 21 (1975), 160-71.

_____ *Tammany, The Evolution of a Political Machine, 1789-1865* (Syracuse 1971).

Myers, Gustavus, *The History of Tammany Hall* (NY 1917).

Nevins, Allan, *The Evening Post: A Century of Journalism* (NY 1922).

_____ *Ordeal of the Union* (2 vols., NY 1947).

_____ *The Emergence of Lincoln* (2 vols., NY 1950).

_____ *The War for the Union* (4 vols., NY 1959-71).

Nichols, Roy R., *The Democratic Machine, 1850-1854* (NY 1923).

_____ *The Disruption of American Democracy* (NY 1948).

_____ *Franklin Pierce* (Philadelphia 1931).

Niven, John, *Gideon Welles* (NY 1973).

O'Brien, Frank M., *The Story of the Sun* (NY 1927).

Parton, James, *The Life of Horace Greeley* (NY 1855).

_____ *The Life of Andrew Jackson* (3 vols., NY 1961).

_____ *Famous Americans of Recent Times* (Boston 1867).

Payne, George H., *History of Journalism in th United States* (NY 1924).

Pearson, Henry G., *James S. Wadsworth of Geneseo* (London 1913).

Pessen, Edward, 'Moses Y. Beach Revisited', *Journal of American History,* 58, 415-26.

_____ 'The Wealthiest New Yorkers of the Jacksonian Era: A New List', *New York Historical Society Quarterly,* 54 (1970), 145-72.

Phelps Stokes, Isaac N., *The Iconography of Manhattan* (6 vols., NY 1915-28).

Pickett, Calder M., 'Technology and the New York Press in the Nineteenth Century', *Journalism Quarterly,* 37 (1960), 398-407.

Pleasants, Samuel A., *Fernando Wood of New York* (NY 1948).

Pollard, James E., *The Presidents and the Press* (NY 1947).

Poore, Ben Perley, *Perley's Reminiscences of Sixty Years in the National Metropolis* (2 vols., Philadelphia 1886).

Potter, David M., *The Impending Crisis, 1848-61* (NY 1976).

_____ *Lincoln and His Party in the Secession Crisis* (Yale U.P. 1942).

Pratt, John W., 'Governor Seward and the New York City School Controversy, 1840-42', *New York History,* 42 (1961), 351-63.

Randall, James G., *Constitutional Problems Under Lincoln* (Urbana 1951).

_____ *Lincoln the Liberal Statesman* (NY 1947).

_____ & Current, R.N., *Lincoln the President* (4 vols., NY 1944-5).

_____ 'The Newspaper Problem in its Bearing upon Military Secrecy during the Civil War', *American Historical Review,* 23 (1918), 302-23.

Randall, Ruth P., *Mary Lincoln, Biography of a Marriage* (Boston 1953).

Rauch, Basil, *American Interest in Cuba, 1848-55* (NY 1948).

Rawley, James A., *Edwin D. Morgan, 1811-1883, Merchant in Politics* (NY 1955).

Rayback, Robert J., 'New York State in the Civil War', *New York History,* 42 (1961), 56-70.

Reilly, Tom, 'Early Coverage of a President Elect: Lincoln at Springfield, 1860', *Journalism Quarterly,* 49 (1972).

Remini, Robert V., 'The Albany Regency', *New York History,* 39 (1958), 341-55.

Rhodes, James Ford, *History of the United States from the Compromise of 1850* (London 1893).

Richardson, James F., 'Mayor Fernando Wood and the New York Police Force, 1855-1857', *New York Historical Society Quarterly,* 50 (1966), 5-40.

Robinson, Elwyn B., 'The Dynamics of American Journalism from 1787 to 1865', *Pennsylvania Magazine of History and Biography,* 61 (1937), 435-45.

_____ 'The Press, President Lincoln's Philadelphia Organ', *Pennsylvania Magazine of History and Biography,* 65 (1941), 157-70.

Rorabaugh, W.J., 'Rising Democratic Spirits: Immigrants, Temperance and Tammany Hall, 1854-60', *Civil War History,* 22 (1976), 138-57.

Rosebault, C.J., *When Dana was the Sun: A Story of Personal Journalism* (NY 1931).

Rosewater, Victor, *History of Cooperative Newsgathering in the United States* (NY 1930).

Sandburg, Carl, *Abraham Lincoln: The War Years* (4 vols., NY 1939).

Schlesinger, Arthur M., *History of U.S. Political Parties* (NY 1973).

Schroth, R.A., *Brooklyn and the Eagle* (Westport, Conn., 1974).

Schudson, Michael, *Discovering the News: A Social History of American Newspapers* (NY 1978).

Schwarzlose, Richard A., 'Early Telegraphic News Despatches: Forerunner of the A.P.', *Journalism Quarterly,* 51(1974), 595-601.

_____ 'Harbor News Association: The Formal Origin of the A.P.', *Journalism Quarterly,* 45 (1968), 253-60.

Scisco, Louis D., *Political Nativism in New York State* (NY 1901).

Silbey, Joel H., *A Respectable Minority: The Democratic Party in the Civil War Era 1860-1868* (NY 1977).

Skidmore, Joe, 'The Copperhead Press and the Civil War', *Journalism Quarterly,* 16 (1939), 345-55.

Smith, George W., & Judah, Charles, *Life in the North During the Civil War: A Source History* (Albuquerque 1966).

Smith, William E., *The Francis Preston Blair Family in Politics* (2 vols., NY 1933).

Spencer, Ivor D., *The Victor and the Spoils: A Life of William L. Marcy* (Providence 1959).

Stampp, Kenneth M., *And the War Came: The North and the Secession Crisis, 1860-61* (Chicago 1950).

Starr, Louis M., *Bohemian Brigade: Civil War Newsmen in Action* (NY 1954).

Stebbins, Homer A., *A Political History of the State of New York, 1865-1869* (NY 1913).

Stenberg, Richard R., 'An Unnoted Factor in the Buchanan-Douglas Feud', *Illinois State Historical Society Journal*, 25 (1933), 271-84.

Still, Bayrd, *Mirror for Gotham: New York as seen by contemporaries from Dutch days to the present* (NY 1956).

Swanberg, W.A., *Sickles the Incredible* (NY 1956).

Thomas, Benjamin P., & Hyman, H.M., *Stanton* (NY 1962).

Thompson, Robert L., *Wiring a Continent: The History of the Telegraph Industry in the United States, 1832-66* (Princeton 1947).

Townsend, George A., *Campaigns of a Non-Combatant* (NY 1866).

Van Deusen, Glyndon G., *Horace Greeley: Nineteenth Century Crusader* (Philadelphia 1953).

——— *William H. Seward* (NY 1967).

——— *Thurlow Weed: Wizard of the Lobby* (Boston 1947).

Villard, Henry, *Memoirs, 1835-1900* (2 vols., Boston 1904).

Villard, Oswald Garrison, *Some Newspapers and Newspaper-Men* (NY 1923).

Wainwright, N.B., 'Loyal Opposition in Civil War Philadelphia', *Pennsylvania Magazine of History and Biography*, 88 (1964), 294-315.

Weed, Thurlow, *Autobiography of Thurlow Weed* (2 vols., Boston 1883).

Weisberger, Bernard A., 'The Newspaper Reporter and the Kansas Imbroglio', *Mississippi Valley Historical Review*, 36 (1949-50), 633-56.

——— *Reporters for the Union* (Boston 1953).

Wikoff, Henry, *The Adventures of a Roving Diplomatist* (NY 1857).

——— *Reminiscences of an Idler* (NY 1880).

Williams, T. Harry, *Lincoln and his Generals* (NY 1952).

——— *Lincoln and the Radicals* (Madison 1965).

Wilmer, Lambert A., *Our Press Gang: A Complete Exposure of the Corruptions and Crimes of the American Newspapers* (Philadelphia 1859).

Wilson, James G., ed., *The Memorial History of the City of New York, from its settlement to the year 1892* (4 vols., NY 1893).

Wilson, James H., *Life of Charles A. Dana* (NY 1907).

Wilson, Quintus, 'Voluntary Press Censorship During the Civil War', *Journalism Quarterly*, 29, 251-61.

Winks, Robin, *Canada and the United States: The Civil War Years* (Baltimore 1960).

Wood, Forrest G., *Black Scare: The Racist Response to Emancipation and Reconstruction* (Berkeley, Cal., 1970).

Young, James Harvey, *The Toadstool Millionaires: A Social History of Patent Medicines in America before Federal Regulation* (Princeton 1961).

Young, John Russell, *Men and Memories* (2 vols., NY 1901).

Zornow, William F., *Lincoln and the Party Divided* (Norman, Oklahoma, 1954).

Unpublished Theses and Dissertations

Ferree, Walter L., 'The New York Democracy: Division and Reunion, 1847-52' (University of Pennsylvania 1953).

Freeman, Rhoda G., 'The Free Negro in New York City' (Columbia 1966).

Furer, Howard, 'The Public Career of William Frederick Havemeyer' (New York Univ. 1963).

Hodnett, Mary P., 'Civil War Issues in New York State Politics' (St. John's Univ. 1971).

Hubbell, John T., 'The Northern Democracy and the Crisis of Disunion, 1860-61' (Univ. Illinois 1969).

Lee, Basil Leo, 'Discontent in New York City, 1861-1865' (Catholic University of America, Washington D.C., 1943).

Lichterman, Martin, 'John Adams Dix, 1789-1879' (Columbia Univ. 1952).

Long, David F., 'The New York News, 1855-1906: Spokesman for the Underprivileged' (Columbia 1950).

McClain, Russell H., 'The New York Express: Voice of Opposition' (Columbia 1955).

Ryan, Joseph F., 'Abraham Lincoln and New York City, 1861-5' (St. John's Univ. 1969).

INDEX

As Journalist: founds *Herald,* 1, 13, 18, 19ff.; editorial influence, 4-9,
74, 83, 90, 98, 105, 116, 152, 153-4, 171, 185-6, 189-90, 194, 195n.,
197, 214, 287, 290-1, 302, 315, 315n., 317; editorial techniques, 6-7,
20, 28, 38-40, 96, 133n., 141, 305-6, 307-8, 317; as newsgatherer,
21ff., 33-5, 140-1, 199-202, 206, 208-9, 315, 317; advertising policy,
20, 26, 78, 285; literary style, 13, 36, 38, 119n.; working day, 39-41;
ambition for *Herald,* 20, 30, 43, 44, 96, 311-12; historical
importance, 1-9, 317-20
Correspondence: with Biddle, 15; with Van Buren, 16; with Woodbury, 16n.; with Hoyt, 16-17; with Jackson, 17; with Pierce, 27, 44,
83-5; with Marcy, 88, 317; with Seymour, 78, 246n.; with
Buchanan, 96, 98, 100, 104, 106, 143-4, 162; with A. Lincoln, 78,
214, 216-17, 216n., 220, 237, 243, 249, 283, 293-4; with Mary
Lincoln, 214-15, 225n., 295; with Johnson, 54, 54n., 297, 300, 301-
2, 303-4, 309
Visitors: Parton, 40; royal entourage, 53; Japanese princes, 54; F.
Wood, 75n; Sickles and Cochrane, 94; Ives, 95-6; Fremont, 98;
Republican agents, 132-3, 287; Fogg, 132; Villard, 195-6; Weed,
196-8; Jewett, 264; Blair, 266; Wakeman, 286; Bartlett, 288;
McClellan, 291; Croffut, 328-30. For other personal and political
relationships *see* under individual names.
See also New York Herald. For editorial views *see* subject headings
Bennett, James Gordon Jr., (1841-1918), 1, 1n., 3, 26n., 27, 27n.,
313n.; naval service, 196, 196n., 215; assumes management of
Herald (1867), 311-13, 311n.
Bennett, Jeanette (JGB's daughter), 1n.
Bennett Guard, 237n.
Biddle, Nicholas, 15, 332
Bigelow, John, 284, 296n.
Black Codes, 301
'Black Republicans', *see* Republican Party
Blackwell's Island, 110
Blair, Francis P., 16, 19n., 266
Blair, Montgomery, 282, 284-5, 295n.
Blockade, 181, 219
Bobo, Wm. M., 40n., 77n., 337
'Bogus Proclamation', 259, 259n.
Boole, Francis I. A., 77, 280
Bordeaux, 100, 285n., 294
Border States, 130, 169, 173-4, 177, 182, 184, 185, 193n., 222, 275
Boston, 33, 72, 147, 164, 300; JGB in, 1n., 13, 28n., 45, 72n.
Bounty System, 243-4
'Bourbons', 299n.
'Bowery Boys', 229